To Make Democracy Safe for America

To Make Democracy
Safe for America

☆

PATRICIANS AND
PREPAREDNESS IN
THE PROGRESSIVE ERA

☆

Michael Pearlman

UNIVERSITY OF ILLINOIS PRESS
Urbana and Chicago

Publication of this work has been supported by a grant from the
Oliver M. Dickerson Fund. The Fund was established by Mr. Dickerson
(Ph.D., Illinois, 1906) to enable the University of Illinois Press
to publish selected works in American history, designated by the
executive committee of the Department of History.

This book is printed on acid-free paper.

Library of Congress Cataloging in Publication Data

Pearlman, Michael, 1944–
　To make democracy safe for America.

　Bibliography: p.
　Includes index.
　1. Military service, Compulsory—United States—
History—20th century. 2. United States—Politics and
government—20th century. 3. Military education—United
States—History—20th century. II. Title.
UB353.P42　1983　　355.2′2363′0973　　83–1107
ISBN 0-252-01019-1

To my mother's memory of my father

Contents

Acknowledgments

Before I began to write this book, I thought that authors' acknowledgments were like Oscar acceptance speeches: public occasions for vain people to pretend to be humble. If I have learned nothing else, I learned I was wrong. So many people have helped me that I must limit my thanks to a few. Of the numerous friends and relatives who housed and fed me while I mined archives around the country, I particularly thank Sam and Clara Herman of Washington, D.C. Jim Sack, of the University of Illinois, Chicago, and Bill Widenor and Fred Jaher, of the University of Illinois, Urbana, read the entire manuscript and made many valuable suggestions. Julie Baskis of Highland Park, Nancy Krueger and Ann Prisland Thorpe of Urbana, and Jerry Taft of Chicago edited my work and hopefully turned my writing into readable English. Zoe Doyle of Chicago Circle's Interlibrary Loan found arcane material that I thought had perished years ago. My wife Lois and my daughters Alicia and Wendy performed the Herculean task of lifting my spirits, no small task in these hard days for academics. Finally, I thank my mother and father. My mother has always been supportive in every conceivable way and has never failed to demonstrate what preparedness leaders called courageous moral character. My father recently died after a very long illness. Although this book is a pale shadow of what he achieved in his few healthy years, I hope he would be pleased.

Introduction

☆

THE MOVEMENT to prepare America to fight in World War I has been examined in several excellent monographs, most of which have concentrated on political activities supporting specific legislative bills. For example, John Garry Clifford's narrative history of the Plattsburg movement, *The Citizen Soldiers,* investigated the organization of the Military Training Camps Association (MTCA), a major lobby for universal military training (UMT). John W. Chambers's "Conscripting for Colossus" told how pressure from preparedness groups influenced President Woodrow Wilson's 1917 decision to use federal conscription on an unprecedented scale. Still another study, John P. Finnegan's *Against the Specter of a Dragon,* indicated that these lobbyists perceived military preparedness as an end in itself, rather than an instrument fashioned to achieve the immediate objectives of a foreign policy.[1]

Rather than rehash these thoroughly examined subjects in another narrative about the preparedness movement, my work, a social and intellectual history, emphasizes some relatively unexplored issues—the personal ambitions and domestic motivations of this movement's civilian leadership. In my sometimes speculative investigation of these men and General Leonard Wood, their anomalous ally in the regular army, I do not emphasize strategic issues and national defense concerns. The central theme of my study is, instead, the social reformation which was of prime importance to these particular advocates of preparedness. Those men, although certainly not provincial, generally shared the notion that scholars have found typical of almost all Americans, civilians and soldiers alike: that is, the belief, before mid-1917, that America's vital interests were already safe from sustained foreign attack. Until the Germans launched their late-war offensives, the Allies, with 250,000 more men on the line, seemed to be holding a stable Western front. English propaganda in America then exuded confidence. Americans, believing their margin of safety was intact, could emphasize reform, not security.[2] While Wilsonians sought "to make the world safe for democracy," my protagonists fought "to make democracy safe for the world" (put more bluntly: "democracy safe for elites"). These civilian preparedness leaders not only avowed this domestic motivation, they were frequently at odds with professional soldiers, perhaps the only body of Americans directly concerned with military defense per se. Most of those officers preferred a large standing army of *selected* conscripts serving multiyear enrollment periods to the alternative program which these civilians sponsored: six months of universal military training for all but the hopelessly handicapped, after which virtually all adult males would join, in some capacity, a citizen-soldier reserve. Those relatively few officers who supported UMT before 1916, mainly Wood and his followers, were admitted exceptions, by no means the rule.[3] Hence UMT, in the early twentieth century, was certainly not *the* acknowledged path to military security. It gathered more thorough support from civilian elites than it often did from professional soldiers because those civilians thought it, and repeatedly called it, a panacea for the great domestic problems of their time.

In the late nineteenth century, representative preparedness leaders such as Wood and Theodore Roosevelt felt that they were living in a "country of political cataclysms." I contend that the roots of the social crisis they perceived lay deep in the nation's past. The belief that abundant goods would ensure "the good life" has often led Americans to maximize economic growth without considering the public problems that excessive enterprise can create. Recently, studies about the ecological impact of modern production and consumption have revealed the bio-environmental dangers threatening a society which attempts to unite people by what they buy and where they buy it. In earlier times, when people were supposed to be united through the moral discipline and common social purpose articulated by a traditional elite, inordinate material development had other effects: if furthered divisions within government, society, and culture that challenged the ideals of that elite. To ward off this divisiveness, adding to the danger of Indian attacks and imperial wars, the patriarchs of Puritan New England tried to prevent economic transactions which might undermine their stated purposes. For the sake of orthodoxy, harmony, and military security, real estate purchases were often limited to men of proven faith and character.[4]

However, since the decrease of external dangers helped release private ambitions that sundered this colonial commonwealth, the public problems of development have grown with growth itself. Usually, this has not aroused most citizens, who, absorbed with a market price, have ignored the social costs. Nonetheless, a fervent neo-puritan minority has rarely been completely mute.[5] During the first half of the nineteenth century, certain transcendental pundits and Congregational preachers, such as Ralph Waldo Emerson and Horace Bushnell, argued that uncontrolled development would bear bitter fruit. In 1860 their predictions were upheld when, contrary to the majority's faith in the beneficence of growth, territorial expansion helped cause a civil war. Approximately forty years later, economic expansion through industrial technology seemed to be creating another social clash. As men grasped at new marketplace opportunities for unprecedented productivity and profits, they progressively weakened what Emerson had called "the ties and ligaments once supposed essential to civil society": equity, nationality, family, tradition, community, moral purpose, and binding principles. Since economic busts followed economic booms, a public dedicated to material growth appeared precariously unified. This being the case, old social elites, like those active in the military preparedness movement, came to believe that they were witnessing a "social, economic, and moral revolution" which was producing "great destruction, in both the physical and the intellectual world, of old buildings and old boundaries and old monuments and, furthermore, of customs and ideals."[6]

By the 1890s, one-eighth of America owned more than one-half of its aggregate wealth. Roosevelt, Wood, and other future preparedness leaders then worried that "class hatred" was separating their countrymen into mutually hostile, and potentially violent, plutocrats and proletariats. On one of these sides stood the "selfish rich" who "put wealth above everything else"; on the other was the "lunatic fringe" who wanted radical change. Besides causing some 1,400 labor strikes in 1894, this dichotomy seemed to exacerbate sectional disputes over financial credit and the monetary supply. Consequently agrarian debtors in the South and West, plagued by their over-production of cotton and wheat, were increasingly hostile to their creditors in the industrial East.[7]

Already divided by income and region, America's North Atlantic Protestant culture seemed to be dissolving into different ethnic enclaves when, to work their industries, entrepreneurs recruited tens of millions of immigrants, many of whom were Jews and Catholics, from southern and eastern Europe. Nativists like Wood, feeling that these newcomers fueled urban corruption and crime, believed they had migrated solely to make money. Yet the general did not feel that these immigrants were entirely to blame for the nation's lack of binding social principles. He and his colleagues maintained that industrial growth had nurtured marketplace moral standards that upheld accumulation as the main purpose of society.[8]

Until the 1820s, economic success still seemed largely attributable to that combination of aggressivity and order now known as the Protestant ethic. In this period, Benjamin Franklin and other pundits who felt that prosperity was organically tied to frugality, diligence, perseverance, and sacrifice proclaimed that "a wise man will desire no more than what he may get justly, use soberly, distribute cheerfully and live upon contentedly." The Whartons of Philadelphia, the Lowells of Massachusetts, and similar northeastern manufacturers and merchants spent considerable time and money disseminating this code through Bible tracts, Sunday schools, religious missions, and YMCAs. In addition to organizing these "moral militias," they gave their employees comfortable housing that was "neat and clean, peaceable and sage." Then technical growth in transportation and industry dramatically expanded manufacturing and markets. This development, creating new potentials for profit, helped move capitalism out of its early stage of limited needs into its later stage of near limitless wants. Corporations with great investments in heavy industry had to wipe out huge initial debts by enlarging their volume of business to lower unit costs. In the process of turning deficits to assets, they weakened many of the country's solidifying traditions and settling institutions. To generate adequate supply, they required a fluid work force of mobile men ready to assume new occupations in different locales. To ensure commensurate demand, they penetrated the distant markets previously furnished by local and less innovative businessmen who were integral members of the communities they served. In either case, the entrepreneurial process, which caused new companies and products to expand and old ones to contract, released people from the customs of the past and the tutelage of traditional elites. For example, as the factory labor system removed production from the hearth by displacing cottage industries and yeoman agriculture, divorce rates climbed 35 percent per decade from 1870 to the mid-1920s. The decline of the patriarchal family, whose paternal structure confined a dynamic economy, suggested that industrialism challenged practices that once sustained the so-called "compact, united and friendly community" in which people "felt involved in each other's welfare."[9]

This expansion of industry and contraction of communion seemed to separate financial success from moral rectitude and personal initiative from social discipline. Now in contrast to Benjamin Franklin, men like William Vanderbilt and J. P. Morgan maintained that the "public be damned" and "I owe the public nothing." Because most of the nation's talented and adventurous citizens went into business enterprise (not into government, the army, or the arts), these "heroes of our material growth" set social standards that accentuated economic accumulation, not moral direction and civic purpose. Consequently the country as a whole appeared increasingly prone to divisions arising from uncontrolled industrialization. To future preparedness leaders who still cherished old puritan principles of cohesion, America seemed to be degenerating into a "mere strip of land on which a crowd is struggling for riches."[10]

Throughout American history this lament, which was the very essence of New England's jeremiads, has often been followed by war depicted as this nation's social purgatory. To John Adams, disturbed about "corruption" on the eve of U.S. independence, war was a "furnace of affliction [that] produces refinement in states, as well as individuals." To Abraham Lincoln, in 1863, it was "a punishment inflicted ... for our presumptuous sins [so] that our whole people might be redeemed." But before enough Americans to constitute a movement would accept the contention that military action was "a crucible burning out selfishness," they would have to admit to social problems so serious as to think combat a commensurate cure. By the turn of the twentieth century, that conviction increased as social disintegration appeared to accompany industrial growth. A reaction then took place to the disturbing specter of an atomistic citizenry lacking moral unity. At Chicago's 1893 World's Fair, a thirty-five million dollar industrial embodiment of the faith in utopia through technology, jeremiads on social sins from alcoholism to prostitution upset what critics called "the boastful Philistinism of our times."[11] Here and elsewhere, admonitions arose from different ideologists. Some would-be reformers, from Henry Adams on the right to George Herron on the left, withdrew into medievalism or advanced towards socialism. But the forty-five to fifty-five leading civilians in the military preparedness movement sought less radical solutions. Virtually all these activists, and their thousands of followers, as successful business and professional men from old East Coast families, did not want to abolish private property. They hoped instead to stem the disunity that challenged their social principles and position by reestablishing a moral code reminiscent of the puritan tradition that restrained materialism but motivated work in the early stages of American development. Herein lay the paradox: civilians turned to the army, often thought a home for wastrels, to revitalize the character forged in scarcity capitalism. In their eyes wealth was now undermining the Protestant ethic from which it had sprung.[12]

The preparedness movement, as a moral supplement to economics, philosophically resembled other social reforms proposed in the 1900s. Heretofore in political economy, the state rarely did anything but stimulate growth, giving tax exemptions, tariff protection, and land grants to "internal improvements" such as transportation projects. Now that

the rigors of competition no longer appeared to ensure moral character, uplift had to proceed outside the business process. Therefore some progressives, who felt "no established harmony . . . existed between the free and abundant satisfaction of private needs and the accomplishment of a morally and socially desirable result," sought to unify the nation through governmental regulations. Activists in other movements also advocated "a large measure of individual subordination and self-denial." Americanizers and nativists respectively sought to create a consensus by educating or excluding the foreign born. Social gospel preachers and settlement house social workers, hoping to build Christian fellowship and a cohesive community spirit, tried to "break down the partitions between rich and poor in church and social life." At various times individual advocates of universal military training participated in many of these Progressive Era programs. However, to the dismay of future preparedness leaders, different progressive proposals, in various fields from politics to education, emphasized democracy more than social discipline. Consequently, even the members of this group who supported progressive reforms were wary of their radical populist potential. This helped motivate temperate reformers like Theodore Roosevelt to shift their hopes for domestic reformation to socially "safe" preparedness programs such as UMT. In the process, they could and did ally themselves with political conservatives like David Jayne Hill. For Roosevelt, military training culminated the type of progressivism he supported: an elite-led search for social stability. For Hill, preparedness promised to forestall what he opposed: the populistic programs of the radical progressives, such as direct democracy and income confiscation.[13]

Of course, this does not mean that conservatives or reactionaries alone supported war against Germany. By mid-1917, many liberals like John Dewey agreed that this military crisis could help reconstruct America. Nonetheless these men who thought that democracy was already safe for the world were, compared to Hill, reluctant warriors at best. Their own hopes that industrial mobilization would make the United States a "semi-socialistic state" was just the consolation they imagined for the "moral desolation" of combat. In short, their prediction sugar-coated what seemed an unavoidable war. Preparedness leaders, by contrast, were much more receptive to battlefield hostilities. By 1915, at the latest, they generally felt that a national military experience was the best and the politically most prudent way for America to counteract the divisive effects of its material growth. Since they reasoned that ordeal might provide common goals eliciting a common sacrifice, they renewed the belief, often held by past elites, that war could resolve domestic problems by morally "crushing the Economic

Man." Without endangering social stratification, a seemingly self-indulgent body politic would thereby be transformed into heroic patriots and selfless citizens.[14]

To document my hypothesis, I shall discuss internal problems and their quasi-military cures, from junior police force programs to college preparatory schools. These phenomena, predating and postdating World War I, have not been emphasized in other studies of the military preparedness movement. By tracing its history from its inception during the Spanish-American War to its flirtation with isolationism in World War II, I hope to show that the Great War did not raise all the issues nor did victory furnish all the benefits that the universal military training movement hoped to provide, because external security alone was not its raison d'être.

While the individuals to whom I pay special attention were influential in at least one preparedness organization, other students of this subject might emphasize other men. In fact, when these scholars picked their protagonists, they limited my options. John Garry Clifford has already written the definitive narrative on Grenville Clark's activities during World War I. A complete character study of Clark, the secretary of the MTCA, must await the release of many personal papers now reserved by his family for an authorized biographer. Still other activists, like Archibald Thacher and Delancy K. Jay, deserve more extensive investigation. But since they, unlike some others, left few personal sources, opened or closed, many of their thoughts remain inaccessible. Where I deal with well-researched individuals, such as Roosevelt and Wood, I have attempted to elucidate aspects of their lives through the prism of preparedness, thus trying to shed new light on these old figures.

NOTES

1. John Garry Clifford, *The Citizen Soldiers: The Plattsburg Training Camp Movement, 1913–1920* (Lexington: University of Kentucky Press, 1972); John W. Chambers, "Consripting for Colossus: The Adoption of the Draft in the United States in World War I" (Ph.D. diss., Columbia University, 1973); John P. Finnegan, *Against the Specter of a Dragon: The Campaign for American Military Preparedness, 1914–1917* (Westport: Greenwood Press, 1974).

2. For civilians, even Theodore Roosevelt, see Robert Osgood, *Ideals and Self-Interest in America's Foreign Relations: The Great Transformation of the Twentieth Century* (Chicago: University of Chicago Press, 1953), esp. pp. 80, 142, 199. For professional soldiers, see James L. Abrahamson, *America Arms for a New Century: The Making of a Great Military Power* (New York: Free

Press, 1981), pp. 171–74; Richard Challener, *Admirals, Generals and American Foreign Policy, 1898–1914* (Princeton: Princeton University Press, 1973), p. 32.

3. For brief periods after World Wars I and II, more professional soldiers favored UMT as a defense policy. This does not disprove that civilians, as early as 1913, supported the same program for social reform. The difference in the respective motives of these two groups *does* help explain the difference in the intensity of their commitments to UMT. Whereas the civilians I study enthusiastically supported it for decades, the army's favor never lasted very long. In 1920, as I discuss in Ch. 9, the service soon abandoned its anomalous support for a citizen-soldier component. In 1948, a period beyond the time scope of my study, strategic planners gladly accepted selective service: a program that promised a large standing army as an alternative to UMT. Even Army Chief of Staff George C. Marshall, the most important military proponent of universal training, privately described it as a *"gesture* of determination" (italics mine). He had supported this policy, which he damned with faint praise, because he thought that postwar America would never support what he really wanted, a generously funded professional force. Once the Cold War disproved this assumption, the officer corps abandoned UMT. In contemporary America, when they criticize the voluntary army, they call for the reinstatement of the selective service draft. I have yet to hear any of them ask for UMT. For evidence of the post–World War II army's *tepid* support for UMT, see Forrest Pogue, Marshall's multivolume biographer, to Michael Pearlman, Sept. 12, 1974, copy in possession of this writer; Marshall quoted in Walter Millis, ed., *The Forrestal Diaries* (New York: Viking, 1951), p. 337; Michel Sherry, *Preparing for the Next War: American Plans for Postwar Defense, 1941–45* (New Haven: Yale University Press, 1977), esp. pp. 38, 50, 88–90, 115–16, 234.

4. Elting E. Morison, ed., *The Letters of Theodore Roosevelt* (Cambridge, Mass.: Harvard University Press, 1951), 1:391; Michael Zuckerman, *Peaceable Kingdoms: New England Towns in the Eighteenth Century* (New York: Vintage Books, 1970), passim.

5. The lower-case "puritanism" used frequently in my work refers to a philosophy of life, not a specific Protestant church.

6. W. David Lewis, "The Reformer as Conservative: Protestant Counter-Subversion in the Early Republic," *The Development of an American Culture*, ed. Stanley Coben and Lorman Ratner (Englewood Cliffs: Barnes & Noble, 1970), passim. For evidence that Emerson and Bushnell, despite some "unorthodox" notions about salvation, held puritan ideas about community, see George M. Frederickson, *The Inner Civil War: Northern Intellectuals and the Crisis of the Union* (New York: Harper & Row, 1965), pp. 25–26, 176–80. Emerson quoted in Burton Bledstein, *The Culture of Professionalism: The Middle-Class and the Development of Higher Education in America* (New York: Norton, 1976), p. 177; unnamed figures quoted in Elting E. Morison: *From Know-How to Nowhere: The Development of American Technology* (New York: Basic Books, 1974), p. 88, and *Men, Machines and Modern Times* (Cambridge, Mass.: Massachusetts Institute of Technology Press, 1966), p. 16.

7. Statistics on the division of wealth and the number of strikes are from Charles Spahr, *An Essay on the Present Distribution of Wealth in the United*

States (New York: Thomas Crowell, 1896), p. 129; James Edward Barber, *The Pulse of Politics: Electing the President in the Media Age* (New York: Norton, 1980), p. 30. Morison, ed., *Letters of Theodore Roosevelt,* 2:1427; Leonard Wood to J. E. Gaujot, Nov. 5. 1913, Wood MSS, Box 66, Library of Congress; Roosevelt quoted in John Morton Blum, *The Republican Roosevelt* (New York: Atheneum, 1963), pp. 34, 60.

8. Barbara Solomon, *Ancestors and Immigrants: A Changing New England Tradition* (Chicago: University of Chicago Press, 1971), p. 183.

9. For the quotation from Franklin and the stages of capitalism, see Werner Sombart, *The Quintessence of Capitalism* (New York: Howard Fertig, 1967), pp. 153–89. For Lowell and the quotations from Lyman Beecher and Michael Chevalier, see Paul Boyer, *Urban Masses and Moral Order in America, 1820–1920* (Cambridge, Mass.: Harvard University Press, 1978), pp. 13, 35–36, 58, 142, 308. On the general social effects of industrial enterprise, see David C. McClelland, *The Achieving Society* (New York: Free Press, 1961), and Karl Polanyi, *The Great Transformation* (Boston: Beacon Press, 1957). Divorce statistics are from Ernest Groves and William F. Ogburn, *American Marriage and Family Relations* (New York: Henry Holt, 1928), p. 346. The final quotation is from George Ticknor as cited in Stanley K. Schultz, "Breaking the Chains of Poverty: Public Education in Boston: 1800–1860," *Cities in American History,* ed. Kenneth T. Jackson and Stanley Schultz (New York: Knopf, 1972), p. 307.

10. The first three quotations from Vanderbilt, Morgan, and Walt Whitman respectively, are cited in Herbert J. Muller, *The Children of Frankenstein: A Primer on Modern Technology and Human Values* (Bloomington: Indiana University Press, 1970), pp. 57, 66, 75. The last quotation is from Owen Wister, *Owen Wister Out West: His Journals and Letters,* ed. Fanny Kemble Wister (Chicago: University of Chicago Press, 1958), pp. 181–82.

11. For the jeremiad and the quotes from Adams, Lincoln, and a Civil War veteran, see Sacvan Bercovitch, *The American Jeremiad* (Madison: University of Wisconsin Press, 1978), pp. 51, 119, 174; Wallace Evan Davies, *Patriotism on Parade: The Story of Veterans' and Hereditary Organizations in America, 1783–1900* (Cambridge, Mass.: Harvard University Press, 1955), p. 336. For the World's Fair and the quote from architect Henry Van Burt, see Thomas Beer, *The Mauve Decade: American Life at the End of the Nineteenth Century* (New York: Vintage Books, 1960), pp. 21, 87–88, 157–58; Alan Trachtenberg, *The Incorporation of America: Culture and Society in the Gilded Age* (New York: Hill & Wang, 1982), p. 215.

12. For more detailed social profiles of the leadership corps, see Chambers, "Conscripting for Colossus," pp. 61–63, and Michael Pearlman, "To Make Democracy Safe For The World: A History of the World War I Military Preparedness Movement in America" (Ph.D. diss., University of Illinois, 1978), pp. 17–19, 672–681. For the followers, see Ralph Barton Perry, *The Plattsburg Movement* (New York: E. P. Dutton, 1921), pp. 38, 271–72, and Clifford, *Citizen Soldiers,* pp. 65–66. An appendix following the final section of my text presents a list of most of the preparedness leaders and a chart delineating their social characteristics.

13. The quotations are from Herbert Croly, *The Promise of American Life*

(New York: E. P. Dutton, 1963), p. 22, and from a social gospeler cited in David P. Thelen, *The New Citizenship: Origins of Progressivism in Wisconsin, 1885–1900* (Columbia: University of Missouri Press, 1972), p. 102.

14. Liberals Frederic Howe and Stephen Wise quoted in Jean B. Quandt, *From the Small Town to the Great Community: The Social Thought of Progressive Intellectuals* (New Brunswick: Rutgers University Press, 1970), p. 143; Stuart I. Rochester, *American Liberal Disillusionment: In the Wake of World War I* (University Park: Pennsylvania State University Press, 1977), esp. pp. 47–49, 55, 59. The last quotation, in a slightly different context, is from Theodore Roosevelt cited in Richard Hofstadter, *The American Political Tradition and the Men who Made it* (New York: Vintage Books, 1948), p. 220. Some previous moral endorsements of war in American history are cited in Nathan O. Hatch, "The Origins of Civil Millennialism in America: New England Clergymen, War with France, and the Revolution," *William and Mary Quarterly* 31 (July, 1974): 408, 422; Michael Paul Rogin, *Fathers and Children: Andrew Jackson and the Subjugation of the American Indian* (New York: Knopf, 1975), pp. 140–41, 147, 156; Frederickson, *Inner Civil War,* passim.

CHAPTER 1

Theodore Roosevelt, the Spanish-American War, and the Search for a National Community

☆ *"megaphone of mars"*

THEODORE ROOSEVELT, dubbed the "megaphone of Mars," was the most prestigious spokesman for the World War I preparedness movement, an undertaking that would use military institutions to achieve internal reform as well as external defense. The future President developed this policy in the late nineteenth century when, between 1876 and 1898, the United States underwent considerable class, geographic, and ethnic conflict. In reaction to this disruption, Roosevelt proposed that common endeavor and struggle could unify America: a country then lacking national institutions of sufficient strength to consolidate the republic through political, religious, or educational means. Whereas those whom he called "emasculated humanitarians" might have redistributed private wealth and public power, Roosevelt hoped to regenerate society through his own moral trinity of "effort, pain and difficulty." He therefore promoted, successively, as this chapter will show, wilderness camping, strenuous athletics, heroic literature, and finally war itself.[1] Neither he, Leonard Wood, nor any other future preparedness leader caused the Spanish-American War.[2] Yet Roosevelt used it in a way that subsequently enticed the military preparedness movement to exploit World War I for domestic purposes. First, he and his Rough Rider regiment created the heroic legend he envisioned, a saga that encouraged later colleagues to believe that a divided country could be united and uplifted through military training and war. In addition to its legend, the regiment contributed its men, many of whom assumed leadership positions in future preparedness organizations.[3] Roosevelt, of course, was its outstanding contribution. He not only transmitted a vision of unifying and purifying military institutions, he inspired other preparedness leaders with an example of how an insecure personality could use the test of battle to prove himself to himself.

Roosevelt's Preparation for Preparedness: The Wilderness, Athletics, and Heroic Literature

Although Roosevelt endorsed moderate governmental reforms, both his ideology and his ambition led him to think that politics was a relatively ineffective way to improve society. Particularly before 1910, his class interest in "the rights of property" and his personal concern for electoral success predisposed him to compromise with those who defended the economic and political status quo. These cares aside, feasibility was a factor driving him to "keep on good terms with the machine." His recent experience indicated that even the "temperate" reforms he supported were likely to fail. While commissioner of the U.S. Civil Service and the New York City Police (1889–97), his "disheartening" fight against patronage and "the steady increase of corruption" proved to be "grimy drudgery." Adroit precinct captains and "indifferent" citizens made his office a "beastly job" and swayed him towards becoming, as he once put it, "thoroughly practical in politics." Therefore, on the eve of America's altercation with Spain, Roosevelt thought that combat, not legislation, was the opportune path to civic improvement. Both the politicians and the public, so immovable at home, seemed ready and willing to be militant abroad.[4] War thus seemed possible and, furthermore, effective. Whereas politics evoked apathy or anarchy, arms could stimulate the moral change that he deemed necessary.

As an essentially conservative man who would say, "I have been called a reformer but am a Republican," Roosevelt believed that economic programs alone could not resolve the "terrible social problems" confronting "the civilized world." Because he thought that a malaise of materialism divided the country, he emphasized individual reformation, not radical alterations of institutional power. His dictum accordingly read: "My problems are moral problems and my teaching has been plain morality." To him, this doctrine indicated that capitalists, day laborers, and farmers all needed to strengthen their "character." Too many businessmen, exploiting workers and customers alike, were preoccupied with "mere money getting," while too many employees, questioning private property and the work ethic, threatened "to abandon the stern morality without which no man and no nation can permanently succeed." As for the agrarian populists, he feared that they also emphasized "class and sectional hatred" instead of the national good.[5]

To Roosevelt, greed and sloth were symptomatic of the fundamental decline in national character accompanying increasing urban affluence. Although by the 1870s farmers and peasants from Kansas to Sicily were no longer pillars of conservatism, gentry throughout Western civilization still liked to think that an "appreciation of property [and] love of the native soil makes [those who work the land] the natural enemy of urban revolutionary ideas." Roosevelt, applying this doctrine to the United States, felt that the Dakota cowboys, "Americans through and through," would love to have "a chance with their rifles at one of the [radical] mobs." All in all, he believed that a rugged life in the wilderness produced the moral strength that could heal the general flabbiness then threatening the nation.[6]

While preparedness leaders like Roosevelt may have preferred nature to the city, that in itself did not distinguish them from pacifists such as Albert Schweitzer. However, these different nature lovers loved different forms of nature for very different reasons. Pacifistic people prized the outdoors as an organic nursery, "soft and comforting and sweet," and preserved it because they cherished life itself. Meanwhile warriors, who loved "the grim and rugged woods," preserved them because they sought severity. While the former looked for tranquility in a garden, the latter pursued exertion in an "abode of iron desolation" whose "furious gales" ensured "there is no peace save the peace of death." Rather than protect the wilderness simply because it has life, they conserved it because they believed that a purgative arena of "severe toil and hardship" developed moral character through sacrifice and suffering. Since Roosevelt felt that modern Americans "need a greater and not a lesser development of the fundamental frontier virtues," he tried to preserve the wilderness and its physical ordeals.[7]

TR must have felt that his own life confirmed his theory that struggle engenders physical and moral strength. In 1884, when ailing members of the upper class sought sedation and sympathy in leisurely tours and luxurious spas, he disregarded longstanding medical advice to live a sedentary life or face imminent death. Although suffering chronic asthma, heart, and stomach problems, Roosevelt refused to return to "a select collection of assorted cripples and consumptives" at "that quintessence of abomination, a large [Catskill] summer hotel." He fled, instead, to his "hero land" of Spartan North Dakota, where he lived with hardened cowboys who believed that infirmities reflected a "defective moral character." There, despite a diet of alkaline drinking water, canned pork, and starch, a "slight and somewhat delicate looking"

Roosevelt, who lost twenty thousand dollars worth of cattle in blizzards of −40°, gained thirty pounds of muscle and the resolve to resume his political career. In time, he also developed a social policy. The "toil and hardship" of Dakota that gave him, in turn, a broken arm, a fractured rib, and "supreme [all-around] health," suggested solutions for public as well as personal problems. Because the cowboys' "stern and unend- ing struggles with iron-bound surroundings" seemed to have created their vitality, Roosevelt searched for urban equivalents to the vanishing frontier for all Americans.[8]

He found one such equivalent in strenuous athletics. Roosevelt did not promote or participate in "games": spontaneous play for mirthful diversion. Although involved in most sports, he showed no interest in baseball, America's favorite game. Baseball is a pastoral activity played in spring and summer while the garden is in bloom. In an urban society, its "parks" and "fields" can be bucolic; in an industrial society ruled by the clock, its indefinite duration could seem so soporific that its major justification was that it helped its fans relax. Amateur baseball, like other "games," may be played by pacifists in a meadow.[9] Perhaps Roosevelt was thinking of a martial struggle in the wilderness when he became football's foremost booster. To him, that particular sport, build- ing self-control and self-reliance, was an "excellent revival of old-time American ways." No mirthful diversion, it was moral instruction. And because Roosevelt felt that "no amount of culture, refinement or intel- lectual force can atone for the lack of the virile virtues essential to the welfare of the nation," he thought that sports like football should be- come a basic part of civic education.[10]

Roosevelt also recommended heroic literature for its moral influence. His own aesthetics were an anomalous blend of genteel style and nat- uralistic vision. Far from complacent about national conditions, he perceived "very unhealthy symptoms" in American society. Yet he still favored the idealized stories of "less critical ages" to the "morbid" ex- posés of the modern mind. This man, who removed all suggestions of sin from his private diary, let alone his memoirs, felt that art's special function was to preserve the vision of nobility that daily life denied. He also thought that the "prophetic imagination" should be used to envi- sion the "grandeur of the nation [as it] looms up, vast and shadowy through the advancing years." In both instances, Roosevelt believed that inspirational art, "presenting [an] ideal," might supersede mun- dane reality in the creation of consciousness. Thus far, his position was not unusual for upper-class idealists and romantic poets living through industrialization. However, the themes and subjects Roosevelt favored were far more combative than were those supported by most bluebloods in the Gilded Age. They built urban parks, orchestra halls, and art mu-

seums to "calm" the masses' "dangerous inclinations" with soothing
gardens, melodies, and murals. Roosevelt, endorsing a different mission for culture, felt that the humanities should convey a vicarious
struggle, not a sensuous peace.[11]

Once again Roosevelt's personal development helped shape his public policy. The adolescent adventure stories which he had read motivated a "sickly and timid" young Roosevelt to emulate heroes. Later,
using similar literary resources on his siblings and children, he told
them the stirring stories he retold in his books, particularly *Hero Tales
from American History* (published 1895). Roosevelt. a devotee of inspirational historiography, believed that a heroic past motivated men to
create an equally heroic present, just as family traditions inspired the
upper class to assume public service. Prior to the mid-1880s, the American creed, which said that all men should compete on their own merits
and all generations improve on their forefathers, generally neglected
tradition. Then, in the ten years preceding 1895, as the country grew
more urban and industrialized, some thirty-five hereditary societies
were founded to help the upper crust find ancestral roots that shored
up their egos in the midst of social change. But although Roosevelt felt
that his own "good [blue] blood . . . had flowed through generations of
[men with] self-restraint and courage . . . in mind and the manly virtues,"
he himself was not content with the exclusivity of the Colonial Dames
(founded in 1894). While other bewailed "the presence of foreign born
banana sellers . . . whose aspirations would make a dog vomit," Roosevelt democratized tradition by writing histories to inspire everyone to
build a great nation. "It is," he said, "a good thing for all America and
it is an especially good thing for young Americans . . . to keep in mind
the feats of daring and personal prowess done in the past . . . [for] no
people can be really great unless they possess . . . the heroic virtues."[12]

If nothing else, the sagas which Roosevelt wrote might turn adolescents from "the mendacious, the sensational and the inane" stories
then available in "the yellow press." These "hideous" publications,
said to create delinquents by glorifying gangsters, threatened to undo
the good work once done by his own father. Each week that Presbyte-
rian Sunday school teacher had conscientiously preached "patriotism,
good citizenship and manly morality" to the residents of the New York
City Newsboys' Lodging House. In the mid-1890s, his devoted son, a
former mission school teacher himself, conveyed the same principles
through written narratives that were proxies for Scripture in this secular age. Then, many urban churches, having failed with Bible classes,
organized paramilitary clubs to teach moral virtues to the young. Concurrently, Roosevelt, New York City's police commissioner, wrote
about soldiers, not about saints. Specifically, he replaced the ineffective

religious tracts traditionally used in child reformatories with adventure tales that lionized the heroes of military history.[13]

Roosevelt differed from the typical military historian by neglecting logistics, tactics, and strategy to concentrate on the semimythical virtues of individual combatants. Most of those technical experts, believing that "military history [provides] the source of all military science," write for officers, not for adolescents. Thus they often are indifferent to human drama and even when they are not, they lack sufficient source material. Soldiers in the field rarely have time to put their thoughts on paper and when they do, the army may censor their letters and prohibit their diaries lest the enemy capture the pages before any publisher can. Consequently, as Roosevelt himself recognized, the most "human" stories of war must often come from novelists.[14] But scarce documentation did not discourage him since here he was more concerned with inspiration than with accuracy.

Roosevelt never would neglect athletics, wilderness camping, and heroic literature. Nonetheless, as the depression of 1893 intensified social disintegration, he veered towards moral uplift through armed combat with Spain. For him, war resembled the domestic programs that he also tried to sponsor and therefore was a new project for his old principles. Like his faith in football and camping, his affirmation that battle would sweep vice away "like chaff" was anchored in his notion that physical hardships produce virtue. Like his faith in didactic historiography, his assertion that war would present "something to think of which isn't material gain" was based on his belief that heroism inspired emulation. America itself had been suffering from indigenous hero depletion ever since former President Ulysses S. Grant squandered his prestige and the Republican Party's luster in corruption and speculation. Roosevelt sought to rectify this domestic shortage in a nation then seeking idols beyond its shores in a revived interest in tales about Napoleon and the stories of Sir Walter Scott. To create new *American* heroes for its own historians to celebrate, Roosevelt promoted a new war that would be invaluable simply because "the memory of every triumph won by Americans . . . helps to make each American nobler and better."[15]

The Rough Riders and the Dream of National Unity

Roosevelt felt that war could build national accord as well as national character. He not only thought that belligerence would heal the old divisions deriving from the War Between the States, he believed it could resolve those class and sectional hatreds (finance versus agriculture, East versus West) recently expressed in the last presidential election.

In 1896 he called the political contest between Bryan and McKinley "the greatest crisis in our national fate, save only the Civil War." However, in 1897, his personal faith that war with Spain would erase social fissures was certainly not assured. The special sympathy that southern congressmen showed for the Cuban rebels forebode a disturbing possibility: If America intervened to support a provincial revolution against a central government, it seemed as likely that attention would refocus on the constitutional issue that once caused its own South to secede. Nonetheless, Roosevelt's optimistic prediction of reunification through war appears to have been right. In 1898, President William McKinley, an Ohio Republican, chose two old Confederate generals (because they *were* old Confederate generals) to serve in the campaign. Reciprocating, the South generously welcomed the new union army whose bands played "Dixie" as they passed again through Georgia towards their Florida embarkation ports. "The cost of this war," said Rough Rider Leonard Wood, "is amply repaid by seeing the old flag as one sees it today in the South. We are indeed once more a united country."[16]

Citizens with different political persuasions, observing common incidents such as these, agreed that "the blare of [this war's] bugle drowned" domestic controversies. McKinley, an obliging orator whose "one great anxiety [was] to express [popular] sentiments and desires," told the country what it wished to hear: "From camp and campaign there comes the magic healing which has closed ancient wounds and effaced their scars." But no assessment of the cause of reconciliation should ignore expanding gold supplies and urban markets. The Spanish-American War, coinciding with renewed prosperity, received credit for the harmony it did not create. Nonetheless, what men think is true may be more important than reality itself. Roosevelt, who once recorded the legends of the past, now carefully nurtured this belief that the Spanish-American War "completed the reunion of the country." Indeed, the greatest symbol of this faith was his own Rough Rider troop—"the most unique aggregation of fighting men ever gathered together in any army."[17]

Although the Rough Riders were predominantly sectional (103 easterners, 1,133 westerners), they had a symbolic nationalism that gripped the imagination of a country then afraid of its own disunion. The West's "hatred" of the East, its bluebloods in particular, had long alarmed Roosevelt. As if to disprove the expressed "local fear...that the simple manners, morals and customs of the New Mexico cowboy may be contaminated by contact with New Yorkers," he and Colonel Leonard Wood, the regiment's initial commander, scattered eastern "swells" through their entire unit. Purposely bunking cowhands with capitalists, they "looked to the amalgamation of certain elements in two classes of men opposed to each other in every respect save [their] quality of manhood." Thus the regiment appeared to integrate America's disparate interest groups. Sons of New York bankers, East Coast industrialists, and agrarian debtors lived as friends in war as they had not lived in peace. Lieutenant Colonel Roosevelt's dearest comrade and best subordinate officer was Bucky O'Neil, two-time Populist candidate for Congress. One sergeant from New York was a leading Gold Democrat; another from Colorado was a prominent Socialist.[18] But despite their political and social differences, the Rough Riders were more than a regiment; they became a community. Sociological studies establish that military objectives produce a common purpose, that shared discomforts create solidarity, and that physical dangers cause men to ignore each other's social class. The war consequently "welded" the few "swells" and the many plainsmen "into one large family." As one Dodge City resident said: "If it wasn't for the look of intelligence on the face of them dudes, you'd think they was all cowpunchers."[19]

Roosevelt the citizen had hoped that the war would foster an inspirational memory. When it ended, Roosevelt the historian recorded the deeds performed by Roosevelt the soldier. Saying that the same "vitality makes men fight well and write well," he emphasized the social cohesion of his own command: "There could be no more honorable burial than that of these men in a common grave—Indian and cowboy, miner and packer, and college athlete—the man of unknown ancestry from the lonely Western plains and the man who carried on his watch the crests of the Stuyvesants and the Fishes, one in the way they had met death, just as during life they had been one in their daring and their loyalty."[20]

Roosevelt was a master story-teller but he alone could not have created the legend of the Rough Riders. According to one writer from the *New York Journal,* who fought in the war himself, "no regiment has ever received the newspaper space that was devoted to them." Indeed, the public press showered the unit with so much attention that some citizens openly "wondered what had become of the [14,412] regular soldiers" who were 85 percent of the expeditionary force. To be sure, the Rough Riders made good copy: mixing social celebrities, bankers, and athletes together with a Wild West show. But their eccentricities were not their main attraction. Both eastern and western newspapers, worried about the country's viability, dwelt on the regiment as a microcosm of the nation. They said that it was "the most representative body of men on American soil" for in it were "cowboys and millionaries, side by side, all men equal." It was "democracy . . . the highest and the lowest, the rich and the poor, the young and the old, ready to fight side by side" and "mingle their blood on a Cuban trail." However, few professional soldiers were nearly this euphoric. When asked "Are you a hero?" General Henry W. Lawton sardonically replied: "No, I am only a regular."[21]

Roosevelt always felt that the Spanish-American War was "a golden hour" that shone even brighter than his presidency. And well he might for, as journalists then observed, he returned home "as the most popular man in the army, if not in the nation." If no one else captured the public imagination quite as he did, it probably was because no other man so vividly embodied the articulated hope that war, "as a moral educator," would stabilize society, unify the country, and glorify the nation. Ironically, however, Roosevelt's great triumph with his regimental unit, which seemed to be a "luck stone to all who touched it," helped create his greatest disappointment: the rejection of his proposed World War I division. In 1917, General Hugh L. Scott, Army chief of staff, remembered how the Rough Riders, as the symbol of national unity, publicly eclipsed the country's professional soldiers. Determined to prevent this from recurring, Scott and the War Department helped ensure that Roosevelt did not go overseas again.[22]

The Pursuit of Heroism: The Tactics of Roosevelt's War

For Roosevelt, athletics and the wilderness had been a personal (as well as a public) policy—and so was war. Like many other preparedness leaders, he would commit himself to combat along with the nation. Political opponents were unfair when they claimed that he pursued publicity in Cuba in the spring of 1898 to run for governor of New York later that year. Major newspapers, government superiors, his family, and his closest friends "all" warned that resigning from his present position as assistant secretary of the navy, when he was needed to mobilize every available ship, would surely "end his political career." But despite the frenetic preparations his office was making for war, no one could change Roosevelt's conviction that his "heart would chafe out" if he did not "abandon everything and go to the front." As the secretary of the navy recorded: "[Roosevelt] has lost his head to this unutterable folly of deserting a post where he is of the most service [in order to] run off to ride a horse. . . . He has gone so far daft in the matter that he evidently regards it as a sacred duty. . . . I called him a crank and ridiculed him to the best of my ability, but all in vain. The funny part of it all is that he actually takes the whole thing seriously."[23]

Still others thought that Roosevelt's enlistment would end his life, not just his career. When he (the only man on horseback) led the charge up San Juan Hill clothed in a Brooks Brothers lieutenant colonel's uni-

form with a polka dot handkerchief tied to his hat, he was far more con-
spicuous to Spanish sharpshooters than he was to any political constitu-
ent. Then, as one Rough Rider put it, the only thing he could have been
running for was governor of Hell. Roosevelt personally went off to war
as he went off to the wilderness, to prove himself to himself. It was, he
said, "my one chance to cut my little notch on the stick that stands as a
measuring rod in every family."[24]

Even his cowboy-troopers, largely inured to violence, found Roosevelt
to be extraordinarily brave. They said that he fought as if he did not
care "whether he got killed or not"; and maybe they were right. Roosevelt, who was "always most unhappy not to have been wounded in
some striking and transfiguring way," seemed to have had a martyr's
courage based on a martyr's faith that posterity would grant him the
glory in death that he had not (yet) won in life. Indeed, his own historical writings on heroism probably encouraged this belief that the future
would commemorate his own deeds as he had done the exploits of the
past. Thus, after battle, Roosevelt wrote that he could now die satisfied
that he had left "a name" to his children "which will serve as an apol-
ogy for my having existed."[25]

Although Roosevelt's heroism was exceptional, his personality was
not unique; his motivation conforms to a well-known psychological
model. His inordinate drive for glory appears to have arisen in reaction
to self-doubt. Only superficially conceited, he confided to friends that he
felt physically and mentally second class. Men usually can accept their
limitations when significant people (particularly their parents) have
first accepted them for what they are. However, a "sickly and timid"
young Roosevelt was raised by a loving but domineering father who insisted that his child become aggressive and strong. This mixture of
affection and reproach from "the only man of whom I was ever afraid,"
engendered neither self-acceptance nor resignation in his son. Consequently this "great little home-boy," heretofore protected by his younger
brother, rejected his "amiable" inclination for "domesticity." Then he
used athletics, the wilderness, and finally war to inflate himself into
the heroic ideal set forth in the adventure stories that he read. Eventually fulfilling his ambition in battle, he was "the happiest man on the
island of Cuba" the day he first fought.[26]

However valuable in itself, war provided Roosevelt with more than a
personal opportunity for fulfillment. It also gave this firm believer in
family traditions, long wishing to "do something to keep up his
[father's] name," a chance to rectify his family's great shame. He admired his parent, a venerated philanthropist, "more than any man in
the world," but he nonetheless was ashamed of him. In the Civil War,
that vast fund "of glorious memories" wherein one Roosevelt cousin

lost a leg but won a Medal of Honor, his young and healthy father, Theodore Roosevelt, Sr., had purchased a replacement. That record had to be erased and the Roosevelt clan redeemed. Thus he, perhaps perceiving a chance to eclipse his father, thought that war was a unique opportunity to "give my [own] children a name."[27]

Roosevelt's battle plans won more than a battle. His tactics functioned to absolve his family name, prove his own character, create venerable traditions, and purify the nation through sacrifice. Believing that hardship creates virtue, he seemed to scorn the kind of cost calculations (more gain for less expense) common to military efficiency and economic growth. Whereas the "cool and sagacious" Leonard Wood attacked the flanks to minimize casualties, Roosevelt admittedly "spent blood like water." He flung his troops, he said, "straight against entrenchments," where they stayed "hour after hour, dropping under fire."[28] His "triumph of bull dog courage" at San Juan Hill exemplified this policy. The expeditionary columns, exposed to a heavy volley in a long zone of fire, retreated from an open valley to the edge of a forest. Roosevelt, breaking "all the rules of modern warfare," charged these disorganized men up a steep slope towards fortified troops supported by artillery. Even he later admitted that the "heavy cost" of this attack helped put the army "within measurable distance of a terrible military disaster." Nonetheless, Roosevelt's own men say that when he "led us up San Juan Hill like sheep to the slaughter," he "had only one idea, and that was to smash on through them." These soldiers, facing a "solid sheet of bullets," paid the price for glory. Of the 400 men who went into action, eighty-six were killed or wounded, six were missing, and forty more suffered heat prostration.[29]

Roosevelt's political opponents said that he was callously indifferent to the welfare of his men. None of the troops, significantly, ever made that charge themselves. Some may have known that Roosevelt jeopardized the Medal of Honor he craved by openly criticizing the War Department for failing to give them adequate supplies. Others certainly remembered him crying over the dead, and well they should. As Roosevelt's sister recalled: Whenever he "spoke of his regiment a note of tenderness came into his voice such as might be heard in a woman speaking of her love." Yet suffering some 33 percent casualties (three times the rate of the rest of the army) the "boys" whom Roosevelt cherished labored under what they called his "absolutely reckless" leadership.[30] More concerned with creating heroic traditions than with preserving the lives of the men he loved, Roosevelt rarely tried to minimize the bloodshed. In both battles that he fought, he ignored directives to assume a rear-guard role covering assaults launched by the regular army, so that he could lead his own troops into more combat and, hence, more casualties. When he finished attacking, largely on "my own accord," one observer noted how "he seemed elated" at the "very heavy losses." Although the average soldier grows demoralized once 10 percent of his unit is struck down, Roosevelt, who continually begged that he and his "boys" be "sent [back] to the front," was proud that "I commanded my regiment with honor. We lost a quarter of our men." Thereafter, he always cited his large casualty rate as his major qualification for future commissions. In 1911, asking for permission to raise a cavalry division if America fought Mexico and Japan, he explained that he had "lost" one-fourth of his enlisted men and over one-third of their officers, "and all this within sixty days."[31]

Although the hunger for glory can be fulfilled through domination, Roosevelt never used military rank to vent authoritarianism. To be sure, he had good reason to be a martinet if he chose to be one. While Roosevelt admired the strength demanded by the wilderness, he retained an eastern prejudice about so-called western anarchy. In fact, he himself had written that pioneer-soldiers, as "archetypes of freedom," need a strong disciplinarian whose "unyielding temper and iron hand" can control "the lawless characters of the frontier." Under weaker men, he continued, these "reckless desperados" are "as dangerous to themselves and their leaders as [they are] to their foes." Yet this elitist who defended the propriety of social inequality always "treated each man on his merits as a man." He thought that blacks were inferior but Booker T. Washington superior; he scorned Asians as a "worthless race" but admired Nippon. ("What natural fighters they are!") Like the Japanese, Roosevelt's soldiers were a special group. "Putting it mildly," he admitted, they lacked the "decorum that obtains in the East." Nonetheless, he came to feel that his cowboy troopers were a natural elite who won their status by the personal virtues displayed in their heroic deeds.[32]

Roosevelt's self-approval always required support from men he respected: first his father and later his soldiers. Because he needed his troopers' admiration and devotion, he could not fulfill his disciplinary duties. Any man would have had trouble turning free-spirited cowboys into "clean-cut, well-oiled [military] cogs." With Roosevelt in command, this was impossible. True, he was hard on mollycoddles who betrayed regimental gallantry. But if his heroic and "goodhearted, homicidal children" happened to break some of the army's rules, he assumed, they said, "an almost fatherly, kindly attitude of forbearance and forgiveness." He not only freed a private court-martialed by a major general, he sometimes joined directly in the fun "as one of the boys."[33]

No other Rough Rider officer was quite as lax as Roosevelt, but virtually none of them were "spit and polish" soldiers. In Leonard Wood's entire military career, he never asked nor gave unthinking obedience to orders. Alexander Brodie, Roosevelt's immediate subordinate, graduated from the Military Academy but, as one trooper said, "he had none of the gruffness or superciliousness ordinarily associated with a West Pointer." Only Tom Hall, the regimental adjutant, was what one Rough Rider called "that horrible freak known as the military martinet." Naturally, everyone hated him. When he fled from battle "crazed with fear," he was sent home because of "climatic effects on his health" —a ruse that enabled Roosevelt to claim that all his men were brave. Hall himself maintained that he was not afraid of the enemy but was sure that his own men were out to kill him. (Those men confirmed that he was absolutely right.) After Hall left and Wood was promoted to brigadier general, Roosevelt assumed complete control. This was fortunate for the unit's cohesion since Roosevelt's need to monopolize his men's adoration had led him to challenge Wood's authority. This was unfortunate for the army's total demeanor because the Rough Riders then became, in the eyes of a least one newspaper man, the worst disciplined unit he ever saw.[34]

Although the Rough Rider esprit, said to be stronger than that possessed by any other regiment, may have been military anarchy, it also was a formidable battlefield asset. Because soldiers usually fight for their comrades (not for their country), egalitarian armies often produce heroic records. Thus the group solidarity that made the Rough Riders a compelling symbol of national integration also helped make them the heroes whom Roosevelt loved. But while the regiment may have blurred its ranks, it did not relinquish all leadership. Its officers, unsustained by formal hierarchy, led their men because they personally possessed the attributes of command. One general said of Roosevelt, he "had a democracy with his subordinates which is not easily ventured by a lesser personality." One Rough Rider said of his comrades: "We boys are all proud of our leading officers. . . . I believe we were the only volunteer regiment that after having been mustered out has not abused or slandered its officers—and all because they were what we call in Arizona 'the right kind of men.' "[35]

Those officers, paying the price of leadership in battle, suffered over 33 percent casualties. While that would have been a blow to any unit, it left the Rough Riders on the verge of disintegration since general headquarters could not stockpile charismatic personalities as it could requisition "shavetail" lieutenants. By the time the regiment charged up San Juan Hill, Wood had been promoted, Brodie wounded, and Capron and O'Neil killed. Roosevelt, then, was the one great leader left. If he had died leading that assault, as he admitted he should have, the unit, according to one of its officers, "would have fallen into chaos."[36]

Actually, the rest of the army was also near chaos after Spanish artillery fire scrambled the units marching into the San Juan Valley. Colonels should have been at work reassembling their regiments when Roosevelt, in effect, abandoned his rank to become a platoon leader heading the charge up the hill. Whatever the risk to his person, his regiment, and the whole battle, then being fought "without any definite plan," he felt that he had to take that objective himself since nothing but his charisma held his troops together. When criticized for a recklessness that could have destroyed the unit, Roosevelt replied that "the only way to lead a regiment like the Rough Riders was by convincing every member of it that you do not know the meaning of fear." His assessment, although true, overlooked the fact that other units did not need heroes who knew no fear. They only needed officers who knew the military meaning of command.[37]

Although the Rough Rider volunteer regiment survived the war intact, it was never entirely part of the U.S. Army. Its officers, who had to lead their men into battle, never had the time or energy to fulfill their administrative duties. It consequently took the adjutant general years to straighten out their records. This probably did not bother Roosevelt, as neither Generals Lee nor Grant nor anyone else in *Hero Tales from American History* ever seemed to do any paperwork. Besides the army's records, the Rough Riders ignored the rules. As natural elites above and beyond ordinary troopers, Roosevelt's boys could break "some regulation or other," dress "more like tramps than soldiers," and buy or steal supplies of everything from grain to horses to silver. Brandishing their fierce group pride, they were always fighting someone. When the Spanish were beaten, they could turn on other foreigners: the U.S. infantry. Roosevelt could have stopped his soldiers but chose to protect them. In fact, he led a few forays himself. Because they did not recognize rank, no regular officer could prevent their pillaging. A general who demanded a salute was rebuked: "I'm a Rough Rider, not a soldier."[38]

The Spoils of Battle: Glory Now and Tragedy Later

The Spanish-American War fulfilled Roosevelt's fondest dreams. When he showed that he could "lead and handle [his troops] as no other man could," a nation which seemed to lack contemporary heroes made him, its "best loved" soldier, "the Idol of every small boy in the country." His "peculiarly American regiment," giving "an exhibition of dash and valor which will inspire every manly heart throughout the land," also helped show that "the country was indeed one when serious danger confronted it."[39] Yet despite their accomplishments, only auspicious conditions saved Roosevelt from being killed by the Spanish or relieved by the army. Under different circumstances his "golden hour" of triumph would have led to the tragic finale of his own dismissal and his regiment's dissolution.

In America the Republicans were in power. Although their own secretary of war admitted that Roosevelt "has little idea of army discipline," he nonetheless was their war hero. As the administration's first choice among the many applicants seeking to raise a volunteer regiment, he was used to offset damaging Democratic claims that the opposition party of big business cared nothing for heroism and humanity. In 1897, with war fever rising, these partisan charges threatened to "sweep the country like a cyclone" and crush the GOP in "the greatest defeat ever known." Now that the Spanish-American War was over, Roosevelt was used to demonstrate that the party which once "saved the Union" still embodied patriotism. Reminiscent of those Civil War veterans "who worked the Soldier racket for all its worth" through the Gilded Age, he and his entourage of seven uniformed Rough Riders, and a bugler who blew charge before each speech, did more than "save New York for us" Republicans in 1898. In the next presidential election, when McKinley lost strength in the East, they answered a decade of local party prayers by the way they won over the West. During the 1890s, when the aging GAR lost too many members to elect the GOP, Republicans facing agrarian insurgents frequently cried for a new war hero to "stamp out discontent," "make the people patriotic," and lead their party back to victory. By 1900, Roosevelt was performing to perfection the role they requested. His seven-week campaign swing through the Plains States, which thought him "a fellow barbarian," helped return Kansas, Nebraska, South Dakota, Utah, and Wyoming to the Republican fold.[40]

In addition to enjoying partisan protection, the Rough Riders benefited from the great exposure they received as the symbol of national unity. This role made their dissolution unacceptable to the public. Strategically, this drastic step was not necessary since this "splendid little war" contained no serious setbacks. Most military reassessments came after the armistice and then they were largely concerned with mobilization and logistics, rather than deportment.

The regiment was also well served by its immediate superior, General Joseph Wheeler of Alabama, a "regular game-cock" who commanded the cavalry and loved the Rough Riders. In the Civil War, he overcame the handicap of his exemplary West Point education to lead free-lance troopers notorious for aggressive action against enemy forces and their own bureaucracy. Understandably, the Rough Riders were Wheeler's last chance to relive his youth. "This is a mob of men," he told them, "and I'm glad and proud to command [you]. I had such a mob in Tennessee and the Yankees will tell you what that mob did." (In the excitement of first battle, Wheeler would yell: "Come on men, we've got the Yankees on the run.")[41]

Wheeler was especially important because he insulated the Rough Riders from the expeditionary force commander, William R. Shafter, a 300-pound general whom the regiment "loathed and detested." More than any mollycoddle, that "fat old slob" and his staff (one of whom was an Astor with a private valet) belied the gallantry of war and the community of heroes. He not only preferred sieges and negotiated settlements to frontal assaults and "any further sacrifice of life."[42] According to Rough Riders and other embittered subordinates, he bivouacked in a suite of rooms at a "palatial" Tampa hotel, toured the theater in a comfortable coach, avoided the front whenever he could, and had iced champagne shipped to him while sick soldiers awaited medicine. When other men were being shot, his own wounds came from gout and a case of eczema caused by excessive sweating of his corpulent body. Roosevelt, who called Shafter and his staff "the pink tea generals" and "the rocking chair brigade," could not abide his command. Thanks to that egotistical rebel Wheeler, he did not have to. Both collective conceit (often called esprit de corps) and "reckless bravery" are horse cavalry traditions. If the Rough Riders, knowing "nothing but their own superb courage," were not immodest and rash, they and other troopers could never have performed their unique mission by launching "blind stampedes" on entrenched positions. Roosevelt's men, who could "charge like demons" when outnumbered four to one and still die "amazed that a mere Spaniard could hit them," had that cocky cavalry attitude and so, of course, did Wheeler. When that "courteous Southern gentleman" received Shafter's orders to halt, he ignored that "blankety-blank pot-bellied son of a blank" and conspired with Roosevelt for the greater glory of the cavalry. Hence, at least initially, their private battle plans reflected the Rough Rider resolution that "a handful of Americans [could] clean out the Spanish Army."[43]

In other and larger wars, Rough Rider egotism could have been disastrous. In this one, it was only irritating. Most of this conflict was fought with army regulars already so indoctrinated as not to be disrupted by Rough Rider behavior. Those citizen-soldiers who were allowed to participate had been sifted from over 200,000 applicants so eager for induction that they and their neighbors, entreating Washington, politically prevented "the standing army of the United States [from] fighting this war" by themselves. Moreover, since this conflict was waged on Cuban jungle trails that forbade complicated maneuvers, neither regulars nor volunteers had to perform precisely executed operations in conjunction with Rough Riders—an unconstrained military clan.[44]

Two wars later, Theodore Roosevelt's oldest son and namesake was the assistant commander of another eminently successful combat unit. Although a full division, it also had a fierce family pride that led it to steal supplies, fight with other troops, and treat virtually everyone else with disdain, from the military police to the theater commander himself. While its soldiers came mainly from New York and New Jersey, they too were said to be "a bunch of wild cowboys."[45]

Theodore Roosevelt, Jr.'s, 1st Infantry Division reinvoked the old Rough Rider spirit, but it had to wage its war within a context long unfavorable to the cavalry. Forty-eight years before they fought in World War II, Thomas Edison, whose brother-in-law was killed in the Rough Riders, declared: "The horse is doomed." Within a decade, during the Philippine insurrection, the cavalry launched its last major charge and Wheeler was at last relieved for insubordination. By 1913, once-proud troopers, "like whipped curs," were "going around Washington with their tails between their legs." By 1943, most of these men, their branch of the service, and its state of mind were all too dead to protect a Roosevelt from the demands of regular military discipline. Then Dwight Eisenhower and other West Pointers who thought "Infantry first, Infantry second and Infantry third" would command, and Roosevelt and his fellow remnants of the cavalry tradition would have trouble operating in the type of army which they ran.[46]

The Spanish-American War could be fought with a professional force supplemented by highly motivated volunteers scrambling among themselves for a chance to go to war. World War II, however, required a highly organized effort from several million draftees, nearly all of whom were "civilians at heart." This created enormous training and discipline problems. Roosevelt's division, the oldest and best in the army, was supposed to teach these recruits how to behave like seasoned soldiers, not like wild cowboys. After America's defeat at the Kasserine Pass in 1943, when the army's senior commanders grew obsessed with formal discipline, Roosevelt, Jr.'s, dismissal became inevitable. Unwilling to restrain his division's bravado, he sinned, General Omar Bradley wrote in a phrase that could have described Roosevelt's father, "by loving his men too much."[47]

NOTES

1. Roosevelt described by Henry Blake Fuller in Howard Mumford Jones, *The Age of Energy: Varities of American Experience, 1865–1915* (New York:

Viking Press, 1973), p. 212. Robert Wiebe, *The Search for Order: 1877–1920* (New York: Hill & Wang, 1967), pp. 11–38. Roosevelt quoted in Edmund Morris, *The Rise of Theodore Roosevelt* (New York: Coward, McCann & Geoghegan, 1979), p. 344; Daniel T. Rogers, *The Work Ethic in Industrial America: 1850–1920* (Chicago: University of Chicago Press, 1978), p. 7.

2. For Roosevelt's admitted political impotence, see Morison, ed., *Letters of Theodore Roosevelt,* 1:607–8, 798, 2:904, 811, 814.

3. Besides Roosevelt and Leonard Wood, other former Rough Riders active in the World War I military preparedness movement included Gordon Johnston who, as Wood's aide, helped build the Plattsburg military training camp. Arthur Cosby became the executive secretary of the Military Training Camps Association, the civilian organ of the Plattsburg camp. Dave Goodrich and George McMurty were both on this association's finance committee. Goodrich and John Greenway were founders of the American Legion. Guy Murchie and Edgar Knapp were chairmen of National Security League branches.

Still other preparedness leaders inherited Rough Rider traditions from their relatives. Delancey K. Jay and Langdon Marvin, executive members of the training camp's association, were nephews of Rough Riders. Senator James Wadsworth of New York, the leading congressional spokesman for universal military training, was Sergeant Craig Wadsworth's brother. Hamilton Fish, active in almost every preparedness organization, was the cousin of the first Rough Rider killed in action. Finally, there was Theodore Roosevelt, Jr., who, before age ten, decided that he too was going to be a Rough Rider when he grew up.

4. On Roosevelt's political philosophy, see Blum, *Republican Roosevelt,* p. 70. Roosevelt quoted in Morison, ed., *Letters of Theodore Roosevelt,* 1:10, 75, 464, 495, 516, 542, 545; William Henry Harbaugh, *The Life and Times of Theodore Roosevelt* (rev. ed.; New York: Collier Books, 1963), p. 217. To Roosevelt's joy, the political bosses would grant him his wish "in such trivial matters as war" as long as they retained their "appointment of street sweepers," see Morison, ed., *Letters of Theodore Roosevelt,* 1:500–503, 2:963.

5. Roosevelt quoted in Carleton Putnam, *Theodore Roosevelt: The Formative Years, 1858–1886* (New York: Scribner's, 1958), p. 448. Roosevelt, "American Ideals," *The Works of Theodore Roosevelt,* ed. Hermann Hagedorn (New York: Scribner's, 1925), 15:10. Roosevelt quoted in Hofstadter, *American Political Tradition and the Men Who Made It,* pp. 229–30; Roosevelt: "The Menace of the Demagogue," *Works of Theodore Roosevelt,* 16:404–5; *Letters from Theodore Roosevelt to Anna Cowles, 1870–1918* (New York: Scribner's, 1924), p. 195.

6. On the gentry, see E. J. Hobsbawn, *The Age of Capital, 1848–1875* (New York: Scribner's, 1975), pp. 182–84, 190–91. For Roosevelt on the cowboy and the frontier, see Morison, ed., *Letters of Theodore Roosevelt,* 1:100–101, 363.

7. Roderick Nash, *Wilderness and the American Mind* (rev. ed.; New Haven: Yale University Press, 1973), pp. 20, 48, 115–16, 242, passim. Critic of "masculinity" quoted in Joe L. Dubbert, *A Man's Place: Masculinity in Transition* (Englewood Cliffs: Prentice-Hall, 1979), p. 283. Roosevelt on the wilderness quoted in Nash, *Wilderness and the American Mind,* p. 150; Putnam, *Theodore*

Roosevelt: Formative Years, pp. 74, 512; Roosevelt, *A Book-Lover's Holiday in the Open: Works of Theodore Roosevelt*, 3:360.

8. G. Edward White, *The Eastern Establishment and the Western Experience: The West of Frederick Remington, Theodore Roosevelt and Owen Wister* (New Haven: Yale University Press, 1968), pp. 52, 65–90; Morris, *Rise of Theodore Roosevelt*, pp. 129, 199, 200, 221. For quotes by and about Roosevelt, see ibid., p. 212; Putnam, *Theodore Roosevelt: Formative Years*, pp. 307, 388, 514, 530; Roosevelt to Mrs. Gerado Immediato, May 18, 1917, Roosevelt MSS, Library of Congress; Morison, ed., *Letters of Theodore Roosevelt*, 1:411, 424.

9. William Roscoe Thayer, *Theodore Roosevelt: An Intimate Biography* (Boston: Houghton, Mifflin, 1919), p. 14. For baseball, see Murray Ross, "Football Red and Baseball Green," *American Way* 4 (Oct., 1971):31–36; Steven Riess, *Touching Base: Professional Baseball and American Culture in the Progressive Era* (Westport, Conn.: Greenwood Press, 1980), pp. 22, 108. In World War II, the star pitcher on the Danbury Federal Prison baseball team was an incarcerated conscientious objector; see Lawrence S. Wittner, *Rebels Against War: The American Peace Movement, 1941–1960* (New York: Columbia University Press, 1970), p. 86.

10. Theodore Roosevelt: "Professionalism in Sports," *North American Review* 61 (Aug., 1890): 188–90; "The Value of Athletic Training," *Harper's Weekly* 38 (Dec. 23, 1893): 1236. Roosevelt quoted in unidentified newspaper clipping in Leonard Wood MSS, Box 255.

11. On TR's diary, see Morris, *Rise of Theodore Roosevelt*, pp. 88, 114. TR's *Autobiography*, not accidentally, does not mention his father's failure to fight in the Civil War and his brother's profligate life with alcohol and women. Roosevelt quoted in Putnam, *Theodore Roosevelt: Formative Years*, p. 576; Roosevelt: "Dante and the Bowery," *Works of Theodore Roosevelt*, 12:98–99; *Foes of Our Own Household: Works of Theodore Roosevelt*, 19:181; Morison, ed., *Letters of Theodore Roosevelt*, 1:410, 620. For art, upper-class idealism, nationalism, and the fragmentary quotes from Emerson and Frederick Law Olmstead, see Trachtenburg, *Incorporation of America*, pp. 106–11, 142–45, 154, and Hobsbawn, *Age of Capital*, p. 285.

12. Theodore Roosevelt, *An Autobiography* (New York: Scribner's, 1929), pp. 14–16; Corinne Roosevelt Robinson, *My Brother, Theodore Roosevelt* (New York: Scribner's, 1921), pp. 1–2, 35; Theodore Roosevelt, Jr., *Average Americans* (New York: Putnam's, 1919), p. 3. For hereditary societies and the quote about "foreigners," see Davies, *Patriotism on Parade*, pp. 44, 294. Roosevelt quoted in Blum, *Republican Roosevelt*, p. 28; Roosevelt and Henry Cabot Lodge, *Hero Tales from American History* (New York: Scribner's, 1927), p. x.

13. Roosevelt quoted in Edward Wagenknecht, *The Seven Worlds of Theodore Roosevelt* (New York: Logmans, 1958), p. 67. The quote on TR's father is from Robinson, *My Brother, Theodore Roosevelt*, p. 5. On art as a substitute for the church, see Hobsbawn, *Age of Capital*, pp. 385–87. On juvenile delinquency during this period, see Joseph W. Hawes, *Children in Urban Society: Juvenile Delinquency in the Nineteenth Century* (New York: Oxford University Press, 1971), pp. 118, 123–25, 229; Henry Drummond, "Manliness in Boys—By A

New Process," *McClure's Magazine* 2 (Dec., 1893):68–77.

14. Denis Mahan quoted in Russell F. Weigley, *History of the United States Army* (New York: Macmillan, 1967), p. 151. Morison, ed., *Letters of Theodore Roosevelt,* 1:700.

15. Theodore Roosevelt to W. W. Kimball, Nov. 19, 1897, Roosevelt MSS; Roosevelt: "The Law of Civilization and Decay," *Forum* 12 (Jan., 1897):588; Roosevelt, "Washington's Forgotten Maxim," *Works of Theodore Roosevelt,* 15:247, 258. For Grant and the cults of Napoleon and Scott, see Dixon Wecter, *The Hero in America: A Chronicle of Hero-Worship* (New York: Scribner's, 1941), pp. 331, 336, 489–90; James C. Malin, *Confounded Rot about Napoleon: Reflections upon Science and Technology, Nationalism, World Depression of the Eighteen-Nineties, and Afterwards* (Lawrence, Kans.: privately printed, 1961), pp. 185–204; Henry Seidel Canby, *American Memoir* (Boston: Houghton, Mifflin, 1947), pp. 94–103.

16. Walter Millis, *The Martial Spirit: A Study of Our War with Spain* (New York: Viking, 1965), p. 220. Roosevelt quoted in Morison, ed., *Letters of Theodore Roosevelt,* 1:566. For southern sympathy, see David F. Trask, *The War With Spain In 1898* (New York: Macmillan, 1981), p. 505. Wood quoted in Virgil Carrington Jones, *Roosevelt's Rough Riders* (Garden City: Doubleday, 1971), p. 48.

17. Radical Populist Tom Watson quoted in C. Van Woodward, *Tom Watson: Agrarian Rebel* (New York: Macmillan, 1938), p. 334. McKinley described by Roosevelt in Harbaugh, *Life and Times of Theodore Roosevelt,* pp. 143–44. McKinley quoted in Gerald Linderman, *The Mirror of War: American Society and the Spanish-American War* (Ann Arbor: University of Michigan Press, 1974), p. 35. Roosevelt, "The Cuban Dead," *Works of Theodore Roosevelt,* 9:340; *Brooklyn Standard Union,* June 21, 1899. The final quotation is from John H. Parker, *History of the Gatling Gun Detachment: Fifth Army Corps, at Santiago* (Kansas City: Hudson-Kimberley, 1898), p. 215.

18. The Rough Rider roster is printed in the back of Theodore Roosevelt, *The Rough Riders* (New York: New American Library, 1961), pp. 150–85. The three quotations are from Morison, ed., *Letters of Theodore Roosevelt,* 1:412, 558; *Santa Fe New Mexican* cited in John K. Herr and Edward S. Wallace, *The Story of the U.S. Cavalry, 1775–1942* (Boston: Little, Brown, 1953), pp. 218–19; Leonard Wood cited in *New Orleans Picayune,* Jan. 14, 1899. Charles Herner, *The Arizona Rough Riders* (Tucson: University of Arizona Press, 1970), pp. 15–16. Among the sons of New York bankers were Roosevelt and Hamilton S. Fish; the East Coast industrialists included Dave Goodrich of the Goodrich Rubber Company.

19. For some of the findings of military sociology, see Robert C. Stone, "Status and Leadership in a Combat Fighter Squadron," *American Journal of Sociology* 50 (Mar., 1946):383–93; Samuel Stouffer et al., *The American Soldier, 2: Combat and Its Aftermath* (Princeton: Princeton University Press, 1949), pp. 96–99. On solidarity in the Rough Riders, see statements by David L. Hughes and Fred Herrig, n.d., Roosevelt Collection MSS, Harvard University; C. D. Scott to Hermann Hagedorn, Nov. 18, 1925, Hagedorn MSS, Box 14, Library

of Congress. Dodge City resident quoted in *New Orleans Picayune*, Jan. 14, 1899.

20. Morison, ed., *Letters of Theodore Roosevelt*, 1:621; Roosevelt, *Rough Riders*, p. 74.

21. The quotations are from Charles J. Post, *The Little War of Private Post* (Boston: Little, Brown, 1960), p. 203; *New York Tribune*, June 6, 1898; *Havana (Ga.) Press*, Feb. 27, 1899; unidentified newspapers in White, *Eastern Establishment and Western Experience*, p. 162, and in Roosevelt Collection MSS; Edward Marshall, *The Story of the Rough Riders* (New York: G. W. Dillingham, 1899), p. 102. On the press ignoring the regular army, see *Harper's Weekly*, July 9, 1898. Lawton quoted in *Havana (Ga.) Press*, Feb. 27, 1899.

22. Roosevelt, *Autobiography*, p. 253. On Roosevelt's popularity, see Ray Stannard Baker, "Theodore Roosevelt: A Character Sketch," *McClure's* 12 (1898):24; newspaperman William Archer cited in Jones, *Age of Energy*, p. 39. *Baltimore Sun*, July 30, 1898. For various ideas on war and reform, see David Axeen, "Romantics and Civilizers: American Attitudes Toward War, 1898–1902" (Ph.D. diss., Yale University, 1969), pp. 23–24, 27–30, 134–37, passim. The quotation on luck and the Rough Riders is from *San Francisco Bulletin*, Jan. 28, 1899. Statement of General Scott, Apr. 13. 1930, Hermann Hagedorn MSS, Box 20.

23. Roosevelt, *Autobiography*, p. 213; Morris, *Rise of Theodore Roosevelt*, pp. 612, 616; Morison, ed., *Letters of Theodore Roosevelt*, 1:795, 2:808, 816. The quotes about Roosevelt "abandon[ing] everything" and losing "his head" are from John D. Long as cited in Trask, *War with Spain in 1898*, p. 58, and in John A. S. Grenville and George Berkeley Young, *Politics, Strategy and American Diplomacy: Studies in Foreign Policy, 1873–1917* (New Haven: Yale University Press, 1966), p. 279.

24. Herner, *Arizona Rough Riders*, p. 146; Jones, *Roosevelt's Rough Riders*, p. 182. Roosevelt quoted in Archie Butt, *The Letters of Archie Butt*, ed., Lawrence Abbot (Garden City: Doubleday, Page, 1924), p. 146.

25. Statement by Scott, n.d.; "Memories of Oscar Wagner," n.d.; Arthur Cosby Scrapbook: all in Roosevelt Collection MSS. Roosevelt quoted in Irving C. Norwood, "Exit—Roosevelt, The Dominant," *Outing Magazine* 53 (Mar., 1909):722. On martyrs, see Theodor Reik, *Masochism in Modern Man* (New York: Farrar, Straus, 1944), p. 336. Roosevelt quoted in Morison, ed., *Letters of Theodore Roosevelt*, 2:860.

26. On Roosevelt, see "Owen Wister's Journal," Jan. 15, 1921, Owen Wister MSS, Library of Congress; Roosevelt, *Autobiography*, pp. 7–8; Morison, ed., *Letters of Theodore Roosevelt*, 2:804, 1443. For TR and his family, see David McCullough, *Mornings on Horseback* (New York: Simon & Schuster, 1981), pp. 35, 113. On self-deprecating personalities, see Karen Horney, *Neurosis and Human Growth: The Struggle for Self-Realization* (New York: Norton, 1950), pp. 22–25, 159, 221, and Harold Lasswell, *Power and Personality: A Framework for Political Inquiry* (New York: Norton, 1948), pp. 41–55. The last quotation on TR is from an unidentified newspaper clipping in Leonard Wood MSS, Box 252.

27. Roosevelt quoted in McCullough, *Mornings on Horseback*, p. 191, and in

Joseph Lash, *Eleanor and Franklin: The Story of Their Relationship* (New York: New American Library, 1973), p. 35; Roosevelt and Lodge: *Hero Tales from American History*, p. 185; *Selections from the Correspondence of Theodore Roosevelt and Henry Cabot Lodge* (New York: Scribner's, 1925) 1:325–28.

28. Statements by Rough Riders Frank Hays, Feb. 7, 1927; David L. Hughes, n.d.; Thomas Laird, Dec. 20, 1925; Kenneth Harris, n.d.: all in Roosevelt Collection MSS. Morison, ed., *Letters of Theodore Roosevelt*, 2:862.

29. The first quotation is from Richard Harding Davis, *The Cuban and Puerto Rican Campaigns* (reprinted; Freeport: Books for Libraries, 1970), p. 172. Statements of Oscar Wagner, n.d.; N. A. Vyne, n.d., Roosevelt Collection MSS. Unidentified Rough Rider quoted in Harbaugh, *Life and Times of Theodore Roosevelt*, p. 113.

30. For the love between Roosevelt and his troopers, see *Washington Star*, Jan. 12, 1899; *Scranton Tribune*, Jan. 7, 1899; statement of Frank Hays, Feb. 7, 1927, Roosevelt Collection MSS. The quotations are from Robinson, *My Brother Theodore Roosevelt*, pp. 169–70; statement by Frank Hayes.

31. C. D. Scott to Hermann Hagedorn, Nov. 18, 1925; Thomas Taylor to Hagedorn, Aug. 30, 1929: both in Hagedorn MSS, Box 14. The quotation on Roosevelt is in an unidentified newspaper in Leonard Wood MSS, Box 255. Roosevelt quoted in Morison, ed., *Letters of Theodore Roosevelt*, 2:846, 850, 892; Roosevelt to William Howard Taft, Mar. 14, 1911, Roosevelt MSS.

32. Theodore Roosevelt, *The Naval War of 1812* (New York: Scribner's 1906), 2:218, 221–22; Morison, ed., *Letters of Theodore Roosevelt*, 1:109, 2:831, 1396, 1423, 4:221–29.

33. The quotation on cogs is from an unidentified source in Jack Dierks, *Leap To Arms: The Cuban Campaign of 1898* (Philadelphia: Lippincott, 1970), p. 47. For Roosevelt's relief at not "becoming a cog in a gigantic machine," see Roosevelt, *Rough Riders*, p. 38. For Roosevelt on his military "children," see Morison, ed., *Letters of Theodore Roosevelt*, 2:1042. For his soldiers on TR, see C. D. Scott to Hermann Hagedorn, Nov. 18, 1925; statements of Fred Herrig, n.d.; Frank Hayes, Feb. 7, 1927: all in Roosevelt Collection MSS. Roosevelt, *Autobiography*, p. 228.

34. Statements of Clarence Edwards, Oct. 25, 1928; Gen. Kilbourne, Nov. 11, 1928; Alvin Ash to Hermann Hagedorn, Feb. 2, 1929: all in Hagedorn MSS, Boxes 14, 20. Statements of R. E. Morrison, n.d.; David L. Hughes, n.d.: both in Roosevelt Collection MSS. Oswald Garrison Villard, *Fighting Years: Memoirs of a Liberal Editor* (New York: Harcourt, Brace, 1939), pp. 154–55.

35. On the Rough Riders, see Davis, *Cuban and Puerto Rican Campaigns*, p. 284. Alexander L. George, "Primary Groups, Organization and Military Performance," *Handbook of Military Institutions*, ed. Roger W. Little (Beverley Hills: Sage Publications, 1971), pp. 299–301, 305; Maj. Gen. James G. Harbord, "Theodore Roosevelt and the Army," *Review of Reviews*, 119 (Jan., 1924):72; Harry Nash to Leonard Wood, Jan. 12, 1900, Wood MSS, Box 28.

36. Statement of Oscar Wagner, n.d.; "T. R.'s Premeditated Recklessness," n.d.: both in Roosevelt Collection MSS; C. D. Scott to Hermann Hagedorn, Nov. 18, 1925, Hagedorn MSS, Box 14; Morison, ed., *Letters of Theodore Roosevelt*, 2:851.

37. Leonard Wood on lack of "plan" quoted in Trask, *War with Spain in 1898*, p. 239; statement of N. A. Vyne, n.d.; "TR's Premeditated Recklessness," n.d.: both in Roosevelt Collection MSS; Herner, *Arizona Rough Riders*, p. 151.

38. Statement of L. H. Mattingly, Sept. 20, 1929, Hagedorn MSS, Box 14; Arthur F. Cosby, "The Rough Riders," *The Santiago Campaign*, ed., J. T. Dickman (Richmond: Society of Santiago de Cuba, 1927), p. 102; statements of Oscar Wagner, n.d.; David L. Hughes, n.d.; "On Board for Miami," n.d.; "Well It Was Nervy!": all in Roosevelt Collection MSS; Roosevelt, *Autobiography*, pp. 249–53; unidentified Rough Rider quoted in Jones, *Roosevelt's Rough Riders*, p. 62.

39. Roosevelt, *Letters from Theodore Roosevelt to Anna Cowles*, p. 222; Marshall, *Story of the Rough Riders*, p. 104; Mrs. W. S. Miller quoted in Wecter, *Hero in America*, p. 381; Roosevelt quoted in Morris, *Rise of Theodore Roosevelt*, p. 673; *Washington Post*, June 26, 1898; Roosevelt, "Annual Message, Jan. 2, 1899," *Works of Theodore Roosevelt*, 17:5–6.

40. Russell Alger quoted in H. Wayne Morgan, *William McKinley and His America* (Syracuse: Syracuse University Press, 1963), p. 394. For the three quotations on the Democratic challenge, see *Chicago Times-Herald* cited in Millis, *Martial Spirit*, p. 124; Elihu Root and others in Ernest May, *Imperial Democracy: The Emergence of America as a Great Power* (New York: Harper & Row, 1973), ch. 10–12; Henry Cabot Lodge quoted in Frank Freidel, *The Splendid Little War* (Boston: Little, Brown, 1958), p. 6. For the GAR vote and the quote from a disgruntled Democrat, see Davies, *Patriotism on Parade*, pp. 79, 198. Lodge to Leonard Wood, Nov. 11, 1898, Wood MSS, Box 26. For the Plains States, war, and TR, see Malin, *Confounded Rot about Napoleon*, pp. 159–80; *Kansas City Star*, June 6, 1900; Morison, ed., *Letters of Theodore Roosevelt*, 2:1339, 1358, 1448, 1452.

41. On Wheeler and the Rough Riders, see John P. Dyer, *'Fighting Joe' Wheeler* (Baton Rouge: Louisiana State University Press, 1941), pp. 347–48; Graham Cosmas, *An Army for Empire: The United States and the Spanish-American War* (Columbia: University of Missouri Press, 1971), p. 147. Wheeler quoted in statement of Frank Hayes, Feb. 7, 1927, Roosevelt Collection MSS.

42. The quotations on Shafter are from statement of Bardshar, n.d., Roosevelt Collection MSS; unidentified soldier quoted in Laurence Stallings, *The Doughboys: The Story of the AEF, 1917–1918* (New York: Harper & Row, 1963), p. 43. The "gilded gang" of East Coast Rough Riders, being more democratic, sent their own valets home, see Marshall, *Story of the Rough Riders*, p. 43. Shafter quoted in Trask, *War with Spain in 1898*, pp. 289–90.

43. Roosevelt on Shafter quoted in statement of Frank Hayes, Feb. 7, 1927, Roosevelt Collection MSS. The quotations on Rough Rider egotism and courage are from Parker, *Gatling Gun Detachment*, p. 179; Davis, *Cuban and Puerto Rican Campaigns*, pp. 170–71; *Chicago Inter-Ocean*, Dec. 31, 1899; Maj. Baston quoted in Trask, *War with Spain in 1898*, p. 222. For the spirit of the cavalry, see Edward L. Katzenbach, Jr., "The Horse Cavalry in the Twentieth Century: A Study in Policy Response," *Public Policy: A Yearbook of the Graduate School of Public Administration, Harvard University*, ed. Carl Friedrich and Seymour

Harris (Cambridge, Mass.: Harvard University Press, 1958), passim. Wheeler described in Davis, *Cuban and Puerto Rican Campaigns,* p. 55, and then quoted in statement of Thomas P. Ledwidge, n.d., Roosevelt Collection MSS.

44. For statistics on volunteers, see Trask, *War with Spain in 1898,* pp. 155–56. For popular pressure for induction and the quote from an unnamed congressman, see T. Harry Williams, *The History of American Wars: From Colonial Times to World War I* (New York: Knopf, 1981), pp. 324, 326, 332.

45. Drew Middleton, "The Battle Saga of a Tough Outfit," *New York Times Magazine,* (Aug. 8, 1945), pp. 8, 41. Hanson Baldwin, "Introduction," *Danger Forward: The Story of the First Division in World War II,* ed. H. R. Knicker-bocker (Atlanta: Albert Love Enterprises, 1947), n.p.; Omar Bradley, *A Soldier's Story* (New York: Henry Holt, 1951), pp. 110–11. The quotation is from this writer's interview with Col. Joseph Kohout, Twenty-Sixth Infantry regimental adjutant, Dec. 26, 1972.

46. George S. Patton quoted in Martin Blumenson, ed., *The Patton Papers, 1885–1940* (Boston: Houghton, Mifflin, 1972), p. 268. Eisenhower quoted in Gary Willis, *Nixon Agonistes: The Crisis of the Self-Made Man* (New York: Signet, 1971), p. 119. The epilogue of my book discusses these events in detail.

47. The first quotation is from William C. Menninger, *Psychiatry in a Troubled World: Yesterday's War and Today's Troubles* (New York: Macmillan, 1948), p. 95. Alfred D. Chandler, ed., *The Papers of Dwight David Eisenhower: The War Years* (Baltimore: Johns Hopkins Press, 1970), 2:770, 1040, 1063–64, 1150, 1343; Bradley, *Soldier's Story,* pp. 155–57.

CHAPTER 2

Leonard Wood and the Universal Military Training Movement: The Soldiers, the Doctors, and William Muldoon

☆

UNIVERSAL MILITARY TRAINING was the major goal of the World War I preparedness movement. General Leonard Wood (1860–1927), heading pressure groups for defense legislation and a model training camp at Plattsburg Barracks, New York, was the movement's major spokesman for UMT. He not only was an ally of the Roosevelts and first commander of the Rough Riders, he was a graduate of the Harvard Medical School, one source of his special interest in reform. His medical background distilled his military experience into a moral perspective that transcended the technical concerns of most modern professional men, be they army officers or doctors. A "soldier, prophet and preacher," he believed that martial discipline would develop citizens physically, morally, and politically.[1] Thus, for him, it was a public health project in an old and broad sense of the term. Before most physicians and public health practitioners came to rely on surgical and pharmaceutical cures, a regulated life was felt to be the key to human health. By the turn of the twentieth century, as medical practice grew less concerned with regimen, UMT came to represent that point of view. This chapter relates this military program to the evolution of the healing arts by focusing on the transition of the therapy of regimen out of social medicine into the armed forces. It traces this process to Leonard Wood's medical school education and his subsequent attempt to reform the living habits of post-revolutionary Cuba. Then, after studying his failure to interest professional soldiers in citizen-soldier training, the section examines why his ideas were endorsed by medical practitioners. One of the foremost supporters was William Muldoon, a health camp proprietor and a leading exponent of military therapeutics. With Wood and others, he would try to turn the preparedness movement into a public health program retaining the tonic of regimen which medicine itself no longer emphasized.

Leonard Wood, "Christian Pathology," and the Sociology of Health

By 1912, when Leonard Wood, U.S. Army chief of staff, began to promote UMT publicly, he had already won rank, seniority, fame, and power. He nonetheless was willing to jeopardize his position by championing an expensive, inconvenient, and time-consuming program that was unpopular with most civilians, politicians, and army officers. Wood was certainly an unusual citizen and a most unusual soldier.

Wood's closest aides stated that the general possessed "intense ambition," a "hunger for power," and an "infinite capacity for believing in himself." These attributes helped sustain him through the bureaucratic conflicts and controversies which punctuated his career. Many of those disputes concerned Wood's interest in domestic issues that rarely bothered most of his military colleagues, who were preoccupied with national security. The majority of the post–Civil War officer corps had learned to avoid the political errors of General Winfield Scott, a Mexican War White House aspirant whose battlefield tactics were overruled by a wary President James K. Polk. These men, "scarcely conscious" of their right to vote, believed that if they dabbled in politics then politicians, citing civilian supremacy, would closely monitor them. Partly because such officers welcomed their detachment as the best guarantee of their institutional autonomy, they ridiculed Wood, who shunned their apolitical, if not antisocial, point of view. In disdain they called him "a pill mixer," a pejorative term among army regulars who felt that medical officers, being "nobody but doctors," did not merit military rank. Nonetheless, Wood never hid his medical background. Far from being defensive, he acknowledged that it strengthened his tendency to favor unconventional programs like UMT. "Although no longer an active medical man," he wrote "the old profession is still very near my heart, and has perhaps been the most valuable asset in the work I have had to do ... in judging and handling men."[2]

Wood attended Harvard Medical School in the 1880s, before new laboratory methods focused therapeutic attention on diseased cells (as opposed to the whole patient) and before clinical training largely replaced the didactic lecture system. He therefore learned his medical craft directly from an inbred faculty nearly all of whom descended from "a line of respectable [New England] ancestors." According to one of his classmates, these professors "taught us not only our profession but behavior; social customs, morality, patriotism, personal dress, politeness, and all the influences that would be necessary in a young man's life." As "bulwarks of all that was best in Boston," they sustained an atmosphere which, in George Santayana's words, "was not that of intelligence or of science, it was that of duty." Thus they were concerned with the same broad public health questions that stirred young Dr. Wood as an intern at Boston City Hospital. Later, Wood's Army Medical Corps service furthered his interest in social issues. Unlike civilian practitioners who usually apply curative procedures to individual patients, army doctors, concentrating on the well-being of entire units, have had authority and responsibility for community preventive care. When Wood was an army post surgeon with the power "to make men clean," he himself handled public health projects from garbage cans to football teams. Although later transferred to the fighting branch, he remained part doctor at heart. As Army chief of staff in 1910, he ordered the vaccination of every American soldier thereby enabling the service to control typhoid fever some thirty years before civilian society did. More importantly, he championed a military training program reflecting the etiology of what might be called "Christian pathology": a philosophy postulating that sin caused disease.[3]

Before modern medical innovations from penicillin to plastic surgery weakened the "indissoluble union between moral, political and physical happiness," virtue and vigor were usually considered cause and effect. Seventeenth-century Puritan clergy, who often dispensed both medical and religious advice, believed that strength was (and should be) God's reward for fidelity. Hence, these "pastor-physicians" feared that secular science someday might free people from the physical penalties of sin. Their nineteenth- and twentieth-century successors modernized that faith in the "corrective afflictions" bestowed by "Israel's great Physician" when they said that "much of the ill-health of the world . . . may be directly traced to a positive disobedience of the laws of nature." Thus they felt, in Theodore Roosevelt, Jr.'s, words, "that illness is always a shame and usually a crime." These representatives of the "medical mind of New England" rejected the impulse to overmedicate. They proclaimed, instead, that "the aim of all judicious medical treatment . . . is to lay the best foundation for relief from disease by a thorough change of life, diet and regimen." Leonard Wood, obeying this code taught by Dr. John Bigelow at the Massachusetts General Hospital, brought "every part of his [own] physique to its highest perfection." A direct descendant of the first Puritan born in America, the soldier did not "smoke, drink, chew or curse." As for pharmaceutical cures, he told one congressional committee: "I never take medicine myself."[4]

Wood applied this etiology to social problems as well as personal health. With it, he "diagnosed the case of a nation as he could that of an

individual and dealt with the roots of disease instead of their results."
Indeed, this philosophy buttressed his plans for a "character-building"
system of universal military training whose principles of "regularity,
thoroughness, promptness, respect for authority, etc." would provide
preventive medicine for the body politic. The general's supporters said
that the "physical culture features of military training [would] develop
a new and better [form of] American manhood." Meanwhile Wood
himself compared pacifists to "moral syphilis" and to "typhoid carriers
[who] poison the very life of the people."[5] In so doing, the doctor who
was a soldier became a soldier who was a doctor.

Leonard Wood, Colonialism, and the Practice of Uplift

From 1898, when he commanded the Rough Riders, to his death in
1927, Wood never altered his belief in military training. Before World
War I began, he claimed that it would promote the work ethic, lower
the crime rate, Americanize the immigrant, teach "responsibility" to
the young, and "bind together all classes of society into one common
purpose."[6] But while UMT was Wood's major proposal, it was not his
only uplift project. He also expressed his missionary ideology and ambition when military governor of post-revolutionary Cuba. There, in
1899, he would try to cure a colony with military therapeutics.

President William McKinley sought a lawyer when he made Elihu
Root his secretary of war. Root, in turn, hoped that a doctor could
"clean-up Cuba" when he made Wood America's proconsul there. This
soldier, inspired with a "holy zeal for cleaning," subsequently proved
to be the man Root wanted. Most other colonial administrators, "handling and governing [the natives] according to their genius and character," were content to promote trade, protect property, and defend
strategic positions. But it was apparent to Wood's colleagues that he
thought he had "a mission—was charged with a great reformation."
Assisted by a staff of "modern Knights of the Round Table [out] on an
experiment in altruism such as the world has never seen," Wood felt
anointed "to infuse new life, new principles and new methods of doing
things" into "naturally indolent" Cubans who have "been going down
[hill] for a hundred years."[7]

Most Europeans knew better. As experienced colonialists they recognized that uplift would actually strengthen opposition to empire.
Hence, they denied Wood's premise that "character" allayed conflict.
Whereas the general tried to instill the "ambition to work and get
ahead," they practiced "indirect rule" through indigenous overlords
with their own vested interest in native subservience. Wood himself
knew that since Cuban elites desired economic access to American

markets and physical protection from black agrarians, only the "undisciplined and ignorant low-class Latin" supported the "extreme and revolutionary" independence movement. He consequently limited voting to the "better class of people representing the churches, business, education [and] the learned professions." However, this man, who "delighted in the difficult job" of moral reformation, could not remain consistently imperial. While he never disputed his colleagues' contention that most Cubans were "treacherous, lying, cowardly, thieving, worthless, half-breed mongrels," he still tried, as he once said, to "teach [the natives] to stand upon their own feet independent of petty chieftains."[8]

Americans, both for and against imperial expansion, praised Leonard Wood's program for Cuban uplift: a broadly defined public health project whose efficiency "would shame many an American city." To those Yankees who recently had hoped that war could purge the nation of material greed, Wood's regime was especially assuring. It appeared to be proof that America, long thought "great in the chase of the Almighty Dollar but small in all the other affairs of life," had "a reserve force of hitherto unknown men who can be trusted to do their duty and to meet the needs of every emergency with credit to themselves and their country." His construction and surveillance of public works and utilities inspired progressives from California to New York. His school system, enrolling 256,000 pupils in student self-governing programs, practiced the most advanced pedagogy. But to Wood's American public, nothing he did seemed nearly so great as the medical projects he undertook, whether the eradication of yellow fever from some of the dirtiest cities in the world or his personal inspection of public school privies. For this he was cheered as a "modern Hercules" who, "cleaning the Augean stable" of Cuba, performed deeds "that are obviously beyond the powers of mere mortals."[9]

Leonard Wood's Cuban character-building curriculum included more than education and sanitation. To the consternation of many conservatives, it also had a military training component. U.S. government officials, wary of rebels, never recognized the "so-called Cuban Republic" that fought against Spain. In fact, to eliminate the main obstacle to "peace and prosperity" and American rule, they had recently given this army of "degenerates" three million dollars to disband. No wonder federal authorities, still facing a Philippine insurrection in the Pacific, were dismayed at Wood's plan to reorganize 1,604 native veterans into a self-led rural guard armed with Remington rifles. They feared that this might resurrect that insurgent band of guerrillas whom Wood himself described as "black people, only partially civilized, in whom the old spirit of savagery has been more or less aroused by years of warfare." His critics, pessimistic imperialists, worried about the military consequences of military training. The general himself had faith in its social effects.[10]

Wood's own occupation army apparently demonstrated "the [beneficial] results of military training." In contrast to those Yankee hustlers who came down to make the Cuban colony another boom town rich with saloons and speculation, their "thoroughness and obedience" were said to have "formed a splendid basis for constructive work." This army, Wood now argued, could instill law and order in Cuban "brigands" who lacked "normal and wholesome pursuits." Military training, creating "common interests" out of anarchy, would surely "be of immense value in building up sentiment and respect for American institutions and American officials." Ever since the Rough Riders convinced Wood that the army could unite his country's regions and classes, he seemed to feel that it also possessed the power to "obliterate the differences of opinion which exist" between nationalities. Wood, who took his post saying that he would bring Cuba into the Union voluntarily, maintained that the army would assimilate the natives and make them "loyal to us."[11]

Along with the general's philosophy of moral uplift and the military training he used to teach it, Wood's Cuban tour of duty demonstrates his enormous missionary ambition. To keep his 109–hour work week, "the hardest service day ever spent by an American," he rejected the presidency of a national traction company wanting to buy his public image and Washington connections for $20,000 a year plus stock. Economically meager and physically unhealthy though it was, Wood's $5,500 a year job as "a veritable Pooh-Bah" ("judge, jury, dictator, scavenger, inspector, military leader, physician and friend") paid him with a generous amount of ego satisfaction. As newspapers observed, it fulfilled Wood's "wish to put his stamp directly on the history of the age in which he has lived."[12] Consequently, his advice on America's colonial policy varied directly with his own tenure of office. He firmly advocated indefinite American occupation of Cuba until China's Boxer Rebellion offered new possibilities for military action. Then, saying that informal control would suffice, he recommended holding the Cuban Constitutional Convention that would free him for duty in the Orient. When the Boxer Rebellion ended abruptly, Wood again maintained that America's government of the island was imperative. However, by then (1901–2), the United States had decided to retrench its empire. Even Wood's friends Elihu Root and Theodore Roosevelt were now content to control Cuba's foreign policy and its strategic position without assuming the internal political problems which he himself was so eager to bear. Hence, Wood admitted that he had failed to change either Cuba's Latin character or America's sluggish colonialism. Of his Hispanic wards he said: "The great mass of public opinion is perfectly inert. . . . It is hard to get them out of the old ruts and grooves." Concerning himself he was, for once, equally sober. When Englishmen told him that his service deserved an earldom and gratuity, Wood replied: "We do things differently in America. I venture to prophesy that within two years I shall have to fight even to hold my commission." Nonetheless, Wood always thrived on imperial responsibility. Some twenty years later, in 1921, after suffering serious disappointments in the United States, he would return to colonial administration, this time in the Philippines. Although those islands had become rather trifling to America, they still were dear to Leonard Wood. By then, colonialism once again became the best way for him to exercise his will-to-power.[13]

In 1910, eight years after America's occupation of Cuba ended, the old governor-general became the new army chief of staff. As Wood's colonial past indicates, he undertook this assignment believing in the domestic benefits of military training, moral solutions to social problems, and his personal destiny to direct a nation's uplift. No doubt agreeing with the Latin admirer who wrote him: "I hope you may accomplish as much for your country as you have for Cuba," Wood turned his attention to the elevation of America.[14]

The Regular Army and the Citizen-Soldiers: The Development of a Professional Officer Corps

In the early 1900s, continental Europe's development of large armies filled with conscripts sparked a debate over how America should recruit, train, and organize its own defense. Leonard Wood, believing that military instruction was based on common sense, supported a six-month period of universal training that would make the army into "a greater mill through which the population is passed." In this way the service would have a large reserve and society would have an uplifting institution. Yet most professional soldiers, despite their cry for more manpower, continued to endorse the old West Point dictum that "to make a good army out of the best men will take three years." By the early twentieth century, the growth of technical knowledge in industrial society turned many old jobs into new professions. Members of the standing army, however, remaining to much of the public a miserable band of mercenaries, still struggled for status as scholars of the great "science of war." Because the military's prerogatives were so insecure, it disputed all claims that civilians could do its job. If in fact they could, the service would never become a profession: an organization that monopolizes a function through its monopoly of some esoteric skill. Consequently, most career soldiers favored (by two-to-one in one poll) a large standing army with five-to-six-year enlistment periods.[15]

These professional soldiers, whom Wood called "old pinheads," had a professional interest in a professional army. They believed that it would maximize their salaries, promotions, and prestige, whereas Wood's campaign for a citizen-service threatened their sinecures, their rewards, and even their way of life. The task of recasting "luxury loving" civilians into a disciplined guard seemed difficult, if not an impossible duty. This assignment, moreover, was likely to disrupt the culture of "clannish" military communities notoriously resistant to change. In a bailiwick service stationed on hitching-post forts, career men were "expected to 'corn' up after dinner and go to bed mellow every night." They also could practice corporal discipline along with moral vice. In Wood's amateur army, however, instructors might have "to persuade, coddle and cajole" recruits rather than continue to jam in obedience "as we used to load an old field gun." Thus the service would have to reform itself lest it alienate the populace on which it had to rest. Wood's proposal, finally, would be unrewarding as well as disruptive, since it considered appointing citizen-soldiers to active command. That feature, advocated to stimulate public interest in the program, was itself a grave insult to the professional pride of "a number of high officers" who, like guildsmen in any line of work, "believe in mystery and not in publicity."[16]

The military had been voicing its desire for a large standing army since at least 1815. But before the Civil War, the theory of Jacksonian democracy delayed professionalization by enforcing open entry into the officer corps, approximately one-fourth of whom were commissioned directly from civilian society. However, after the Gilded Age growth of producer monopolies offered "soldiers of fortune" more money in industry than they could ever pillage on the battlefield, few satisfied consumers of national security argued even theoretically for a citizen-soldier service. Henceforth both academic and popular thought, both laissez-faire and the left, tended to agree that military and economic organizations embodied different stages of social development. Intellectuals, articulating this consensus about the antithesis between war and industry, outlined historial progress from combat to commerce: "In the modern world," said William Graham Sumner, philosopher for laissez-faire, "ferment is furnished by economic opportunity and hope for luxury. In other ages it has often been furnished by war." War, according to Scott Nearing, an economist on the left, was a relic of the past, "defunct" in the present, with "no part to play in the future" of mankind.[17]

The army itself, while denying that it was an artifact, used Sumner's assumptions to support its own plan to build a professional force. It

maintained that irreconcilable differences separated martial selfless-
ness and self-concerned civilians. However, its claims to the contrary,
the service was not truly Spartan. Its top West Point graduates, from
Robert E. Lee to Douglas MacArthur, invariably chose to join the Corps
of Engineers, generally considered the apex of the army. There, inter-
meshed with real estate developers, they and the rest of the service
built America's commercial arteries, sometimes spending twice as
much on river and harbor improvements as they did on coastal defense.
Many other West Pointers, fleeing rural poverty, enrolled in the Academy (the nation's "cheap school of science") to improve their future
career opportunities through a government-subsidized education. Later,
as officers, they frequently sought assignments that would allow them
to enter some local business or a War Department bureau. Far from
feeling that a Washington staff appointment was ignoble duty, these
and other soldiers, hoping to "get a bootlick on people of note," fought
one another for a chance to join the "businessmen in blue"—that 33
percent of the officer corps who imposed a cost-accounting calculus on
nearly every army action. (For example, the quartermaster corps required twenty-nine officers to sign twelve different statements explaining a $28 loss of army property.) Those who entered this "privileged
class" in Washington, deserting "the flagpole" at the fort "to play
around the throne," augmented their rank, pay, creature comforts,
and "political pull." Thus, its corporate code to the contrary, the army
seemed rent with a "rivalry, envy, [and] jealousy that precludes all possibility of brotherliness."[18]

Nonetheless, the military spirit was not completely sham. Although a
real warrior, like young George Patton, would pledge never to "degenerate into a commonplace officer," Leonard Wood and his supporters
sincerely criticized individual indulgence. This ambitious general, who
had also gone to Washington to cultivate political friends of his own,
honestly but naively felt that the army could not abide commercial self-
concern. Yet he and his entourage would not conclude, as did so many
sociologists and soldiers, that the service should therefore segregate
itself from society. They hoped, instead, that the flower of the army,
serving "without thought of private gain," would reintroduce martial
virtues to modern civilization. By reforming the materialists who entered its ranks, the armed forces would help both themselves and the
nation avoid distasteful stages of development: barbarism on the one
hand, overrefinement on the other. Whereas either stage, alone, was
unhealthy for society, military energy, when mixed with civil order,
would revitalize the principles of the Protestant ethic.[19]

But despite Wood's desire to integrate and thereby change the army
and America, his plans for UMT were not implemented. Politicians,

promising budget reductions to inflation-ridden voters, would not advocate this program in war, lest alone peace. Most senior officers, concurring, thought that six months of citizen-training was a virtually useless expense. In 1912, with Wood's plans thus blocked, he began what few soldiers would ever dare do, least of all at a time when the Taft and Wilson administrations threatened to punish any officer taking a "public part in [any] political matter." Wood, having long felt himself to be an outcast in the service but a hero to the nation, took his project directly to the people, eventually making over 100 speeches in six months' time. Upon becoming the catalyst who transformed an intra-army argument about UMT into a political debate and a social movement, his public message once again coalesced with his personal ambition. Not unlike those rivals who criticized Wood's "notoriously undisciplined attitude" and his "overwhelming [drive] for notoriety," the general's own aide later observed: "His impulse was not unrelated to that which drives an actor who has tasted the wine of popular applause and is driven once more back to the blaze of the footlights. He liked the attention, he liked the feeling of power, having a message to deliver and an audience eager to receive it; he liked the headlines next morning."[20]

Modern Medicine: The Evolution of the Healing Arts

When Leonard Wood after 1912 sought to mobilize a constituency for universal military training, he received public support from numerous doctors who apparently possessed more faith in the therapeutic efficacy of army service than most professional soldiers ever had. In 1916, for example, seventy-nine presidents of state medical organizations, nineteen presidents of national medical societies, ten chairmen of American Medical Association divisions, and representatives of ninety-five medical schools went on record favoring UMT. Some of these physicians, sons of Civil War veterans, had studied military history or gone through training themselves. In fact, they still identified their profession with their idea of the army. Rejecting the Red Cross image of medicine as international and pacifistic, they called their therapies "weapons" for "hand-to-hand conflict" with disease. Minimizing the economic motivation in their occupation, they saw the surgeon and the general as two dedicated servicemen courageously performing life-or-death operations. However verbose, their military analogues had some sociological merit. Unlike diagnosticians and general practitioners, who were small, competitive businessmen in client-centered enterprises, the most promilitary doctors were generally surgeons, medical school professors, hospital administrators, or asylum psychiatrists. Akin to military officers, they worked in institutional settings where nurses, like enlisted men, gave "absolute and unquestioning obedience" to the orders of superiors. Perhaps because their own dependent patients resembled docile recruits undergoing basic training, some of these doctors, following the lead of Leonard Wood, seem to have perceived the army as a potential sanatorium able to perform the social function which hospitals themselves had once assumed.[21]

Until the late nineteenth century, the best available medical care could usually be dispensed at home by the family physician carrying all his instruments in his own black bag. Children's Hospital (Boston) and other medical centers, stressing "the moral benefit" of "Christian nurture," were largely built to bring the poor "under the influence of order, purity and kindness." Then a series of innovations, such as the X-ray machine built in 1895, changed these clinics to reflect America's near dogmatic faith in salvation through science. Hospitals became (and have remained) committed to advanced-technology care even when some prestigious machinery (like that used in cardiac intensive-care units) has actually had minimal results. To buy, maintain, and manage the expensive new equipment that hospitals craved, they had to deemphasize their eleemosynary image lest potential benefactors, with reputations to protect, refuse to be treated in such stigmatizing institutions. Hence clinics relinquished many of their social uplift interests to concentrate strictly on medical training, research, and care. A new agency consequently was needed to correct and control deviant behavior. As Dr. Charles W. Burr, Professor of Mental Diseases at the University of Pennsylvania, declared: "Unless the American boy is taught obedience, unless he learns to submit to authority, unless he learns that the highest manhood is to obey, unless he learns that work is a blessing, not a curse, this country is doomed. . . . Universal military training will do much to stiffen up, to make firm-fibered and manly the boys of America."[22]

Dr. Burr and others who followed Leonard Wood may have fancied the martial life largely because social discipline was increasingly irrelevant to their daily practice. Licensed physicians in the early twentieth century justified their newly won monopoly of the healing arts by their specialized training in scientific principles which maintained that "pathology is the physics of disease." A mechanistic concept of "the biological man" thus became prevalent in research and care. Earlier, in 1861, when organic models were more widely used, Dr. Oliver Wendell Holmes, Wood's favorite teacher at the Harvard Medical School, wrote that the telegraph was "a network of iron nerves" uniting America "into a single living body." Now, inverting the metaphor, life came to copy the machine. According to this "medical materialism," taken to its extreme, cardiology concerned a pump and pipes, metabolism was a chemical plant, and the central nervous system was said to be a telegraphic network where "the brain is the central office." Because machines do not have souls, modern physicians who based their authority on impersonal science ignored the old counselor role of the family physician whose influence derived from years of intimate acquaintance with the private lives of their clientele. Instead of using a ministerial form of medicine to reform their neighbors' moral habits, as did Leonard Wood, therapists now frequently treated their patients as one repairs an engine, but using scalpels and drugs rather than wrenches and fuels. Consequently they often shifted their primary concern from the sick to a sickness, from the man to his disease. As for the patient himself, he grew ever less responsible for his own health. The client who believed that a doctor could save him, or a manufactured drug could cure him, became a passive consumer of a health-care commodity which was a service that he bought rather than a plan by which he lived.[23]

The "science" of medicine affected the practice of public health in much the same manner. At the time of the American and French revolutions, when doctors throughout the Western world were social activists, the field of public health was broadly concerned with issues like political corruption. In fact, until the 1850s, its American practitioners often felt they were fulfilling a "religious duty" for the elevation of humanity and "the sanitary regeneration of society." However, by the late nineteenth century, they narrowed their domain from general reform to epidemiology and sanitation. In response to the population influx straining urban facilities, public health became primarily preoccupied with drainage, sewage, and waste disposal. In the 1900s, it added the study of bacteriology and immunology. Whether attentive to garbage or germs, public health, like private practice, thus became progressively divorced from moral life. Often ignored by modern medicine, the ethical tenets once emphasized in "the Christian pathology" were increasingly lodged in certain healing cults, one of which was the Leonard Wood-led military training movement. Perhaps some clinicians joined this "happy Latin scholar," thoroughly educated in the humanities as well as science, because his auspices allowed them to endorse old principles growing professionally passé.[24]

In retrospect, it seems naive to have believed that the army would inform the young about "their physical make-up and what it means to take care of this temple which God gave us." Military life is not only vulnerable to communicable diseases like those that killed seventeen American soldiers for each combat fatality in 1898. Military medicine is extremely "impersonal" and rarely didactic. Because war inflicts wounds irrespective of any soldier's hygenic habits, it undermines the belief that virtue is rewarded. "Blind," as veterans say, "in its human destruction," war's "great bloody wave" of casualties have to be treated in mass with the utmost haste. Consequently, medical corps personnel often acquire the "habit of regarding a man and his wound as separate institutions." They even "seem rather annoyed that the former should express any opinion on the latter, or claim any right in it." Thus army medicine, which has had an appreciable impact on modern public health practice, emphasizes surgery and drugs, not counseling and virtue. Although Leonard Wood wanted "clean-in-mind" soldiers who would treat their uniforms like clerical robes, the mass-produced condom became standard World War I equipment. Notwithstanding Wood's plea for the prophylactic of temperance, other officers felt that "people who are going to be killed deserve as much pleasure as they can get." Military training advocates like Wood, who hoped that men would not "go to their death from the arms of a prostitute," were deceived by a misguided faith or a desperate trust in martial morality.[25]

Acting on that faith, some doctors before the war recommended the therapy of army life. To them, forts resembled the old hospitals of Philadelphia and Boston within whose guarded walls patients, upon penalty of expulsion, were forbidden to act rudely, play cards, receive gifts, or communicate with members of the outside world. Both institutions, medical and military, were sanctuaries from the injurious seductions of civilization, especially excessive wealth. This variant of "Christian pathology," transferring condemnation from the individual patient into a critique of society, is an etiology as old as American medicine. In contemporary life, tranquilizers and barbiturates consumed by the ton have become the technologically discovered prescriptions for technologically induced problems like insomnia, hypertension, and nervous strain. (As Lewis Mumford remarks: These opiates are becoming "the religion of the masses.") Before the new age of drugs, which began with the introduction of aspirin in 1899, nonpharmaceutical cures were recommended for these ailments. Some physicians, who emphasized the ill-effects of endless competition for material success, prescribed rest cures like travel and resorts. Others, who primarily opposed luxury, indolence, and self-indulgence, advised work cures: the most extreme of which was war. Civil War statistics, indicating a decrease in insanity, seemed to them to prove "that the mind of the country was raised by the war to a healthier tension and more earnest devotion to healthier objects than was largely the case amid the apathies and self-indulgence of the long-continued peace and national prosperity that preceded the great struggle."[26]

Neo-puritan complaints that Americans were a "soft, fat, flabby emotional and kindhearted but mush-headed race" remained common among a post–Civil War generation of promilitary physicians, one of whom was Leonard Wood's own neurosurgeon, Dr. Harvey Cushing of the Harvard Medical School. As a volunteer at Passchendaele, after facing a German attack, Cushing explained: "The savage in you makes you adore [the bombardment] with its squalor and wastefulness and danger and strife and glorious noise. You feel that, after all, this is what men were intended for rather than to sit in easy chairs with cigarette and whisky, the evening paper or the best-seller, and to pretend that there is no barbarian behind your starched and studded shirt." Yet even Cushing seems moderate when compared to the editor of *Boston Medical and Surgical Journal* who said that certain patients would stand a better chance of recovery if "they were sent to the battlefield instead of the sanitarium."[27]

William Muldoon and the Therapy of Pain

Years before Leonard Wood inaugurated citizen-soldier training in World War I, one physician suggested that the country adopt Spartan-like communities with "well devised rules [for] training the young." Another doctor, echoing the family physician who sent Theodore Roosevelt's "nerve"-sick brother to a Texas army post, urged upon the country military drills to prevent dementia praecox (schizophrenia) and other infirmities. Yet medical men were not General Wood's sole source of support. Others also endorsed his endeavor to use military preparedness to improve the public's health. Aside from Wood himself, a professionally trained physician who brought a medical perspective to the army, the therapist with the most influence on the military training movement was William Muldoon (1845–1933), a lay clinician who introduced a martial approach to medicine. Those citizens attending Wood's experimental program in UMT recognized that Muldoon's own health camp had set a precedent for Plattsburg. After completing a three-hour cavalry drill, New York's Mayor John Purroy Mitchel returned to his pup tent and exclaimed: "Muldoon's has nothing on this." George Wharton Pepper, an upper class Philadelphia lawyer, told audiences that men enrolled at Plattsburg for the same reason that they went to Muldoon's. Both being reactions "against excessive civilization," they were "akin to the emetic corrective after the feast in the days of Roman decadence." Two years later, in 1918, when a fifty-one-year-old Pepper could not enlist as a private in the army under Leonard Wood's banner, he went to Muldoon's "for reconditioning."[28]

A Renaissance man, William ("Billy") Muldoon was, at different times, a soldier, wrestler, bartender, policeman, entrepreneur, physical trainer, and social philosopher. Sometimes called "the Professor," this grade-school-educated Irish Catholic resembled Harvard alumnus Theodore Roosevelt in his fear that industrial America was suffering from excessive luxury and leisure. To help cure this problem, in the early 1890s he built a health camp in Purchase, New York, where, for $600, he gave the rich and powerful cold showers, simple food, strict discipline, and strenuous exercises, one of which involved a pain-inducing sphere that he dubbed a "medicine ball." Yet, like others in the military training movement, Muldoon damned opulence while praising private property. This self-made millionaire in the banking, coal, sports, and health industries took no vows of poverty. He, instead, focused his scorn on indulgence, which he defined as wealth without "discipline and control." Although he lived in palatial splendor "like the President of a South American Republic," Muldoon honored restraint, regulation, and work by imposing them on his clientele through a paramilitary coercion.[29]

Muldoon, who reminded reporters of General Pershing, was active in military societies and eventually became president of the Sixth New York Cavalry (Civil War) Veterans' Association. Because this former Union army trooper ran his sanatorium on military principles, his patients (who included Generals Chaffee, Bell, and Lawson) often called him "the Colonel." When those and other men came to him for help, Muldoon dressed them in khaki pants and blue army shirts, housed them in barracks, and treated them with the contempt of a drill instructor. Ordering his charges to sleep, bathe, and eat at his command, he made them "as prompt and orderly as so many old soldiers of the regular army."[30]

A bruising wrestler who had trained heavyweight boxing champion John L. Sullivan by intimidation, Muldoon browbeat some of the most powerful men in America whom he bluntly told: "You are a proven failure; I will manage you while you are here." As one patient put it: "No one was really any one however much he might be outside. Our host was all. He had a great blazing personality which dominated everybody." His customers, however, disagreed with doctors who criticized "Muldoon's abusive profanity." Swearing by him (not only at him), they helped create the long waiting list of men eager to pay his high fee. According to George Wharton Pepper, who came to Muldoon suffering exhaustion but returned home "hard as nails": "Muldoon was rough, rude, sarcastic and unfair but 99 percent of the people who go there deserve to be treated with roughness, rudeness, sarcasm and unfairness and it does them a lot of good. . . . It was a rough experience but one I never regretted."[31]

Certainly Muldoon was successful but exactly what he did (as well as how and why it worked) is a complicated question. Muldoon himself, talking the language of "Christian pathology," claimed that he trained his customers to develop the disciplined habits that ensured their health. Others said that his patients, consumed with hate for Muldoon, committed themselves to recover enough strength to kill "the Colonel." While both these opinions have some elements of truth, they overlook Muldoon's particular genius. As one of his clients said: "His real bent was as a trainer and conditioner of men. He had an uncanny instinct about it, seemed to know, just as a good trainer knows, how much the animal will stand without injury, when to start and when to stop."[32]

This talent enabled Muldoon to nurture the same pride that men felt when they survived Plattsburg, West Point, or some other military training program. His customers feared they would collapse from this "premonition of Dante's Inferno." When they did not break, they developed a therapeutic self-confidence. Muldoon's health camp specialized in treating neurasthenia, a symptom of acute self-deprecation. After a neurasthenic withstood Muldoon, he apparently found enough confidence to face the rest of the world.[33]

Roger Alden Derby, a future Plattsburger, was a rich patrician leading a seemingly purposeless life when he "had a pretty severe nervous breakdown." As he recalled: "I was really in good condition and [only] needed somebody *I* had confidence in to tell me I was sound." He went to Muldoon's, where one day "the Colonel" asked him to spar in a gentlemanly fashion. Honored to get into the ring with a champion, Derby agreed. Muldoon then proceeded to beat him to a pulp. Derby was too angry to quit but when Muldoon thought his opponent could stand no more, he stopped, hugged him, and declared that Derby was tough enough to be the middleweight champ. Those words, Derby said, "did more for me in about ten seconds than all the nerve specialists and doctors had done for me in weeks."[34]

From pride in pain (which the army symbolizes with combat medals) to khaki uniforms, Muldoon's method was highly military. It actually resembled nothing so much as the frontline psychotherapy that he, as a Civil War sergeant, certainly witnessed and probably practiced. Then, enlisted men were treated for exhaustion, depression, and cramps, summarized as "combat fatigue." Now Muldoon faced the same symptoms in America's "ceaselessly scheming" civilian society. There, business, political, and professional men who debased the work ethic in the pursuit of money were commonly said to suffer neurasthenia: a diagnostic label that soldiers would later use interchangeably with "shell-shock." (In World War I, many doctors and laymen said that virtually all combatants, disabled or not, had "a condition of profound neurasthenia.") But neither Muldoon, who dealt with senators, nor the army treating soldiers, considered these casualties to be "sick men." That diagnosis, rationalizing their symptoms, would have justified their breakdowns. Instead, both Muldoon and the army, making "torture" into treatment, exploited the guilt and pride their patients felt by using humiliation and reassurance to compel "'neurotics' to flee [from them] to health." First using mortifying methods like bed checks for urine, they insulted the afflicted's self-respect. They thereby shamed men into relinquishing their "ticket out of combat"—the neuropsychiatric symptoms that necessitated their relief from the pressures of business or the dangers of battle. The army simultaneously emphasized the glory of the soldier's unit, its jeopardy in his absence, and its dependence on his service. Appealing to a patient's pride, it tried to convince him that he had the courage to return to action. Muldoon, on the other hand, had to create a combat experience before he could evoke a similar reaction of moral restoration. When he pushed men beyond what they thought they could endure, he did exactly that.[35]

The main difference between the army's neuropsychiatric evacuation tents and Muldoon's health camp lay not in method but in monetary cost. While the military provided "socialized" medicine free to any emotional casualty, the trainer treated only those prosperous men who could afford his fee. But like other therapists, licensed or lay, Muldoon's success with a select clientele caused him to think that his healing method was applicable to the world outside his practice when, in fact, it was not. Patients, whether lower-class ethnics or Yankee elites, tend to choose practitioners who share their values. Since Muldoon's customers believed in his theory that they proved their worth once they survived his ordeal, his regimen was often efficacious for them. Misled by his success, Muldoon thought that his etiological philosophy about the danger of wealth with the absence of discipline was relevant to the nation, not just the upper class. Consequently, he tried to democratize his system by asking Congress and some philanthropic millionaires to endow Muldoon training camps for the general public. When that failed, he came to pin his hopes on the military preparedness movement. "The country," Muldoon said, "has got to sweat itself back to a state of purity . . . by work and discipline which is backed by an authority that nobody can defy or question. I know of no system that will do this other than one of universal military training."[36]

NOTES

1. The quotation is from Henry L. Stimson Diary, May 21, 1919, Stimson MSS, Yale University.

2. Statements of Gordon Johnston, Jan. 25, 1929; Frank McCoy, May 16, 1929: both in Hermann Hagedorn MSS, Boxes 19, 22, Library of Congress. Archie Butt, *Taft and Roosevelt: The Intimate Letters of Archie Butt* (Garden City:

52   To Make Democracy Safe for America

Doubleday, Doran, 1930), pp. 781–82; Samuel P. Huntington, *The Soldier and the State: The Theory and Politics of Civil-Military Relations* (New York: Vintage Books, 1957), Chapters 8, 9, 10; *The Military Services Journal* quoted in Barbara Tuchman, *Stilwell and the American Experience in China, 1911–45* (New York: Bantam Books, 1972), p. 21; unnamed soldiers quoted in Columbus (Ohio) *Dispatch*, Dec. 8, 1899; Cosmas, *Army for Empire*, p. 264. Leonard Wood to Dr. J. M. T. Finney, Feb. 16, 1913, Wood MSS, Box 70.

3. For the Harvard Medical School, see Thomas Francis Harrington, *The Harvard Medical School* (New York: Lewis Publishing, 1905), pp. 765, 1023–34; George Santayana, *Character and Opinion in the United States* (Garden City: Doubleday Anchor, 1956), pp. 36–39. For the army medical corps, see Stanhope Bayne-Jones, *The Evolution of Preventive Medicine in the United States Army, 1607–1939* (Washington: Office of the Surgeon General, 1968), pp. 1–2. The quotations are from William T. Councilman as cited in Morris J. Vogel, "Boston's Hospitals, 1870–1930: A Social History" (Ph.D. diss., University of Chicago, 1974), p. 152; Dr. Pfeiffer to Hermann Hagedorn, Feb. 21, 1929, Hagedorn MSS, Box 12; Lincoln (Neb.) *Courier*, July 15, 1899.

4. The first quotations are from Benjamin Rush as cited in George Rosen, *From Medical Police to Social Medicine* (New York: Science History Publications, 1974), p. 248. For Puritans and medicine, see John Duffy, *The Healers: The Rise of the Medical Establishment* (New York: McGraw-Hill, 1976), p. 36, Paul Starr, *The Social Transformation of American Medicine* (New York: Basic Books, 1982), pp. 39–40, and quotations from Puritans in Bercovitch, *The American Jeremiad*, pp. 58–59. On New England medicine and Christian pathology, see Robert Tomes, "Why We Get Sick," *Medical America in the Nineteenth Century*, ed. Gert H. Brieger (Baltimore: Johns Hopkins Press, 1972), pp. 256–57, and Gerald Grob, *Mental Institutions in America: Social Policy to 1875* (New York: Free Press, 1973), pp. 153–59. Theodore Roosevelt, Jr., to Arthur Lee, June 29, 1927, Roosevelt, Jr., MSS, Box 44, Library of Congress. The quotations from medical practitioners are from Dr. Henry A. Christian and the managers of Boston's Children's Hospital as cited in Vogel, "Boston's Hospitals," pp. 37, 136. On New England medicine, see Jacob Bigelow, "On Self-Limited Diseases"; Austin Flint, "Conservative Medicine," in Briger, *Medical America in the Nineteenth Century*, pp. 101, 135–38. The quotations on Leonard Wood are from Nelson A. Miles, *The Personal Recollections and Observations of Nelson A. Miles* (Chicago: Werner, 1896), p. 488; statement of Johnston Hagood, n.d., Hermann Hagedorn MSS, Box 17. Wood quoted in *Springfield (Mass.) Republican*, Jan. 14, 1899.

5. Wilson Gill to Hermann Hagedorn, Feb. 10, 1929, Hagedorn MSS, Box 17; Wood to C. P. J. Mooney, Sept. 3, 1917, Wood MSS, Box 96; Howard Gross, president of the Universal Military Training League, quoted in Chambers, "Conscripting for Colossus," p. 218; Leonard Wood, *Our Military History: Its Facts and Fallacies* (Chicago: Reilly & Britton, 1916), pp. 183–84; Wood to Military History Society of Massachusetts, Jan., 1913; Wood MSS, Box 70.

6. Wood to E. W. Nichols, Sept. 29, 1913; Wood to Lyman Abbott, Sept. 27, 1913; Wood, "Address to the Association of American Agricultural Colleges and Experimental Stations," Nov., 1913: all in Wood MSS, Boxes 66, 67, 68.

7. Statement of Elihu Root, Dec. 3, 1928, Hermann Hagedorn MSS, Box 14; Wood quoted in David Healy, *The United States in Cuba: 1898–1902* (Madison: University of Wisconsin Press, 1963), p. 179. The characterization of other colonialists is by General Robert Bullard as cited in Allan R. Millett, *The General: Robert L. Bullard and Officership in the United States Army, 1881–1925* (Westport: Greenwood Press, 1975), p. 145. General Adna Chaffee quoted in Howard Gillette, Jr., "The Military Occupation of Cuba, 1899–1902: Workshop for American Progressivism," *American Quarterly* 15 (Oct., 1973):414; statements of Frank McCoy, Apr. 30, 1929, Hermann Hagedorn MSS, Boxes 14, 15.

8, On Wood in Cuba, see Herman Hagedorn, *Leonard Wood* (New York: Harper & Brothers, 1931, 1:237–39, 392, 2:14; James H. Hitchman, *Leonard Wood and Cuban Independence: 1898–1902* (The Hague: Martinus Kijhoff, 1971), passim. On European colonialism, see V. G. Kiernan, *The Lords of Human Kind: Black Man, Yellow Man and White Man in an Age of Empire* (Boston: Little, Brown, 1969), pp. 52–53, 95, 211. Wood quoted by Rene Bache in the *Dispatch,* Jan. 19, 1899. Cubans described by Parker, *Gatling Gun Detachment,* p. 78.

9. For American editorial response to Wood's rule in general, see *Watertown (N.Y.) Times,* Nov. 10, 1899; *Brooklyn Times,* Dec. 15, 1899. For Wood's "progressivism," see Gillette, "The Military Occupation of Cuba," pp. 410–25; Hitchman, *Leonard Wood and Cuban Independence,* passim. For some American editorial responses to Wood's public health projects, see *Albany Times-Union,* Dec. 7. 1899; *Mississippi Times,* Mar. 20, 1899; *Washington Star,* Feb. 8, 1899.

10. For American policy towards the rebels and successive quotes from President McKinley, Henry Cabot Lodge, Whitelaw Reid, and Gen. S. B. M. Young, see Trask, *War With Spain In 1898,* pp. 53, 56; Lodge to Leonard Wood, Sept. 28, 1898, Wood MSS, Box 26; Millis, *The Martial Spirit,* pp. 47, 50–51, 141–43, 362. Healy, *The United States in Cuba,* pp. 33–34, 46–47, 68–69, 104–5. John H. Napier, "General Leonard Wood: Nation-builder," *Military Review* 12 (Apr, 1972):81. Wood quoted in Linderman, *Mirror of War,* p. 318.

11. Charles M. Pepper, *To-morrow in Cuba* (New York: Harper & Brothers, 1899), pp. 335–39; *New York Tribune,* July 22, 1899. Wood quoted in *Chicago Tribune,* Oct. 4, 1900; *New York Times,* Feb. 9, 1903. Leonard Wood, "Memorandum: General Scheme for Replacing to a Great Extent the United States Troops in Cuba with Native Regiments," Oct. 27, 1899, in Hermann Hagedorn MSS, Box. 15.

12. *St. Louis Dispatch,* Jan. 15, 1899; *Troy (N.Y.) Times,* Dec. 2, 1898; *Lewiston (Me.) Journal,* Dec. 31, 1898; *Buffalo Commercial News,* Dec. 5, 1899. As to Wood's health, he exacerbated a cerebral swelling by continuing to work eighteen hours a day despite a typhoid fever of 103 degrees. By 1927, this injury grew into the neurological tumor that killed him.

13. Healy, *United States in Cuba,* pp. 144–49. Wood quoted in ibid., p. 188; in Henry Stimson to Dr. Abbott, June 14, 1928, Hermann Hagedorn MSS, Box 16. Wood in the Philippines will be discussed at length in Ch. 9.

14. Gonzalo Jorrin to Wood, May 20, 1902, Records of the Military Governor of Cuba, Letters Received, National Archives.

15. Wood quoted in Clifford, *The Citizen Soldiers,* p. 10. Sylvanius Thayer, the "Father of West Point," quoted in R. Ernest Dupuy, *The Compact History of*

the United States Army (New York: Hawthorn, 1956), p. 124; Stephen B. Luce, founder of the Naval War College, quoted in Abrahamson, *America Arms for a New Century,* p. 48. I obviously disagree with Abrahamson's belief that a large body of professional soldiers supported UMT, at least before 1916. For documentation he quotes John McAuley Palmer and George Van Horn Mosley, relatively junior officers whom I believe to be unrepresentative. For the results of the poll of more typical soldiers, see Jack C. Lane, *Armed Progressive: Leonard Wood* (San Rafael: Presidio, 1978), pp. 174–75, 181.

16. For Wood on professional soldiers, see Hagedorn, *Leonard Wood,* 1:45, 124; Wood to Benjamin Wheeler, Oct. 7, 1914, Wood MSS, Box 88. The quotations on traditional military discipline are from Gen. Robert Bullard as cited in Millett, *The General,* pp. 156, 209, 287. The quotation on traditional military morality is from statement of Dr. Davis, June 9, 1929, Hermann Hagedorn MSS, Box 18. The final quotation on military professionalism is from the *Danville (Ill.) News,* Aug. 29, 1910.

17. Huntington, *Soldier and the State,* pp. 203–11, 222–26. For statistics on commissions, see Marcus Cunliffe, *Soldiers and Civilians: The Martial Spirit in America, 1775–1865* (Boston: Little, Brown, 1968), pp. 134, 269, 361. William Graham Sumner, "War," in *War: Studies from Psychology, Sociology and Anthropology,* ed. Leon Bramson and George W. Goethals (New York: Basic Books, 1968), p. 223. For Nearing and other "leftists," see Rochester, *American Liberal Disillusionment,* pp. 7, 18, 90.

18. The 1848 West Point Board of Visitors quoted in Cunliffe, *Soldiers and Civilians,* pp. 127–28. Forrest Pogue, *George C. Marshall: Education of a General* (New York: Viking Press, 1963), pp. 88–89, 286. Army Officers quoted in Millett, *The General,* pp. 227, 290; Heath Twichell, Jr., *Allen: The Biography of an Army Officer, 1859–1930* (New Brunswick: Rutgers University Press, 1974), pp. 159, 213; Blumenson, ed., *Patton Papers, 1885–1940,* 144, 171.

19. Ibid.; Morison, ed., *Letters of Theodore Roosevelt,* 1:738–39; Thomas G. Dyer, *Theodore Roosevelt and the Idea of Race* (Baton Rouge: Louisiana State University Press, 1980), p. 42.

20. Gen. Peyton C. March, *The Nation at War* (New York: Doubleday, Doran, 1932), pp. 256–57; Challener, *Admirals, Generals and American Foreign Policy,* pp. 53–56; Millet, *The General,* pp. 4, 177. Generals George Duncan and John Pershing describing Wood in Frank E. Vandiver, *Black Jack: The Life and Times of John J. Pershing* (College Station: Texas A. & M. University Press, 1977), 2:772; Daniel R. Beaver, *Newton Baker and the American War Effort, 1917–1919* (Lincoln: University of Nebraska Press, 1966), p. 154. Statement of Gen. Kilbourne, Nov. 26, 1928, Hermann Hagedorn MSS, Box 22.

21. U.S., Congress, Senate, Military Affairs Committee, *Hearings on Universal Military Training,* 64th Cong., 2d Sess., 1917, pp. 250–65; John F. Fulton, *Harvey Cushing: A Biography* (Springfield: Charles C. Thomas, 1946), pp. 12, 60, 670, 679; Harvey Cushing, *Consecratio Medici* (Boston: Little, Brown, 1928), p. 48; Hugh Hampton Young, *A Surgeon's Autobiography* (New York: Harcourt, Brace, 1940), pp. 33–34, 526–27, 532, 534; Eliot Freidson, *The Profession of Medicine: A Study of the Sociology of Applied Knowledge* (New York: Dodd & Mead, 1970), p. 107. The instructions to nurses are quoted in Duffy, *The*

Healers, p. 281. Comparing medical to military operations: in both, the privates and patients are often kept purposely ignorant to make them more manageable. Appreciating this discipline, the surgeon who treated General George S. Patton said of his charge: "He took orders without question—in fact, he was a model patient," see Friedson, *Profession of Medicine*, p. 53; Martin Blumenson, ed., *The Patton Papers: 1940–1945* (Boston: Houghton, Mifflin, 1974), p. 831.

22. For the evolution of the hospital, see Ivan Illich, *Medical Nemesis: The Expropriation of Health* (New York: Random House, 1976), pp. 106–7, 113, 172; Vogel, "Boston's Hospitals," passim. Reports of Children's Hospital (Boston) quoted in ibid., pp. 38, 39, 115. Burr quoted in Senate, *Hearings on Universal Military Training*, 64th Cong., 2d Sess., 1917, p. 255.

23. Early twentieth-century physicians quoted in Charles Rosenberg, *No Other Gods: On Science and American Social Thought* (Baltimore: Johns Hopkins Press, 1976), pp. 5, 102. Oliver Wendell Holmes, "Bread and the Newspaper," *Atlantic Monthly* 8 (Sept., 1861):348. For the evolution of the physician, see Richard Shryock: *Medicine in America* (Baltimore: Johns Hopkins Press, 1966), pp. 149–162; *Medicine and Society in America: 1660–1860* (New York: New York University Press, 1968), pp. 175–179.

24. For the changing political attitudes of doctors, see R. R. Palmer, *The Age of Democratic Revolution: The Struggle* (Princeton: Princeton University Press, 1964), pp. 375, 405, 467, 523; Starr, *Social Transformation of American Medicine*, p. 83; Illich, *Medical Nemesis*, pp. 155–59. Leading figures in early America's public health movement quoted in Rosenberg, *No Other Gods*, pp. 113, 120. For the changing nature of the public health movement, see George Rosen, *A History of Public Health* (New York: M. D. Publications, 1958), pp. 214–17, 244–47, 332–35. Wood described in statement of Mrs. Wood, Feb. 5, 1929, Hermann Hagedorn MSS, Box 11. For evidence that doctors who supported UMT were uneasy with modern medicine, see Dr. E. N. Brush, "The Physician as a Citizen," *American Medicine* 9 (May 17, 1905):872–73, (June 3, 1905): 917; Harvey Cushing, *The Medical Career and Other Papers* (Boston: Little, Brown, 1940), 5–6, 13, 20, 34–35, 94–95; Senate, *Hearings on Universal Military Training*, 64th Cong., 2d. Sess., 1917, pp. 260–90.

25. Karl Compton quoted in Denis S. Philipps, "The American People and Compulsory Military Service" (Ph.D. diss., New York University, 1955), p. 447. Millis, *Martial Spirit*, p. 367. The quotations on the impersonal nature of wounds and army medical treatment are from Post, *Private War of Private Post*, p. 65; Red Cross worker George Kennen quoted in Freidel, *The Splendid Little War*, 179; Louisa May Alcott quoted in Shyrock, *Medicine in America*, p. 99. Wood quoted in Hagedorn, *Leonard Wood*, 2:255. Edward M. Coffman, *The War to End All Wars: The American Military Experience in World War I* (New York: Oxford University Press, 1968), pp. 81, 133; George S. Patton quoted in Blumenson, ed., *Patton Papers, 1885–1940*, p. 548.

26. Vogel, "Boston's Hospitals," pp. 43, 55, 78–79, 81–82; Roy Harvey Pearce, *Savagism and Civilization: A Study of the Indian and the American Mind* (Baltimore: Johns Hopkins Press, 1953), p. 152; Lewis Mumford, *The Pentagon of Power* (New York: Harcourt, Brace, Jovanovich, 1970), pp. 38, 307. The long quotation is from the Government Hospital for the Insane, "Report for 1864–

1865," as cited in Albert Deutsch, "Military Psychiatry: The Civil War," *One Hundred Years of American Psychiatry,* ed. D. K. Hall, Gregory Zilboorg, and Henry Alden Bunker (New York: Columbia University Press, 1944), p. 383.

27. Statement of Dr. C. W. Burr in Senate, *Hearings on Universal Military Training,* 64th Cong., 2d Sess., 1917, p. 255; Harvey Cushing, *From A Surgeon's Journal: 1915–1918* (Boston: Little, Brown, 1937), p. 241; "Therapeutic Value of War," *Boston Medical and Surgical Journal* 159 (Mar. 13, 1913):400.

28. For testimony from doctors, see Senate, *Hearings on Universal Military Training,* 64th Cong., 2d Sess., 1917, pp. 267, 872–73, 917. On Eliot Roosevelt, see McCullough, *Mornings on Horseback,* pp. 146–48. Mitchel quoted in unidentified newspaper clipping in Leonard Wood Scrapbook, Wood MSS, Box 258. George Wharton Pepper, "The Moral Value of Preparedness," May 2, 1916; Pepper to Henry Stimson, Sept. 24, 1940, Pepper MSS, Boxes 8, 11, University of Pennsylvania. Although Muldoon's clientele was small (he never took more than twenty patients at a time) and his register was confidential, one can find other concrete links between his camp and Plattsburg. Muldoon's select alumni included Plattsburg advocates Elihu Root and Theodore Roosevelt and Plattsburg soldiers Roger Derby and Elihu Root, Jr. Leonard Wood's aide, Frank McCoy, entrusted a close friend to Muldoon's care and another Plattsburg advocate, Franklin D. Roosevelt, was a strong admirer of Muldoon himself, see Elihu Root to A. Cox, Dec. 4, 1908, Root MSS, Box 189, Library of Congress; Frank McCoy to George Marvin, Nov. 7, 1933, McCoy MSS, Library of Congress; Franklin Roosevelt to William Muldoon, Oct. 3, 1921, Gen. Corr. 14, Box 8, Roosevelt Presidential Library.

29. Nellie Bly, untitled story, *New York World,* June 24, 1894; Edward Van Every, *Muldoon: The Solid Man of Sport* (New York: Frederick A. Stokes, 1929), pp. 206–7, 264–65, 272, 280; *New York Times,* Apr. 29, 1917, 4:10; Roger A. Derby, *Memoirs of Roger Alden Derby* (privately printed by Elizabeth Derby, 1959), p. 202; M. K. Wisehart, "William Muldoon Has Brought Thousands Back To Health," *American Magazine* 98 (Dec., 1924):15.

30. Muldoon to Theodore Roosevelt, Apr. 18, 1917, Roosevelt MSS, Reel 228; Van Every, *Muldoon,* pp. 26, 272; John D. Williams, "An American Admirable Crichton," *Century Magazine,* 104 (Oct., 1922):904–5. The quote is from "A Physical Culturist Who Steadies 'Jumpy' Nerves by Treating 'Em Rough'," *Literary Digest,* 65 (Apr. 3, 1920):84.

31. Van Every, *Muldoon,* pp. 168–69. Muldoon quoted in Garnet Warren, "Making Over Men at Muldoon's," *New York Herald Magazine,* (Feb. 28, 1909). Theodore Dreiser, *Twelve Men* (New York: Boni & Liveright, 1919), p. 150; Dr. Alexander Lambert to Dr. Richard Cabot, Feb. 29, 1916, Cabot MSS, Box 26, Harvard University; Pepper to Louis Robey, Apr. 2, 1927, Pepper MSS, Box 7.

32. Williams, "An American Admirable Crichton," pp. 900–901; Dreiser, *Twelve Men,* p. 160. The long quote is from Derby, *Memoirs of Roger Alden Derby,* p. 201.

33. Austin Brennan quoted in W. A. Swanberg, *Dreiser* (New York: Scrib-

ner's, 1965), p. 106. James C. Coleman, *Abnormal Psychology and Modern Life* (n.p.: Scott Foresman, n.d.), pp. 201–5.

34. Derby to Endicott Peabody, Mar. 3, 1909; May 31, 1909, Peabody MSS, Box 41, Harvard University; Derby, *Memoirs of Roger Alden Derby,* pp. 202–5.

35. Edward A. Strecker, "Military Psychiatry: World War I, 1917–1918," in Hall et al., eds., *One Hundred Years of American Psychiatry,* pp. 391–96; Albert J. Glass, "Psychotherapy in the Combat Zone," *American Journal of Psychiatry* 60 (Apr. 1954):725–30. For neurasthenia as the affliction of American materialism, see James B. Gilbert, *Work without Salvation: America's Intellectuals and Industrial Alienation* (Baltimore: Johns Hopkins University Press, 1977), esp. pp. 12, 36, 190. The quotations on neurasthenia in WWI, army medicine, and combat fatigue are in Eric J. Leed, *No Man's Land: Combat and Identity in World War I* (Cambridge: Cambridge University Press, 1979), pp. 81, 176; Menninger, *Psychiatry in a Trouble World,* p. 92; Roger W. Little, "The 'Sick Soldier' and the Medical War Officer," *Human Organization* 15 (1956): 23–24.

36. Freidson, *Profession of Medicine,* pp. 269–70; David Mechanic, *Medical Sociology* (New York: Free Press, 1968), pp. 155, 164–65. For Muldoon, see *Boston Globe,* Jan. 19, 1892; Van Every, *Muldoon,* p. 317; *New York Times,* May 19, 1916; *New York Times Magazine,* Apr. 29, 1917, 4:10.

CHAPTER 3

Plattsburg: The Men, Their Lives, and Their Sparta

☆

IN 1913, WHEN Leonard Wood, general and doctor, began to prescribe military training for civilians at summer instruction camps, most professional soldiers thought the enrollment would be too small to test the idea of universal service. Even Wood and his own supporters wondered whether men would ever volunteer to spend their summer vacations undergoing army drills, By 1916, when 16,000 men went to Plattsburg Barracks and the other training camps, the attendance had exceeded everyone's expectations. While German submarine warfare aroused some recruits, many others entered largely because they were "susceptible to the peculiar attraction which the military seems to hold for a certain type of personality."[1] This chapter examines Robert Bacon, Theodore Roosevelt, Jr., and other civilians who possessed that Plattsburg personality. It asks what the camp did for its recruits and how it complemented other aspects of their lives, from athletic endeavors to wilderness camping, from the search for moral meaning to their Protestant ideals. These men who worried, like Puritans once did, about their ethical condition and corruption through wealth, felt that Plattsburg's physical hardships would help them develop personal integrity. For those citizen-soldiers, as for Wood himself, the military fort became a social health camp.

Plattsburg: A Sparta for the Rich

Cynics to the contrary, Plattsburg was definitely not an upper-class leisure resort. To prove Wood's theory of UMT to the many skeptics who ridiculed it, the general made sure that his camp was so demanding that its "discipline and work would make the regular army buck." He therefore concluded six weeks of intense training with a nine-day hike on which was carried a forty-two pound pack. Several prominent men, aware of this ordeal, excused their absence by saying that while their spirits were willing, their bodies were unable. Franklin Roosevelt pleaded that an appendectomy prevented any fifty-mile maneuvers for the next few weeks, and Columbia University Professor Douglas Johnson claimed that with a weak heart he could march only twenty-five miles a day. More to the point, President Edmund James of the University of Illinois said that he would like to attend but thought it would kill him.[2]

Most Plattsburgers, however fatigued from this ordeal, thrived on its severity. Wood and his aides, Spartans themselves, were amazed that of 6,300 men who hiked with full packs in a blistering heat, just two fell out. Of another 6,500 men attending one encampment, only three left early. The rest, recruits who wanted the most rigorous training possible, made one instructor exclaim: "I've never heard of men so enthusiastic for work."[3]

This intense austerity, far from driving men away, actually attracted them to Plattsburg. Their enrollment there was, in part, a reaction to the social trait distinguishing them from some prominent pacifists. Leaders of the peace movement like Jane Addams, while also well educated and bred, often worked in low-paying occupations such as social work.[4] Many Plattsburgers, on the other hand, inherited or made large fortunes that left them uneasy and perplexed. They had been reared in the Protestant ethic of scarcity capitalism which damned Mammon while it sanctioned private property. This code's ambivalence bred anxiety since men who are thoroughly indifferent to their material assets, holding what they have (in Roger Williams's words) "with dead and weaned and mortified affections," will not have to fear wealth's malignant consequences. Rich Brahmins, worried about the "pernicious effects of luxury," previously consoled themselves by claiming that while "zealous in business," they were Christian stewards dedicating their fortunes "to the needs of the community." The Plattsburg camp provided another escape from the moral dilemma of money by giving its recruits a new opportunity to atone for the riches that they kept. As one of them put it: "We all feel instinctively that the life of ease and luxury of the present generation is wrong, it is destructive of moral and physical fiber, it tends to degeneracy. Nearly every man who goes to Plattsburg goes with the knowledge that he must give up all the comforts and convenience of life and endure hardships and I believe that he does so freely and readily as a kind of silent protest against the easygoing life he ordinarily leads."[5]

Placed in historical perspective, this Plattsburg exaltation of abstinence was a moral protest lodged against the change in the common meaning of ascetic discipline. After nineteenth century industrial technology helped inflate the intensity of economic motivation, a marketplace psychology increasingly portrayed man as inherently materialistic.

Hence utilitarianism supposed that a self-denying Christian character was eccentric to modern civilization which presented the idea that "material advancement and prosperity are the end, the aim and general purpose of human life." Military training advocates, upholding pre-modern puritan ideals, rejected this standard of behavior which they found pervasive from 1914 to 1917. Then many businessmen, during this period of military neutrality and commercial boom, said that the European war "is not our trouble, it is our opportunity." Plattsburgers, by contrast, shamefully lamented that America "turned the other cheek to the buffet, not in weakness but in order to use both hands for grabbing money." Thus these recruits, despite their own economic resources, were ill-at-ease in a commercial culture which glorified those who magnified their wealth. As in the past, such men adopted Spartan ideals and methods in hope that austerity, order, and unity could replace the social trinity of luxury, license, and faction. Certainly idiosyncratic Plattsburgers, like elite combat troops, felt themselves superior to others and were proud to have "an esprit de corps of our own." One member of this modern Christian Sparta said that "our crowd is a very decent sort of thing, a thing even thrilling to touch shoulders with for a little time, a thing to inspire great hope and confidence in thinking over later." The camp, said Leonard Wood, "is the most hopeful and inspiring thing imaginable. . . . It does a lot to remove the impressions which one gets from contact with the great crowd of money chasers."[6]

Pride in being at Plattsburg helped mitigate anxiety about one's affluence, thereby producing recruits who looked "the picture of health." Because the camp seemed to succeed with these individuals, its advocates believed that its regimen should be extended to all society. They specifically felt that a policy of compulsory military training, which would democratize the Plattsburg camp of volunteers, could purify a country seemingly committed to spreading comforts and commodities from plumbing to meat.[7]

Plattsburg, Purification, Puritanism, and the Frontier:
Charles Henry Brent, George Wharton Pepper, Henry Stimson,
and Owen Wister

Plattsburgers, as proselytizers, were secular heirs of the nineteenth-century evangelists who hoped to preserve moral and spiritual principles from a marketplace oblivion. Those clergymen preached a religion of restraint; these citizen-soldiers advocated social controls. Each group, pitching their respective camps in sections of upstate New York, stirred the remnant guilt feelings of the Calvinist conscience in America.

One of the great expositors of Plattsburg's Protestant purgatory was the camp's unofficial chaplain, Episcopal Bishop Charles Henry Brent (1862–1929) of the Philippine Islands. This man, who entreated his God: "Beat me into a comely form upon thy anvil," believed that the "glad embracing of penalty is the height of penitence." In particular, he seemed to feel that the mortifications of war, "more thoroughly hell than Dante's inferno," were penance for sins that baptism could not expiate. As head chaplain of the American Expeditionary Force, he would write about men emerging from "the burning fiery furnace" of battle "purified and refined." He would also speak of man's "spiritual vision" which, by God's will, was inversely correlated "to the ease and calm ... of prosperity and peace."[8]

Before America declared war in 1917, Brent embraced Plattsburg as a combination of the two most formative experiences in his life—his childhood in the Canadian woods and his monastic education with the Cowley Fathers of Boston. He cherished both these austere environments and now praised Plattsburg for placing men "under obedience" as it invigorated their manhood. International relations aside, he said that "wholesomeness" alone justified the camp, whose unique degree of "discipline and mode of life were the very things needed by men of our day and generation." As for himself, Brent, who rejected church placements in Washington because of their "material advantages," always regretted that a serious heart problem prevented him from taking the complete Plattsburg training course.[9]

Bishop Brent, who was the spiritual mentor of several Plattsburgers, among them Robert Bacon, went to the camp at the behest of his "devoted friend," George Wharton Pepper (1866–1961). The latter, a wealthy patrician, also exemplified the Plattsburg spirit of rehabilitation through sacrifice. Although he helped organize and administer the camp's civilian arm, his comrades in the Military Training Camps Association felt that "his big contribution" lay in the "powerful inspiration" of his personal example. They said that he "struck exactly the right note; namely the obligation of the individual to be willing to sacrifice something of his own comfort and time, as the only satisfying proof of his own sincerity."[10]

In 1944 Pepper recalled that he had been a World War I interventionist because he then believed in America's "manifest destiny to reform the world." However, the statements which he made in 1915 indicate concern for self-purification, not world reformation. This forty-nine-year-old rookie wondered if he had "any real military value." Whether he did or did not, he was still convinced that we "well-to-do" Americans "are becoming disgustingly luxurious" and need compulsory military training as "a course in real hardship." Pepper, practicing the doctrine

he preached, used all his special influence to win admission to Plattsburg in 1915. Once there, termination was his only disappointment.
Back in Philadelphia, he found himself "wishing for the regular life,
strenuous exercise and pleasant companionship of the camp." As he
told one audience: "Once you have been up at Plattsburg you count the
days until you return."[11]

By 1916, however, Pepper had developed a new goal: to serve as
a private in the Mexican border campaign. Although the army there
was suffering through broiling hot days, freezing cold nights, blinding
sandstorms, and inadequate supplies, he still wished to experience the
"strenuous conditions of guerilla warfare." When Leonard Wood assured him a commission on the staff of any expedition the general might
head, Pepper corrected his leader. "What is needed," he said, "is a
readiness on the part of men of privilege to join the ranks." Once rejected for Mexican duty, Pepper could only resign his Plattsburg rank
and return as a private to the 1916 camp. "There is," he explained,
"great value to the cause [when] older men who have more or less 'made
good' . . . are entirely content to do the work of enlisted men."[12]

In 1917, still wanting to go "into the line without a commission,"
Pepper again tried and failed to enlist as a private. Only a Colonel William Muldoon would accept a Private George Wharton Pepper.[13]

Although the regular army dashed Pepper's hopes for an enlisted
man's duty, he always cherished his Plattsburg experience, as did his
good friend Henry Stimson (1867–1950). "One of the most enthusiastic
men in camp," this former secretary of war (1911–13) also had to pull
strings just "to get in and work like any other man." Once there, he too
enjoyed himself so thoroughly that he was "quite anxious" to schedule
Plattsburg "as a regular kind of vacation."[14]

Actually, Stimson had been taking training camp vacations most of
his life. Suffering indigestion and insomnia in New York City, where he
lucratively practiced law, he spent his holidays, from ages 17 to 73,
hunting big game or camping in the untamed wilderness. Like his mentor, Theodore Roosevelt, seeking "days of toil and hardship," Stimson
embraced nature as a severe test of character, rather than a scene of
peace and harmony. "I yearned," he said, "to show that I was able to
support my life in that wild country in spite of the difficulties and dangers that might confront me."[15]

Stimson, emphasizing the warlike ordeal of life on the frontier, concluded that the ethical principles of the outdoorsmen are "similar to the
code of honor learned by the soldier in the field." However his ideas
about the wilderness-warrior nexus overlook the fact that war often
alienates more pacific men from nature. Phrases such as "no man's

land" and "enemy territory" indicate that combat, especially artillery attacks, can engender an enormous fear of the outdoors. Some twenty-five years after discharge, a different veteran, less critical of creature comforts, confessed that he always painted landscapes from the window of a house because "I like looking out on the world from a reasonably sheltered position." This man probably cherished arcadia's ability to soothe the ill-effects of litter, noise, and polluted air: phenomena most toxic in bombardments. Yet the reduction on the battlefield of "stately trees" to "graveyards of splintered stumps" did not traumatize Stimson, an artillery officer in World War I. Nor was he aggrieved by the deafening sounds of explosive shells and the fumes of poison gas. Having vacationed in the woods for difficulty and danger, in war he could enjoy the "satisfaction of hearing" his big guns ("my beauties") "boom out their grand old anvil chorus." Some combat soldiers, who "make love to the earth" on which they live and dive for cover, may deeply regret fighting in an earth-scorching war. Because preparedness leaders like Stimson did not go to nature for tranquility and beauty, they did not feel this guilt. While he, for one, noted the "desolate" battlefield strewn with "gruesome" destruction, he nonetheless said that war evoked memories of his cherished vacations. To Stimson, it seemed "much [like] a good grizzly hunt in my younger days."[16]

Once Stimson made his transition from wilderness to war, he hoped that America might follow suit through a national program of universal military training. Before World War I, he feared that "modern city life" threatened the "hardy outdoor virtues of mind and body" that sustained the republic. Yet he could not envision a viable solution to the moral crisis caused by urban affluence. He long thought that war, as an antidote to "materialism and mercantilism," might be "a wonderfully good thing for this country." Nonetheless, it seemed unlikely to occur. Compulsory military training could also be invaluable, but it too did not seem to be "within the realm of political possibility." Stimson, doing what seemed feasible, therefore emphasized governmental reforms. He believed that the disappearance of free land on the frontier, the proverbial "safety-valve," necessitated political means of social control if the nation were to escape agitation and turmoil. He consequently campaigned for the Republican Party ("the richer and more intelligent citizens of the country") and for constitutional reforms that centralized power in elite executive hands. But once the military training movement gathered some momentum, Stimson could redirect his energies from institutional change to moral reform. The army then became a wilderness surrogate able to correct the "evil effects of indoor life." As such, it might become "the salvation of our democracy." Because Stimson felt that UMT inculcated loyalty, obedience, and patriotism, he hoped that military preparedness would not become a strictly military issue. If that happened, he said, "the nation will have lost a great opportunity. The real need of the country is a change of ideals in all respects."[17]

To an outdoorsman like Stimson, war was a "great opportunity" for himself as well as the nation. This man, who had overcome the hardships of nature, could now seek "one of the strongest feelings in life"— "mastery over the souls of fighting men." He first used his War Department knowledge of army personnel to recruit officers for Theodore Roosevelt's abortive World War I division. Then he left his leader lest aid to President Wilson's political rival jeopardize his own chance to "stand up to the shelling." By 1917, Stimson, now commissioned, was being trained to help fill America's critical shortage of division-level tacticians. But to prevent being considered "a staff officer and nothing else," he asked for duty in the line, "the real soldiering [that] no one can doubt or gainsay." When he got it as a colonel in the artillery, he experienced the "great satisfaction in actual command" which made him "feel more like a man than anything else." This assignment, he concluded, was "incomparably more attractive to most manly men than the higher forms of staff duty requiring much more intellect." Theodore Roosevelt, Jr., did not like Stimson but, seeing this fifty-one-year-old officer in action, exclaimed that "it was really splendid [for someone] of his age to go into the line when everyone is naturally telling him to do all sorts of other jobs. . . . He has more than lived up to everything that could have been expected."[18]

Once Stimson proved himself in combat, he could attend to the task of beating the Germans. Hereafter, he was "only anxious to do the work which I can do most usefully towards winning the war." With some regret, but without much protest, he left Europe in August, 1918, to train a stateside regiment.[19]

In battle Stimson had said, "I want always to be considered a line man." If anybody forgot it, he was "tremendously irritated." Although he became secretary of state and secretary of war once again, he took more pride in his month of combat than he did in political decisions that helped shape world history. To him, the cabinet was just another staff officer position, for "to give the order" to contest the Japanese invasion of the Philippines in 1941 "was a matter of duty. . . . It was in its loyal execution that true glory would be found." Mr. Secretary Stimson always "liked to be called Colonel."[20]

In popular culture, Henry Stimson's concept of the regenerative struggle, waged in warfare or the wilderness, is most often expressed in the Western: a genre shaped by another preparedness advocate—

Owen Wister (1860–1938). Although he never went to Plattsburg, in both pen and person he was active in propaganda for military training. Furthermore his writings, especially *The Virginian,* helped establish sentiments that nourished the camp. That all-time best-selling novel, reprinted seventeen times in 1902, ends with the hard-fighting cowboy wed to the well-mannered "schoolmarm." Together, they unite virility and order: the combination UMT promised to create. Professor Frank Mather, Jr., found *The Virginian* seriously flawed as art. As drama, however, he thought it an "indubitably heroic" work. Thirteen years after writing this review, Mather returned from Plattsburg praising the "health, order and spirit" of that army fort.[21]

Like the narrator of *The Virginian,* Wister periodically collapsed in the East to be revived in the West, the "true fountain of youth." Praising the "psychological effect" of this land, he should have known that his breakdowns were not physical. "Sturdy, broad-shouldered [and] vigorous," there was "something," he admitted, "wrong with my insides that no doctor was able to name." If he had consulted any literary critic he would have been told that his stories about the noble cowboy reveal that Wister suffered from leading a life he deplored. He disliked the effete East yet lived in Philadelphia. He condemned materialism yet haggled over "every penny" that his potboiler fiction could get. He mourned the commercialization of the West but called the Southern Pacific Railroad an "enormous benefactor." Although convinced that the "life of action" was nobler than that of the mind, he thought himself "too intellectual [with] not enough guts." He was a devoted family man with a "perfect marriage" to an angelic woman, and yet he was a misogynist whose masculinity complex ensured that his happiest hours would be spent in the womanless world of ranches and clubs. Finally, he was an anti-Semite who hated Jews for the very social traits he possessed—for being intellectual, commercial, deceptive, ostentatious, and clannish. By projecting his unacceptable sins onto them, he could get some psychic relief.[22]

Projection, however, was not Wister's only therapy. To assuage a conscience that condemned luxury but not property, Plattsburgers spent their vacations in an army camp. To escape his own inner conflicts, Wister sought to redeem himself in a Wyoming "holiday leavened by hard bodily work and manly deeds." Once revived in the West, he returned to the East to await his next emotional breakdown in that land of "alien vermin . . . [who] turn our citizenship into a hybrid farce."[23]

Yet however noble the primitive West might be, Wister knew that the Great Plains would eventually "New Yorkify and rot." Despairing of a national reformation, this neurasthenic, like others with his "illness," spent much of his time in prolonged travel, making expatriate trips into the dying cultures of the pristine West, aristocratic Charleston, patrician Europe, and Brahmin Massachusetts. Despite his chronic fatigue, he always could find some excuse to go to Boston. Unlike other American locales that had "known no real pain since 1865," that city's spirit had been so completely purged in the "fiery furnace of the Civil War" that it remained "deepened by adversity instead of shallowed by prosperity."[24]

Nonetheless Wister did not wallow in total resignation. When World War I began, he seized combat as an opportunity to transform America into Boston and Uncle Sam into the Virginian. Convinced that suffering produces moral growth, he warned the nation that neutrality would destroy "the greatest opportunity [it] will ever meet."[25]

The New England Tradition and the Puritan Roots of Plattsburg

Along with a Spartan love for the wilderness, a Puritan heritage nurtured the sentiments that created the military training camps. Actually, Plattsburg and Tudor-Stuart Puritanism were analogous reactions to urban growth, commercial development, and social mobility. They both believed that these forces triggered a moral declension to be met with greater self-denial and social discipline. Those seventeenth-century saints often prepared for grace like these twentieth-century soldiers prepared themselves for war. They both used military drills to strengthen the will to fight the "irreconcilable war" against material seduction. When Puritans migrated beyond Cromwell's New Model Army, they deemphasized martial training in favor of nature's purgatory. In America they hoped that the forest wilderness would elevate their faith like the desert cleansed Israel of the fleshpots of Egypt. Their Plattsburg descendants, who were also knit together by a trust in social purity from trials and tribulations, transferred the arena of moral restitution from nature back to the military camp.[26]

Plattsburgers, their friends, and their biographers all recognized this affinity to Puritanism. Theodore Roosevelt, Jr., a founder of the 1915 training camp for business and professional men, used John Bunyan's *Pilgrim's Progress* ("a great consolation to me") as a moral roadmap through World War II. That allegory told this descendant of Jonathan Edwards that the combat front was "The Valley of the Shadow of Death" and as such, was the only righteous path back to the "Delectable Mountains" of Oyster Bay. Supply work at the rear of the line, "Doubting Castle under Giant Despair," was the real danger since it imperiled Roosevelt's struggle for integrity. Thus, he explained, he had to "stay at the front until all is finished, for my soul's peace depends on it." He stayed until he was finished—a combat fatigue fatality on July 12, 1944.[27]

Plattsburg leader and Harvard professor Ralph Barton Perry (1876–1957) praised the Puritan Saint for "bracing [his] character . . . against the indulgence and improvidence of [his] times." During the preparedness campaign, he worked for UMT: Perry's moral equivalent to this religious creed. Feeling that the "weak willed American nation [was] clamoring after the sweetmeat of wealth," he maintained that the "physical and moral qualities" instilled by army drill would help improve the country's "personal character."[28]

As a component of New England's puritan customs, the military training camps were successful in the East, where old elites concerned with cultural traditions did not concentrate excessively on commerce and comfort. However, the camps were relative failures in the West, where a nouveau riche elite, with a "utilitarian" outlook, lived a more polyglot life-style leavened with Latin manners. Considering foreign affairs alone, California should have been optimum territory for the Plattsburg movement. It not only shared the national concern with German militarism, it possessed special sectional fears of the "the Yellow Peril" on the Pacific and the Mexican revolution in its own backyard. Yet notwithstanding political and journalistic reports that the state was taking a "real interest" in military preparedness, the Presidio (Monterey) encampment lacked the proper puritan spirit. West Coast Plattsburgers, according to their East Coast counterparts, pitched their camp on the grounds of a luxurious hotel that "radiated peace and ease and the comfort of life." There, they maneuvered in their Rolls Royces and had champagne picnics with their girl friends. Camp instructors had to tolerate all this lest the volunteer recruits get mad and quit.[29]

One exasperated officer cursed "the peculiar crust of self-satisfaction and indifference that surrounds Californians." Benjamin Dibblee, this camp's civilian organizer, thought that men must have enrolled there "on the theory that they were to have a free vacation." But even Dibblee, a native Californian, lacked the East Coast commitment to Spartan puritanism. He would volunteer for training but not for combat. Because Dibblee had been captain of the 1899 Harvard football team, Theodore Roosevelt, Sr., when recruiting for his World War I division, assumed that he would emulate those twenty Rough Riders who left the Ivy League gridirons to charge up San Juan Hill. Apologetically, Dibblee had to confess that while he would join the army if called, he was "not so keen that [he] would want to fight to get into the first batch of troops which might be sent to Europe." While the man to whom he confessed, Theodore Roosevelt, Jr., was fighting his own way onto the first troop transport bound overseas, Dibblee himself was spending the war as an assistant adjutant in a stateside training camp. Safe and secure, he lived to grow old, rich, and fat in southern California.[30]

Theodore Roosevelt, Jr.: The Making of a Plattsburg Recruit

Plattsburg was more than a component of cultural configurations like puritanism. Biographical sketches of its recruits reveal that its program also reflected individual personality patterns. Theodore Roosevelt, Jr.'s, life (1887–1944) is one case in point.

Any sensitive son and namesake of a United States president, caught between flattery and partisan criticism, is likely to question his own worth. When the nation's foremost politician is also its greatest celebrity, hollow-sounding praise and invidious judgments are apt to be especially intense. But even before these effects of fame bestirred self-doubt, the pressure to prove his virtue afflicted TR's son. Born before his father's soaring career directed much of his attention from his family, Roosevelt, Jr., was raised by this demanding parent who swore he would not "have any weaklings in my household." He should have been satisfied with his son for by all accounts of newspapers, family, and friends, the child was "very manly and very bright." Tragically, however, his assets became liabilities. Seeing his son's talents develop, Roosevelt, Sr., demanded further excellence. Loving his father, this eleven-year-old boy had a nervous breakdown trying to fulfill parental expectations. Temporarily chastened, the parent swore never again to "press Ted either in mind or body. The fact is that the little fellow . . . had bidden fair to be all the things I would like to have been and wasn't, and it has been a great temptation to push him." These verbal vows to the contrary, Roosevelt would tolerate shortcomings in his younger sons but not from his eldest. When disappointed with that child, he openly called him "a mucker."[31]

Roosevelt loved Ted, the boy "who is particularly dear to me." Yet inconsistent affection can be more damaging than consistent rejection; it can preoccupy a child with fear of the sudden loss of love. Moreover, if the parent had been less affectionate, the son might have discarded his excessively high standards. As it was, Roosevelt, Jr., always felt compelled to "prove worthy of the father whom he adored." However, members of his family rarely revealed their gut emotions and this lad, like his parent, chose to mask his self-doubt by flaunting his physical honor. Described as "a regular bull terrier" who "licked all the boys" in his class, the *Groton School Verses* immortalized his pugnacity as follows: "To punch a fellow's head he's ready/ . . . This sweet thing's name is Teddy."[32]

When he was not punching noses, he was playing football. The smallest player on his prep school and college teams (126 pounds at Harvard), he combined mediocre ability with an incomparable will to take physical punishment. Thirty years after Groton, witnesses still recalled that his eyes were weak and his body was small but he had "an indomitable spirit," "untiring energy," and "all the courage in the world." His father, who once boasted that he would disown any offspring who would not play football "for fear of breaking his neck," now worried that his son would be permanently "battered." When Roosevelt, Jr., ended his college freshman season with a broken ankle, two broken ribs, a broken nose, and water on the knee, his proud parent thanked fortune that his son was too light to proceed to his varsity annihilation.[33]

Roosevelt, Jr., reared by his father to believe that physical prowess would "certainly secure" "respect for his virtues," obviously thought that football was an excellent way to prove his worth. He consequently cherished the symbol of his exploits: the freshman football letter that made him feel "so large." Almost forty years later he still lamented the broken ankle that susequently cost him a prized varsity "H." By then, however, he had many other medallions. As a soldier who won every combat decoration, he cherished those medals like he once prized his athletic letter. His aide said that he wore "all his ribbons every chance he got."[34]

Roosevelt, Jr., certainly proved himself to others. But he, like his father, could never quite prove himself to himself. After college he continued his self-imposed testing and training. Impatient to build the economic foundation of an independent political career, he raced through school, skipping one year at both Groton and Harvard. Then, when he was ready to win his fortune, the "first boy of the land" ignored numerous opportunities to market his name. He became, instead, a wool sorter in a carpet factory paying seven dollars per fifty-hour work week. The *Independent* magazine, which praised his act as a symbolic illustration of the democratic principle that all men shall start life equal, predicted that "young Roosevelt will probably stay but a brief time at the bench." Because he stayed there a year and a half, his salary was raised to $8.50 a week. "Intolerant of any outside aid," he lived within his own income, preferring boardinghouse isolation to society events. As he must have known, this won the admiration of his father, who was now convinced that his son would not lead "a perfectly silly and vacuous life around the clubs and sporting fields."[35]

Yet all Roosevelt's accomplishments in fighting, football, and the factory were only preliminaries to the great test of war. More than any other boy in America he was brought up on *Hero Tales from American History*. What he did not hear from his father, he read on his own. Isolated by his pugnacity and sensitivity, he spent much of his childhood, armed with tin sword, memorizing Sir Walter Scott and playing out his characters. He even wrote a little poetry of his own: "Would God I might die my sword in my hand . . . / O'er matched yet killing in death."[36]

Along with romantic literature, young Roosevelt had an overdose of the Rough Riders, whose regimental mementos decorated his home. Rough Riders themselves escorted him through their camp and played with him when, in a "continuous stream," they visited their colonel. (They also attended his wedding and stole most of the cake.) At age twelve, dressed in his father's army boots and hat, he was clicking his heels before his headmaster's wife, saluting his father, organizing the local boys into a regiment, and fighting "with a 'Mick' who dared call him a toy soldier." By thirteen, he decided "to become a great soldier" himself. But dissuaded by his father, who apparently felt that the peacetime army suited bureaucrats like General Shafter, not warriors like his son, Roosevelt, Jr., did not enroll at West Point. Nonetheless, like his parent before him, he still craved a combat experience against virtually anybody. In 1908, while President Roosevelt was trying to deescalate tensions with Mexico and Japan, his son was hoping "to enlist the first moment that war is declared."[37]

By 1915 Roosevelt, Jr., was obviously ready for Plattsburg. A member of the three-man delegation that first implored Leonard Wood to extend the training beyond college students, he took the course with relish—avoiding newspaper reporters, his wife, and anyone else who might upset his concentration. For his efforts he received the highest possible rank, a recommendation for a reserve commission, and his father's acclamation that he had "done better than any other man in camp." Plattsburg publicly advertised itself as peace through preparedness. Roosevelt himself was so eager for combat that he impressed at least one recruit with his "spirit of blood lust."[38]

Previously, when Roosevelt had sought employment, he shunned all family help. When America declared war in 1917, he mobilized his entire clan. While Cousin Franklin smoothed the way through President Wilson's War Department, his father besought John Pershing, whom he had made a general, for an immediate assignment for his son. Meanwhile his wife, a family friend of the officer in charge, was busy arranging the earliest possible transportation overseas. Soon Roosevelt, Jr., was a major assigned to combat duty in the 1st Infantry Division. People in Washington and his own regiment justifiably charged nepotism. One sardonic veteran even suggested that revised army rules explicitly state that no one command a battalion "without the consent of his parents or guardian." But whatever was said, Roosevelt, Jr., readily "proclaimed his complete satisfaction with the army, the war and the world in general."[39]

The complaints once voiced all quickly vanished for, as one of Roosevelt's superiors wrote, "I have never known a harder working, more conscientious leader." He not only impressed others; for once he seemed to satisfy himself. Repeating the poem that his father had used to appraise his own ordeal in Dakota, he now said that "I have lived and toiled with men . . . [and] played my part whatever the outcome." When he died mattered less than how he died, and if he died, this "is the finest way in the world to go." By the time the war was over, Roosevelt, Jr., had established a combat record that gave him a "contentment and happiness which has never failed." Then the 1st Division's operations officer, a laconic soldier named George Catlett Marshall, wrote him:

> With no idea of flattery and with absolute honesty I will tell you that my observation of most of the fighting in France led me to consider your record one of the most remarkable in the entire AEF. Based on personal knowledge of conditions, I consider your conduct as a battalion commander . . . among the finest examples of leadership, courage and fortitude that came to my attention during the war. . . .
>
> I do not believe I have ever before indulged myself in such frank comments of a pleasant nature to another man, but I derived so much personal satisfaction as an American from witnessing the manner in which you measured up to the example of your father.

Roosevelt must have treasured Marshall's letter for he put it in the military file that was "to be handed down to [his own] children."[40]

Robert Bacon: A Plattsburger's Search for Moral Satisfaction

The affairs of Robert Bacon (1860–1919) also show that the Plattsburg experience was part of a total life and personality pattern. Unlike Roosevelt, Jr., this fifty-five-year-old "Greek God" of Wall Street enrolled for military training after already completing an apparently brilliant career in school, business, and government. He certainly had numerous admirers: among them Harvard Professor Albert Bushnell Hart, patrician Peter Bowditch, writer John St. L. Strachey, and President Theodore Roosevelt. Respectively, they said that Bacon was "the handsomest man I knew," the "finest specimen of American manhood," "the whitest of the white men," and "one of the best fellows alive." Even William Muldoon, who made a fortune insulting the rich and powerful, professed to revere men "of the Robert Bacon type." It would seem that Bacon's only critic was Bacon for he thought himself "a shameless dun." Despite all his triumphs in several fields, he lived a frustrated life. This "Don Juan of achievement" ran from one success to another in a fruitless search for satisfaction. Eventually, he turned toward military training and the army where he hoped to discover the gratifying accomplishment that heretofore eluded him.[41]

Bacon began his long string of disappointing triumphs at Harvard College, where he was the most accomplished and popular man on campus. At a time when the Crimson's athletes were the best in the country and its students really directed their squads, he, the school's heavyweight boxing champion, was captain of the crew, baseball, and football teams. Only twenty years old, this first marshal of the Class of 1880 completely eclipsed an idolater named Theodore Roosevelt, who might have hated Bacon out of pure jealousy if he had not succumbed to a classmate "as pleasant as he is handsome." Yet all his talents did not save Bacon from a prolonged personality crisis with roots in the Protestant ethic that drove men to Plattsburg. After graduating from college, he did not want to go into business, which he called a "money grabbing vain search after riches." However, he mistrusted his own desires, fearing indolence caused his distaste for commerce. Bacon's father, like the fathers of other ambivalent Brahmins, moved to solve his son's perplexity by placing him in an investment banking career, where he eventually became a J. P. Morgan partner and the legator of a $7,500,000 estate. Nonetheless, banking never satisfied his sensibilities, especially his need to work without procuring luxuries. By 1902, after a nervous breakdown in business, Bacon was "aching to give the rest of my poor life to the service of my country." President Roosevelt, responding to this plea, offered to make his old friend the new assistant secretary of state to Elihu Root. Newspapers thought that Bacon would not accept an appointment to this laborious post with little chance for glory. Bacon himself was overwhelmed at the "great honor [and] opportunity to do some useful work."[42]

Secretary Root combined "tender-hearted warmth" with hard-hearted advice about a "selfish, money-making world." His strong but sympathetic personality inspired filial piety in Bacon who immediately found Root to be "one of the most attractive men I have ever met." In time Bacon wrote his chief: "As usual, when I am in trouble I cried to you for help. I don't see how I can possibly get along any longer unless I come and live next door to you somewhere. There is never a day for me that I do not feel the need of you and your help." But despite Root's presence, State Department duty failed to fulfill Bacon's attempt to justify his life. Roosevelt had said that his friend's "sweetness of temper" would be a great diplomatic asset. Hence the department, searching for a courtier to relieve Mrs. Root of the social duties she deplored, exploited Bacon's wealth, charm, and looks. When he was not entertaining, he was apt to be thoroughly engaged in what Dean Acheson has called the "utter triviality" of ordinary State Department operations. Hence he defused "the danger of an international incident" by placing the Duke of Abruzzi in front of Great Britain's ambassador at the Harvard commencement. He also perfunctorily protested Russian pogroms for the sake of the New York vote, soothed candy producers demanding duty-free sugar, restrained bureaucratic raids on the Commerce Department's right to print extra copies of trade reports, and arranged special consular tests to satisfy senators hungry for patronage. During World War I, the moralistic Bacon would tell an aide that any man with influence could get anything he wanted from the State Department.[43]

Devoted to Roosevelt and Root, Bacon stayed on the job and then, with mixed feelings, accepted President Taft's offer to become ambassador to France. He was tired of diplomacy and did not want to move away from Root but he was "thankful for the chance to be kept at work." This embassy post also enabled him to fight his battle for Liberia, a nation then facing bankruptcy, tribal revolts, and external encroachments from England and France. Two decades before that land became an important source of crude rubber, Bacon, a future Hampton Institute trustee, devoted himself to protecting "the only country in the world where the Negro had a chance to prove himself capable of government." Committed as he was, he would not await the naval officers on whom he and the State Department usually relied for facts and firsthand reporting. Before they could assess Liberia to be a corrupt, political "travesty," Bacon, a romantic seeking moral purpose, urged his colleagues to come to its defense. Secretary Root, a realist seeing no national interest at stake, passed the issue onto the incoming Taft administration. As interim secretary of state between Root's resignation and Taft's own appointment, Bacon did what little he could for Liberia when he took the domestic risk of sending Booker T. Washington, then considered a political liability, on an official American commission of support. Shortly thereafter as Taft's ambassador to France, Bacon continued his minicrusade by negotiating a nebulous international recognition of Liberian sovereignty. Following that, he spent most of his time protecting his patrician privacy from nouveau riche Americans seeking French recognition as an entree into proper American society. Bacon, after two years, was anxious to leave his post but stayed one year more because Root said "Don't be a quitter." Henry Lee Higginson, the Boston banker who had given Bacon his first job, met the ambassador in Europe and came away convinced that he would rather be on the Harvard Corporation than in the American embassy. Bacon was, Higginson noted, obsessed by "his duties to his country and his fellow man"; he was "hankering after some occupation [that would] fill the life of a high minded honorable man."[44]

When the Harvard Corporation subsequently offered Bacon his "field marshall's baton" as a university trustee, he came home in 1912, telling reporters that "America needs earnest and sincere men on the firing and fighting lines." Bacon, besides exhibiting self-deprecation, had a political anxiety which led him to think that the United States was close to disintegration. Perhaps his personal and public perceptions reinforced each other since paranoia can result from projected self-hatred. But whatever the source of his alarm, Bacon's fear was real in itself. In 1902, he said that the United Mine Workers' anthracite strike was a greater crisis than the Civil War. Although real radicals called union leader John Mitchell the "little tin god of the capitalist class," Bacon felt compelled "to fall in behind [Roosevelt] with a musket or coal shovel in defense of personal liberty, law and order." Later, Bacon's dread of trade unions abated, but his fear for society still remained strong. He would therefore write that Western civilization "was riding for a fall" and that the "excesses" of the "organized masses" would "drag us through decades of misery."[45]

To save America from this ominous future, Bacon turned again to Root. He once wrote him that "I wish I had the power to place away in the back of my head for future use, the chunks of wisdom which always come to me from contact with you." Now, outraged, at "miserable lying papers like the *World* and *Herald,*" he planned to buy control of the *New York Post.* Then, after using it to spread Root's wisdom throughout the country, he would project this great oracle into the White House. From there, Bacon's personal mentor would be the nation's father figure. To that end, Bacon said, "I would give the rest of my worthless life." When his newspaper plans nonetheless failed, he compensated by convincing Harvard University Press to publish the seven-volume Root public papers. Guaranteeing all expenses, he lost $12,000 in three years' time.[46]

Once again Bacon had failed. Instead of entering the White House, Root retired to New York. Meanwhile, his compiled wisdom gathered dust in warehouse storage. As for Bacon himself, his great moral purpose became the monthly meetings of the Harvard Corporation and a South American lecture tour on international law.

For years Bacon considered war a unique opportunity for social service and personal justification. Theodore Roosevelt's exploits in the Spanish-American War inverted their relationship, making Roosevelt the idol and Bacon his worshipper. While still in the State Department, the latter drew this one conclusion: combat was an American gentleman's only worthy enterprise. Thus Bacon, psychologically predisposed for fighting, was "war ready" when hostilities began in Europe. Yet, in 1914, it seemed that self-deprecation would overcome his last chance for vindication. On his first trip to wartime France he wrote home: "I seem to be conscious of a sort of feverish desire to do something for somebody, with not enough aggressiveness or ability to make it worthwhile. . . . Perhaps it's a weakness, a lack of the preeminent attributes of the masculine animal. . . . My dream of being sometime somebody to serve as an inspiration, and to awaken a big ambition, is past."[47]

Despite this fear, Bacon did not languish in despair. Like the late George Apley, the literary archetype of the frustrated Boston Brahmin, he made the war his hope for self-fulfillment. He sailed back to France to spend Thanksgiving with the "splendid fellows . . . bleeding and suffering at the front" and did ambulance work as "an excuse for keeping in touch with the armies." Ceasing to worry about his own decay, he began to anticipate combat service in a martial passion play that, in his mind, pitted the Anglo-Franco spirit against Germany's "scientific, soulless war machine." He told friends "of the pride I should feel if I were only fighting and suffering" with the French army, and they found him "absolutely obsessed over the war." Even Leonard Wood thought that Bacon's eagerness for overseas duty "was almost pathetic."[48]

Once too shy for public speaking, Bacon had judged himself "unfit for leadership." Now, submerged in his crusade, he had the "courage to brave public opinion and [become] a leader." In the 1916 New York senatorial primary, he lost while running on a preparedness platform and still felt "quite contented." Campaigning for self-vindication, he was glad just "to have made the fight [and] felt a better man for it." As chairman of the Plattsburg Military Training Camps Association, second president of the National Security League, and executive member of virtually all the other military training societies, Bacon became, so one historian has said, the "linchpin of the whole civilian preparedness movement." Thus he finally had what he always wanted—a satisfying role in a great moral enterprise.[49]

When America finally declared war in 1917, this "dreadful nightmare of sacrifice and suffering" became the "crucible" by which Bacon would cleanse "the national soul from selfish material interests." He immediately wrote General Pershing pleading to give his "service in any capacity." While he dreamed of "the real thing," commanding "men in the line," his age foreclosed such duty. Pershing consequently made him garrison commander of his general headquarters at Chaumont. There, technically unqualified for this assignment, Bacon spent his time censoring letters and giving French lessons. However he was not bitter. The man who once loyally assisted J. P. Morgan and Elihu Root now declared that he was willing to serve another great commander and "sweep out Pershing's office if that will give him peace of mind." The general must have had other janitors around for he transferred Bacon back to diplomatic duty as chief liaison officer to the British general staff. There, resuming his old role as a social functionary, he greeted King George, organized Allied officer clubs, hosted dinner parties, and "soothed over natural friction." While this job may have resembled his old State Department post, Bacon still cherished his new position. Living each day in an "atmosphere of wonderful British heroes," he felt himself a link in the Anglo-American alliance that would save civilization in war and peace. Although he was not a combat hero, pilgrim Bacon finally reached his own "Delectable Mountain" of self-satisfaction. And it came none too soon. Ignoring a dangerous lesion when he entered the service, he contracted mastoiditis, which killed him six months after the armistice.[50]

NOTES

1. For statements on the initial skepticism about Plattsburg, see statement of Gen. Hagood, n.d., Hermann Hagedorn MSS, Box 19; Grenville Clark to Theodore Roosevelt, Nov. 19, 1914, Roosevelt MSS, Reel 215. The quotation is from Samuel R. Spencer, Jr., "The Selective Training and Service Act of 1940 from Inception to Enactment" (Ph.D. diss., Harvard University, 1951), p. 15. Because Spencer had extensive personal contact with Plattsburgers when serving as personal secretary to Grenville Clark, this may be considered a primary source.

2. Wood to Gen. E. St. J. Greble, Oct. 8, 1916; Franklin Roosevelt to Wood, Aug. 16, 1915; Douglas Johnson to Wood, Apr. 18, 1916; Edmund James to Wood, Aug. 16, 1915: all in Wood MSS, Boxes 80. 83, 85, 90.

3. Wood to Frank McCoy, Sept. 26, 1916, McCoy MSS, Box 14; Perry, *The Plattsburg Movement,* p. 119; Lt. Halstead Dorey quoted in *New York Herald,* Aug. 16, 1915.

4. However, some volunteer (rarely full-time) social workers favored UMT, see Ch. 5, pp. 110–11, 118n29. As to the peace movement: here I refer to organizations during World War I, not to the movement that preceded the war. The former was politically radical, the latter was a movement for social control similar to the preparedness movement, see Ch. 6, pp. 122–24, and Ch. 8, pp. 172–73.

5. For the pacifist leadership, see Chambers, "Conscripting for Colossus," p. 16. For an example of training in the Protestant ethic, see James Brown Scott, ed., *Robert Bacon: Life and Letters* (Garden City: Doubleday, Page, 1923), pp. 7–12. Brahmins quoted in Frederic Cople Jaher, *The Urban Establishment: Upper Strata in Boston, New York, Charleston, Chicago, and Los Angeles* (Urbana: University of Illinois Press, 1982), pp. 35, 64; John Collins Warren, *To Work in the Vineyards of Surgery: The Reminiscences of John Collins Warren* (Cambridge,

Mass.: Harvard University Press, 1958), pp. 185–86. Rev. F. L. Finchbeaugh quoted in *Cincinnati Enquirer,* Sept. 17, 1916.

6. On capitalism and asceticism, see William James, *The Varieties of Religious Experience* (new ed.; New York: New American Library, 1958), pp. 85, 235. On the conflicting cults of business and Sparta, see Sigmund Diamond, *The Reputation of the American Businessman* (New York: Harper & Row, 1966), pp. 44, 70, 92, 131; Gordon Wood, *The Creation of the American Republic, 1776–1787* (New York: Norton, 1972), pp. 51–53, 64. The quotations are from magazine writer Frederick Hoffman as cited in Gilbert, *Work without Salvation,* p. 9; A. Barton Hepburn as cited in C. Roland Marchand, *The American Peace Movement and Social Reform, 1898–1918* (Princeton: Princeton University Press, 1972), p. 173; Theodore Roosevelt, Jr., *Rank and File: True Stories of the Great War* (New York: Charles Scribner's Sons, 1925), p. 262; Archibald Thacher to John Prentice, Apr. 19, 1916, Grenville Clark MSS, Dartmouth College; Quincy Mills, "Plattsburg Eulogy," 1915, Mills MSS, University of North Carolina; Wood to Frank McCoy, Oct. 6, 1916, Wood MSS, Box 93.

7. Description of Arthur Woods in *New York Times,* Aug. 24, 1915. For the democratization of consumption, see Daniel J. Boorstin, *The Americans: The Democratic Experience* (New York: Vintage Books, 1974), pp. 307–59.

8. Charles Henry Brent Diary, Aug. 9, 1918, Brent MSS, Library of Congress; Alexander C. Zabrinski, *Bishop Brent: Crusader for Christian Unity* (Philadelphia: Westminster Press, 1948), p. 202; Charles Henry Brent, *The Mount of Vision* (New York: Longmans, Green, 1918), pp. 98, 110; Brent to Leonard Wood, Mar. 16, 1917, Hermann Hagedorn MSS, Box 19.

9. Zabrinski, *Bishop Brent,* pp. 15–16, 27–28; Brent to Leonard Wood, Aug. 29, 1916, Wood MSS, Box 86; Brent to Walter Hichman, Aug. 16, 1916, Brent MSS, Box 12.

10. Arthur Cosby to Langdon Marvin, Mar. 17, 1922, Grenville Clark MSS; Archibald Thacher to Pepper, Mar. 1, 1916, Pepper MSS, Box 15.

11. George Wharton Pepper, *Philadelphia Lawyer: An Autobiography* (Philadelphia: J. B. Lippincott, 1944), pp. 70, 110, 316, 376; Pepper to F. S. Wood, n.d., Pepper MSS, Box 8; *New York Times,* Mar. 1, 1916; Pepper, "The Moral Value of Preparedness," May 2, 1916, Pepper MSS, Box 8.

12. Pepper to Wood, June 26, 1916; Wood to Pepper, June 27, 1916; Pepper to Wood, June 28, 1916: all in Wood MSS, Box 90; Pepper to Grenville Clark, June 28, 1916, Clark MSS; Pepper to Halsted Dorey, May 2, 1916, Plattsburg Barracks File, Box 1783, National Archives.

13. Pepper to W. W. Atterburg, Dec. 26, 1917, Pepper MSS, Book 10, Box. 8.

14. *Plattsburg Daily Press,* Aug. 3, 1916; Stimson to Wood, Oct. 3, 1916, Wood MSS, Box 102.

15. Elting E. Morison, *Turmoil and Tradition: A Study of the Life and Times of Henry L. Stimson* (New York: Atheneum, 1964), pp. 72–73; Roosevelt quoted in Wagenknecht, *Seven Worlds of Theodore Roosevelt,* p. 19; Henry Stimson, *My Vacations* (n.p.: privately printed, 1949), p. 2.

16. Henry Stimson and McGeorge Bundy, *On Active Service in Peace and War* New York: Harper & Brothers, 1948), p. xvi. For war causing fear of nature, see Paul Fussell, *The Great War and Modern Memory* (New York: Oxford Uni-

versity Press, 1975), pp. 79, 108, 144. Unidentified soldier quoted on the destruction of the woods in D. Clayton James, *The Years of MacArthur: Vol. 1, 1880–1941*, (Boston: Houghton, Mifflin, 1970), pp. 213–14. Stimson to Theodore Roosevelt, July 28, 1918, Roosevelt MSS, Reel 287; Stimson Diary, July 11, July 22, 1918, Stimson MSS. For combat soldiers and nature, see J. Glenn Gray, *The Warriors: Reflections on Men in Battle* (New York: Harper & Row, 1970), pp. 206, 235–38; Philip Caputo, *A Rumor of War* (New York: Holt, Reinhart & Winston, 1977), pp. 265, 288. Morison, *Turmoil and Tradition*, p. 191; Henry Stimson, "Artillery in a Quiet Sector," *Scribner's* 65 (June, 1919):713.

17. Henry Stimson, *The Issues of the War* (New York: National Security League, n.d.), pp. 17–21; statement of Stimson in Senate, *Hearings on Universal Military Training*, 64th Cong., 2d Sess., 1917, pp. 825–26; Stimson quoted in Morison, *Turmoil and Tradition*, p. 32; Stimson to Theodore Roosevelt, Dec. 14, 1915, Roosevelt MSS, Reel 203; Stimson and Bundy, *On Active Service in Peace and War*, pp. 22, 59–62, 79, 208; Stimson to George Slater, Mar. 20, 1916, Stimson MSS.

18. Stimson quoted in Morison, *Turmoil and Tradition*, p. 195; Henry Stimson, "Roosevelt and the World War," *Works of Theodore Roosevelt*, 21:xviii–xix; Stimson and Bundy, *On Active Service in Peace and War*, p. 92; Wade Chance to Theodore Roosevelt, May 2, 1917; Stimson to Roosevelt, Feb. 7, 1918, July 28, 1918: all in Roosevelt MSS, Reels 234, 263, 287; Stimson Diary, May 12, 1918, May 21, 1918, June 3, 1918, Stimson MSS; Roosevelt, Jr., to Roosevelt, Sr., Aug. 9, 1918, Roosevelt, Jr., MSS, Box 7.

19. Stimson to Theodore Roosevelt, Feb. 7, 1918, Roosevelt MSS, Reel 263; Morison, *Turmoil and Tradition*, pp. 193–95.

20. Stimson to Theodore Roosevelt, May 13, 1918, Roosevelt MSS, Reel 276; Claude Fuess, "The Reminiscences of Claude M. Fuess," pp. 83–84, Oral History Project, Columbia University, New York, N.Y.; Stimson and Bundy, *On Active Service in Peace and War*, p. 404.

21. Frank J. Mather: letter in *Forum* 34 (Oct., 1902):223; "Rear-Rank Reflections," *Unpopular Review* 5 (Jan., 1916), p. 17.

22. Owen Wister, *The Virginian* (New York: Airmont, 1954), p. 11; Wister quoted in White, *The Eastern Establishment and the Western Experience*, p. 123; Wister, *Roosevelt: The Story of a Friendship* (New York: Macmillan, 1930), pp. 50, 84–85, 158, 227–28, 271; George T. Watkins III, "Owen Wister and the American West: A Biographical and Critical Study" (Ph.D. diss., University of Illinois, 1959), pp. 119, 227–28, 264, 315; Wister to Lanier, Aug. 16, 1926, Houghton Library, Harvard University; Wister Journal, Feb. 2, 1921, Wister MSS, Library of Congress.

23. Owen Wister, *Members of the Family* (New York: Macmillan, 1911), p. 11; Wister quoted in Watkins, "Owen Wister and the American West," p. 231.

24. Wister quoted in Gene M. Gressley, *Bankers and Cattlemen* (New York: Knopf, 1966), pp. 60–61; Watkins, "Owen Wister and the American West," pp. 43, 372; Wister, *Roosevelt*, pp. 20, 104, 110, 119; Wister Journal, May 23, 1919, Wister MSS.

25. Owen Wister: *The Pentecost of Calamity* (New York: Macmillan, 1915),

pp. 139, 148; "Preface," in Edward Toland, *The Aftermath of Battle* (New York: Macmillan, 1916), p. ix.

26. Michael Walzer, *The Revolution of the Saints, A Study in the Origins of Radical Politics* (New York: Atheneum, 1972), esp. pp. 285–87, 290, 297; Peter N. Carroll, *Puritanism and the Wilderness: The Intellectual Significance of the New England Frontier, 1629–1700* (New York: Columbia University Press, 1969), pp. 2, 15–16, 61–62, 89; Bercovitch, *American Jeremiad,* pp. 51–52. 101–2.

27. Roosevelt, Jr., to Eleanor B. Roosevelt, n.d., Jan. 1, Feb. 1, Mar. 13, Apr. 22, June 3, 1944: all in Roosevelt, Jr., MSS, Family Papers, Library of Congress.

28. Ralph Barton Perry: *Puritanism and Democracy* (New York: Vanguard, 1944), p. 266; "What is Worth Fighting For?," *Atlantic Monthly* 116 (Dec., 1915): 829; *The Plattsburg Movement,* p. 4.

29. For a comparison of regional elites, see Jaher, *Urban Establishment,* esp. pp. 653–54. Franklin Roosevelt to Leonard Wood, June 23, 1915, Wood MSS, Box 82. Clifford, *Citizen Soldiers,* pp. 94–95; Pogue, *George C. Marshall: Education of a General,* pp. 136–37; *San Francisco Examiner* quoted in ibid., p. 136.

30. James G. Harbord to Frank McCoy, Aug. 23, 1914, McCoy MSS, Box 14; Dibblee quoted in "Plattsburg Committee Meeting of Nov. 24, 1916," Grenville Clark MSS; Dibblee to Theodore Roosevelt, Jr., May 19, 1917, Roosevelt, Sr., MSS, Reel 209; *New York Times,* Nov. 12. 1945; W. Cameron Forbes, "The Journal of W. Cameron Forges," ser. 2, 2:181.

31. Hermann Hagedorn, *The Roosevelt Family of Sagamore Hill* (New York: Macmillan, 1954), pp. 50–51; Roosevelt, Sr., quoted in *Washington Times,* July 6, 1902. *New York Herald,* Sept. 2, 1900; Morison, ed., *Letters of Theodore Roosevelt,* 1:392, 2:803–4; William H. Allen, "The Reminiscences of Dr. William H. Allen," pp. 140–41, Oral History Project, Columbia University.

32. For inconsistent affection and self-deprecation, see Otto Fenichel, *The Psychoanalytic Theory of Neurosis* (New York: Norton, 1945), pp. 41, 44. The four quotations are from Eleanor Butler Roosevelt, *Day Before Yesterday: The Reminiscences of Mrs. Theodore Roosevelt, Jr.* (Garden City: Doubleday, 1959), pp. 59–60; Morison, ed., *Letters of Theodore Roosevelt,* 2:1442, 3:490; William A. Gardiner, *Groton School Verses: 1886–1903* (Boston: n.p., 1904), n.p.

33. For Roosevelt, Jr.'s, football heroics, see letters from teachers and classmates written to Glenn McCord in 1940, quoted in Glenn McCord, "The Revelation of a Great Man's Son" (manuscript in possession of Mr. McCord: Arlington, N.J.). Roosevelt, Sr., quoted in *New York World,* Nov. 20, 1905; Morison, ed., *Letters of Theodore Roosevelt,* 3:613–14, 652, 5:76, 81–82.

34. Ibid., 2:1444, 5:93–94; Roosevelt, Jr., to Terry Allen, Jr., Oct. 19, 1942, Terry Allen File, Army War College, Carlisle, Penn.; personal interview with Marcus O. Stevenson, Nov. 15. 1972.

35. "From College to Business," *Independent* 65 (Oct. 8, 1908):846–47; Morison, ed., *Letters of Theodore Roosevelt,* 4:1034, 1236–37, 1330, 1373–74, 7:392, 417.

36. Roosevelt, Jr., *Average Americans,* p. 3; Roosevelt, Jr., to Irving Gladwin, Dec. 31, 1921, Roosevelt, Jr., MSS, Box 20; Roosevelt, Jr., "A Boy's Book

Rambles," *Bookman* 60 (Feb., 1925):689–91; Roosevelt, Jr., "The Norman Baron's Prayer," 1902, Roosevelt, Jr., MSS, Box 7.

37. *Philadelphia Telegram,* Sept. 14, 1898; Alice Roosevelt Longworth, *Crowded Hours: The Reminiscences of Alice Roosevelt Longworth* (New York: Scribner's, 1933), pp. 24–25; Glenn McCord, "The Revelation of a Great Man's Son," p. 131; *New York Herald,* July 6, 1902. The quotations are from Morison, ed., *Letters of Theodore Roosevelt,* 2:1135, 3:693–94, 5:824; Hagedorn, *Roosevelt Family of Sangamore Hill,* p. 145; Roosevelt, Jr., to Leonard Wood, June 19, 1916, Wood MSS, Box 90.

38. Morison, ed., *Letters of Theodore Roosevelt,* 8:965; unidentified newspaper clipping, Aug. 9, 1915, in Leonard Wood MSS, Box 258.

39. Roosevelt, Jr., to Roosevelt, Sr., n.d., Roosevelt, Jr., MSS, Box 85. Morison, ed., *Letters of Theodore Roosevelt,* 8:1193. The disgruntled veteran was quoted by Heywood Broun in *New York World,* n.d., clipping in Roosevelt, Jr., MSS, Box 80. Roosevelt, Jr.'s, reaction to war is described in George C. Marshall, *Memoirs of My Service in the World War, 1917–1918* (Boston: Houghton, Mifflin, 1976), p. 51.

40. Gen. George B. Duncan quoted in Coffman, *War to End All Wars,* pp. 136–37; Roosevelt, Jr., to Eleanor B. Roosevelt, May 22, 1918; Roosevelt, Jr., to Albert Lappen, Aug. 27, 1937; George Marshall to Roosevelt, Jr., 1920; Roosevelt, Jr., to Marshall, July 14, 1920: all in Roosevelt, Jr., MSS, Boxes 7, 37, 68. Marshall said that he never spoke this way before. By repute, he never did so again. To say the least, he was not known for his flattery.

41. *Boston Advertiser,* Sept. 6, 1905; A. B. Hart to Mrs. Robert Bacon, Sept. 29, 1919, Houghton Library, Harvard University; Peter Bowditch to Frank McCoy, Oct. 15, 1920, McCoy MSS, Box 16; George Van Horn Mosley, "War Diaries," Oct. 10, 1917, Mosley MSS, Library of Congress; J. L. Strachey to Leonard Wood, Oct. 26, 1915, Wood MSS, Box 90; Theodore Roosevelt to General S. M. B. Young, Nov. 27, 1915, National Association for Universal Military Training MSS, Box 7, Library of Congress; William Muldoon to Theodore Roosevelt, Apr. 18, 1917, Roosevelt MSS, Box 228; Robert Bacon to Bernard Baruch, Aug. 4, 1916, Baruch MSS, Box 171, Princeton University. For the concept of the Don Juan of Achievement, see Fenichel, *Psychoanalytic Theory of Neurosis,* p. 502.

42. Scott, ed., *Robert Bacon,* pp. 25–29, 57; Morison, ed., *Letters of Theodore Roosevelt,* 1:20; *Boston Herald,* May 30, 1919; Bacon to Theodore Roosevelt, Oct. 4, 1902, Roosevelt MSS, Reel 329; *Boston Advertiser,* Jan. 16, 1909; Bacon to Elihu Root, July 10, 1905, Root MSS, Box 40.

43. Bentley T. Mott, *Twenty Years as Military Attache* (New York: Oxford University Press, 1937), p. 120; Philip Jessup, *Elihu Root* (New York: Dodd & Mead, 1938), 1:455, 2:137–38; Bacon to Root, July 23, 1907, Jan. 30, 1914, Root MSS, Boxes 60, 118; Bacon to J. J. Jusserand, Feb. 7, 1907; Bacon to Mr. Carr, Dec. 20, 1907; Bacon to Root, n.d.; Bacon to Smith, June 22, 1907; Smith to Bacon, June 22, 1907: all in State Department Numerical Files 358, 389, 493, National Archives. Bacon cited in Blumenson, ed., *Patton Papers, 1885–1940,* p. 406,

44. Bacon to Theodore Roosevelt, Sept. 3, 1909, Roosevelt MSS, Reel 89;

Bacon quoted in Abbott, ed., *Letters of Archie Butt*, pp. 341–43; H. Hatzfeldt to Bacon, July 7, 1908; Bacon to Whitelaw Reid, July 17, 1908, Feb. 17, 1909, Sept. 3, 1910; Bacon to State Department, Aug. 29, 1910: all in Whitelaw Reid MSS, Reel 71, Library of Congress; Challener, *Admirals, Generals, and American Foreign Policy*, pp. 63–64, 119, 319–23; Mott, *Twenty Years as Military Attache*, pp. 83–85, 185; Bacon to Root, Nov. 20, 1910, May 27, 1911, Root MSS, Boxes 68, 78; Higgenson to Charles F. Adams, Apr. 12, 1909, in A. Lawrence Lowell MSS, File 176, Harvard University.

45. *New York Times*, Jan. 13, 1912, May 30, 1919; Horney, *Neurosis and Human Growth*, p. 38; Bacon to Theodore Roosevelt, Oct. 4, 1902, Roosevelt MSS, Reel 329. Mitchell described by radicals in John Laslett, *Labor and the Left: A Study of Socialist and Radical Influences in the American Labor Movement, 1881–1924* (New York: Basic Books, 1970), p. 214; Scott, ed., *Robert Bacon*, p. 435.

46. Bacon to Root, June 23, 1911, Sept. 6, 1911, Sept. 7, 1911, May 17, 1913: all in Root MSS, Boxes 78, 104; A. Lawrence Lowell to Mrs. Robert Bacon, Sept. 2, 1919, Lowell MSS, File 1868.

47. Bacon to Roosevelt, Feb. 11, 1899, Roosevelt to Bacon, Feb. 16, 1899, Roosevelt MSS, Reel 320; Bacon cited in Wister, *Roosevelt*, p. 90; Scott, ed., *Robert Bacon*, p. 204.

48. John P. Marquand, *The Late George Apley* (New York: Grosset & Dunlap, n.d.), pp. 236, 263, 266, 272; Bacon to Root, Oct. 29, 1914, Root MSS, Box 118; Scott, ed., *Robert Bacon*, pp. 217, 228, 253; *New York Times*, Oct. 3, 1915. 2:3, Dec. 19, 1915; W. Cameron Forbes, "Journal of W. Cameron Forbes," ser. 2., 1: Nov. 29, 1914, Forbes MSS.

49. Scott, ed., *Robert Bacon*, pp. 204, 225–26; Bacon to Theodore Roosevelt, "Primary Day," 1916, Roosevelt MSS, Reel 218; Finnegan, *Against the Specter of a Dragon*, pp. 169–70.

50. Scott, ed., *Robert Bacon*, pp. 297, 322, 325, 368, 399–400; John J. Pershing, *My Experiences in the World War* (New York: Frederick A. Stokes, 1931), 1:23, 2:60–61; Bacon quoted in statement of Gen. Kilbourne, Nov. 26, 1928, Hermann Hagedorn MSS, Box 20; Frank McCoy to Mrs. Robert Bacon, Oct. 15, 1920, McCoy MSS, Box 16; "Robert Bacon: A Reminiscence," *The Review* 1 (June 7, 1919):75.

CHAPTER 4

Military Training:
The College Experience

☆

IN 1913, WHEN Chief of Staff Leonard Wood inaugurated
citizen-soldier training at Plattsburg Barracks, New York, the government would give him neither money for equipment nor conscription for
enrollment. College students, for whom the camp was founded, would
therefore have to volunteer to pay for the privilege of spending their
summer vacations obeying drill instructors. The general, obviously
needing all the help he could get if he were to gather a respectable number of recruits, appealed to the presidents of America's most eminent
universities by telling them that military training would improve their
students' citizenship, discipline, and character. Except for Columbia's
Nicholas Murray Butler, a self-proclaimed pacifist, all those whom
Wood contacted, from Yale to the University of California, "enthusiastically supplied their support." Without these academics to guarantee
Plattsburg's moral purity, the public might have continued to think the
service was "a school of iniquity." These men, dissolving the perceived
link between the army, brothels, and saloons, probably ensured enough
recruits to keep Wood's camp from closing.[1] This chapter explores the
pedagogic arguments they made for army drill by placing them within
the larger history of higher education. The martial attitudes of educators and alumni cannot be understood without focusing concurrently
on the institutional decline of the college and the rise of the university,
on the new role of the president and his old interest in moral uplift.
This context reveals that military training, as a course in discipline,
was a response to an identity crisis felt by higher education on the eve
of World War I.

In the late nineteenth-century, academic institutions which sought
financial solvency had to accommodate America's practical desire for
greater productivity. To secure enrollment, they changed their basic
structure from denominational colleges stressing moral nurture to secular universities teaching occupational expertise. Before World War I,
however, many educators who still cherished Christian traditions of in-

struction had not fully adjusted to this new orientation. They therefore tried to graft moral requirements onto a curriculum that generally emphasized utilitarian electives. At first they sponsored a program of conservative humanism featuring uplift and discipline through mandatory courses and social supervision. When this failed, they tried to preserve a Christian environment through extracurricular activities such as religious revivals and football teams. Finally, when football turned commercial, some of these pedagogues adopted military training as an antidote to the contemporary university's moral neutrality. To educators who still emphasized traditional didactic duties, army drill became a twentieth-century opportunity to express nineteenth-century beliefs that higher learning had a moral responsibility.

The Moral Argument of Military Training: College Presidents in Search of Virtue

The most active member of Plattsburg's Advisory Committee of College Presidents was its secretary, Henry Sturgis Drinker (born in 1850; appointed president of Lehigh University in 1905). A descendant of Philadelphia's merchant grandees, he was a civil engineer, an attorney, and now head of a school of railroad and mining technology. But whatever his occupation, paternalism was his true vocation. Having joined academia to "look after boys" once his own grown sons had left his home, he declared that "the development of sturdy manliness [was his] highest duty." So despite lineage from colonial Quakers jailed for pacifism and his own involvement in the Carnegie Foundation for Peace, in 1913 he became interested in the "enormous educational value" of military training. Thereafter the promotion of this "hard disciplinary experience in obedience and clean living" became "the most important business [that he had] in the world." In fact, the advisory committee's chairman, John Grier Hibben of Princeton, said that Drinker's efforts on behalf of Plattsburg were largely responsible for "all that we were able to accomplish in assisting General Wood." Moreover, that assistance outlived Wood himself. In 1932, Drinker still was praising military camps for "their great value in the training of our young men."[2]

Although Drinker was the most active, he was only one of many presidents who promoted Plattsburg training as a course in social discipline. Other devotees included Cornell's Jacob Gould Schurman (born 1865; appointed 1892), Yale's Arthur T. Hadley (born 1861; appointed 1899) and Princeton's Hibben (born 1861; appointed 1912). They said, in turn: that military training, irrespective of defense, should be retained "for its moral, mental, social and civic effects"; it instilled "discipline, cleanliness and efficiency"; it taught the "order, system and punctuality" that Americans need "more than any other people." These educators, however outspoken, were not unique. Despite Woodrow Wilson's indifference to most military issues, Hibben's predecessor temporarily reverted from President of the United States to president of Princeton when he endorsed military training camps for teaching "discipline and regularity" to the nation's college students. Other academic presidents, in a 1915 poll, favored military drill in their schools by 33 to 10. Even Nicholas Murray Butler, whom a colleague called "a weathercock showing which way the wind is blowing," now reversed his prior stand to affirm that military camps provided an "exceptional opportunity for a much needed training in the essentials of citizenship."[3]

Of course, there were exceptions. Neither Stanford's President Emeritus David Starr Jordan (born 1850; appointed 1891) nor Harvard's A. Lawrence Lowell (born 1856; appointed 1909) supported military training for character development or social control. Jordan, a pacifist, opposed all army service while Lowell, a preparedness advocate, promoted a strictly "military policy" for the military purpose of preventing serious shortages of junior officers. Although Lowell shared his colleagues' concern that their students were growing "frivolous and pleasure seeking," he did not believe in a military training reformation, As he saw it: "Military discipline, which means obedience to orders, is a very different thing from the self-discipline needed in civil life, and it seems on the whole to diminish the sense of responsibility for one's own conduct."[4]

Because Lowell was interested in military efficiency without moral uplift, Harvard developed the best collegiate army course in the country. Rather than spend time on close-order marches and other disciplinary drills "of little or no advantage [for] political soldiering," it maximized proficiency by emphasizing lectures on the technical problems of the European war. Its cadets certainly learned their lessons. Leonard Wood thought that they were at least 50 percent better prepared than the average American soldier. Consequently, he later used them to help instruct his own 89th Infantry Division, one of the best trained units in the American Expeditionary Force.[5]

Its technical merits notwithstanding, Lowell's program did not appeal to those college presidents more concerned with moral improvement than with military competence. When Harvard tried to curtail the army training corps' requirements for military drill, Cornell's Schurman protested that this exercise was necessary "for the physical and moral development of the individual student." Even in war, many presidents continued to emphasize the ethical state of their schools, not the physical defense of their country. Schurman discouraged wartime enrollments in the regular army by charging his undergraduates to remain in college for the sake of the nation's "intellectual and spiritual life." Meanwhile Hibben stopped talking about countries emerging from the battlefield "chastened and purified" and introduced new Princeton-based military courses admittedly designed to prevent any precipitous "rush into enlistment."[6]

Institutional Change in Higher Education: The New Role of the President and Demoralization of the Campus

Many college presidents obviously hoped to use military training for moral reform. But if one momentarily discounts institutional change in higher education and the crisis in the role of the college president, it is difficult to grasp why administrators felt that their relatively well-behaved students needed moral reformation at all. Henry May's seminal study, *The End of American Innocence,* posits that the old guard used military training to control the bohemians who suddenly surfaced in the 1910s. In turn, spokesmen for that avant-garde—Max Eastman, Randolph Bourne, John Reed, and company—damned preparedness, perhaps because traditionalists endorsed it. (In Europe, where "the Establishment" seemed more pacific, artists whom Bourne admired welcomed war to shame bourgeoise timidity.) In America, if one accepts May, the bohemians and their stand for peace explains why the preparedness movement issued many jeremiads condemning youth for "its small regard for obedience and discipline." Nonetheless, it still seems unlikely that college presidents panicked over an incipient cultural rebellion since their writings do not reveal great concern for Greenwich Village. To be sure, traditionalists objected to social change which emphasized consumption and free choice at the expense of abstinence and self-control. But being a long evolutionary process, this transformation did not suddenly bloom in the early 1900s. Some 250 years before Plattsburg, its Puritan progenitors were also blaming moral declension on affluence, urbanization, and the young. Moreover, "spoiled" adolescents have been aggravating college administrators for centuries. In 1740, the first president of Columbia (then King's College) declared that parents must begin to restrain their offsprings' "debauchery and uncontrolled indulgences."[7]

Rarely angels in the past, the college students of the early twentieth century were actually rather compliant. Many certainly supported military training with an enthusiasm that discredits charges of "rebellion" and "degeneracy." In 1916 campus polls on UMT, Yale's students voted 1,112 for and 228 against, Harvard favored it 860 to 339, Princeton by 503 to 92, and the University of Pennsylvania, despite its Quaker tradition, by 936 to 50.[8]

It was ironic that college presidents should have contended that their students needed military training as a course in social control. A brief review of the history of higher education shows that their own campuses had been quiet since the mid-nineteenth century because they had relinquished discipline-inducing subjects, from compulsory Greek to mandatory chapel. Many of these schools, founded to develop Christian gentlemen, had not intended "to prepare their students directly for business or [a] career." Nonetheless, to attract enough enrollment to maintain their solvency, they came to reflect and sustain America's commitment to economic growth. As late as 1875, most of the nation's 7,000 engineers could still learn their trade while building railroads, factories, or canals. But by 1915, after "the [productive] cream had been skimmed off the [existing] body of knowledge," a professional training in this field meant graduation from one of the 194 universities now offering courses to America's 115,000 engineers. Students, then free from the drills in Latin grammar and moral philosophy, which were thought to be drawbacks in the innovative world of enterprise, were no more dutiful than their predecessors; they were simply less frustrated for having received the "useful" courses they craved.[9]

Outside the classroom, campus life was even more autonomous and practical. As schools increasingly stopped acting in loco parentis, social activities escaped the administrative supervision that had been more restrictive than the average home. Once largely religious, extracurricular programs now comprised a rugged competition for the power, prestige, and well-connected friends that prepared collegians for a business career. Consequently students, satisfied with the social life that was their primary concern, no longer were "imbued," after the 1860s, "with hostility to the college government." They then stopped rolling cannonballs at professors, fomenting lethal riots, and committing "crimes that were [said to be] worthy of the penitentiary." When a few campuses did errupt, social control was more cause than cure. Disturbances took place at a few old New England colleges that still tried to enforce paternalism or at larger universities whose administrators interfered with established student freedoms.[10]

Their hyperbole to the contrary, modern college presidents were not witnessing a social rebellion by students educated in their institutions. Because those collegians were being trained to succeed in industrial society, they were not as defiant as were young Europeans "magnificently unprepared for the long littleness of life." In America, the alienation which caused these foreign intellectuals to greet war as a purification rite typified not students but college presidents, much less comfortable with campus life. They, after all, had undergone a disturbing change of role and function. In nearly all institutions interested in greater productivity, structural differentiation accompanied physical expansion. As the "local puritan college" (Santayana's words for Harvard) grew into the secular university, the resulting specialization in large-scale administration meant that presidents rarely taught courses in ethics and morality. Instead, men generally selected for their "perfect acquaintance with business and political matters" devoted their time and energy to raising funds, reconciling interest groups, and coordinating academic departments that taught morally neutral skills in science, commerce, and industry. But since traditions live on after functions change, some college presidents still honored the moral duties they no longer performed. Military training gave them a new opportunity to perform their old mission—to teach virtue and build character.[11]

A comparison of academia's policy positions in World Wars I and II indicates the following: because army exercises helped resolve the tension between the traditional purpose and the contemporary function of higher education, they became less attractive as time reduced that tension. In the 1910s, Harvard, Yale, Princeton, and the universities of Chicago and California were among the leading exponents of military drill. By the mid-1940s they were the leading opponents of this suddenly popular policy. Opinion polls then showed that over 60 percent of the nation's students and 70 percent of the public, anticipating future wars, favored UMT. Meanwhile the military high command, repeating an old argument that once appealed to academics, claimed that their discipline-inducing regimen would "fit" students for "the opportunities that college offers." Nonetheless, educational institutions, despite special White House conferences and briefings, consistently rejected the War Department's pleas. This widespread reversal of academic opinion suggests that the ideals and self-images of higher education had changed between the wars. By World War II, most American college presidents had adjusted to their ethically neutral role of conciliator, coordinator, and fund-raiser. These self-interested members of the "college-lobby," on the eve of the great post-war "take-off" into sustained enrollment growth, frankly viewed the army as a rival bureaucracy competing for the same young men and government money. Although old Plattsburg leaders desperately "tried to educate the [new] educators" as to the "great educational and moral" meaning of military training, most academic administrators were more concerned with the fact that in World War II their enrollments had decreased by as much as 50 percent. When it came to gathering up the ninety million dollars worth of research grants and subsidies that the Pentagon disbursed in 1950 alone, many college executives were apt to declare that their schools were "bastions of our defense as essential . . . as supersonic bombers." But when it came to endorsing the type of military draft lacking student deferments that ensured high enrollments, these men were much more reticent. Reluctant to risk his clientele, President Harold W. Dodds, Hibben's successor at Princeton, would only say that he might support UMT if it proved to be a clear "military necessity."[12]

The Pursuit of Moral Rearmament: Conservative Humanism and Military Training

Military training during World War I was not the only attempt to preserve moral values in the university system. Before the war, future army drill enthusiasts advocated other didactic programs whose failure, by 1914, led them to promote UMT as an alternative method of moral reform. Protesting elective curricula, utilitarian education, and student social freedom, these men tried to resurrect mental discipline and spiritual development through a policy of conservative humanism. More a general attitude than any specific course, this persuasion expressed itself both inside and outside the classroom. Some educators tried to restore paternal supervision to college life. In the past, Schurman and Hibben, two Protestant philosophers, would have taught the mandatory senior course in moral philosophy, an exhortative survey of the social sciences culminating four Christian years of "character education." However, by the 1890s, presidents left the classroom and this subject left the curriculum as psychology dropped ethics, stressing moral instruction, to join mental testing for efficient job placement. Nonetheless preserving their personal commitment to their obsolete responsibility, both men, as well as their colleague Henry Sturgis Drinker, allocated their spare time for counseling individual students. Schurman visited the sick to encourage their recovery and Drinker asked "his [poor] boys" home for supper. Meanwhile Hibben kept whole faculty committees waiting while he personally advised an incoming freshman. His predecessor at Princeton, Woodrow Wilson, a man who later cited the "advantages [of military training] to the youth of the country," had built a preceptor-residential system whose "discipline of an ordered life" promised to promote the optimum collegiate gentleman. Actually, Wilson described his ideal students the same way that Plattsburgers would describe their fellow volunteers—all loyal, dutiful comrades bound by esprit de corps and committed to selfless service. His campus and their camp were both alleged to be Spartan oases free from the corruption of normal civilian life.[13]

While Wilson, Hibben, and company tried to restore paternal influence to the American university, others hoped to reform the elective system itself. George Wharton Pepper, an upper-class Philadelphia lawyer, was one of those who strenuously opposed utilitarian education and vigorously supported military training. Between 1911 and 1914, as he began his forty-seven year tenure as a trustee of the University of Pennsylvania, that old Philadelphia college, where he had studied Greek and majored in the arts, was becoming a modern university. In 1914, 90 percent of the student body attended professional or technical programs. By 1915, Pepper thought that his alma mater had become "an undigested mass of courses, a miscellaneous crowd of instructors, and a pathetic rabble of students." To him, "mere intellectualism" and "vocational training" were disgorging "streams of young men and young women steeped in materialism." Appalled, Pepper contended that academic departments competed for enrollment by "tickling undiscriminatory palates" with easy classes. He therefore fought to retain the school's most "dreaded" requirements. Whatever their intellectual merits, he felt that those courses developed character by preventing movement "along the line of least resistance."[14]

Despite Pepper's efforts to defend "dreaded" subjects, whatever they might be, university life failed to reform. Try as he might, he could not convince most trustees, let alone students and faculty, that higher education was becoming an "intellectual joyride." So, like other alienated moralists trapped in a university age that emphasized utility to ensure solvency, Pepper seized upon military training as an "antidote for the abuse of elective" courses. He readily proclaimed that it should be "permanently incorporated into our educational system" as the best way to turn "unrestrained individualism" into "polite, efficient and law-abiding" citizenship.[15]

The presidents of some major public and semipublic universities joined Pepper and other private college traditionalists in the military training movement. Although they presided over institutions largely founded to develop specific and marketable skills, they themselves thought practicality meant public service as well as economic growth. They therefore tried to nurture different forms of civics within the university system. Like Drinker at Lehigh, Edmund James at the University of Illinois and Schurman at Cornell integrated conservative humanism with vocational education when they made "disciplinary and cultural studies" in the arts and the humanities basic requirements of their curricula. In so doing, they exposed new professions to an old moral training. Still, these neohumanist reforms failed to upset the universities' vocational and research priorities. Consequently, a moral vacuum developed that made military training attractive. As one agricultural and mining school president later said: Army drills taught "promptness, obedience and self-command as no other course in college can teach it."[16]

The Pursuit of Moral Rearmament: The Failure of Religion and Football and the Rise of Military Training

George Wharton Pepper, Edmund James, and their colleagues tried to develop moral virtue through extracurricular activities: first religion, then football, and finally military training. Afraid that university education was feeding the students' "mind and body at the cost of their souls," they initially attempted to surround their schools with ministerial agents such as evangelists, chaplains, and YMCAs. But since this was not a religious age, Plattsburgers had to secularize their morality to help it survive. First, conservative humanism restated denominational college values. Then strenuous athletics, which purportedly taught self-control and obedience, supplemented revivals: the admitted tool for "discipline and government in [old] institutions of learning." Because "no minister . . . begins to have the opportunity of the coach in the higher education for life," religion endured at Pennsylvania State College through a joint appointment in an interdisciplinary program. The chaplain there coached sports as "a very valuable door through which to gain the hearts of the students." At other schools, football virtually supplanted religion altogether. Before preparedness leaders took up the army as an alternative way to build character, they in particular felt that the gridiron could fill the moral void left by the demise of the senior course in philosophy, compulsory chapel, and Greek. In contrast to pacifistic presidents wanting activities "gentler and finer" than this game played by the "methods of war," Schurman welcomed football "as an ally in the moral training of students" at Cornell. Meanwhile Benjamin Ide Wheeler (the University of California's contribution to Plattsburg) singled out this sport for producing "manly character, punctuality and unhesitating action."[17]

Unfortunately, football failed to fulfill the moral expectations of its advocates. Like other Gilded Age businessmen who overbuilt their capital plants, academic entrepreneurs from 1870 to 1900 created a supply that exceeded all demand when they expanded the number of American universities by 60 percent. Since no pedagogic J. P. Morgan could "trustify" the education industry, schools had to compete in a buyer's market by advertising aggressively their most prestigious products. Hence, their recently built press and publicity bureaus used football teams to attract profitable shares of student fees, alumni funds, and public contributions. As do all potential investors, these solicited subscribers first inspected the ledger, in this case the scoreboard. The "passionate interest" which President Drinker had in the small-time football that his four sons played was not typical of his profession. Except at a few places such as Lehigh, whose president never "bought a ticket to 'a big game' in his life," big-time college athletics were becoming box-office spectacles in which the minority played and the majority watched.[18]

Once commercialized, the business in football inexorably grew. A successful team, like any other big enterprise, required a large capital investment: in stadiums, equipment, players, and coaches. Moreover, this particular operation had but ten market days a season to climb out of debt. Because American consumers do not believe "it is how you play the game that counts," bad football teams lost money. Then universities, hoping to recoup their losses (and show "practical" Americans they were smart enough to turn a profit) borrowed still more capital to present still better squads. As for the average student and other "mere spectators," they were supposed to pay off the debt, not play on the team.[19]

Harvard exemplified this college football quagmire. Its gentlemen sportsmen consistently fell before the semiprofessional players coached by Yale's Walter Camp. Finally, the men of Harvard, demanding less virtue and more victory, raised funds to begin (but not complete) construction of a magnificent new stadium. That "veritable Pandora's box" shackled the school with a $100,000 liability. To attract enough spectators to liquidate this debt, in 1908 it hired Percy Haughton, the Ivy League's first full-time coach. He subsequently ran his team the way efficiency expert Frederick W. Taylor managed factories: diagramming operations, synchronizing manpower, and discharging anyone who failed to perform. Also like Taylor, a former athlete whose stewardship began by directing sports tems, Haughton fulfilled all his production quotas. In the next eight years Harvard lost just two games to Yale and one to Princeton.[20]

Pre-Haughton Harvard had asked Yale to deescalate its varsity teams, but Yale, then the supreme power, refused its request. By 1913, having grown much weaker, the Sons of Eli wanted peace. Walter Camp, their athletic ambassador at large, asked Dean LaBarron R. Briggs, the chairman of Harvard's faculty committee on athletics, for the mutual removal of coaches from the football field. Briggs, who once hoped that amateur football would "humanize" its players, was probably sympathetic, but trapped by his winning teams and outstanding debts, he declined to negotiate. "Once in pursuit of money," Briggs latter admitted, "you are tempted by all the devices of business. It pays to advertise; it pays to pay enough for securing coaches who will turn out teams that people will pay to see." For players, football might be the moral equivalent of combat: doing for participants "what the [Civil] War did for their predecessors." For administrators, this sport better resembled the collegiate equivalent of disarmament negotiations. Unable to reach a political settlement, Yale had to surrender or increase its playing field commitment. Soon thereafter it hired its own full-time professional coach, thereby escalating the costs of commercial football.[21]

In the Progressive Era, business expansion often stimulated social criticism. As the football industry grew, its critics multiplied. Some rebuked football as they did meatpacking, demanding physical protection for anyone who labored in the stockyards or on the playing fields. (In 1903 alone forty-three men were killed playing football.) But unlike those who would abolish bloodsports—"logical vegetarians of the flabbiest Hindoo type"—other reformers did not want the game played on a "too lady-like basis." Future military training leaders in particular wished to spread participation, rather than protect the participants themselves. Publicly and privately they worked to change football from an "un-American" spectator sport into a basic part of civic education. They wrote muckraking articles, tried to negotiate commercial deescalation agreements, and sat on the school committees that sought to police the game. Finally, Theodore Roosevelt and future Plattsburg advocates Robert Bacon and Endicott Peabody organized a White House conference to reform football.[22]

Yet none of this protest against commercialization did much good since winning teams produced the money and publicity which every school needed. Even future military preparedness leaders were caught up in this web. George Vincent of the University of Chicago, Arthur Hadley of Yale, and A. Lawrence Lowell of Harvard, all of whom supported "physical training for the mass of students," criticized the "shameless professionalism" of intercollegiate athletics. Nonetheless, they hired and supported commercial football's three greatest coaches —Amos Alonzo Stagg, Camp, and Haughton. Other devotees of military training were also seduced. Enthusiastic alumni contributed to their alma maters' athletic funds; President Theodore Roosevelt gave his school its assistant coach. Explaining why he personally transferred one West Point instructor to Cambridge football duty, he said: "I was a Harvard man before a politician." All these men—Roosevelt, Vincent, Lowell, Hadley, and others—disliked box-office sports but their schools needed a favorable won-lost record. They were riding a tiger and could not get off.[23]

About the time World War I began, football jersey numerals were introduced to aid consumer identification. No subsequent occurrence, not even the formation of a professional association for college press and publicity agents, could better symbolize the spectacle nature of the sport. In November, 1914, *Puck* magazine began to invert a well-known adage by implying that war should now become the moral equivalent of football. Since these "gladiatorial contests" featured a "few athletic stars and a great many tipsy betters," it endorsed UMT as an effective alternative for producing a "uniformly high average of physically fit and mentally disciplined men." More than one hundred class presidents and football captains themselves supported *Puck's* plan by a 4 to 1 margin. Their preference, moreover, was not unique. Although some star athletes, even Percy Haughton, went to Plattsburg, a flock of preparedness leaders explicitly endorsed compulsory drill as a moral improvement upon commercial football. One of those who argued that induction would substitute exercise for entertainment, concluded that this generation of "stoop-shouldered, cigarette-smoking, physically degenerate youth" just "sits on the side lines and hysterically cheers its favorites."[24]

NOTES

1. Clifford, *Citizen Soldiers*, p. 2–13; statements of Gen. Hagood, n.d., Frank McCoy, May 26, 1929, both in Hermann Hagedorn MSS, Box 19. Wood to John G. Hibben, Oct. 1, 1913, Wood to J. K. Priest, Jan. 13, 1913, Wood to Lyman Abbott, Sept. 17, 1913, Nicholas Murray Butler to Wood, Feb. 10, 1913: all in Wood MSS, Box 90. Unidentified soldier quoted on "iniquity" in Cunliffe, *Soldiers and Civilians*, p. 112.

2. For Drinker's background and career, see Catherine Drinker Bowen, *Family Portrait* (Boston: Atlantic-Little, Brown, 1970), passim; *National Cyclopedia*, 15:114; *New York Times*, July 28, 1937. Henry Sturgis Drinker: "New Phases of Education," *New York Times*, Aug. 10, 1912; "The Students' Military Instruction Camp at Gettysburg," *New York Times*, Aug. 17, 1913. Drinker quoted in Clifford, *Citizen Soldiers*, p. 133; Bowen, *Family Portrait*, pp. 16, 38. Hibben to Hermann Hagedorn, May 10, 1929, Hagedorn MSS, Box 19; Drinker to Herbert Hoover, Feb. 17, 1932, Presidential Papers, Hoover Presidential Library, West Branch, Iowa.

3. Jacob Gould Schurman, "Every College Should Introduce Military Training," *Everybody's Magazine* 32 (Feb., 1915):181; Schurman quoted in *New York Sun*, June 18, 1916; Arthur T. Hadley, "Education in Germany," *Youth's Companion* 80 (Jan. 6, 1910):4; "Extracts from the Annual Report of President Hadley, 1915," Edmund James MSS, Box 94, University of Illinois; John G. Hibben, "The Colleges and the National Defense," *Independent* 82 (June 28, 1915):532; Wilson quoted in Clifford, *Citizen Soldiers*, p. 21; *New York Times*, Jan. 24, 1915, 3:5; Butler described by A. Lawrence Lowell to William Howard Taft, Mar. 28, 1919, Taft MSS, Reel 207, Library of Congress; Butler to Thompkins MacIlvaine, Apr. 27, 1916, Butler MSS, Columbia University.

4. Lowell to Ralph Lowell, Mar. 6, 1924, Lowell MSS, Harvard University;

Plattsburg Camp of Instruction News, Aug. 9, 1915, copy in Plattsburg Barracks File, Box 1780, National Archives; Henry Yeomans, *Abbott Lawrence Lowell* (Cambridge, Mass.: Harvard University Press, 1948), pp. 68, 165–66, 380, 398–99, 413. The long quotation is from Lowell to Gen. Clarence R. Edwards, Mar. 8, 1920, Lowell MSS.

5. "Massachusetts. [1915] Commission on Military Education," *School Review* 25 (Mar., 1917):169–76; Leonard Wood to Lowell, Aug. 13, 1917, Wood MSS, Box 103; statement of Col. J. C. Lee, n.d., Hermann Hagedorn MSS, Box 22; Leonard Wood Diary, Sept. 12, Sept. 13, 1917, Wood MSS, Box 9; George C. English, Jr., *History of the 89th Division* (War Society of the 89th Division, 1920), p. 21.

6. Lowell to "Dear President," Sept. 30, 1916, Schurman to Lowell, Oct. 9, 1916, Lowell MSS, File 1283; Schurman quoted in Eugene Hotchkiss, "Jacob Gould Schurman and the Cornell Tradition" (Ph.D. diss., Cornell University, 1960), pp. 271–72; Hibben quoted in *Literary Digest* 49 (Oct. 17, 1914):741; Hibben to Struthers Burt, Jan. 6, 1919, Hibben MSS, Princeton University.

7. Henry F. May, *The End of American Innocence: A Study of the First Years of Our TIme, 1912–1917* (Chicago: Quadrangle Books, 1964), pp 361–67. For young European intelligentsia, see Robert Wohl, *The Generation of 1914* (Cambridge, Mass.: Harvard University Press, 1979); Roland N. Stromberg, *Redemption by War: The Intellectuals and 1914* (Lawrence: Regents Press of Kansas, 1982). "Discipline and the Will," *New York Times,* Nov. 1, 1915. King's College president quoted in Max Savelle, *Seed of Liberty: The Genesis of the American Mind* (Seattle: University of Washington Press, 1966), p. 254.

8. Senate, *Hearings on Universal Military Training,* 64th Cong., 2d Sess., 1917, pp. 891, 919, 925, 934.

9. For the institutionalization of technical education and the quotation, from the *London Times,* see Morison: *Men, Machines and Modern Times,* pp. 103–4, 135–36: *From Know-How to Nowhere,* pp. 106, 116. For the quotation on educational aims, from President Guy P. Benton of Miami University, and the growth of engineering schools, see Jones, *Age of Energy,* pp. 170, 172, 230.

10. For the decline of in loco parentis and student social life, see David Allmendinger, *Paupers and Scholars: The Transformation of Student Life in Nineteenth-Century New England* (New York: St. Martin's Press, 1975), passim; Canby, *American Memoir* pp. 160–71. The quotation on student rebellion is cited in Bledstein, *Culture of Professionalism,* p. 229. George E. Peterston, *The New England College in the Age the University* (Amherst: Amherst College Press, 1964), pp. 86, 117, 146–47; Laurence R. Veysey, *The Emergence of the American University* (Chicago: University of Chicago Press, 1965), pp. 277, 295.

11. For Europeans and the quotation describing the poet Rupert Brooke, see Wohl, *Generation of 1914,* pp. 87, 200, 235–36. University of Michigan presidential search committee cited in Bledstein, *Culture of Professionalism,* p. 307. Frederick Rudolph, *The American College and University: A History* (New York: Vintage Books, 1962), p. 423. One university president, Daniel Coit Gilman of Johns Hopkins, summarized the tension in his role in the 1900s: "We have broken away from the restricted notions of the past; we have not yet learned

how to adjust ourselves to the broader domains in which we are walking" (see Bledstein, *Culture of Professionalism,* p. 48).

12. For statistics, War Department pleas, and university responses to UMT, see Frank Cunningham, "The Army and Universal Military Training, 1942–1948" (Ph.D. diss., University of Texas, 1976), pp. 132–68; William Spencer to George C. Marshall, Mar. 7, 1945, Tom Wyles to Max Lilienthal, Mar. 29, 1945, Irving Allen to William Spencer, Mar. 9, 1945: all in Military Training Camps Association MSS, Chicago Historical Society. Kenneth Budd to John McAuley Palmer, Apr. 21, Apr. 27, June 2, 1944, Grenville Clark MSS; John McAuley Palmer to Horace Kallen, Mar. 26, 1945, Palmer to James Wadsworth, May 24, 1944, Palmer to Kenneth Budd, May 11, 1944; all in Palmer MSS, Library of Congress. President of Michigan State University quoted in Richard J. Barnet, *Roots of War* (Baltimore: Penguin Books, 1973), pp. 42–43; President Dodds quoted in Kenneth Budd to John McAuley Palmer, Apr. 27, 1944, Palmer MSS.

13. Veysey, *Emergence of the American University,* pp. 180–233. Veysey, using the term employed by the historic protagonists, calls this orientation "the liberal culture" movement. I prefer to label it "conservative humanism." For moral philosophy, which implanted the precepts of "Christian pathology" described at length in Ch. 2, see D. H. Meyer, *The Instructed Conscience: The Shaping of the American National Ethic* (Philadelphia: University of Pennsylvania Press, 1972), passim. For Schurman, see Hotchkiss, "Jacob Gould Schurman and Cornell Tradition," pp. 71–78, 294. For Drinker, see Bowen, *Family Portrait,* pp. 38, 99. For Hibben, see George McClellan, Jr., *The Gentleman and the Tiger: The Autobiography of George McClellan Jr.,* ed. Harold C. Syrett (Philadelphia: J. B. Lippincott, 1956), pp. 326–327; Steven Buenning, "John Grier Hibben: A Biographical Study (1919–1932)" (Senior Honors Paper, Princeton University, 1971), pp. 6, 20, 22. Woodrow Wilson cited in *United States Congressional Record,* 66th Cong., 2d Sess., 1919, p. 5387; Laurence R. Veysey, "The Academic Mind of Woodrow Wilson," *Mississippi Valley Historical Review* 49 (Mar. 1963):622, 628–29

14. Statement of Charles Reinhart, n.d., George Wharton Pepper to Effingham Morris, Dec. 27, 1915, both in Pepper MSS, Box 10; George Wharton Pepper, "The Trustee and His Place in Academic Life," *General Magazine and Historical Chronicle* 37 (July, 1935):400–402. Pepper quoted in *New York Times,* Oct. 18, 1913; *New Haven Journal,* Mar. 19, 1914. Pepper: "A Plea for the Highest Education," Oct. 16, 1909; "Education and Religion," Oct., 1913; Pepper to Joseph Buffington, Mar. 16, 1916: all in Pepper MSS, Boxes 10, 12.

15. Pepper to Nicholas Murray Butler June 21, 1920, Butler MSS; Pepper, "Commencement at Trinity College," July 17, 1918, Pepper, "Liberty Loan Address," Apr. 18, 1918, both in Pepper MSS, Box 14.

16. For Cornell as a semipublic university, see Rudolph, *American College and University,* p. 253. For Drinker, Schurman, and James, see Bowen, *Family Portrait,* pp. 49, 114; Hotchkiss, "Jacob Gould Schurman, and the Cornell Tradition," pp. 110, 119; Richard Allan Swanson, "Edmund James, 1815–1925: A 'Conservative Progressive' in American Higher Education" (Ph.D. diss., Uni-

versity of Illinois, 1966), pp. 111–15, 187–94, 215–20. Veysey, *Emergence of the American University*, p. 256. The final quotation is from Bradfor Knapp to James Wadsworth, Apr. 28, 1926, Wadsworth MSS, Library of Congress.

17. Unidentified newspaper clipping in George Wharton Pepper Box, University of Pennsylvania Archives; Swanson, "Edmund James," pp. 187–94; Veysey, *Emergence of the American University*, p. 195. For the quotation on revivals as a means of discipline, see Allmendinger, *Paupers and Scholars*, pp. 119–20. For quotations on athletics, see L. B. R. Briggs, "Intercollegiate Athletics and the War," *Atlantic Monthly* 122 (Sept., 1918): 307; E. E. Sparks, president of Pennsylvania State College, to Joseph Raycroft, Jan. 20, 1915, Amos Alonzo Stagg MSS, Box 12, University of Chicago; peace advocates David Starr Jordan and Charles William Elliot quoted in Jordan, "The American Game of Football as Related to Physical Education," *National Education Association: Journal of Proceedings and Addresses,* 48 (1910):357, 362; Schurman quoted in *Cornell Era* 25 (Oct. 1, 1892):6; Wheeler quoted in Walter Camp, *Football Facts and Figures* (New York: Harper & Brothers, 1894), p. 11

18. Veysey, *Emergence of the American University*, pp. 309, 324–27, 346–48, 355–57, 443, For Drinker and Lehigh, see Bowen, *Family Portrait*, pp. 11–13, 83; Drinker, "New Phases of Education," *New York Times,* Aug. 10, 1912. Scott Cutlip, "'Advertising' Higher Education: The Early Years of College Public Relations," *College and University Journal* 9 (Nov., 1970):21–28; Guy Lewis, "The American Intercollegiate Football Spectacle" (Ph.D. diss., University of Maryland, 1954), pp. 38–48.

19. John R. Tunis, *The American Way of Sport* (New York: Duell, Sloan & Pearce, 1958), p. 59; Jesse F. Steiner, *Americans at Play* (New York: McGraw-Hill, 1933), p. 91; Canby, *American Memoir*, p. 139.

20. Lewis, "American Intercollegiate Football Spectacle," pp. 32–35, 49–50, 203–4, 261–62, 283–86. The quotation on the stadium is from James R. Angell in National Collegiate Athletic Association, *Proceedings of the Twenty-Fifth Annual Convention,* Dec. 31, 1930, p. 104. Frank Barkley Copley, *Frederick W. Taylor: Father of Scientific Management* (New York: Harper & Brothers, 1923), 1:56–57, 72.

21. Walter Camp to Howard McClenahan, Oct. 29, 1913, L. B. R. Briggs to Camp, Oct. 15, 1913, Camp to Channing Frothingham, Nov. 25, 1913: all in Camp MSS, Box 49, Yale University; Briggs quoted in Veysey, *Emergence of the American University,* p. 306; Briggs, "Intercollegiate Athletics and the War," p. 307. *Century Magazine* (1887) quoted in Dubbert, *A Man's Place,* p. 180.

22. Lewis, "American Intercollegiate Football Spectacle," pp. 212–14; Roosevelt quoted in ibid., p. 233; Morris, *Rise of Theodore Roosevelt,* p. 24. Endicott Peabody, "Ideals of Sport in England and America," in National Collegiate Athletic Association, *Proceedings of the Eighth Annual Convention,* Dec. 30, 1913, p. 55; Jacob Gould Schurman, "Are Football Games Educative or Brutalizing?," *Forum* 16 (Jan., 1894):646–47; Roosevelt, "Professionalism in Sports," pp. 188–89.

23. George Vincent to Ernest D. Burton, Nov. 17, 1924, University of Chicago Presidential Papers MSS, Box 15; "President Lowell's Annual Report,"

Harvard Graduate's Magazine 21 (Mar., 1913):477; Roosevelt quoted in Lewis, "American Intercollegiate Football Spectacle," p. 244.

24. *Puck* 76 (Dec. 19, 1914):5; Leonard Wood to Nathan Straus, Nov. 21, 1914, Wood MSS, Box 75; William Muldoon quoted in *New York Times,* Aug. 29, 1917, 4:10; statement of George Vincent in National Collegiate Athletic Association, *Proceedings of the Twelfth Annual Convention,* Dec. 28, 1917, p. 79; Senate, *Hearings on Universal Military Training,* 64th Cong., 2d Sess., 1917, pp. 259, 928, 935.

CHAPTER 5

Military Training:
The School Experience

WHEN LEONARD WOOD founded Plattsburg in 1913, he planned to train only college students. By 1915, other groups were requesting access to the camp. University alumni wanted instruction for older men; certain school teachers and administrators wanted it for younger boys. These educators were working in primary and secondary schools that were changing their format because of economic growth. As factories and offices replaced the family labor unit, fewer sons worked beside their parents. The school, substituting for these absentee fathers said to have become "almost strangers to their children," grew more responsible for the total "physical, mental and social training of the child." At the same time, advanced industrialization, having increased the need for formally educated managers and technicians, prolonged schooling and thereby postponed work-site discipline imposed upon the young. Many progressive educators then began to feel that it was "a moral offense to snatch [the boy] from the natural life of boyhood and place him in what ought to be a man's job." They thereupon reduced the "military air" observed in many schools in order to "make learning fun." This dual development in education perplexed preparedness leaders who could not reconcile increased responsibility with decreased discipline. In search of a solution, these citizen-soldiers sponsored prep schools, Boy Scout troops, and other reform programs substituting strenuous conditions for the effeminizing leisure thought to distinguish adolescent life. However, the educational projects they proposed failed to fulfill their ideals. After 1910, for example, the private schools of the wealthy grew less didactic as they trained their students for high scores on the college boards.[1] Meanwhile, the poor rejected the Gary school plan that would have brought new courses for social control into public education. While all this was occurring, preparedness educators endorsed junior military training to help the nation by forestalling what they called a deleterious tendency towards permissiveness.

The Evolution of the Prep School and the Use of the Army

A small and homogeneous group of men initiated the junior military training movement. Impressed by what they saw at Plattsburg, headmasters, trustees, and alumni from America's upper-class preparatory schools—Groton, St. Mark's, St. Paul's, St. George's, Exeter, and Phillips Academy (Andover)—asked General Wood to organize similar camps at their own institutions. And why not? The college prep schools, although run by Episcopal clergy, expressed the same puritan value system as did Plattsburg and Muldoon's, two boarding schools for adults. All these facilities enforced austerity to prevent the immorality of wealth without work. The idle rich, whom they often treated, affronted many Americans, some of whom responded by advocating the abolishment of estate inheritance. Prep schools, enrolling young heirs themselves, devised an alternative to radical taxation: an educational regimen eliminating languor without confiscating wealth. At Groton, for example, the sons of millionaires, living in six-by-ten cubicles in their formative years, had a weekly allowance of twenty-five cents and a snack of milk *or* crackers. Its headmaster, Endicott Peabody (1857–1944), shielded his students from leniency and luxury by providing a school that preserved the old Puritan practice of placing young males outside their families. He did this because he felt that the weak-willed "modern parent does not dare refuse his child's slightest request." Rather than emphasize the development of intellect or skill, his prep school program of asceticism, classics, and compulsory athletics reflected another of his puritan beliefs that "suffering is good for a man," it being God's way of building character. That curriculum (which one Darwinian called "the struggle for existence in a Groton school career") was meant to teach its pupils the responsibility, chivalry, and self-control that they would need if they, potential members of a passive leisure class, were to grow into a true governing elite. If so trained, the upper class (like their fellow blue-blooded Rough Riders) would perform social services of such "sterling worth" that radicals would be diminished. Thus Theodore Roosevelt, who constantly criticized material indulgence in the rich, not only ignored economic determinism when he wrote about the heroes of military history, he sent his own sons to Groton where they might learn to be the heroes of society — selfless public servants whose behavior would belie left-wing doctrines about upper-class greed.[2]

The prep school creed resembled the military code by mixing a patrician esprit de corps with a puritan austerity and an episcopal chain of command. In substance as well as style, these schools had a martial nature. Alumni said that Groton, unable "to distinguish breaches of discipline from lapses in morals," was run "much like a military academy." Indeed, generals William M. Black and Leonard Wood sent their sons there because they felt it provided excellent preparation for West Point. Certainly most Grotonians had no difficulty adjusting to army life. The school sent numerous alumni to Plattsburg—"perhaps 10 times" the normal representation. And to its headmaster's immense satisfaction, some four-fifths of its eligible graduates later served in World War I. One of them was Robert McCormick, whose *Chicago Tribune* led the nation in the number of newspaper editorials (sixteen published) for UMT. Ruing the military incompetence of America's "idle rich," he anonymously funded Groton scholarships for army brats. According to him, this "tie-up" between the school and the service would benefit both of them as well as the country.[3]

Prep schools certainly prepared their students for the army but belatedly adopted such training for themselves. In the late nineteenth century, when some fifty military academies were being founded, they usually ignored the "concerted effort" to use army drills to develop "mental discipline and moral rectitude." Groton abandoned its short-lived training program in 1894 concluding that it did "not bring sufficient benefit." Concurrently its fellow prep schools simply refused to form corps of their own. Because these institutions were secure in their traditional curricula, they apparently felt no need for army exercises. Then, as the American college changed its priorities from moral virtue to academic competence, the college preparatory school had to follow suit. By 1914, academies which once trained boys for a Christian life admittedly trained them for their college boards. Once even the English teacher was "little better than a drill master." Now problem solving skills supplanted memorization, and modern languages displaced Greek. As this occurred, the Plattsburg movement began. Formerly indifferent headmasters, like so many college presidents, then embraced military training to "teach the value of duty" within "modern schools" that failed to "inculcate respect for authority."[4]

Leonard Wood, unlike most professional soldiers, strongly encouraged this educational interest in military training. He not only impressed prep school teachers with his "power and personality," he reflected their common philosophy when he claimed that "moral and physical conditioning" was necessary "from the standpoint of discipline which American boys need above all [other] things." In fact, Wood was something of a headmaster himself since he too was a didactic educator molding male virtue within the confines of a total institution.[5]

Perhaps Wood's concern for adolescent morality partly stemmed from his own problems as a parent. A devoted father, this "prodigiously busy man" spent his sparse free time trying to elevate his two sons to his level of excellence. Neither one made the grade. At Groton they compiled mediocre grades and engaged in such "dishonorable conduct" as hiding "trash literature" and rifling a teacher's desk. Those acts foretold their later lives. After completing unsatisfactory collegiate careers (Harvard dismissed Leonard, Jr.; Osborne dismissed West Point), they went on to become national scandals who cost their father, the "best friend" they had, more pain than his unsuccessful (1920) presidential campaign. In the 1920s, while their parents toiled away in the Philippines, Osbore resigned from the army "to live as I pleased." He made a fortune in stock speculation and lost it at baccarat. He paid for his night life with illegal checks, had a nervous breakdown, and was divorced for infidelity. Leonard, Jr., utilized his father's name to promote common stock speculation schemes. After that enterprise ended in bankruptcy, he went into theatrical productions, organizing a stage company and writing plays like *Sin Tax*—"an emotional drama of the tropics."[6]

Just as some seventeenth-century English gentlemen sent their prodigal sons to the New World and nineteenth-century Anglo-American elites sent them out West, Leonard Wood shipped his boys to Plattsburg where they could get a "wholesome bit of discipline in the way of doing things as told, when told." Military life may have failed to change Wood's sons but, according to Harvard Dean B. S. Hurlbert, it made other frivolous boys into "bigger and better men." Two militarily renovated personalities, documenting the belief in reformation through war, were Hamilton Stuyvesant Fish (1872–1898) and Henry Augustus Coit (1888–1916). Fish, a member of a prominent New York family, was the first Rough Rider killed in Cuba. Coit, a grandson of St. Paul's first rector, was a World War I volunteer in the British army. They both died heroes, after living as failures who squandered their time drinking, brawling, and drifting. Their families, who later led junior military training programs, felt that their honorable deaths redeemed their wasted lives. Nicholas Fish thanked the regiment's surviving officers and Joseph Howland Coit kept his pride, if not his son, when Henry sustained in battle the St. Paul's tradition. Although the Wood boys, along with Fish and Coit, were extreme examples, they symbolized the wayward sons whom the upper class feared they were raising. This fear helped create the prep schools and the prep schools created the junior Plattsburg movement as "an enforced period of right living and good training" devised to help students "overcome the easy conditions which surround them."[7]

Dr. Samuel Drury (1878–1938), headmaster of St. Paul's, was this movement's initial leader. Before his arrival in 1910, that old church school had degenerated into a modern country club where "manners counted more than morals." Committed to rebuilding St. Paul's intellectual and social discipline, he grasped Leonard Wood's argument that military training would improve the "morals, physique and character of our youth." At first, the schoolmaster wished to introduce army drill into his own academy but, after consultation with Wood, he decided to hold instead "a purely military camp." When it opened in the summer of 1916, fifty-three of his charges made up its largest delegation.[8]

Although St. Paul's initiated the camp, two graduates from Groton and two from St. Mark's were also on its executive committee. Its chairman, Horace Stebbins (??–1947), graduated from Groton in 1892 where he, according to its football coach, was the greatest athlete in the school's history. Stebbins, however, never had a chance to win collegiate gridiron glory because, when his classmates went off to the Ivy League, he himself went into poverty. For two years thereafter he survived on Headmaster Peabody's direct support—an "extraordinary kindness" which he never forgot. After Stebbins made his fortune in the textile business, this bachelor made Groton School his heir, endowing it with a thousand dollars a year and two million dollars in his will. The junior military camp, as an "efficacious lesson in accuracy, promptness and obedience," was another of his gifts to Groton. Stebbins, reinstituting the military drills that he took at the school in 1891, administered the camp's organization, instructed its cadets, and paid two-thirds of its expenses with a fifteen-thousand-dollar check.[9]

Other loyal alumni also worked for junior military training. Henry Stimson felt that affluent urban youth, "forever sheltered from disagreeable duty," needed the army to show them that "vital stores of energy, grit and courage" can overcome "the hard facts of life." He therefore gave his own alma mater, Phillips Academy (Andover), a military endowment. A trustee for forty-two years, he willed two-thirds of his estate to this "one educational institution that I love." Its "rapid firing instructors" built his own resolve, and, "grateful to the school for the revolution it worked in my character," he wished to make some appropriate repayment. He apparently believed that Andover would appreciate a Plattsburg-type program since, to him, they certainly were analogous institutions. Periodically Stimson returned to his school for the same reason he enrolled at Wood's training camp. In each instance he sought a Spartan relief from commerce and comfort. When he returned to Andover in 1914, he took Wood with him. That visit inaugurated the school's martial curricula of battalion drills, rifle practice, overseas ambulance work, and a twenty-two-man delegation to the military summer camp.[10]

Stebbins, Drury, Stimson, and others designed a strictly military summer camp at Ft. Terry (Plum Island), New York. Their project, which opened in 1916, fulfilled their plans. The lieutenant colonel in charge told his cadets that since "military life is [built on] military discipline," they would be drilled until they gained the "prompt and subconscious obedience to orders [that is] essential to military control." Then he delivered the regimen he promised—calisthenics, close-order drill, the manual of arms, military protocol, and the strict regulations which forbade one father from withdrawing one son one day early.[11]

One of this officer's assistants was Henry S. Hooker (1879–1964), a Groton alumnus and Franklin Roosevelt's law partner. In 1914, when Hooker saw Germany's military camps filled with "clean cut boys of 19 and 20, quiet, wonderfully well mannered and respectful," he felt that he had witnessed "the most exalted [display of] patriotism, unselfishness and sacrifice." To emulate the Germans he went to the junior military camp. Looking "the picture of health" when he returned, he exclaimed that it was "the most inspiring thing I have ever seen." It surely was the most indelible. For the next twenty-six years of his life, UMT was his admitted "obsession."[12]

Parents and other observers of the cadets were equally impressed with the Plum Island camp. They endorsed the commanding officer as a fine "schoolmaster" and begged General Wood to prevent his impending transfer to Hawaii. Promising to subscribe again next year, they encouraged the camp's executive committee to launch a national movement for junior military training. This committee publicized its project by circulating 200,000 copies of an *Outlook* magazine article as the "best expression of the [camp's] true spirit, purpose [and] ideal." The author of the essay was Ernest Hamlin Abbott, whose grandfather, Jacob Abbott, was the mid-nineteenth century's foremost expert on child care. In this role, he was a source of the prep school principle that privileged children must be trained to withstand the temptations of wealth. Publications like his well-known Rollo books aside, Jacob raised his son Lyman, the editor-publisher of the *Outlook,* and his grandsons Lawrence and Ernest by this creed he helped create. In 1913, his descendants became interested in military drills which incorporated his dictum that "obedience is doing what is commanded because it is commanded." Later, after Lawrence helped organize the Plum Island camp and Lyman joined its advisory committee, Ernest followed his own sons there to observe their "marvelous" progress. His article, which was read before the Senate's Military Affairs Sub-Committee on Universal Military Training, summarized the prep-school argument for army drill: "These boys [it said] have received [what] this country needs. Chief among the faults of the American people are lawlessness . . . love of ease, and willingness to avoid trouble at the cost of duty. Chief among the virtues inculcated at Plum Island are the opposites of these faults—prompt obedience of law [and the] acceptance without complaint of hardship and simple living.... Universal military training would develop these qualities in the boys of the Nation, and therefore, in time in the Nation itself."[13]

This kind of copy was effective advertising. By early 1917, over 70,000 boys had applied for the upcoming summer training course. Unfortunately, when America declared war in April, the War Department faced more pressing priorities. A host of commercial training camps then arose to fill the educational void by promising to inculcate "loyalty, discipline, initiative [and] resourcefulness" for three hundred dollars per cadet.[14]

Para-Military Training and the Prep School: From Hamilton Fish to John Wanamaker.

Although Junior Plattsburg was a prep school production, its founders never voiced the fears expressed by some elites before the Spanish-American War: that training "the children of the masses . . . in the use of arms will endanger property." In fact, the camp's organizers purposely recruited public school students from different classes and locales whom they interspersed in each cadet company. This practice, reminiscent of the old Rough Riders, was supposed to provide a "lesson in democracy" that would "obliterate" class conflict, but not classes themselves. Dave Goodrich, former Rough Rider and present New York City elite, helped collect $1,135.50 to send the poor to military training camps. Not to be outdone, Hamilton Fish (1888–   )— Plattsburg veteran, all-American football player, and first cousin of the martyred Rough Rider hero—organized the Junior Patriots of America to provide military scholarships to the needy. "Heartily endorsed" by Theodore Roosevelt, Fish's own hero, the officers of its adolescent companies raised over ten thousand dollars via solicitations, "military teas," and public exhibitions of their close-order drill.[15]

This philanthropic plan to use military training to uplift the poor along with the rich was part of the greater upper-class tendency to ignore some class distinctions in America. Within academic psychology, Professor G. Stanley Hall, another proponent of military drills for "rigid discipline," popularized the term "adolescence" to suggest generational (not economic) causes of social conflict. In the preparedness movement per se, other devotees of UMT were likewise oblivious to certain class phenomena. Overlooking the long hours labored by the children of the poor, they maintained that superfluous leisure was a pervasive problem compelling prep school programs for everyone. Samuel Drury, for example, felt that the working-class, just like the rich, should be drilled to suppress their inclinations towards indulgence. To spread his doctrine of prep school puritanism, he democratized St. Paul's through scholarships, exchange students, and competitive entrance exams. Joseph Howland Coit (??–1930), chairman of the American Defense Society, tried to do the same thing through UMT. Son of the first rector of St. Paul's and nephew of its second, Coit taught Greek and coached cricket there for some twenty years. After the school's family dynasty finally fell in 1907, he moved to New York and entered the publishing business. But wherever he was he never abandoned his family's educational mission. When he was not distributing didactic literature of the Theodore Roosevelt variety, he was chairing St. Paul's alumni meetings and the boards of associated charities. During the preparedness movement, Coit organized public high school military units designed to teach the "habit of obedience" to a "flabby, avaricious" society.[16]

Just as Coit brought St. Paul's principles into the inner city, Roger Alden Derby (1884–1949) carried Groton's creed out to the country. Educated by Endicott Peabody and revived by William Muldoon, this heir of Hudson River patricians feared the fate of those "unfortunate enough to inherit means and follow the herd to Wall and State Streets." Although knowing next to nothing about real agriculture, his "Puritan conscience" drove him to become a farmer. He consequently fled the Northeast, "too rich and luxurious" for him, to settle in the hills of North Carolina. This land saved him from wealth but not from crop failure. By 1928, having lost his "dreaded inheritance" and gained a "growing family," he too had to join the "herd" at Dillon, Read and Company.[17]

In 1913, fifteen years before the misfortune befell him, Derby expressed his Groton "spirit of service" in community development programs built to stem the flow of rural workers to the city. Alienated from his own upper-class affluence, he admired his yeomen neighbors for having "nothing decadent about them." Because they were "as fine a lot of people as I have ever known," Derby wished to rear his own sons on the farm, the best means "ever devised to train boys [in] the correct principles of moral conduct." But the yeoman virtues he admired became social liabilities when agrarian individualism hindered the growth of the hospitals, roads, and schools that might preserve and protect the farm population. To "transform [the] straggling, individualistic [backwoods] into an intelligent and coherent community," he built a "public boarding school" in the Carolina hills. There, he simultaneously prepared local children for farming and citizenship by combining vocational education with the creed of Grotonian civics. In time, military training became a new means to further Derby's didactic goals.[18]

Although Derby was a descendant of West Point instructors, he was said to have been the most recalcitrant Plattsburger in the 1915 camp. Perhaps because his own rebellious nature squirmed under a martial regimen, he thought it was the solution to "a hundred difficulties that beset me in the development work I am trying to do." Therefore, in 1916, he sent his school's principal to Plattsburg and four of its pupils to Plum Island. When the students, "worthwhile raw material," returned home with "more orderly" personalities and a "broader" outlook on life, Derby put the whole school "under military discipline." Hereafter the boys awoke to bugles, dressed in khaki, assembled in companies, "marched to and from mess," were drilled by a wounded Canadian army sergeant, and were put to sleep by taps. By now Derby had concluded: "To make democracy discipline itself is a difficult task, yet it can be done."[19]

Coit and Derby, although influential, were far less important disseminators of prep school principles than was Arthur Woods (1870–1942), special advisor to Junior Plattsburg, executive member of the Junior Patriots of America, and general spokesman for UMT as a program of "the greatest physical and moral value" to "the young manhood of the country." Woods's family tree produced many moral educators, the most notable being great-grandfather Leonard Woods, the first professor of Christian theology at Andover Theological Seminary. During the Jacksonian era of political democracy and economic individualism, he preached deference and memorialized missionaries who displayed their "character" by renouncing wordly pleasures. His son, President Leonard Woods, Jr., of Bowdoin College, protected traditional Christian education from modern university encroachments in the late nineteenth century. However his own son, Arthur Woods's father, shunned the cloth and went into textiles, founding Joseph Woods and Sons of Boston and Chicago. Young Arthur himself was about to join the family firm when he, as a church counselor to a newspaperboys' club, resumed the family mission of moral education. Part swaggering hooligans, part hardworking entrepreneurs, newsboys personified both the promise and the danger of the young, urban poor. Woods must have saved more boys than he lost for Endicott Peabody, the demanding headmaster of Groton School, asked him to join his staff in 1895.[20]

Although Groton's defenders and critics agree that Woods was an excellent prep school teacher, he was not content with guiding the rich. As director of the school's summer camp for disadvantaged youth, he remained concerned with the urban poor as well. Founded in 1893, that summer camp (like the future Plattsburg camps) was a sanatorium for group discipline, strenuous exercise, and conservative social work. Avoiding any hint of redistributing wealth or power, it chose instead to encourage simplicity in its well-to-do staff, amity between rich counselors and poor campers, and "moral strength" in the needy, who were sent back "to their poor, squalid homes" ethically transformed by their camp experience. Woods hoped to train his assistants for future social service. He certainly trained Franklin Roosevelt, a "most satisfactory" Grotonian, Benjamin Joy, and others for whom Plattsburg policies would clothe prep school principles in military garb.[21]

Despite Woods's excellent teaching record, by 1905 he wished to move out of the classroom and into the world. At the turn of the century, when churches were shifting their missionary resources from foreign outposts to urban America, he resisted his initial inclination to go to the Philippine Islands and took a position in New York. With help from his friend and fellow reformer Jacob Riis, Woods became a police reporter and then a deputy police commissioner. Yet he did not "intend to be a cop all my life. My biggest, almost my whole interest," he confessed, "is in education. My best years have been at and for the Groton School." Not content to bring the poor to the Groton camp, Woods joined the police to bring Groton to the poor. However, while he wished to remain in the city on active service for the school and the public, Dr. Peabody wanted him to return to the academy after beginning his program of placing their students in urban welfare institutions like the Henry Street Settlement House. Their ideas in conflict, Woods permanently left the Groton prep school but not his Groton mission.[22]

In 1914, Mayor John Purroy Mitchel's administration came to power in New York City with Arthur Woods as its police commissioner. Always the schoolmaster, his foremost concern was juvenile delinquency. Department statistics reporting a 9 percent annual increase in adolescent crime and a predominantly young criminal population documented his prep school conviction that the urban environment threatened the republic by demoralizing the child. Hoping to rectify this problem with more prep school pedagogy, Woods devised programs to build character without redistributing income. He would take delinquents out of the pool hall (but not out of the slums) and place them in gymnasiums, churches, and settlement houses where they could find "other boys of better character."[23]

As part of this policy Woods initiated "one of [his] most satisfactory" projects, a junior police force program that used army drills to foster "sturdy manhood" in the young. There were several precedents for this paramilitary treatment of adolescent criminality, most of them occurring in the late-nineteenth century. Then, after 500 "Boy's Brigades" were busy instilling "reverence, discipline, and self-respect," Jacob Riis wrote that summer "camps under military rule will come near to solving the delinquency problem." Concurrently, as the agricultural depression of the 1890s prevented social agencies from sending rowdy boys west to work on Spartan farms, the New York and Philadelphia houses of refuge, along with the Colorado State Industrial School, appointed former army officers to impose martial regimens implanting "obedience to authority." Shortly thereafter, in 1895, New York City municipal reformer Colonel George E. Waring, Jr., won national attention by organizing and training 2,500 children in his uniformed Juvenile Street Cleaning League. Ostensibly an aide to his sanitation workers, it really existed to develop "the sturdy, upright citizen which the times demand." Arthur Woods, as heir to all these programs that "compelled [adolescents] to live decently," was the ideal man to perpetuate their point of view. A protégé of Riis and a former staff members of Waring's (New York) City Club, he also was a veteran of military training in the 1880s at the Boston Latin School. There, attending one of the few school systems retaining a cadet corps after the Civil War, First Lieutenant Woods drilled his classmates at least twice a week. Later, his junior police force program, like his old student troop, built another "law and order" haven inside the city, "the very worst place in the world" for the young. Begun in 1914, it used meetings, lectures, and military drills to teach Lower East Side immigrant children public health, social discipline, and loyal citizenship. In turn its members, having learned that "the soldier who executes his captain's command is no less valuable than the captain himself," taught these virtues to their peers and their own parents. On occasion, they even brought offenders into a special advisory court, State Supreme Court Justice Samual Levy presiding.[24]"

Woods, who attended many junior police force meetings with his wife, vigorously applauded his own pet project. Other military training advocates concurred. Ex-Police Commissioner Theodore Roosevelt, who supported a paramilitary "Law and Order Gang" in his own administration, enthusiastically endorsed the cadets. Meanwhile, *Outlook* magazine glorified the program for "instilling law and order into the minds and hearts of the children of the city."[25]

Although some 6,000 youngsters eventually joined the junior police force, it was not New York City's most ambitious attempt to extend prep school principles. Mayor John Purroy Mitchel (1879–1918)—Plattsburg lieutenant and Junior Plattsburg advisor—felt that UMT should become an "essential element of general education." He simultaneously supported the Gary school system as a civic training program able to disseminate the "advantages enjoyed hitherto by children of the well-to-do in private schools." The Mitchel administration was a coalition of budget-cutting businessmen, social progressives, and military training advocates. The Gary plan, dividing an extended school day into equal components of work, study, and play, provided something for each group. For budget cutters, it substituted inexpensive playgrounds for costly classrooms. For progressives, it made the school a public settlement house that allowed pupils more opportunities to pursue their own interests. For military training advocates disturbed by effeminate aspects of education, the Gary program of organized recreation and manual work made school a "rough and hardening experience" which would prevent the growth of "a generation of tame, white-collared, white-handed slaves of theory and clerical routine."[26]

The Gary plan resembled those playgrounds, prep schools, and manual training programs that also tried to uplift a "flabby, underdeveloped, anemic, easy-living city youth." The team games stressed in its play component were supposed to be "a Moral Equivalent of War." They taught street urchins to obey their captains and "sacrifice" themselves for the common cause. Much the same was said about Gary's work component: a "factory for building character." It taught the Protestant ethic allegedly missing in immigrant subcultures, not the vocational skills needed in a specific trade. The program, as a whole, provided New York with preventive detention inside the public schools. Its lengthened school day and extended school year (8:15 to 4:15 for ten full months) was supposed to protect the "life, limb [and] morals" of the "wholesomely busy" child from the nefarious city in which he lived. The plan thereby anticipated arguments made for the military training that would "keep boys off the streets." Arthur Woods, "a hard boiled sentimentalist," thought that urban vice was probably irrevocable. Yet he felt that the Gary school system, like the Groton summer camp, could strengthen a child's will "to resist the temptation insistent to city life." Whereas Groton stood in loco parentis for the adolescent rich, the Gary plan superseded the immigrant poor whose offspring constituted 71 percent of the city's public school enrollment.[27]

But however patriotic, Mayor Mitchel's educational plans came to naught. Public school teachers, like most army officers, felt someone else should handle the ill-behaved. Consequently they disliked the Gary system's commitment to long hours of social control. Meanwhile ambitious parents, unwilling to surrender their children to the schools, disliked Americanization through manual instruction, especially after Tammany Hall, ridiculing the work ethic, told them U.S. Steel devised the program to train "wage slaves." Nonetheless, Mitchel stuck with his unpopular Gary school plan. If nothing else, this project cost him enough votes in 1917 to free him to join the army.[28]

The Gary school system and the New York City Junior Police were both offshoots of another moral training camp—the social settlement house. Like the Groton summer camp and the Plattsburg army camps, the settlement house provided hard work and physical austerity for the rich (in this case, full or part-time social workers "sickened with advantages"), character development programs for the poor, and a common meeting place in a stratified society. Consequently, many settlement house workers would come to express an affinity for military camps. Even Jane Addams, on occasion, contrasted "the high resolve" of the Union Army's heroes with the city-bred urchins' "lust for vice." Yet she, becoming a pacifist, stopped short of her colleagues who wrote about the "spiritual gains of war." That group of settlement house workers unequivocally endorsed military service for "creating new and desirable conceptions of national unity." One of these militarists, George W. Alger of New York's Henry Street Settlement, said that army life could be "a training school for democratic discipline [and] a means for union of all classes of men."[29]

In 1884, St. George's Church of New York City built the nation's first denominational settlement house in order to bring Congregationalism directly to the masses. Rev. William Rainsford, a gentleman reformer who was a close friend of Arthur Woods and Endicott Peabody, used gymnasiums, social clubs, and workshops to entice boys off the streets and into his church. By 1916, his program added a uniformed battalion of armed cadets trained in the manual of arms and close-order drill. "We are," said one Rainsford disciple, "very proud of the organization. [It is] the crack company of the state."[30]

Outside the city, the George Junior Republic (begun in 1890) and the Berkshire Industrial Farm (founded in 1886) developed moral character and social control through a program of physical labor, strict obedience, and paramilitary drill. These rural reformatories thus fortified the pedagogic point of view that nourished the Gary school system and the Junior Plattsburg movement. In fact, the reformatories, prep schools, and military camps shared an interlocking directorate. For example, the *Outlook* magazine, whose editor maintained that the proper aim of education should be "character," published fifteen articles in praise of the Junior Republic, an institution whose active supporters included Peabody, Woods, and Franklin Roosevelt. Accompanied by Woods, Theodore Roosevelt had a "thoroughly" enjoyable time there, visiting cadets who were "the type of men I would like to have with me in any kind of work, military or civil." The Berkshire Industrial Farm, although supervised by an ex-Groton master, was more of a St. Paul's production. Its directorate included Richard Hurd, a St. Paul's alumnus and secretary-treasurer of the American Defense Society, Samuel S. Drury, and Joseph Howland Coit.[31]

William R. George, the former drill sergeant who founded the Junior Republic for moral and social training, devised its program of military exercises and maneuvers, but he eventually came to use manual work more than infantry drill. Conversely, department store magnate John Wanamaker (1838–1922), the chairman of Philadelphia's National Security League, came to affix military training to work itself. Wanamaker, like the defenders of the Gary plan, lamented the demise of the apprenticeship system wherein artisans supervised the religious and moral development of the young, teaching them God and the Protestant ethic along with a trade. In lieu of such instruction in 1890, this YMCA worker, Sunday school teacher, and temperance reformer built a commercial institute to provide his young employees with compulsory training in business principles, religious codes, and military drills instilling "good citizenship."[32]

Wanamaker, who loved martial institutions, felt that his failure to pass the army physical in the Civil War was the "greatest humiliation of his life." His commercial institute, using militia drills to develop Christian character, merged his military and religious avocations into a department store Plattsburg. Although, in 1916, an increase in consumer demand and factory employment created a labor shortage in retail outlets, all Wanamaker "cadets" still had to attend a two-week summer camp "under full military discipline." America's youth needed "greater respect for existing conditions and authority," and this training, a Wanamaker executive told the Senate, was an excellent course in "reliability."[33]

William T. Hornaday: The Bronx Zoo, the Boy Scouts, and Military Training

William Temple Hornaday (1854–1937) was another advocate of junior military training with prior involvement in civilian education programs—particularly urban zoos, the Gary school system, and the Boy Scouts of America. While still in college, Hornaday, the son of a "comfortable" Iowa farmer, decided to become a "museum builder." But because he loved observing and training animals even more than dissecting them, in 1892 he forsook taxidermy in favor of planning a grand zoological garden in Washington, D.C. However, the same populist bloc in Congress that opposed appropriations for the navy also thought that disposessed humans had more pressing claims than animals on the public purse. Blocking funds to shelter all the "creeping things of the earth," they drove Hornaday into the real estate business where he remained until 1895, the initial year of his three-decade reign as the first director of the Bronx Zoological Park.[34]

Doing a "roaring trade" in real estate, Hornaday would not have returned to the zoo business if "the magnificent possibilities" of the Bronx park had not aroused his sense of social mission. Proud to be a public education and recreation leader who "served out natural history for the millions," he wanted to make plants and animals "available to the masses" in an accessible and attractive zoological garden. Like the Gary school system, which Hornaday vigorously supported, his Bronx park would serve as an asylum within the disgusting and dangerous jungle of city life. "Larger and finer than any other zoo in the country," it could be an invaluable recreational alternative to the ubiquitous saloons that were "worse than all the other scourges of the earth." It would also be a "natural world in miniature," showing wild beasts in habitat rather than cages. In it uncorrupted animals, which Hornaday felt were morally superior to most humans, could exemplify integrity to mankind.[35]

Hornaday not only wished to bring the wilderness into the city, like other "child savers" he hoped to bring the young out to the frontier. There, whether on the sea or in the woods, adolescents could not be seduced by urban vice. In 1916, Hornaday directed the U.S. Junior Naval Reserve and before that he was active in the Boy Scouts of America: "a great national antidote for the devilish spirit of anarchy now cropping up like rank and poisonous weeds all along the path of the nation's progress." Hornaday, who loved the Scouts, also loved the army. As a boy he organized "a 'company' of junior soldiers." In college he "loved" the military training he took. ("I ate it all alive.") In fact, with man and beast alike he often played soldier at the zoo. He uniformed his employees (brave men who performed "heroic deeds"), assembled them in ranks, and held them to a "soldierly discipline." Impressed with elephants who performed "imitation military drill . . . with true military promptness," he treated the animals much like their guards.[36]

Army enthusiast that he was, Hornaday believed that the "military element" in the Boy Scouts was the cornerstone of its program. He therefore supported its use of uniforms, Rough Rider hats, company organizations, and military mottoes such as "be prepared." This point of view he shared with other preparedness leaders who were active in scouting, among them Theodore and Franklin Roosevelt, Leonard Wood, John Wanamaker, Robert Low Bacon, George Wharton Pepper, Arthur Woods, Benjamin Idle Wheeler, and Ernest and Lawrence Abbott. Nevertheless, the regular scouting program, which officially forbad military drill, was too cautious to satisfy most of these men. The Boy Scouts, like a college football team, was an expensive operation to run. Besides equipment and transportation costs, the organization had to recruit numerous volunteers willing to spend their free time out in the woods with the neighborhood boys. Furthermore, scouting's ambition was even greater than its overhead. Mixing messianic and bureaucratic goals, it hoped to build a nationwide movement large enough to uplift the morals of the young and to protect the jobs of the agency's executives. However, working-class youth, often employed and at least semi-independent, had no time for nor interest in such ascetic programs, least of all in one begun by adults to occupy the leisure of more wealthy adolescents. Consequently scoutmasters only reached a small group of docile and dependent boys already anxious to do their good deeds. To expand their clientele beyond its present 1.3 percent of the adolescent population, scouting launched a public relations campaign designed to alienate no one. Straddling controversial issues, it claimed to be "neither [pro]-military nor antimilitary." It was simply training "in the old fashioned pioneer virtues"—a nebulous phrase that could temporarily unite militarists like Hornaday with pacifists like Earnest Thompson Seton.[37]

Seton also advocated the preservation of the wilderness but unlike Hornaday, who emphasized authority and discipline, he believed in liberty and equality. Feeling that an individual owed his first allegiance to his own conscience, Seton disliked social control through military training or loyalty oaths. The prewar Scouts, by including him and Hornaday, contained two antithetic conceptions of nature. One postulated the gentle garden that nurtured an antinomian resistance to "all social practices based on force." The other favored the puritan notion of purgatory in the rugged wilderness. This fragile coalition could not survive the war. In 1914, when W. P. McGuire and Seton, the chief and associate editors of *Boy's Life* magazine, published anti-war articles in the official Boy Scout publication, the military wing of scouting was outraged. It claimed that this "treasonable literature" subverted the organization's raison d'etre which was, it said, the development of "the spirit of sacrifice" and "the sense of personal responsibility for service to the nation." If not stopped, it could turn the Boy Scouts into a "national menace." Since the warrior wing, whose endorsement was needed in another fund raising drive, held more power than its pacifist opponents, it was able "to cut off the circulation of this rot." Then emphasizing "the question of Americanism," Hornaday, Franklin and Theodore Roosevelt, Leonard Wood, and others forced Seton and his allies off the Boy Scout National Council. Next, they asked other Plattsburgers to join (and thus militarize) the scoutmaster corps, only 8 percent of whom had undergone any military experience. Nonetheless, these preparedness leaders could not turn scouting as a whole into a "fertile field" for future military training. Its bureaucrats, trying to attract boys from all political backgrounds, refused their request for rifle practice nor would they identify their organization as the institutional "feeder" of the Junior Plattsburg movement.[38]

The Boy Scouts was not Hornaday's only disappointment. Many of his other plans to reform America's urban society also failed. To his "deep sorrow," most cities ignored his pleas to build expensive zoological parks. In New York, which had listened to him, the "low-class Jew" and other "human swine," together composing some "50 percent" of the city, waged a "Rubbish War" by heaping garbage on the zoo's grounds and carving grafitti into its walls. Meanwhile, as Washington officials "hilariously dumped" Hornaday's plans for big game preservation, a "Vandal army of destruction," out on the countryside, was wantonly exterminating "all wildlife." Hornaday, now "tired and exhausted," compared "the lawless American spirit" of "too-much liberty and too-much personal sovereignty" with Germany's "solidarity, unity and devotion." He then surmised that war ". . . will do one great and good thing for the young men of America. It will teach them the enormous value of discipline, it will teach them to take orders, and to obey them cheerfully for the good of all. . . . It will teach them the great virtue of loyal obedience to necessary authority."[39]

With this goal in mind Hornaday worked for military preparedness as he had campaigned for wilderness preservation, with nearly total emotional commitment. Assuming the leadership of five different preparedness organizations, he "almost forgot about wild animals" for the duration of the war.[40]

NOTES

1. On general educational trends, see Lawrence A. Cremin, *The Transformation of the School: Progressivism in American Education, 1876–1957* (New York: Vintage Books, 1964), passim. The three quotations are from Abraham Flexner and Frank P. Bauman, *The Gary Schools: A General Account* (New York: General Education Board, 1918), p. 17; educators cited in Joseph Kett, *Rites of Passage: Adolescence in America, 1790 to the Present* (New York: Basic Books, 1977), p. 236; in David Tyack, "Bureaucracy and the Common Schools: The Example of Portland, Oregon, 1851–1913," *Education in American History,* ed. Michael Katz (New York: Praeger, 1973), pp. 164–65, 171. Claude Fuess, *The College Board* (New York: College Entrance Examination Board, 1967), passim.

2. Guy Murchie to Leonard Wood, Feb. 18, 1915, William G. Thayer to Wood, Oct. 28, 1915, A. P. Gardner to Wood, Oct. 27, 1915: all in Wood MSS

Boxes 80, 83, 85. James McLachlan, *American Boarding Schools: A Historical Study* (New York: Scribner's, 1970), pp. 9, 13, 19–49; Endicott Peabody to Theodore Roosevelt, Sept. 30, 1911, May 20, 1914, Roosevelt MSS, Reels 113, 183; Frank Ashburn, *Peabody of Groton* (Boston: Coward-McCann, 1944), passim. The quotation by the biologist is from Henry Fairchild Osborne to Endicott Peabody, Oct. 19, 1925, Peabody MSS, Box 77. For the political effects of the Rough Riders, see Parker, *History of Gatling Gun Detachment,* pp. 182–83.

3. The first two quotations are from Groton alumnus Francis Biddle, *A Casual Past* (Garden City: Doubleday, 1961), p. 194. General W. M. Black to John Biddle, Feb. 5, 1917, Endicott Peabody to Leonard Wood, Sept. 17, 1913, Peabody MSS, Boxes 55, 68; Wood quoted in Ashburn, *Peabody of Groton,* p. 226; Chase C. Mooney and Martha E. Lyman, "Some Phases of the Compulsory Military Training Movement, 1914–1920," *Mississippi Valley Historical Review* 28 (Mar., 1952):654–56; Robert McCormick, "Ripe for Conquest," *Century* 59 (Apr., 1916):837–38; McCormick to Peabody, July 20, Aug. 24, 1926, Peabody MSS, Box 80.

4. Graham Whidden, "Our Schoolboy Soldiers," *Munsey's Magazine* 15 (July, 1896):459, 466; T. B. Bronson, "The Value of Military Training and Discipline in Schools," *School Review* 2 (May, 1894):281; Endicott Peabody to Secretary of War, Apr. 7, 1894, Peabody MSS, Box 16: James McLachlan to Michael Pearlman, Dec. 26, 1972, in possession of this writer; Claude Feuss, *Independent Schoolmaster* (Boston: Little, Brown, 1952), pp. 106–7, 330; statement of Frederick Winsor at *Proceedings of the Congress of Constructive Patriotism,* Jan. 25–27, 1917 (New York: National Security League, 1917), p. 255.

5. Statement of Endicott Peabody, Nov. 17, 1928, Hermann Hagedorn MSS, Box 19; personal interview with Roger Drury (son of Headmaster Samuel Drury) June 24, 1972; Leonard Wood to Lyman Abbott, Sept. 27, 1913, Wood MSS, Box 68.

6. Newton Baker quoted in Josephus Daniels Diary, Mar. 23, 1917, Daniels MSS, Library of Congress; Endicott Peabody to Leonard Wood, Dec. 23, 1909, Osborne Wood to Peabody, Mar. 31, [1916?], Peabody MSS, Boxes 50, 63; Dean B. S. Hulbert to Leonard Wood, Sept. 22, 1915, Wood to Dean H. A. Yeomans, Dec. 11, 1916, Wood MSS, Boxes 88, 100. Osborne Wood quoted in *New York Times,* Apr. 1, 1925. For Leonard Wood, Jr., see *New York Times,* Dec. 29, 1923, Dec. 31, 1923, Apr. 1, 1927.

7. Wood to Endicott Peabody, Dec. 26, 1914, Wood MSS, Box 75; Dean B. S. Hulbert to Endicott Peabody, Mar. 24, 1910, Dec. 22, 1915, Peabody MSS, Boxes 53, 66. For Fish, see "The Paradox of Hamilton Fish," statement of Ledwige, n.d., Roosevelt Collection MSS. For Coit, see Joseph Howland Coit to Theodore Roosevelt, Feb. 8, 1912, Adelene B. Coit to Roosevelt, n.d., Roosevelt MSS, Reels 128, 311: Joseph Howland Coit to Owen Wister, Mar. 9, 1922, Wister MSS, Box 16. Rev. Philip Steinmetz (headmaster of the Episcopal Academy of Philadelphia) to George Wharton Pepper, Nov. 11, 1916, Pepper MSS, Box 15; Henry S. Hooker to Woodrow Wilson, Dec. 1, 1916, Ass. Sec. of the Navy Papers, Box 102, Franklin Roosevelt Presidential Library, Hyde Park, N.Y.

8. Roger W. Drury, *Drury of St. Paul's: The Scars of a Schoolmaster* (Boston:

Little, Brown, 1964), pp. 89, passim; Leonard Wood, *The Military Obligation of Citizenship* (Princeton: Princeton University Press, 1915), p. 66; Drury to Leonard Wood, June 16, 1915, Nov. 15, 1915, Wood MSS, Box 87; *The Rangefinder,* July 15, 1916, Grenville Clark MSS. Like Plattsburg, the junior military training camp was not supposed to be an end in itself. It was built to demonstrate the feasibility of compulsory military training for nearly all male adolescents. Its advocates, who successfully lobbied New York State's legislature for a militarized version of physical education, hoped to convince the nation's schools to require military drills.

9. Frank Ashburn, *Fifty Years On: Groton School 1884–1934* (privately printed, 1934), pp. 112, 198; Stebbins to Endicott Peabody, Mar. 29, 1893, Mar. 6, 1894, Apr. 8, 1907, Jan. 1, Jan. 19, 1916, June 10, 1927, Peabody MSS, Boxes 15, 36, 66, 97; J. D. Williams to Archibald Thacher, Oct. 7, 1916, Horace Stebbins to Grenville Clark, Jan. 16, 1917: both in Clark MSS; Archibald Thacher, *The Cadets of Plum Island* (New York: Junior Division of the Military Training Camps Association of the United States, 1916), p. 5. The secondary education of the four other members of Junior Plattsburg executive committee could not be ascertained. Three, however, were Harvard graduates and thus were also likely to have been prep school products.

10. Stimson, *The Issues of the War,* p. 21; Stimson and Bundy, *On Active Service in Peace and War,* pp. xiii–xiv; Stimson quoted in Claude Fuess, "The Reminiscences of Claude M. Fuess," pp. 185–86; Stimson to Alfred Stearns, Apr. 16, 1924, Stimson MSS; Stimson to Leonard Wood, Nov. 6, 1914, Wood MSS, Box 75; *Rangefinder,* July 15, Aug. 8, 1916, Clark MSS. In 1947, Stimson performed his last great service for Andover when he helped make Col. John Mason Kemper its new headmaster. A West Pointer, Kemper's "whole life had been associated with the Army." See John L. Mott to Stimson and Stimson to Mott, Oct. 31, Nov. 7, 1947, Stimson MSS; *The Handbook of Private Schools* (Boston: Porter Sargent, 1972), p. 82.

11. Lt. Col. Andrew Hero, "Military Discipline Paves Way for Responsibility," *Rangefinder,* July 25, 1916; Kenneth Budd to Grenville Clark, July 24, 1916, Clark MSS; William Scheide to Commanding Officer, Fort Terry, Aug. 9, 1916, Hero to Scheide, Aug. 12, 1916: both in Leonard Wood MSS, Box 88.

12. Henry S. Hooker to Theodore Roosevelt, Sept. 14, 1914, Roosevelt MSS, Reel 190; Hooker to Franklin Roosevelt, Sept. 10, 1914; Langdon P. Marvin to FDR, Aug. 12, 1916, Hooker to FDR, July 9, 1916: all in Ass. Sec. of Navy Papers, Box 102, Franklin Roosevelt Presidential Library; Hooker to Henry Stimson, June 12, 1942, Stimson MSS, Reel 106.

13. Charles Nutter to Leonard Wood, Aug. 19. 1916, Theodore Robinson to Wood, July 8, 1916: both in Wood MSS, Box 90; Archibald Thacher to Joseph Choate, Oct. 25, 1916, Choate MSS, Library of Congress; Bernard Wishy, *The Child and the Republic: The Dawn of Modern American Child Nurture* (Philadelphia: University of Pennsylvania Press, 1968), p. 58. Jacob Abbott quoted in David Rothman, *The Discovery of the Asylum: Social Order and Disorder in the New Republic* (Boston: Little, Brown, 1971), p. 218. Ernest Abbott to Leonard Wood, July 20, 1916, Aug. 1, 1916, Wood MSS, Box 86. Ernest Hamlin Abbott, "The Boys of Plum Island," *Outlook* 103 (Aug. 23, 1916):958.

14. Clifford, *Citizen Soldiers,* p. 222. The commercial camps are quoted in *Boston Evening Transcript,* May 11, 1918, 2:7.

15. Unnamed conservative quoted in Davies, *Patriotism on Parade,* pp. 341–42; Theodore Roosevelt to Endicott Peabody, Dec. 20, 1915, Peabody MSS, Box 60; Archibald Thacher to Albert B. Hart, Oct. 24, 1916, Grenville Clark MSS; Frank Potter to Seth Low, May 30, 1916, Low MSS, Box 111-12, Columbia University; personal interview with Hamilton Fish, June 12, 1972; *New York Times,* May 26 & June 5, 1916; *New York Herald,* Apr. 9, 1917.

16. G. Stanley Hall, "Some Educational Values of War," *Pedagogical Seminary* 25 (Sept., 1918):305–6. For Drury, see Drury, *Drury of St. Paul's,* pp. 83–84, 99, 147, 152–53, 173. For Coit, see Coit to Theodore Roosevelt, Jan. 17, 1911, Nov. 22, 1916, Roosevelt MSS, Reels 97, 216; St. Paul's *Alumni Horae* (Dec. 30, 1930):59–60; Coit: "Universal Service in America in 1917," Dec. 31, 1916; "Train the High School Youth," Feb. 25, 1917: both in Charles Bonaparte MSS, Box 210, Library of Congress.

17. Derby to Endicott Peabody, Mar. 3, 1907, Oct. 21, 1914, Feb. 21, 1928, Peabody MSS, Boxes 41, 61, 79; Derby, *Memoirs of Roger Alden Derby,* pp. 108, 212, 228, 271.

18. Ibid., pp. 228, 244–57, 265; Derby to Endicott Peabody, Feb. 8, 1915, June 12, 1916, Feb. 12, 1920, Peabody MSS, Boxes 61, 65, 70; Derby to Theodore Roosevelt, Roosevelt MSS, Reel 217; Roosevelt, *Foes of Our Household,* pp. 207, 216; Derby to Leonard Wood, Sept. 13, 1916, Wood MSS, Box 87.

19. Derby, *Memoirs of Roger Alden Derby,* pp. 20–24, 44–47, 227, 247, 256; Dorthy Straight to Frank McCoy, Sept. 16, 1915, McCoy MSS, Box 14: Derby to Theodore Roosevelt, May 15, 1916, Dec. 2, 1916, Reels 209, 217.

20. Arthur Woods quoted in *New York Evening World,* Aug. 19, 1915. For Woods's ancestors, see Kett, *Rites of Passage,* pp. 76–77; Claude Fuess, *An Old New England School* (Boston: Houghton-Mifflin, 1917), pp. 152, 195–96, 201; Peterson, *The New England College in the Age of the University,* pp. 76, 253. Unidentified newspaper clipping, July 26, 1907, Woods File (HUG 300), Harvard University Archives; Hawes, *Children in Urban Society,* pp. 95–98; Frank Marshall White, "A Man Who Has Achieved the Impossible," *Outlook* 118 (Sept. 26, 1917):125

21. George Martin, "Arthur Woods," *Groton School Quarterly* (June, 1924), n.p. *The Grotonian* (Oct., 1893):4–6, (Oct., 1899):8, (Mar., 1901):110–11. Circular letter quoted in Elliot Roosevelt, ed., *F.D.R.: His Personal Letters* (New York: Duell, Sloan & Pearce, 1947–1950), 1:72.

22. Woods to Endicott Peabody, Apr. 21, 1906, Jan. 26, 1908, Peabody to Meredith Hare, Dec. 2, 1908, Peabody MSS, Boxes 37, 45.

23. *New York Times,* Nov. 15, 1914, Jan. 17, 1915, 2:13, June 2, 1916, Mar. 30, 1916; Arthur Woods, *Crime Prevention* (Princeton: Princeton University Press, 1918), pp. 101-2.

24. Arthur Woods, "The Police and Social Service," *The Churchman* (Nov. 13, 1917):560; Drummond, "Manliness in Boys," p. 71. Riis quoted in James B. Lane, *Jacob Riis and the American City* (Port Washington: Kennikat Press, 1964), pp. 99–100. Robert M. Mennel, *Thorns and Thistles: Juvenile Delinquents in the United States, 1825–1940* (Hanover: University of New Hampshire Press,

1973), pp. 62–63, 99–100. For Waring see Boyer, *Urban Masses and Moral Reform*, p. 181; Trachtenberg, *Incorporation of America*, p. 126; Richard Skolnick, "George Edwin Waring, Jr.: A Model for Reformers," *New York Historical Society Quarterly* 52 (Oct., 1968):366–67. Arthur Woods Diary, Nov. 25, 1884, Jan. 9, 1885, Feb. 25, 1886, Woods MSS, Library of Congress; *Junior Policeman*, Jan., Feb., & Apr., 1917, New York City Municipal Archives; "Juvenile 'Copettes,'" *Literary Digest* 52 (June 10, 1916):1735–38.

25. *Junior Policeman*, Apr., 1917; Theodore Roosevelt to Chief Inspector of the Junior Police, Mar. 15, 1917, Roosevelt MSS, Reel 388; "The New York City Junior Police," *Outlook* 113 (July 12, 1916):588+.

26. Mitchel quoted in *New York Post*, Feb. 2, 1917; *New York Times*, Sept. 21, 1917. For the Gary school system in general, see Ronald Cohen and Raymond Mohl, *The Paradox of Progressive Education: The Gary Plan and Urban Schools* (Port Washington: Kennikat Press, 1979), passim. The final quotation is from Fusion Committee of 1917, *The Truth about the Gary Schools*, in Mitchel MSS, Box 17, Library of Congress.

27. G. Stanley Hall, UMT advocate, quoted on manual education and child reform in Kett, *Rites of Passage*, p. 219. My discussion of "play" is based not on the Gary schools per se but on the type of recreational activities they incorporated. For the most militant team game enthusiasts, see Dominick Cavallo, *Muscles and Morals: Organized Playgrounds and Urban Reform, 1880–1920* (Philadelphia: University of Pennsylvania Press, 1981), pp. 83, 92–94. The quotations on the Gary plan are from an unidentified supporter in Diane Ravitch, *The Great School Wars: New York City, 1885–1973* (New York: Basic Books, 1974), p. 206; Matilde Ford to Paul Wilson, Dec. 22, 1915, John Collier to Fellow Citizen, Oct. 4, 1917: both in Mitchel MSS, Box 17. Woods described by *New York Times*, Oct. 26, 1930, 9:2. Woods quoted in *Brooklyn Eagle*, Oct. 10, 1917.

28. For opposition to the Gary plan and social control, see Ravitch, *Great School Wars*, pp. 210–26; David B. Tyack, *The One Best System: A History of American Urban Education* (Cambridge, Mass.: Harvard University Press, 1974), pp. 70–71, 250–51; Cohen and Mohl, *Paradox of Progressive Education*, p. 88. One of many letters warning Mitchel that the Gary plan was politically dangerous is from Robert Proctor to Mitchel, Oct. 16, 1917, Mitchel MSS, Box 17. In Ch. 6, this writer deals with Mitchel's 1917 reelection defeat at length.

29. For the settlement house in general, see Allen F. Davis, *Spearheads for Reform: The Social Settlements and the Progressive Movement, 1890–1914* (New York: Oxford University Press, 1967), pp. 35–39, 51–52, 76–80, 146. For "advantages" and the Union army, see Jane Addams: *Twenty Years at Hull-House* (first pub. 1910; New York: New American Library, 1960), pp. 34–37, 65; *The Spirit of Youth and the City Streets* (first pub. 1909; New York: Macmillan, 1926), pp. 10–21. For "militaristic"social workers, see Marchand, *American Peace Movement and Social Reform*, pp. 235–37, 261; George W. Alger, "Preparedness and Democratic Discipline," *Atlantic Monthly* 117 (Apr., 1916):481. Other, mostly part-time, settlement house workers active in military preparedness were James Storrow, William Hard, Richard T. Ely, Francis Kellor, Ever-

ett Wheeler. All of them appear to have been more enthusiastic about these community centers than was Roger Baldwin, a rare, unequivocal pacifist. (Unlike Addams and Lillian Wald, he continued to oppose military mobilization after the United States declared war.) By 1917, Baldwin came to question the settlement work he had done, as revealed by his statement that "social work alone is not enough." For Baldwin, see Donald Johnson, *The Challenge To American Freedoms: World War I and the Rise of the American Civil Liberties Union* (Lexington: University of Kentucky Press, 1963), pp. 10–12.

30. W. S. Rainsford, *The Story of a Varied Life* (Garden City: Doubleday & Page, 1922), pp. 228–29, 233–37, 241, 249, 255; Theodore Price to Leonard Wood, Oct. 19, 1916, Wood MSS, Box 93.

31. Jack M. Holl, *Juvenile Reform in the Progressive Era: William R. George and the Junior Republic Movement* (Ithaca: Cornell University Press, 1971), passim; Lyman Abbott, "The Spirit of Democracy," *Outlook* 95 (July 30, 1910): 741; Arthur Woods to William George, Nov. 10, Nov. 26, 1911, George MSS, Cornell University; Theodore Roosevelt to George, Nov. 10, 1911, Roosevelt MSS, Reel 370; Burnham Carter, The Berkshire Industrial Farm, 1886–1926 (n.p.: n.n., n.d.), passim. Richard Hurd to Arthur von Briesen, Dec. 4, 1917, von Briesen MSS. Princeton University.

32. Holl, *Juvenile Reform in Progressive Era*, pp. 56, 66, 83, 85, 99–101, 191; Herbert Adams Gibbons, *John Wanamaker* (New York: Harper & Brothers, 1926) 1:39, 41, 47, 2:282–86, 294–96; Wanamaker to Leonard Wood, June 25, 1915, Wood MSS, Box 82.

33. Gibbons, John Wanamaker, 1:75–77, 2:403; statement of store official in Senate, *Hearings on Universal Military Training*, 64th Cong., 2d Sess., 1917, pp. 430–48.

34. William Temple Hornaday, "Autobiography," Ch. 1 and 2, unpublished mss in Hornaday MSS, Boxes 16, 18, Library of Congress. For the populist opposition, see Daniel J. Kevles, *The Physicists: The History of a Scientific Community in Modern America* (New York: Knopf, 1977), p. 63.

35. Hornaday, "Autobiography," Chapter 13, Hornaday MSS, Box 18; William Bridges, *Gathering of Animals: An Unconventional History of the New York Zoological Society* (New York: Harper & Row, 1974), p. 24. Hornaday to William Frew, Apr. 25, 1895, Hornaday MSS, Box 13; William T. Hornaday: *Report on the Character and Availability of South Bronx Park*, First Annual Report of the New York Zoological Society, Mar. 15, 1897, pp. 27–34; *The Man Who Became a Savage* (Buffalo: Peter Paul Book Comp., 1896), pp. 27, 31–32, 144. Hornaday to John D. Rockefeller, May 10, 1897, Hornaday MSS, Box 13; William T. Hornaday: *Free Rum on the Congo* (Chicago: Woman's Temperance Publication Association, 1887), pp. 80, 107; "The Rise of the Zoological Society," Hornaday MSS, Box 18. Although Hornaday was obviously a bit eccentric, like a good literary character he only magnified what other men in the preparedness movement also felt.

36. Hornaday quoted in "Boy Scout Statement," Dec. 6, 1915, Leonard Wood MSS, Box 91; Hornaday to Daniel Carter Beard, July 21, 1910, Beard MSS, Box 21, Library of Congress. Hornaday, "Autobiography," Ch. 2, Hornaday

MSS, Box 16; *The Mind and Manners of Wild Animals* (New York: Scribner's, 1922), pp. 109–11, 106–8, 212, 228, 302; Bridges, *Gathering of Animals,* pp. 87–89, 118, 198, 253–54, 299.

37. Harold Levy, *Building a Popular Movement: A Case Study of the Public Relations of the Boy Scouts of America* (New York: Russell Sage Foundation, 1944), pp. 18–21, 86–87, passim; Daniel Carter Beard to Theodore Roosevelt, May 9, 1913; James West to Roosevelt, May 3, 1918, Roosevelt MSS, Reels 173, 274; Daniel Carter Beard to George D. Pratt, Apr. 24, 1912, Beard MSS, Box 99. Jeffry Hantover, "Sex Role, Sexualiy, and Social Status: The Early Years of the Boy Scouts" (Ph.D. diss., University of Chicago, 1976), pp. 252–53. According to General Leonard Wood, there was something of a Boy Scout caucus at the 1916 Plattsburg camp; see Wood Diary, Sept. 5, 1916, Wood MSS.

38. Brian Morris, "Ernest Thompson Seton and the Origins of Woodcraft," *Journal of Contemporary History* 5 (1970):186–94; nature lover, pacifist, and civil libertarian Robert Baldwin quoted against "force" in Johnson, *Challenge To American Freedom,* p. 13. David Starr Jordan, "A Challenge! Do You Want to Fight?" *Boy's Life* 9 (Nov., 1914):3; Leonard Wood to Theodore Roosevelt, Nov. 23, 1915, Roosevelt to James West, Sept. 8, 1917, Roosevelt MSS, Reels 202, 395; Franklin Roosevelt to James West, June 23, 1916, FDR to Leonard Wood, June 23, 1915, Ass. Sec. of Navy Papers, File 86, Roosevelt Presidential Library; DeLancey K. Jay to Leonard Wood, Oct. 18, 1916, Wood MSS, Box 88.

39. Hornaday to Henry Fairchild Osborn, Oct. 8, 1918, Hornaday MSS, Box 13; "Men," *Ladies Home Journal,* 34 (Jan., 1917):6: Hornaday to Theodore Roosevelt, July 7, Aug. 17, 1917, Roosevelt MSS, Reels 239, 243; Bridges, *Gathering of Animals,* pp. 102, 115; Hornaday quoted in Steven Fox, *John Muir and His Legacy: The American Conservation Movement* (Boston: Little, Brown, 1981), p. 158; Hornaday: *Wildlife Conservation in Theory and Practice* (New Haven: Yale University Press, 1914), pp. 110–11, 162, 183; *A Search-Light on Germany* (New York: American Defense Society, n.d.), p. 13; *Awake! America* (New York: Moffat, Yard, 1918), pp. 99, 185.

40. Hornaday to Henry A. Moe, Apr. 7, 1934, Hornaday "Autobiography," Ch. 19, Hornaday MSS, Boxes 13, 17.

Theodore Roosevelt, John Greenway (on his right), and other Rough Riders in the Spanish-American War: "cowboys and millionaires side by side, all men equal." (courtesy Theodore Roosevelt Collection, Harvard College Library)

General Leonard Wood: "a strange combination of kindness and severity." (from Joseph H. Sears, *The Career of Leonard Wood*, 1921)

William Muldoon: prescribing a "premonition of Dante's *Inferno*." (from *Literary Digest*, June 17, 1933)

SECURITY OR DOUBT—WHICH?

That the terrific sacrifices to Win the War may not be in vain, will you dedicate some time to constructive thought now and join in decisive action during the week of January 14th to 20th?

★　　　★　　　★

August 15, 1916

Thousands upon thousands of weak, listless, hopeless, ineffective boys like this, of little value in the up-building and strength of the nation, annually begin to take part in the government of the United States. Many become narrow, vicious, irresponsible dead weights, the victims of prejudice and ignorance. They endanger our liberty, limit progress and weaken our defense. Universal training will contribute to their future welfare.

Consider—Shall the human liberties of our children be safeguarded by a democracy universally trained in youth to know and respect the obligations and service of citizenship, or be left to the mercy of theorists and a mob subject to alien and vicious influences?

It will give to all, courage, strength and the determination to win regardless of sacrifices—

To know now, that the United States will be safe from its future enemies from within and without;

To know now, that a regenerated citizenship, strong, alert, without distinction of class, race or privilege, with respect for authority and capable of thinking nationally, will be able to defend its liberties;

To know now, that there is a dependable prospect of the realization of the highest aspirations for posterity.

January 20, 1917

The same young man after five months of training at Camp Stewart had gained thirty-eight pounds in weight. He is strong, alert, ambitious, self respecting and efficient. He has a broader conception of government, and mutual responsibilities. A nation determined to so develop its young men, inculcate the real meaning of liberty and the obligations of citizenship is safe for our children and deserves our supreme sacrifices.

★　　　★　　　★

It is wholly within the power of the people to have such an inspiring ideal of future security and progress before them as will give to all the Will to Win, the Passion for Victory, and, more than ever a country worth fighting for, by now providing for Universal Military Training. Will history show the people [you] failed to act at a supreme moment by not writing their Congressmen to pass the Chamberlain Bill and to save the cantonments to serve a vital purpose when the army no longer needs them and the War Department is ready to undertake the work? The training each year of half a million nineteen-year-old boys in the broad obligations of citizenship, for a period of six months, will insure increased personal efficiency, common understanding and give confidence in the future of democracy in this republic.

IF YOU WILL HELP—REGISTER HERE

MAN AMERICA WEEK
January 14th to 20th

Universal Military Training League—Chicago

President

Preparedness poster: a moral metamorphosis through military training.
(from John Purroy Mitchell Papers, Library of Congress)

Theodore Roosevelt and Leonard Wood at Plattsburg: escaping "contact with the crowd of money changers." (from Hermann Hagedorn, *Leonard Wood*, 1931)

George Wharton Pepper: seeking "a course in real hardship." (from G. W. Pepper, *In the Senate*, 1930)

Henry Stimson in World War I: getting his chance "to stand up to the shelling." (from Elting E. Morison, *Turmoil and Tradition: A Study of the Life and Times of Henry L. Stimson*, 1960, courtesy Houghton Mifflin Co.)

Theodore Roosevelt, Jr., demonstrating bayonet drill at Plattsburg: "a protest against the easy-going life." (from Eleanor B. Roosevelt, *Day Before Yesterday*, 1959)

Robert Bacon: "the whitest of the white men" thinks himself a "shameless dun." (from James Brown Scott, *Robert Bacon, Life and Letters*, 1923)

CHAPTER 6

Motives and Meanings
of Military Training

☆

MILITARY TRAINING, according to most preparedness advocates, was a social program able to resolve such outstanding national problems as unassimilated immigration, slovenly labor, political conflict, and serious crime. This chapter, exploring the roots of this belief, shows how wartime arguments for army service arose from prewar assumptions, policies, and failures. Among the suppositions it examines is the idea that the new immigrants, having migrated solely for money, would need to suffer deprivation for the United States if they were to be Americanized. The proposals investigated include international law and industrial mediation, both of which provide explanatory background for an alternative means of social control, universal military training.

This chapter studies personalities as well as political issues by examining New York City's Mayor John Purroy Mitchel, a man who gained the public office he sought but not the social unity that he hoped to build. Mitchel turned to the army as an alternative to politics. Meanwhile his police commissioner Arthur Woods, also discussed in this section, used military training as an administrative tool to impose discipline and duty on corrupt patrolmen. Finally, this chapter deals with the general business community. Although most of its members pursued commercial success to the exclusion of military preparedness, Henry Alexander Wise Wood, a manufacturer, and S. Stanwood Menken, a lawyer, seized the movement to acquire the public power that heretofore eluded them. By investigating both unfulfilled reforms and frustrated men, one can see that military preparedness was used to realize social and personal goals which civilian practices alone failed to achieve.

The Legacy of Prior Wars: George Haven Putnam, Frederic Coudert, and International Law

Most preparedness advocates had faith in the domestic effects of military institutions but, of course, there were a few exceptions. While they generally felt that the Civil War was a heroic epic, it was just an ugly memory to George Haven Putnam (1844–1930), publisher, executive director of the National Security League, and president of the American Rights League. Having enlisted in the Union army at eighteen, he was the only preparedness leader who had actually fought in a total war. His memoirs, written on the eve of World War I, record his daily battles with influenza, mosquitoes, dust, and mud. As a junior officer, his greatest military problem had been controlling the brawling, gambling, and drinking of enlisted men. He remembered not a postwar millennium, but a moral dissipation so great that it hindered the veterans' capacity to return to work. Putnam, as a gentleman reformer, fought commercial vulgarity, political corruption, immigration, and radicalism yet not by means of war. According to him, preparedness would defend Anglo-American society but never could cleanse it.[1]

The Spanish-American War also left an ambiguous legacy to the preparedness movement. Symbolic unity between the East and West was reassuring, but yellow press demagoguery indicated that war could advance anarchy as well as authority. Consequently some future preparedness leaders were induced to promote international law and arbitration. From 1905 to 1909, Secretaries of State Elihu Root and Robert Bacon, with support from Lyman Abbott's *Outlook,* worked to build a permanent World Court. A few years later, they and Joseph Choate, future honorary president of the National Security League, helped direct the Carnegie Endowment for International Peace, an admittedly "conservative body" that would financially support the campaign for UMT. Ostensibly antithetic, both international law and induction could be agencies of political control. Thus they shared social principles that bridged the gap between war and peace. The law between nations, when sanctioned solely by consent, can be a classic example of participatory democracy. However, Bacon, Root, and other men who mistrusted popular sovereignty (and who opposed war mainly in times of peace), led a mediation movement based on an international tribunal isolated from public participation. Their World Court, somewhat like America's Supreme Court, would issue edicts and decisions restraining the options of democratic diplomacy. Foreign policy aside, this would have important consequences at home. If the World Court facilitated peace, an ensuing growth in the general prestige of the judiciary would fortify the national courts against populist accusations that they functioned to defend a plutocracy.[2]

The preparedness movement's leading international lawyer was Frederic Rene Coudert (1871–1955), partner in the prestigious Coudert Brothers' firm, director of the New York Peace Society, and executive member of the National Security League. As a young man of twenty-five, Coudert accompanied his father, a prominent Gold Democrat, to his party's national convention of 1896. There, he saw the "extraordinary power" of William Jennings Bryan drive that assembly "perfectly crazy." He "never forgot" that awful but "most apt illustration of the psychology of the crowd," and henceforth endorsed such mass society theorists as Alexis de Tocqueville, Gustave La Bon, and Walter Lippmann. Something of a philosopher himself, Coudert eventually came "to the conclusion that the so-called modern psychology, with all its exaggerations, is right in reducing the reasoning element in the so-called *homo sapiens* to the very minimum quantity." Coudert, expressing this theory in jurisprudential form, believed that international law was a process to "suppress exhibitions of popular feeling," not a codification of transcendental justice. As such, in 1898, it failed its function when it did not restrain the public's "frenzy" for the Spanish-American War.[3]

World War I, contrasted to the war against Spain, was a worthy cause for Coudert. In 1915 he became an active interventionist in whose eyes belligerency was the sine qua non of national vitality. Neutrality, on the other hand, had become the policy of a mass society whose "heterogeneous assortment of conflicting racial entities" was "drifting towards some moral oblivion." Mindlessly the masses seemed completely unaware that at the battle front "there is a lack of the sordidness, meanness and petty individualism that makes everyday life so unlovable." But remarks like this, no matter how belligerent, did not banish Coudert from his juridical "peace movement." He and similar interventionists continued to direct international law organizations which would maintain world order by enforcing "cooling off" periods on public opinion. Such activities were, in part, public relations politics, since Coudert later admitted that he encouraged the "American public's curious assumption that international law was an exact science [in order] to claim that our [pro-English] side was in the right." Yet hypocrisy is not the complete explanation for this apparent legalism. Preparedness leaders, in their prewar careers, forcefully controlled turbulent conditions. When Theodore Roosevelt, historian, was not praising the militant imposition of "civilization" upon the "savage" Indian, the President was joining Root the lawyer and Bacon the banker to regulate tooth-and-claw industrial competition. Now Germany's invasion of Belgium and its use of submarines, all of which broke the "rules" of war, presented these men with a unique opportunity to fight the good fight against anarchy. In one great contest they could oppose both bloodthirsty barbarians (in this case the "Huns") and the lawless application of advanced technology. (It may be recalled that Bacon called the German army a "scientific, soulless war machine.") Litigation by combat thus became their program for internal control *and* international law.[4]

John Purroy Mitchel and the Failure of Politics

Military preparedness was supposed to produce unity and patriotism as well as social obedience. When New York's John Purroy Mitchel could not establish these objectives through political institutions, he renounced municipal government in favor of the army. As Mitchel's friends said of him: The "dauntless fighting spirit" that he wore like a "plume" would have made him "an excellent district attorney." Unfortunately, as a mayor who hated "expediency," he was temperamentally unfit for the office he held. Because Mitchel, the beau ideal of the militant reformers eager to do battle with Tammany Hall, would not stoop to be a political broker, in 1917 the electorate would reject him, after he had already rejected them.[5]

Mayor Mitchel's administration (1914–18) emphasized industrial arbitration. Reflecting a Progressive Era premise that ignorance (not interest) precipitated conflict, he tried to nurture economic harmony by the "disinterested investigation and interpretation of facts to both sides." To the consternation of the *New York Times,* he protected the civil liberties of the Industrial Workers of the World, offering them free employment bureaus instead of jail. Venturing beyond the legal neutrality that forbade the police to bust nonviolent picket lines, he also made attempts at mediation that won the "deep gratitude and sincere appreciation" of the International Ladies Garment Workers' Union.[6]

Mitchel's pressure on recalcitrant employers helped build the clothing industry's Council of Conciliation. However, he could not settle his own city's transportation strike. One month after he negotiated a 1916 agreement for union recognition and a board of arbitration, a notoriously autocratic group of transportation companies circulated "yellow-dog" contracts while they imported 3,000 strike breakers. Mitchel, as the guarantor of the original settlement, conceded that management had acted in bad faith. But committed to property rights, he deployed his police to enforce his pronouncement that union violence would not be tolerated. For all Mitchel's efforts to protect "the public interest" now at risk in industrial relations, capital often thought him a meddler while labor viewed him a traitor.[7]

As Mitchel admittedly failed the progressive ideal of the mayor who would mend urban class and ethnic conflicts, he became aroused by the moral potential of military life for America. Already, in 1915, he wrote a friend that war was an "opportune time to awaken the religious spirit" which would create "a larger vision on the part of the people as to their duties and their responsibilities to the city and its government." Shortly thereafter, engulfed in civic conflict, he concluded that military training camps were the best way to establish social harmony in a stratified society. Within them, he said, "the rich and poor, high and low [develop] a reciprocal respect and understanding [that] they get in no other relation of life." Before long UMT had become Mitchel's panacea for social problems from national disunity to unassimilated ethnics, from political corruption to delinquent youth.[8]

Mitchel was still in his first term of office when America, in his words, "passed out of the state of painful neutrality." He probably wished to enlist at once. For the last two years he had preferred Plattsburg ("one of the few worthwhile experiences in life") to the "vexatious" city in which he lived. Indeed, newspapers remarked that while up at camp the mayor was as "happy as a boy." Since the very thought of returning to New York could ruin his day, he ordered Alderman Henry Curran to take his place at an urgent City Board of Estimate meeting. Thus able to remain at Plattsburg, Mitchel could attend to the more important issues at hand. Twenty-four years later, another recruit still remembered Mitchel's "grief and shame" when he did a "left about" turn to a "right about" order.[9]

Mentally preoccupied with preparedness, Mitchel did not want to run again for mayor in 1917. Yet, "as a good soldier" serving on the "Western front" of urban politics, he could not surrender the city to what he honestly thought was a pro-German Tammany Hall. He dreaded another term of office but need not have worried. His work on behalf of the Gary school system, UMT, and frugal government alienated the city's large ethnic vote. Moreover, his campaign was even worse than his record. While Tammany was out pressing the flesh, the mayor, according to his own supporters, was "sitting down and looking wise" and utterly failing "to keep in touch with the masses of voters." If Mitchel were unconsciously sabotaging his reelection, he finally showed some political skill. Carrying only 23 percent of the vote, he lost by the greatest plurality in the history of New York. His devoted followers, some of whom raised two million dollars to buy election officials, newspaper advertising, and editorial support, wrote him their condolences. Mitchel replied that he was "personally relieved beyond expression," glad "to be free from the annoyances and troubles," and happy to be able "to follow my own inclinations—an experience I have not enjoyed in a good many years." His loss, he concluded, "releases me for things that I really want to do."[10]

For the past two years Mitchel, not a wealthy man, had complained that his salary barely paid his expenses. Since March, 1915, newspapers were reporting that he would soon use his experience with municipal franchises to enter a lucrative business career. Nonetheless, when the Guggenheims offered $50,000 a year and a future partnership, Mitchel, finally "free to make some money, engaged in an effort to avoid it." More than wealth, he now craved a line commission in combat. But despite the fact that he held the highest rank at Plattsburg, the thirty-nine-year-old "boy mayor" was no young "soldier boy." Furthermore, his uncompromising stand for preparedness had alienated Woodrow Wilson, his former political mentor. Thus, when Mitchel volunteered for the fighting infantry, he was offered "the dust of a Bureau" at a "rotten" desk in Washington. Then, Army Air Force General George O. Squirer interceded to grant him the rare honor of enrollment in flight school. Although 80 percent of the combat air corps suffered casualties, 38,000 would-be knights still dreamed of engaging in celestial jousts. One might have thought that Mitchel, a political knight-errant with a penchant for high-speed auto driving, would have relished the corps, but he did not. Flying, lacking communitarian gratifications, simply was "not like service with troops." Mitchel, before 1915, never saw "15,000 men under as clean conditions, morally and physically, nor men animated by a higher spirit of patriotism" as he did at Plattsburg. He wished to recapture that camp's "remarkable spirit of genuine Americanism" during "these extraordinary times when sacrifice is a normal duty." But having no choice except a plane or desk, he went off to flight school hoping for eventual transfer to the line. Yet if Mitchel were old for the infantry, he was ancient for a corps whose flyers peaked at twenty-six. In 1918, a training flight accident killed him and his military ambition.[11]

Plans for Stability and Prosperity: Mediation, Americanization, Vocational Discipline, and Commercial Success

John Purroy Mitchel's martial communitarianism was not the only attempt to establish national unity through military preparedness. In 1914, when England's patriotic response to war extinguished threats of a general strike and a rebellion in Ulster, external belligerency seemed to have fostered internal harmony in Britain. England's "new social ideal" had a profound effect on Americans whose National Security League emulated Lord Robert's National Service League. Since 1902 those British gentlemen had argued that UMT would offset "the decay of the national spirit." Now their U.S. counterparts, feeling that their country was divided like prewar England, wanted their own army used "to do away with class feeling." Inequality would continue but the "rich and poor would learn to respect one another. Classes would not be abolished; but they would no longer be barriers to just understanding."[12]

To the preparedness movement, social unity was an ideological objective rather than simple profit-margin politics. It therefore ignored the Tom Mooney case, which presented an excellent opportunity to use national defense to destroy labor unions. Although the American Federation of Labor defended Mooney, a San Francisco union leader alleged to have bombed a preparedness parade, prominent movement leaders chose to support the federation's demands that army training be financed through progressive taxation and that inductees never police industrial strikes. They did this because, as one spokesman wrote, "The more antagonistic elements [such as capital and labor] which we combine in our movement, the nearer we shall [be to] achieving our real purpose—the rebuilding of national consciousness."[13]

Many military training advocates were already in contact with the AF of L through common membership in the National Civic Federation —an organization that supported company welfare programs, conservative trade unions, and industrial mediation in order to reform, and thus preserve, contemporary capitalism. By 1916, the Civic Federation's president and its preparedness committees (manned by Henry Stimson, Robert Bacon, and others) added a new proposal for social control: UMT to inculcate loyal "subordination" in America's work force. Unfortunately, the mere idea of such training aroused "utter" apathy, if not hostility, in the labor movement, which subsequently ignored the federation's military literature, preparedness meetings, and Plattsburg application blanks.[14]

As Plattsburgers occasionally admitted, they campaigned for compulsory induction precisely because most workers had no time, money, or desire to volunteer for their program. The camp, although a "class affair," nonetheless claimed to be a harmonious cross-section of society which proved that "military training would do more than anything else to make the country a real melting pot and build up national solidarity." Not entirely propaganda, such statements were often self-deceptions dreamed by wishful thinkers. Harvard philosophy professor Ralph Barton Perry was not known for sloppy writing, yet his official history of Plattsburg wavers between democratic mythology and elite actuality. He first declared that the camp was "an opportunity to know your fellow man rather than your class, your profession or your type." Then he ruefully acknowledged that it was "almost wholly confined to college, professional and businessmen."[15]

Unrepresentative "in fact," Plattsburg strove to be republican "in spirit" so that in its miniature society men might "learn to judge each other by the way each did his day's work, without reference as to who he was or where he came from." Consequently, its leaders tried to attract at least symbolic delegations from all social groups. When successful, they scrupulously treated all men alike. Thus, Privates Arthur Woods and John Purroy Mitchel dutifully obeyed their 1915 camp superiors: the New York City policemen instructing them in drill. Leonard Wood, for his part, took "special care to see that class or racial groups were never allowed to be together in one tent or company." When the assistant secretary of war asked him to house eight students from the University of Virginia together, Wood refused. "We want," he explained, "the camp to be absolutely democratic"; he was mixing all schools and bunking Robert Bacon with the city police.[16]

For upper-class moralists, military training became the long-awaited "artifice" by which to rebuild the social harmony supposedly existing in Puritan New England's preurban past. In addition to creating a village-like cohesion, it also was an Americanization program. Here too, elites believed that a social problem was a moral lapse. Some of them admitted to commercial concerns that diverted them from implanting patriotic principles. More often they felt others were to blame for the nation's lack of common moral standards. Overestimating their legendary forefathers who braved the wilderness in the name of faith, they naturally underestimated the contemporary immigrants who came in the wake of the pioneer myth. They consequently thought that the newcomers needed an ethical uplift exercise since they, unlike their predecessors, migrated for money. As Leonard Wood maintained, these immigrants had to "undergo a great deal of Americanizing before [they could] speak with people who have been here long enough to have traditions and ideals."[17]

Actually, until Congress prohibited the enlistment of non-English-speaking soldiers in 1894, the army traditionally assimilated immigrants when it filled up to one-half of its depleted ranks with "foreign paupers" whom it employed, educated, and transported West. Many of these men, after discharge, settled there on unoccupied land which, according to legend and Theodore Roosevelt, made them "distinctly American" by forcing them to "wage [an] unrelenting war" against the elements. By 1914, arguments made for UMT as the functional equivalent of the vanishing frontier resurrected the army as an acculturating institution that would make "real Americans of this foreign horde." According to Henry Stimson, its training would inspire "the great stream of immigration composed largely of men who never had the lesson of loyalty which was instilled into our fathers by the wars, the privations and the common experiences of our national growth."[18]

However condescending this point of view might be, it was not really racist. True genetic determinists like Henry Fairchild Osborn and

Madison Grant wanted to save their Nordic race by isolating America from Europe's "dysgenic" war—"class suicide on a gigantic scale." They thereby differed from Theodore Roosevelt, Robert Bacon, Leonard Wood, and the other interventionists who felt that a great patriotic experience could yet redeem the immigrants. This latter group of elites established the National Americanization Committee, which planned to use the army to teach recent arrivals their responsibilities, obligations, and duties. For Jacob Schiff, S. Stanwood Menken, Francis Kellor, and other organization members active in prewar Americanization programs, military training became a new solution to an old problem.[19]

Before the war, when future committee member Nicholas Murray Butler had confidence in America's racial harmony, he felt that the Balkans could solve their own nationality conflicts by adopting American federalism. At that time Butler was a pacifist who said that preparedness was militarism and that munitions dealers started wars. Then so-called hyphen pressure groups began to show him the tenacity of ethnic loyalties. By 1916, fearing that the country was "breaking up" into nationality blocs, he said that the United States had yet to solve "the problem of integrating America." By February, 1917, feeling that ethnicity had eclipsed "genuine patriotism," Butler came to endorse war as a "unifying force of national necessity and conscious national purpose."[20]

Besides assimilating immigrants and unifying social classes, UMT was supported to instill "habits of thoroughness and promptness" as well as "respect for the rights and property of others." It thus was supposed to improve the nation's industrial workers, approximately one-third of whom were foreign-born themselves. Through the nineteenth century and up to World War I, prominent businessmen often affected the army model for large-scale management. In America, former Civil War generals often became the "*captains* of [the railroad] industry." Not to be outdone, the directors of British transportation corporations assumed or maintained a military rank (as did Colonel Edmund Buckner of Standard Oil, Major William Ramsay of Du Pont Chemicals, and Captain William Jones of Carnegie Steel.) Meanwhile the Germans, using more than military titles, praised their army for training their factory labor, the least violent industrial workers in the Western world. This particular lesson was not lost on many Americans who previously approved the "military character" of the Germanic state in which "the men who ran their railroads and those who cleaned the streets went about their duties exactly as if under military direction." According to one magazine writer, Yankee capitalists, once jealous of Germany's technical schooling, now felt that that country's "industrial efficiency is largely due to its compulsory military service." Consequently, emulation was in order for American companies then energetically searching for ways to strengthen "factory patriotism" and "esprit de corps" in a national work force whose annual turnover rate was 115 percent for each industrial plant. By 1913, members of the New York State Chamber of Commerce were claiming that national guard training distinctly improved "the character of their employees." Three years later, a nationwide survey found that 889 commercial organizations were for UMT, with only 56 opposed.[21]

The Plattsburg enrollment committee tried to tap this verbal commitment to military training when it asked management to send its employees to Plattsburg camps "promoting discipline, order and good citizenship." Browne and Sharps Tool Manufacturers, for one, was eager to participate. It wanted to enlist fifty foremen to make them "more efficient leaders in the industrial army." But the most enthusiastic employers were usually Plattsburgers themselves. Robert Bacon, John Purroy Mitchel, and William Cooper Proctor (of Proctor and Gamble's) granted their employees military leaves, while Arthur Woods made army training an essential part of his police administration program.[22]

In 1914, after revelations "of a widespread alliance between police, gamblers and disorderly houses" in New York, Mayor Mitchel made reform of law enforcement a major goal of his incoming administration. The city's three previous police commissioners had been army men (two of them West Pointers) and he, wanting to use military discipline to turn patrolmen into "soldiers of peace," hoped to appoint another officer to office. Because Colonel George W. Goethals "had instilled [the highest] degree of efficiency and personal loyalty" into his Panama Canal work force, the mayor thought the colonel could control the cops. However, personal friends, former police officials, and even city newspapers warned Goethals ("the man who could get anything done") not to tarnish his sterling reputation attempting the "impossible" task of police reform: a job that "would kill any man that took it, in every sense of the word." When Goethals subsequently refused Mitchel's offer, the mayor asked Arthur Woods to handle "the stumbling block of every administration." Newspapers said that Mitchel was throwing a babe to the wolves; Woods himself thought he was entering "the graveyard of hope." Nonetheless, he took the job and triumphed.[23]

Although containing police corruption was an immense task, Woods's ambition transcended the reduction of graft. As a native Bostonian he had imbibed the principles articulated by that city's altruists in the nineteenth century. Then, when police work placed greater emphasis on lodging the homeless, finding lost children, and dealing with beggars, drunks, and tramps, charitable gentlemen felt the force should be "moral missionaries" to people in need. Raised in this tradition, Woods had asked his Groton students to join the urban police. Now outside the prep school, he told police to be, in effect, Groton graduates. But if New York City's "finest" were to become social service workers teaching cleanliness to the poor, Woods would have to do more than reverse the recent trend to focus law enforcement on traffic direction and felony control. He would have to transform cops whom one leading reformer called "the dirtiest, crookedest, ugliest lot of men combined . . . outside of Turkey or Japan."[24]

Undaunted, Woods set out to train his men for "noblesse oblige" by appointing new men to command the old police bureaucracy. Yet that by itself would be insufficient since honest supervision in the past just democratized graft, moving it out of the station and down to the beat. Woods would therefore have to make the whole force "into extraordinary men" who could "remain honest in the face of all temptation." Groton and the Gary school system, also confronting enticing vice, had trained their own charges through physical activity and moral instruction. Now Woods, trying to correct the drinking and gambling habits of the police, used parallel techniques on adults. With help from Groton's old physical education teacher, a retired British cavalryman, this former baseball coach organized a wholesome program of discipline-inducing athletics that placed gymnasiums and instructors in every station house.[25]

In addition to athletic exercises, Arthur Woods's police development program emphasized army instruction. Military discipline was not unprecedented in public administration, especially in New York. There, Elmira State Penitentiary officials had already made their best inmates into officers who marched convicts in martial formation through the prison day. Perhaps thinking that whatever worked with prisoners would also work with the police, Rochester appointed a West Pointer its deputy chief "to elevate the level of the cops." In Woods's own city, in 1895, Police Commissioner Theodore Roosevelt began to give out paramilitary medals for law enforcement heroism. Meanwhile his fellow municipal reformers, Civil War veteran George E. Waring and his staff of former army officers, uniformed their street and sanitation workers, marched them in close formation, and ordered them with martial authority. Yet none of these old soldiers out-soldiered Arthur Woods. (After one year's service in World War I, he was "Colonel Woods" for the rest of his life.) In 1907, when Woods directed the police department's school for recruits, he used a retired sergeant to build a "military carriage and spirit" in cadets who learned to drill better than any group outside the army itself. By May, 1914, after he became commissioner, he was placing an unprecedented emphasis on martial style from regimental parades to medals of honor. The world war only accelerated this prewar program.[26]

In 1915 Woods took forty police supervisors up to Plattsburg to learn "what it means to be an officer" and acquire a "better idea of command." (Apparently they learned by drilling Privates Woods and Mitchel.) The commissioner, delighted with their subsequent progress, declared: "I want to see as many of the force as possible attend [this camp]." For 1916, Leonard Wood and Arthur Woods built a special police encampment at Fort Wadsworth (New York) which accommodated 2,509 men over seven two-week shifts. After it was over, a grateful commissioner wrote the general: "I could not exaggerate the value this Camp has been to the efficiency and morale of the Police Department. The men who have been there have improved not merely in their technical knowledge but in the spirit in which they go at their work, in loyalty to their job. . . . [Your instructors] succeeded in infusing into the policemen who were at the Camp something of the fine spirit of the gentlemen and able officers that they are."[27]

As a schoolmaster, Woods had sent the poor back from the Groton summer camp with "higher ideas of cleanliness, discipline and moral strength." Now a police commissioner, he sent his subordinates back from Fort Wadsworth with "bright eyes, [an] elastic step, and renewed enthusiasm."[28]

Woods, persuaded by these results, increased the military atmosphere at his police training school. First he sent its director up to Plattsburg to "observe the work and draw from it all possible lessons of value to us." Then he obtained General Wood's personal advice on how to apply military protocol to police rank. Finally, he began training all cadets with military drills that purportedly developed "devotion," discipline, "teamwork and brotherhood." In this way a new "military spirit" replaced the traditional apathy, corruption, and collusion which Woods called the department's "inverted esprit de corps."[29]

The commissioner not only gave the department military training, he gave it his own probity, energy, and dedication. At least one of these factors must have been effective for, in the words of two leading scholars, Woods's tenure "set an unmatched record for the city." Virtually all the metropolitan papers, from *The Masses* through the *Brooklyn Eagle* to the *New York Times,* acclaimed Woods's accomplishments as did radicals, pacifists, and militarists alike: be they Lincoln Steffens, Amos Pinchot, or Leonard Wood. But perhaps the greatest possible plaudit came from Theodore Roosevelt, who painfully confessed that Woods was "the very best [commissioner] we have ever had—I speak with knowledge . . . until Woods' administration, I had always regarded myself as the best."[30]

Although Woods was not able to institutionalize his reforms, thus preventing the new patrolmen from becoming old cops after he left office, this only proved that the *Outlook* prematurely wrote that he was "a man who has achieved the impossible." But while Woods was in office, his "soldiers of the city" provided substantial ammunition for the universal military training movement. They seemed to be one work force that the service certainly improved.[31]

Despite the well-publicized military rejuvenation of the New York City police, much of the commercial community remained indifferent to the preparedness movement. Just as some soldiers wished to live apart from the world of business, many businessmen, who thought soldiers were "lazy or crazy," were convinced that the military did not mix with the marketplace. For years, American entrepreneurs felt that their competitive advantage over European industries lay in a pacific diplomacy that reduced taxes and preserved physical resources. Far from disclosing that suffering creates virtue, their cost-keeping calculations indicated to them that "soldiering" is loafing and "war is waste." Therefore most businessmen, primarily concerned with a labor shortage and an export boom, chose not to patronize the Plattsburg camps. Those who did usually let only "a reasonable number" of volunteers enroll. For example, Packard Motor Company President Henry Joy, a military school graduate and state militia officer, repeatedly declared that American society without UMT "was a rope of sand unfit for war or peace." However, he too made camp attendance optional and therefore ineffective. When given the choice between a Plattsburg purgatory or time on the job, most workers chose work. Nonetheless Joy was a relatively committed employer. Many other industrialists told Plattsburg recruiters that they simply had no interest in military camps.[32]

The business community, withholding its money as well as its men, left the whole preparedness movement woefully underfinanced. The National Security League, encountering "the greatest difficulties in getting contributions," raised only $600,000 in three and one-half years. The American Defense Society, gathering $90,000 in 1915, had to hire a professional fund raiser to be more effective. The Navy League received $60,000 in its banner year and the Army League's treasury held a few thousand dollars at most. The Junior Naval Reserve and the Vigilantes were run on shoestring budgets, and the National Association for Universal Military Training had trouble even paying for stenographic help. While "utterly disgusted" patriots railed at the "apathy existing on all sides" of a nation "wallowing in prosperity," Robert Bacon lamented that the preparedness movement "needed money more than anything else." In retrospect, Leonard Wood talked of the "*handful* of businessmen who helped put over the Plattsburg camps." [Italics mine.][33]

The Pursuit of Power: Henry Alexander Wise Wood and S. Stanwood Menken

One businessman who was very active in the preparedness movement was Henry Alexander Wise Wood (1866–1939), member of the U.S. Chamber of Commerce's Committee on National Preparedness, executive director of the National Security League, president of the Patriotic Education Association, and chairman of the Conference Committee on Preparedness. Wise Wood, a contradiction incarnate, was an entrepreneur who hated commercialism, a mass producer who hated mass society, a newspaper press inventor who abhorred most papers, a Nietzschean who condemned Germanic philosophy, and an engineer who wrote poetry. He also was the super-patriotic son of ex-Mayor Fernando Wood, New York City's notorious copperhead politician (a southern sympathizer in the Civil War) who once said soldiers were "vagabonds well paid [for] doing nothing."[34]

At seventeen Wise Wood joined a newspaper machinery company believing it provided a good business, "a great adventure," and a worthy "mission." In America, both church and state were relatively weak and tradition not as strong as innovation. A domestic power vacuum therefore existed for the media to fill. Walt Whitman dreamed that a popular poetry could "permeate the mass of American mentality"; Wise Wood sought power from other pages. Politically, he felt that newspapers would "govern the minds of men" by "creating the fashions [prevailing] in public thought." Personally, he desired to invent machines that could enlarge the editions of these sovereign institutions, thereby expanding their "opportunities for service." Thirteen years after entering the press industry, Wise Wood had married the boss's daughter and ascended to the presidency of what later became the Wood Newspaper Machinery Corporation. There he earned a good fortune, patented six hundred inventions, and won a gold medal from the Franklin Institute. He then turned his attention to poetry and prose, next to aeronautics, and ultimately to military preparedness.[35]

Between 1903 and 1908 Wise Wood wrote four critiques of mass society that were manifestoes for elite control. In a manner more typical of old Boston Brahmins than the son of a big city boss, he indicted America for avarice and indulgence pervading its society from rich to poor. Immigrants, flooding into the city, were exploiting immoral opportunities totally unknown to the "old Anglo-Saxon tenets of fair play." Politicians, seeking public office for private profit, should have led "the unthinking mass mind" but chose to appease the electorate instead. The rich, morally fatigued with pleasure, purchased politicians to do their bidding, churches to parrot their platitudes, and the world's greatest lawyers to be the "Fagins of modern commercialism." In so doing, they brought constitutional authority into contempt and thereby endangered the entire social order.[36]

Wise Wood believed that reform depended on public opinion, which was ultimately controlled by the popular press. Consequently, he zealously attacked the fourth estate. Newspapers, which purportedly pandered to mass vulgarity while they obscured corruption, were the worst of all commercial villains. Indeed, they were Wise Wood's own Carthage—to be conquered but not destroyed. Great concern about the media, such as his, was not uncommon in the Progressive Era. Liberals like John Dewey and Jane Addams felt that modern communications might provide an open forum for citizens to debate their common concerns. When reformed to be responsive, they felt it would create small town democracy on a national scale. Wise Wood, by contrast, had no such plan for free access to print. In principle, at least, he never decried media manipulation of public opinion. He only contested its present management. This, in itself, is understandable once one recognizes his envy of and responsibility for the publications he abhorred. Jealous of those circulation magnates who practiced government by newspaper, he complained that a corrupt few "alone may say in what manner shall be put into play the incalculable forces of suggestion and stimulation which lie in the bowels of these new-found and tremendous engines for the control of thought." At the same time he knew that his own sophisticated inventions made the mass press with its mass audience technically possible. In fact, Hearst and Pulitzer were two of his best customers.[37]

Perhaps Wise Wood wrote his social diatribes about the media for their cathartic effect since he lacked any concrete plan for social change. He talked about exposing immoral transactions and teaching honor over avarice. But he really had no idea how to make the all-mighty newspapers into the nation's tutor since a publicly regulated press could not control the public that regulated it. In lieu of real reform, Wise Wood had to satisfy himself with dreams of "morally regenerating" America's "paralyzed intellectual and moral perceptions." The new outlook he envisioned would replace the speculator's love of quick profit with the craftsman's love of labor and the "blind impulse of the unthinking mass mind" with rule by a natural elite. That elite would have the mental integrity to accept what only reason sanctioned, and reason led them away from Christian ignorance "to the clear dawn of the god-unneeding age of civilization." Like Nietzsche's Zarathustra, they rose to man's full potential by thrusting "back to their graves the grim hordes of the past hugging their implements of terror, worship and propitiation."[38]

War eventually became Wise Wood's instrument for social regeneration—a response foretold in the military analogues that ran through his
writings. In one essay he compared the rationalist's mental strength to
army discipline. In a poem the elite comprehend nature "with a fierce
joy, fierce as the joy of battle, which is sweeter than all of youth's
ecstasies." But before a timely world war gave Wise Wood a social
cause, this discontented industrialist turned to aviation to express his
frustrated will-to-power. He originally investigated aerodynamics to
help solve an atmospheric resistance problem occurring in high-speed
paper folding. From there he went on to preside over airplane clubs and
to found *Flying* magazine. The editorials which Wise Wood wrote for
this publication were nothing less than love poems to aircraft. Besides
declaiming "the thrill of power flight" as a supreme expression of the
warriors' masculine instincts, they announced a "new world of sensation" wherein an elite fraternity of men "extended the dominion of humanity" into the heavens by performing one of the few "deeds that
have dominated time." Later, Wise Wood's wife recalled that "nothing
ever thrilled him [like] rushing on [in aircraft] at those marvelous
speeds."[39]

However, Wise Wood's pleas to the contrary, Orville Wright treated
the "art" of aviation as if it were a business when he strewed his pat-
ents across the "upward struggle of the race." Consequently, aviation's
development had to rely on government subsidies, which were contingent upon its military potential. Hence, while the army air corps used
aeronautical research for military preparedness, Wise Wood used preparedness to promote aeronautics. Filling *Flying* magazine with articles
expounding the strategic importance of airplanes, he even published
one shocking story about a future war with Germany whose outcome
hinged on air supremacy.[40]

Nevertheless, comparative budgets reveal that America paid little
heed to Wise Wood's writings. On the eve of World War I, Italy was
spending ten times (and Mexico three times) U.S. appropriations for
army aircraft. Understandably, when combat broke out in 1914, Wise
Wood desperately welcomed this conflict as a "supreme" opportunity
to arouse a national commitment to flying. War itself, however, soon
became more interesting than airplanes which were, after all, just physical outlets for his socially thwarted will-to-power. By 1915 he was saying that this period had "suddenly become a dynamic age seething with
gigantic action." Since the war forced men to "think in heroic dimen-
sions," it presented a golden chance for leaders with vision to point
their country towards "a new destiny, new purposes and new goals."
The nation was now "rotten with individual selfishness, sectional prejudice [and] class jealousy." Its citizens were "slovenly, undisciplined,

inefficient and unhealthy." But considering the "physical, social and industrial advantages" that universal military service gave Germany, the same program in America would "inculcate habits of high moral value such as *obedience, respect for authority* and mental cleanliness." In this way "an orderly community" could yet arise from near anarchy.[41]

Because preparedness finally provided Wise Wood with a program to change the society he despised, he neglected poetry and planes to take up this crusade. One of his rivals said that Wise Wood, who fought anybody that threatened his position in the preparedness movement, was using the issue for "self-glorification." No doubt this was true. When the movement began, the satiric H. L. Mencken said that Wise Wood was really a hotel waiter and hardly anyone knew who was playing a prank—he or Mencken. Then Wise Wood, making up to seven preparedness speeches a week, began to emerge from the obscurity which heretofore engulfed him. Yet even if he did crave power and prestige, he only took them on his own moral terms. As president of the American Society of Aeronautical Engineers, he was appointed to the Wilson administration's Naval Advisory Board. There, he pleaded for a comprehensive preparedness program. When he failed, he abandoned his entree into government circles with a public resignation that called the secretary of the navy "wholly incompetent" and our national policy "dangerously weak."[42]

Now free from the administration, Wise Wood set out to "remasculate America." While he fought back the urge to send "ladies underwear" to Washington's "squawmen," he could not forego the "great pleasure" of assailing Wilson for pacifism and the country as a whole for "seething with spies." His "agitated" attacks on a ubiquitous Germanic-socialistic-pacifistic "Trinity of Treason" did not help the preparedness movement appear rational, yet it probably satisfied his own emotional need to attack the great body of "national defectives." Conspiracies, by the newspapers or the pacifists, provided a psychologically satisfying excuse for Wise Wood's previous political failures and made tangible targets for his present hostility. While others enlisted for duty overseas, he prepared to search out and destroy the enemy at home.[43]

At least one man whom Wise Wood tried to repress was certainly no pacifist. S. Stanwood Menken (1870–1954), the founder and president of the National Security League (NSL), resembled him so closely that these two frustrated men were bound to compete for leadership in the preparedness movement. Menken, a direct descendant of Haym Salomon, the colonial financier, was a member of a distinguished Jewish family that migrated to America in 1690. After graduating from Columbia University's law school, he became a prominent New York City attorney representing utility companies and local banking institutions. He was also active in the gentlemen-political organizations that claimed to champion municipal administration by expertise and intellect. If they failed to defeat "partisan politics," Menken predicted that property taxes would burden his class and general mismanagement would lead to socialism. But Menken's reforms never quite succeeded and his pessimism consequently grew. The American people, he once said, momentarily arouse themselves to elect an independent, but then let the city drift back to the machine.[44]

Menken's personal ambitions were thwarted along with reform. To no avail he relinquished his religious affiliation, altered his name (from "Solomon S." to "S. Stanwood") and married into a Gentile mugwump family politically close to Theodore Roosevelt. He thus gained admission to the exclusive City Club (the upper-class municipal think-tank) but never could get the judgeship or the congressional seat he craved. As Menken admitted, he simply could not succeed with "the political powers that be."[45]

But Menken reasoned that those powers would not be powers if preparedness triumphed, since America's military problems were "merely symptomatic of a general national inefficiency." Consequently, in December, 1914, he selected the NSL's cofounders from the Reform Club, the City Club, and other patrician political societies. Under his tutelage, the league made preparedness into an "economy and efficiency" issue which underscored, in a nationwide lecture series, the military perils of pork barrel legislation, boss rule, and government waste. Although Henry Alexander Wise Wood complained of this "tendency to set the defense movement to work on innumerable social problems before it finished its work for . . . fighting men and fighting machines," Menken maintained that national security necessitated a thorough public appreciation of "what good government means as developed by the most progressive nations."[46]

His favorite "progressive" nation was the homeland of the Von Briesens, his intensely proud German-born in-laws. Menken, preparing America to fight the nation he admired, illustrated the contemporary observation "that those persons who most loudly curse Germany are most anxious that we should follow her lead." He specifically admired that country's ability to apply "duty to the State" to every aspect of life. If the preparedness movement could inculcate that same spirit in America, thereby educating "the unfortunates to better serve the Nation as citizens in peace as well as war," then "good government" by "the very best people" was still feasible here. War, forcing the United States to emulate Germany in order to defeat her, seemed to present

duty to the state

reincarnation of the national soul

an ideal opportunity to abolish "self-centered politics." This "reincarnation of the national soul" would, Menken concluded, finally enable America "to make democracy safe for the world."[47]

NOTES

1. George Haven Putnam: *Memoirs of My Youth, 1844–1865* (New York: Putnam's, 1914), pp. 287, 295; *Memoirs of a Publisher, 1865–1915* (New York: Putnam's, 1915), pp. 26, 115, 118, 169. Putnam to Theodore Roosevelt, Aug. 6, 1918, Dec. 4, 1918, Roosevelt MSS, Reels 288, 303.

2. Sondra Herman, *Eleven Against War: Studies in American International Thought, 1898–1921* (Stanford: Hoover Institute Press, 1969), pp. 23, 27, 30–31, 42–43; Lyman Abbott to Theodore Roosevelt, May 25, 1907, Roosevelt MSS, Reel 72; Marchand, *American Peace Movement and Social Reform*, pp. 41–45, 55, 63.

3. Frederic Rene Coudert, "The Reminiscences of Frederic Rene Coudert," pp. 21–26, Oral History Project, Columbia University; Coudert to Theodore Roosevelt, Nov. 6, 1911, Roosevelt MSS, Reel 116; Coudert to Nicholas Murray Butler, Jan. 6, 1925, Sept. 8, 1931, Dec. 17, 1934, Jan. 26, 1938: all in Butler MSS; Frederic Rene Coudert, *A Half Century of International Problems* (New York: Columbia University Press, 1954), p. 195.

4. Coudert to Theodore Roosevelt, Dec. 21, 1915, Roosevelt MSS, Reel 203; Coudert to Nicholas Murray Butler, Oct. 2, 1917, Butler MSS. Coudert quoted in *New York Times*, Aug. 26, 1916; Chambers, "Conscripting for Colossus," p. 89. Coudert, "Reminiscences of Frederic Rene Coudert," pp. 69–70.

5. Raymond Fosdick, *Chronicle of a Generation: An Autobiography* (New York: Harper & Brothers, 1958), p. 82; McClellan, *The Gentleman and the Tiger*, p. 292. In describing Mitchel and his followers, military metaphors seemed naturally appropriate to Robert Carro, *The Power Broker: Robert Moses and the Fall of New York* (New York: Knopf, 1974), pp. 62–63, 76.

6. John Purroy Mitchel to Mrs. Robert Balentine, Nov. 16, 1916; Benjamin Schlessinger to Mitchel, July 26, 1915, Mitchel MSS, Box 18; *New York Times*, Apr. 9, 10, 11, 12, 1914.

7. Melvin Dubofsky, *When Workers Organize: New York City in the Progressive Era* (Amherst: University of Massachusetts Press, 1968), esp. pp. 93–97, 126–47; Edwin R. Lewinson, *John Purroy Mitchel, The Boy Mayor of New York* (New York: Astra, 1965), pp. 135–37; Lewis Noschkes to Mitchel, May 1, 1916; William Einhorn to Mitchel, Sept. 27, 1917, Mitchel MSS, Boxes 17, 18.

8. For the progressive ideal and Mitchel's admission of "futility," see Martin J. Schiesel, *The Politics of Efficiency: Municipal Administration and Reform in America, 1880–1920* (Berkeley: University of California Press, 1977), pp. 158. 190; Dubofsky, *When Workers Organize*, pp. 142–43. Mitchel to Rev. Charles W. Welch, Apr. 5, 1915, Mitchel MSS, Box 25; statements of Mitchel in *Proceedings of the National Security Conference*, Jan. 20–22, 1916 (New York: National Security League, n.d.), p. 353; *Proceedings of the Congress of Constructive Patriotism*, Jan. 25–27, 1917 (New York: National Security League, 1917), p. 188.

9. Mitchel to Rev. John W. Page, Apr. 18, 1917, Mitchel MSS, Box 18; Mitchel quoted in unidentified newspaper clipping in Leonard Wood MSS, Box 258; Henry H. Curran, *Pillar to Post* (New York: Scribner's, 1941), p. 192; Theodore Roosevelt, Jr., to Theodore Rousseau, Dec. 29, 1939, Roosevelt, Jr., MSS, Box 139.

10. The first quotations are from Otto T. Barnard to Mitchel, Nov. 7, 1917; Mitchel to Leonard Wood, Oct. 27, 1917; Ernest Cuzzo to Teddy [Rousseau?], Sept. 20, 1917: all in Mitchel MSS, Box 18. Allen, "The Reminiscences of William H. Allen," pp. 376–80. The final quotations from Mitchel are from Mitchel to Theodore Roosevelt, Nov. 12, 1917; Mitchel to Joseph Buhler, Nov. 9, 1917; Mitchel to Eugene Daly, Nov. 12, 1917; Mitchel to Myron T. Herrick, Nov. 8, 1917: all in Mitchel MSS, Box 18.

11. *Brooklyn Eagle,* Mar. 24, 1915; *Boston Evening Transcript,* July 16, 1918; *New York Globe,* Nov. 18, 1916; Mitchel to Capt. John Kelley, Nov. 8, 1917; Mitchel to Leonard Wood, Nov. 21, 1917; Mitchel to Robert Adamson, June 3, 1918: all in Mitchel MSS, Boxes 18, 19. For the air corps, see Charles Genthe, *American War Narratives, 1917–1918* (New York: David Lewis, 1969), pp. 14–15, 47–48, 90–91. Mitchel quoted on Plattsburg in unidentified newspaper clipping, Leonard Wood MSS, Box 258; statement of Mitchel in *Proceedings of the National Security Congress,* p. 351; Mitchel to William Meloney, June 5, 1918; Mitchel to Leonard Wood, June 13, 1918, both in Mitchel MSS, Box 19.

12. For England, see Arthur Marwick, *The Deluge: British Society and the First World War* (New York: Norton, 1970), esp. pp. 47–49, 134–35; Thomas Kennedy, "The Endangered Empire and the Nation in Arms: The National Service League in Edwardian England" (unpublished paper in possession of this writer). Speech by Grace Power in *Proceedings of the Congress of Constructive Patriotism,* p. 12.

13. Robert Bacon cited in *New York Times,* Mar. 5, 1916, 1:18; G. Edward Buxton to Halstead Dorey, Apr. 11, 1916; Dorey to Buxton, Apr. 12, 1916, Plattsburg Barracks File, Box 1785, National Archives.

14. For the National Civic Federation in general, see James Weinstein, *The Corporate Ideal in the Liberal State, 1900–1918* (Boston: Beacon Press, 1968), passim. For its military training activities, see *New York Times,* Jan. 18, Jan. 19, Jan. 23, 1917; Ralph Easley to Henry Stimson, May 18, 1916, Aug. 11, 1916, Sept. 7, 1916; Easley to George Chamberlain, Dec. 15, 1916: all in National Civic Federation MSS, Boxes 53, 79A, 187, New York Public Library.

15. Delancey K. Jay to Grenville Clark, n.d., Clark MSS. The long quotation is from Leonard Wood to Henry Joy, July 28, 1916, Wood MSS, Box 90. Perry, *Plattsburg Movement,* p. 38.

16. The long quotation is from Leonard Wood to C. P. J. Mooney, Aug. 28, 1917, Wood MSS, Box 96. Three unidentified newspaper clippings in Leonard Wood MSS, Box 258; William Ingraham to Leonard Wood, May 11, 1916; Wood to Ingraham, May 12, 1916, Wood MSS, Box 89.

17. Edward George Hartmann, *The Movement to Americanize the Immigrant* (2d. ed.; New York: AMS Press, 1967), pp. 39–43, 56, 93; Solomon, *Ancestors and Immigrants,* pp. 54, 198; statement of John Purroy Mitchel in *Proceedings of*

the *Congress of Constructive Patriotism,* p. 188; Leonard Wood to W. A. Kobbe, July 17, 1916, Wood MSS, Box 89.

18. Bruce White, "The American Military and the Melting Pot in World War I," *War and Society in North America,* ed. J. L. Granatstein and R. D. Cuff (Toronto: Thomas Nelson & Sons, 1971), pp. 37–39; Theodore Roosevelt, *The Winning of the West: Works of Theodore Roosevelt,* 9:18–19. The third quotation is from Leonard Wood in an unidentified newspaper clipping, Wood MSS, Box 258. Stimson, *Issues of the War,* p. 16.

19. Henry Fairchild Osborn, "Preface" in Madison Grant, *The Passing of the Great White Race* (2d ed.; New York: Scribner's, 1923), p. xiii; ibid., pp. 230–32; *New York Times,* Oct. 17, 1915, 2:1–2; John Higham, *Strangers in the Land: Patterns of American Nativism, 1860–1925* (New York: Atheneum, 1966), pp. 242–50.

20. Nicholas Murray Butler, *A World in Ferment* (New York: Scribner's 1917), pp. 28–34, 154, 159; Butler to Frederic Rene Coudert, Nov. 9, 1916, Leonard Wood MSS, Box 87.

21. Leonard Wood to Ernest H. Abbott, July 24, 1916, Wood MSS, Box 86; Hobsbawn, *Age of Capital,* pp. 216–17. For German praise for their military training, see John R. Freeman to George Goethals, Jan. 26, 1917, Goethals MSS, Box 22, Library of Congress. For American praise of German militarism, see John J. Pershing quoted in Donald Smythe, *Guerrilla Warrior: The Early Life of John J. Pershing* (New York: Scribner's, 1973), p. 139; Ellery Sedgwich to Leonard Wood, Oct. 16, 1914, Wood MSS, Box 90. For American businessmen and business conditions, see Thomas Cochran, *200 Years of American Business* (New York: Basic Books, 1971), pp. 54–55, 167; Rodgers, *Work Ethic in Industrial America,* pp. 46, 61, 88, 162–64; New York Chamber of Commerce to "Sir," Dec. 12, 1913, Wood MSS, Box 75; "Press release of July 24, 1916," Henry Stimson MSS.

22. *Washington Post,* May 4, 1916; G. Edward Buxton to Halstead Dorey, Apr. 11, 1916, Plattsburg Barracks File, Box 1785.

23. Aldermanic Report of 1912 quoted in *New York Times,* Dec. 6, 1925, 9:8; Mitchel quoted in *New York Chronicle,* May 20, 1916. On Goethal's reputation, see Stallings, *Doughboys,* p. 206. John R. Freeman to Goethals, Jan. 26, 1914; Mabel Boardman to Goethals, Jan. 24, 1914: both in Goethals MSS, Box 22; *New York Times,* Jan. 24, 1914. Mitchel quoted in *New York Tribune,* Jan. 19, 1915. For initial newspaper reaction to Woods, see *New York Herald,* Apr. 8, 1914; *New York Evening Sun,* Apr. 8, 1914. Woods quoted in *New York Tribune,* Mar. 19, 1915.

24. On old Boston and modern police work, see Roger Lane, *Policing the City: Boston, 1822–1885* (New York: Atheneum, 1971), pp. 48–49, 60–64; Eric H. Monkkonen, *Police in Urban America, 1860–1920* (New York: Cambridge University Press, 1981), passim. Reformer Rev. C. H. Parkhurst quoted in Richard Skolnick, "The Crystalization of Reform in New York City, 1894–1917" (Ph.D. diss., Yale University, 1964), p. 154. For Woods's philosophy, see Woods, *The Policeman and the Public* (New Haven: Yale University Press, 1919), pp. 42, 62–63, 157.

25. *New York Times,* Jan. 2, Jan. 3, 1915; White, "Man Who Has Achieved the Impossible," p. 127; Woods quoted in *New York American,* Feb. 23, 1915; *New York City Police Department Annual Report,* 1915, p. xiv.

26. Gilbert, *Work without Salvation,* p. 145. Maj. F. H. Schoeffel to George Goethals, Jan. 23, 1914, Goethals MSS, Box 22; Skolnick, "George Edwin Waring, Jr.," pp. 356–59; statement of Arthur Woods in New York City Board of Aldermen, *Record and Reports of the Committee to Investigate the Police Department,* 1912, pp. 3946–49; *New York Press,* May 17, 1914.

27. Arthur Woods to Ralph Barton Perry, Perry MSS, Harvard University Archives; Woods quoted in *New York Times,* Aug. 7, 1915; *New York City Police Department Report: 1914–1917,* pp. 90–91; Woods quoted in *New York Sun,* Aug. 24, 1915; Woods to Leonard Wood, Sept. 18, 1916, Wood MSS, Box 75.

28. Arthur Woods et al., *Statement of Groton School Summer Camp Committee,* 1900, copy in Groton School Papers, Franklin Roosevelt Presidential Library; *New York City Police Department Report: 1914–1917,* p. 92.

29. Arthur Woods to Halstead Dorey, Sept. 2, 1915, Plattsburg Barracks File, Box 1780; Woods to Leonard Wood, Sept. 11, 1915, Wood MSS, Box 82; Arthur Woods, "The Making of a Good Police Force," *Weekly Review* 3 (Sept. 29, 1920):643; Woods to Endicott Peabody, Nov. 16, 1906, Peabody MSS, Box 35.

30. The first quotation is from Wallace Sayre and Herbert Kaufman, *Governing New York City: Politics in the Metropolis* (New York: Norton, 1965), p. 693. *Brooklyn Eagle,* Nov. 2, 1916; *The Masses,* Apr., 1915; *New York Times,* Apr. 9, 1915; Ella Winters, ed., *The Letters of Lincoln Steffens* (New York: Harcourt & Brace, 1938), 2:605; statement of Amos Pinchot in Senate, *Hearings on Universal Military Training,* 64th Cong., 2d Sess., 1917, pp. 646–47; Leonard Wood to Douglas Haig, Sept. 5, 1918, Wood MSS, Box 113; Theodore Roosevelt to John J. Pershing, Sept. 6, 1918, Roosevelt MSS, Reel 408.

31. White, "Man Who Has Achieved the Impossible," p. 48. *New York Times,* May 7, 1916, 7:2.

32. Henry Ford quoted on soldiers in David Noble, *The Progressive Mind, 1890–1917* (Minneapolis: Burgess Publishing, 1982), p. 42. For more on the business community and the other quotations, see Marchand, *American Peace Movement and Social Reform,* pp. 80–85. The founder of "scientific [business] management" coined the opprobrious term "soldiering." Henry Joy to Leonard Wood, Dec. 8, 1916; Joy to Nehemiah Boyston, Sept. 4, 1915: both in Wood MSS, Box 88. Horace Stebbins to Endicott Peabody, Jan. 17, 1916, Peabody MSS, Box 66.

33. U.S. Congress, House, Special Committee to Investigate the National Security League, *Hearings on the National Security League,* 65th Cong., 3rd Sess., 1919, p. 2063; American Defense Society, *Confidential Statement of Finances,* n.d., copy in Charles Bonaparte MSS, Box 210; Finnegan, *Against the Specter of a Dragon,* p. 162; Armin Rappaport, *The Navy League* (Detroit: Wayne State University Press, 1962), pp. 77–78; Hermann Hagedorn to Theodore Roosevelt, Dec. 15, 1915, Roosevelt MSS, Reel 211; H. H. Sheets to Frank Depew, Nov. 6, 1917, National Association for Universal Military Training MSS, Box 10, Library of Congress. The quotations are from Horace Stebbins

to Endicott Peabody, Jan. 17, 1916, Peabody MSS, Box 66; William T. Horna-day to Theodore Roosevelt, June 12, 1916, Roosevelt MSS, Reel 211; Robert Bacon to Lt. Gen. Young, Oct. 27, 1916, Nat. Ass. for UMT MSS, Box 6; Leonard Wood to John G. Hibben, May 10, 1920, Wood MSS, Box 152.

34. Wise Wood to Theodore Roosevelt, Sept. 17, 1917, Roosevelt MSS, Reel 246; *New York Times,* June 7, 1915. Fernando Wood quoted in Arthur A. Ekrich, Jr., *The Civilian and the Military* (New York: Oxford University Press, 1956), p. 113.

35. Wise Wood quoted in *New York Times,* July 1, 1928, 9:4; Henry Alexander Wise Wood, *Progress in Newspaper Manufacture and Its Effects Upon the Printing Industry* (New York: Wood Newspaper Manufacturing, 1932), pp. 10, 12; Wise Wood quoted in *New York Times,* Apr. 10, 1939; *The National Cyclopedia,* 91:26–27.

36. Henry Alexander Wise Wood: *A Philosophy of Success* (New York: William Ritchie, 1905), pp. 7–9; *Money Hunger: A Brief History of Commerical Immorality in the United States* (New York: Putnam's, 1908), pp. 8, 46, 51–52, 55, 64, 70, 110.

37. Ibid., pp. 24, 30, 33, 43, 48. For liberals, see Quandt, *From Small Town to Great Community,* esp. 55–56, 66, 116, 140. Wise Wood, *Progress in Newspaper Manufacturing and Its Effects Upon Printing Industry,* p. 11; *New York Times,* July 4, 1918.

38. Wise Wood: *Money Hunger,* pp. 52, 55, 84, 126, 131; *Philosophy of Success,* pp. 10–12; *The Book of Symbols* (Boston: Plimpton Press, 1904), pp. 35–36.

39. Wise Wood: *Philosophy of Success,* p. 20; *Book of Symbols,* p. 33. *Flying* (Sept., 1915):60, (Mar., 1913):20, (Dec., 1915):779, (Nov., 1912):18; Elizabeth Wood to Orville Wright, Apr. 25, 1939, Wright MSS, Box 57, Library of Congress.

40. Wise Wood to Orville Wright, Feb. 4, Feb. 14, Feb. 25, Mar. 14, 1914: all in Wright MSS, Box 57; *Flying* (Nov., 1912):19; (Jan., 1913):18–19; (May, 1914):14.

41. Comparative budgets are listed in I. B. Holley, Jr., *Ideas and Weapons: Exploitation of the Aerial Weapon by the United States During World War I* (New Haven: Yale University Press, 1953), p. 29. Speech by Wise Wood, Mar. 30, 1917, copy in Leonard Wood MSS, Box 100; Wise Wood, *America, Look into Your Heart* (New York: National Security League, n.d.), p. 4; Wise Wood quoted in *Salt Lake Tribune,* Jan. 10, 1917; Wise Wood to Theodore Roosevelt, Nov. 16, 1915, Aug. 4, 1916, Roosevelt MSS, Reels 202, 207; Wise Wood, "What the Army Needs," *Independent* 89 (Feb. 19, 1917): 304.

42. Philip Roosevelt to Theodore Roosevelt, Nov. 26, 1916, Roosevelt MSS, Reel 216. William Henry Harbaugh in "Wilson, Roosevelt and Intervention: 1914–1917" (Ph.D. diss., Northwestern University, 1954) relates this item about Mencken without comment, thereby suggesting that he is not sure if this remark was serious. *New York Times,* Dec. 23, 1915.

43. Wise Wood to Mrs. Wilfred Du Puy, May 22, 1916; Wise Wood to Theodore Roosevelt, June 22, 1916, Oct. 31, 1916: all in Roosevelt MSS, Reels 210, 211, 215. Wise Wood described by unidentified newspaper clipping in Leonard Wood MSS, Box 258. *New York Times,* Jan. 24, 1917, Mar. 14, 1917.

44. Wise Wood to Menken, Nov. 24, Nov. 26, 1917, Theodore Roosevelt MSS, Reel 253; *New York Times,* Sept. 2, 1938; House, *Hearing on National Security League,* 65th Cong., 3rd Sess., 1919, pp. 258–60, 287, 290, 346, 464, 472; S. Stanwood Menken: *A Concept of National Service* (n.p.: National Security League, 1918), pp. 3–5; *Knowledge by the People, True Basis of National Security* (n.p.: National Security League, 1917), p. 7.

45. Menken to Oswald Garrison Villard, Dec. 20, 1924, Villard MSS, Harvard University. House, *Hearings on National Security League,* 65th Cong., 3rd Sess., 1919, p. 319.

46. Menken quoted in *Our Country* (National Security League newsletter) (June-July, 1916), p. 1; Menken to Nicholas Murray Butler, Dec. 15, 1914, Butler MSS; speech by Menken in *Proceedings of the Congress of Constructive Patriotism,* p. 19; Wise Wood to Theodore Roosevelt, Jan. 5, 1917, Roosevelt MSS, Reel 219; S. Stanwood Menken, *Annual Report of the President of the National Security League,* May 3, 1916, p. 5.

47. William Lyons Phelps quoted in *New York Times,* Apr. 9, 1916; S. Stanwood Menken, "National Defense and Efficiency," *Scientific Monthly* 2 (Apr., 1916): 356–58; speech by Menken in *Proceedings of the Congress of Constructive Patriotism,* pp. 15, 19; Menken, *Concept of National Service,* pp. 3–5, 10.

CHAPTER 7

World War I: Victory and Defeat at Home and Abroad

☆

IN 1916, WHEN Woodrow Wilson ran for reelection, emphasizing peace and prosperity, he believed that America desired neutrality "no matter how many lives were lost at sea." On the other side of the partisan aisle, Theodore Roosevelt, stressing war and sacrifice, agreed that "the country is not in a heroic mood." In January, 1917, two months after Wilson's victory conclusively proved that the United States did not want purification through pain, the preparedness movement reconvened at the National Security League's Congress of Constructive Patriotism. Its proceedings record a 340-page jeremiad summarized in Elihu Root's exhortation "to stir" the nation "out of the lethargy into which [it has] fallen. We had," he said, "reached this condition of indifference and sluggish patriotism through decadence. As we have grown rich in material things we have grown poor in spirit."[1]

However, neither Root nor Roosevelt could save America now. Only the Germans could do that and they did it, four days after Root's sermon, by declaring unlimited submarine warfare. This action left the general public perplexed since it wanted neither war nor retreat from the seas. While the country in a quandary sought guidance from Wilson, preparedness leaders organized meetings and letter-writing campaigns to stampede the administration into war. They later believed that their pressure proved decisive, but their true effect remains problematic at best. On a conscious level the president appears to have paid them little heed. Nonetheless, one may speculate that Roosevelt and his colleagues might have influenced Wilson's unconscious calculations since, on other occasions, they affected his stance on military defense and political repression. Because subliminal thoughts lie beyond the realm of historical fact, the ultimate impact of the preparedness movement may never be known. In any case, military training leaders certainly welcomed the war they desperately tried to declare. As one Security League executive recalled: "I breathed freely for the first time [in] months. It seemed to me we were losing our souls."[2] Now he and his comrades would seek to recapture what they feared they had lost.

During the war, preparedness advocates used civilian repression and military education to help purify their country through the crucible of combat. Lest negotiations terminate this golden opportunity, vigilantes from the NSL and the American Defense Society coerced reluctant citizens to support unconditional surrender. Meanwhile Theodore Roosevelt, having failed to unify America through political institutions, hoped to employ the army to consolidate society. Although he did not receive the commission he craved, other proponents of universal military training were more fortunate than he. Henry Stimson, Leonard Wood, Arthur Woods, and Grenville Clark respectively, were senior officers in the 77th and 89th Infantry Divisions, the army air force flight school, and the Student Army Training Corps. There, they practiced the military indoctrination they previously preached. Partly due to their efforts the foreign born, the native born, and the college bound alike experienced the discipline of army life. If the preparedness movement failed to make war an occasion for uplift, it was not for lack of effort.

Unconditional Surrender, Theodore Roosevelt, and the Search for Social Unity

Once war was declared, preparedness movement leaders, feeling that "the nation is to be saved by the very blood and tears that it must shed," worked to preserve their martial purgatory from an early armistice. They favored unconditional surrender, rather than negotiations, because they believed that "we in America have but commenced our share of suffering and sacrifice." From France, Theodore Roosevelt, Jr., wrote his father that a "cancerous growth had formed in all departments of the republic. The war looks as if it could be [another] three months or three years. For our country's sake I hope the latter." From New York, his father wrote the newspapers that "now at last we can hold our heads aloft... [and] cherish forever sorrowful but glorious memoirs of this World War." He consequently reversed his initial belief that "smashing Germany" would create "a disaster." Instead, he now warned America that its "moral salvation" could not withstand a "craven peace" that stopped short of beating the Hun "to his knees."[3]

Although Roosevelt was out of office when the European war began in August, 1914, he still was analyzing international politics from a presidential perspective of enlightened self-interest. Accordingly indifferent to any "abstract right or wrong," he was primarily concerned with the balance of world power. Lest that equilibrium be upset to the advantage of Germany, Russia, or Japan, Roosevelt supported the type of conciliatory peace without victory that he tried to negotiate between the great powers at Portsmouth and Algeciras in 1905 and 1906. He specifically felt that America's armed intervention (a "folly" reaping "bloodshed and misery") would subvert the status quo that protected his country from "a frightful calamity."[4]

Between 1898 and 1915, Roosevelt's geopolitical perspective vacillated from the romantic to the realistic. His domestic policy was far more consistent: always striving to produce national harmony. As a New Yorker with a southern mother and a western ranch, he felt uniquely suited to overcome sectionalism. A Harvard man bred from Dutch, Scotch, and Gallic stock, he thought he symbolized amalgamated Americanism. His goals were consistent, his tactics somewhat fluid. While out of the high echelons of power in the mid-1890s, he hoped that a common struggle against Spain would breed common sentiments. In the presidency in the early 1900s, he felt that the expansion of his executive authority would promote the unity for which he worked. However, the normal political process compromised his efforts to take up the "cause of mankind" and "do battle for the Lord." As would any candidate for office, Roosevelt had to sacrifice some prospective members of his comprehensive consensus. Long feeling it "hopeless" to reconcile blacks and whites, except when they fought together as in the Spanish-American War, he gave up the Negroes, traditionally loyal to him and his party, to make political inroads in the Democratic South. Then, he ignored trust busters from the Middle and Far West to court enlightened capitalists largely from the East. "In politics," he once confessed, "we have to do a great many things we ought not to do."[5]

Roosevelt's Rough Rider legend suggests that as a nation builder he was most successful when a soldier. Perhaps this is why war could still become for him a viable alternative to politics. In late August, 1914, after his country appeared "sick and tired of [his domestic] reforms," he reverted to his prepresidential notion that combat was a consensus creating adventure replete with moral value. He then began to say that the European war was a purification rite bringing out "everything that is best in [England's] national character." Soon, he was writing Britain's ambassador that "your country is passing through the flame and will come out cleansed and refined. Mine is passing through the thick yellow mud-stream of 'safety first.'"[6]

Roosevelt and other preparedness leaders had no illusions about combat conditions in World War I. By the time America intervened in 1917, three years of slaughter had long dispelled all predictions of quick, climactic battles chivalrously fought on the open field. "This terrible cataclysm" was now an "open book" whose tales of heavy artillery, mud trenches, and vermin were well known to any casual reader of the *Harvard Bulletin*. But believing in redemption through "suffering" in "this dreadful fiery furnace," Roosevelt and his colleagues anticipated salutary reactions to martial privations. They felt, in Robert Bacon's words, that combat would exact an "awful price, but the soul of the nation would be tested in the crucible."[7]

To participate in this battlefield purgatory, Roosevelt was willing to sacrifice his chance for another presidential term. Friends worried, and he recognized, that President Wilson could entomb him in the army, tying him up in restrictions to ensure his obscurity. And yet, to command a division in World War I, Roosevelt risked "military lockjaw," temporarily censored his partisan activities, and pledged his loyalty to Wilson, a man whom he "despised." When that "abject coward" would not declare war for Roosevelt nor grant him his commission, he was "quite willing to accept the Presidency." Then he could initiate hostilities and retire into combat.[8]

Although Roosevelt was ready to sacrifice the oval office for a pup tent, he was certainly not renouncing his public ambition. Planning a bigger and better version of his old Rough Riders, he transferred his aspirations from politics to war. To exemplify sectional harmony to America's "parochial people," his new division recruited men from every state and planned to mix them within each regiment. In its officer corps, direct descendents of Generals Lee, Jackson, Grant, and Sheridan would compose a "splendid gesture that makes nations." Sectional integration thereby accomplished, the division assembled a social cross-section of American life by deliberately recruiting stockbrokers and chauffeurs, lawyers and mechanics, actors and miners, bankers and truckdrivers, clubmen and policemen, Joseph Howland Coit, Senator James Wadsworth, and those cowboys who survived their colonel's last command. Ethnically, it contained Russian Jews, Irish Catholics, and "the largest possible" German-born contingent, as evidence that "we are all Americans and nothing else." Racially, it would have at least two "colored" regiments, one to be led by a Negro colonel with full power over all subordinates. Hence Roosevelt would do in the army what he could not do in the White House: appoint "worthy" black men, often barred from civil service, to command positions from which they might win the esteem that would elevate their race.[9]

While Roosevelt's troops would be an American microcosm, his senior officers would be the best in the army. Reflecting subsequent credit on his judgement, virtually all the men he chose compiled outstanding war records. The division's prospective chief of staff, anticipating its exploits, declared that "it will be the greatest and finest experience of a lifetime to serve under the Colonel with the men and opportunities he has bound together." The colonel, of course, agreed. His division, the Rough Riders writ large "on a hundred-fold scale," would enact heroic deeds "greater than any we had established in the past." That, in turn, would bequeath for the future "a heritage of honor to all citizens." Unlike assimilation during peace, which was gradual at best (sometimes "the slow work of centuries"), Roosevelt's new war could make everyone "intensely American"—"no matter how cosmopolitan their origins."[10]

Unfortunately, in trying to assemble his new community of heroes, Roosevelt made the mistake all too characteristic of him and his eldest son. In advancing the glory of their own commands, they actually weakened the rest of the army. America's trained officer corps was so small that the high command would spread it as thin as possible, building regiments and divisions twice the European size, and it would still be insufficient. Roosevelt himself must have known of this shortage for it was the military raison d'être of Plattsburg. Yet he still tried to monopolize America's scarcest military resource, the few outstanding officers who had to turn a mass society into the nation's army. Roosevelt, in pursuit of prominence, probably needed a prestigious reference group to enshrine his ego. As General Pershing observed, his personal "ambition eventually warped his [total] view of things." But whatever his exact motive, Roosevelt's heroic corps d'elite might have inadvertently built its legend at the cost of his country's defeat. He thought that the outstanding quality of his division would force President Wilson to send him to the front. In fact, it gave the administration an excuse to reject his application altogether. The army chief of staff wrote the secretary of war: "Roosevelt proposes . . . to milk the regular army of all its best officers for his one division, to form of the preferred stock the Rough Riders of this war, leaving the great army of millions to be less well instructed and on an inferior status. . . . He is very honest about it but he is not a trained soldier in any respect."[11]

Roosevelt's health had been deteriorating ever since he suffered, on a 1913–14 Amazon exploration, a near fatal and recurrent fever that left him "pretty nearly done out." By 1918, he would be sixty, the age at which he long had expected to die. The charge up San Juan Hill, in an admittedly "little war," remained "the great day of his life." Now, finally active in one of those "rare times" that "indelibly mark history," he looked forward to an even more memorable great day of his death. Through martyrdom in this "supreme crisis," reminiscent of the trials "manfully faced by our fathers in the days of Lincoln," Roosevelt, like his Republican hero, could ensure his immortality in the "imperishable" legends of a country united by war. Wilson's refusal to grant him, as he once put it, "the supreme good fortune of dying honorably on a well-fought field" was "a bitter blow from which he never quite recovered." In 1919, "profoundly unhappy" as a "male Casandra has-been," he perished in his sleep. His coffin was draped with Rough Rider flags.[12]

Using the Army for Uplift: Americanization, the Air Force, and the Student Army Training Corps

Other preparedness leaders besides Theodore Roosevelt tried to use the war to produce national unity. These men, calling the draft the "greatest opportunity ever had for developing national patriotism and a real American spirit," asked government officials not to preoccupy army recruits with just "technical training." As some 300,000 National Security League pamphlets said, an education in the general obligations of citizenship was equally important.[13]

For years those patrician Jews active in the NSL tried to raise their social status by training their Eastern European co-religionists in American cultural standards. To help the army assume this function, financier Jacob Schiff, a member of the league's committee on patriotism through education, chaired the Jewish Welfare Board, an organization teaching citizenship and English to drafted immigrants. By the middle of 1918, S. Stanwood Menken (of colonial Jewish-American extraction) was praising "the marvelous system of our Army" that has transformed "64,000 Russian Hebrews into upstanding disciplined soldiers."[14]

Stateside training, however, was just preliminary education. The ultimate test of martial Americanization came when New York City's "Melting Pot" soldiers from the 77th Division faced machine-gun fire. Its rank and file, speaking forty-two languages, personified its theme song: "The Jews and the Wops, and the Dutch and the Irish cops; they're all in the Army now." Its officer corps, on the other hand, could have held a Plattsburg camp reunion. Besides thirteen past and future executives of the Military Training Camps Association, they included Henry Stimson, Julius Ochs Adler (publisher of the New York Times), Robert Porter Patterson (President Truman's future secretary of defense), A. Lawrence Lowell's cousin, Robert Bacon's son, and at least a dozen other Plattsburgers. Whereas the Rough Riders in 1898 symbolized national solidarity during a decade of sectional strife, the 77th embodied social unity in the 1910s, a time of ethnic conflict. Old Rough Rider Roosevelt, himself a long-time critic of "polyglot, pleasure-loving" New York City, called this unit "a university of American citizenship."[15]

Politically, the 77th was called "the national idea carried into practice." Militarily, it seemed more like a public mess thrown into the army. Its enlisted men, judged by ranking officers to be the "poorest fighting material in the United States," were physically underdeveloped, unfamiliar with firearms, inexperienced in outdoor living, and "entirely ignorant of military discipline." Moreover, their basic training was almost as poor as their background. They lacked weapons to fire (almost half of them went into combat not knowing how to shoot), grounds on which to drill, and proper isolation from New York City. Thus recruits were often drunk or absent without leave. Many of the officers, "all so ridiculously inexperienced," could not understand their French-speaking instructors and many of the men could not comprehend their English-speaking officers. As if all this were not enough, the War Department, feeling the 77th could be only "a mere replacement division," transfered out 5,000 of its best soldiers, including three different commanders in less than a month.[16]

Despite all these problems, the unit came "to bow down before the military God, *Authority*." Secretary of War Newton Baker visited the 77th in New York and found it "as fine a division as was made in any National Army Camp." The demanding General Pershing inspected it in France and declared himself quite pleased with its development. Deserving of reward, it was the first national (as opposed to regular) army division sent to the front. Once there it was still so green that, in the midst of combat, its men had to be told how to take cover. When it came back from initial battle "very ragged and utterly tired," most of its noncommissioned and junior officers were gone and its 4,623 casualties were replaced by more men who "had never fired a rifle in their lives."[17]

The division expected extended relief and got the Argonne Forest, according to Pershing, "the most difficult terrain on the Western front." If the Meuse-Argonne offensive were to end the war, the 77th would have to march straight across a land whose natural swamps and deep ravines had been reinforced with barbed wire, booby traps, pillboxes, and trenches. All this territory was dominated by fortified bluffs providing observation and a withering crossfire. Given no relief and not much direction when lost in the forest, a dense fog, and the rain, it took the division eighteen days, over 5,000 casualties, and an enormous amount of courage to trudge through the Argonne. Because, as its commander confessed, its soldiers lacked military knowledge and technique, it appears that the "polyglot division" ran on simple "Yankee pluck." When it finally was relieved, after capturing 29 percent more territory than any other American division in the war, some 200 men from its 306th Regiment swore out U.S. citizenship.[18]

Those civic affirmations confirmed the martial Americanization that the preparedness movement had planned. Conscription removed over 400,000 immigrants from their ethnic ghettos. Then "iron army discipline" compelled them to adopt a new language, diet, appearance, and role. Aliens, stripped of their old image, were thereby forced into a new national identity. Yet unlike some other total institutions, whose oppressive nature provokes defiance in men with any pride at all, this particular division encouraged positive feelings that expedited assimilation. It not only promised draftees enhanced civilian status if they served honorably in combat companies, its enlisted men could identify with many of their sympathetic Yankee officers. Although some members of that corps continued to make derogatory remarks about Jews, "Polocks," and "Wops," others handled conscientious objectors with consideration and commanded soldiers with respect. For example, Robert Patterson—member of the Harvard Club, the Episcopal Church and the Order of the Distinguished Service Cross—listed Samuel Silverstein and Jacob Drobkin among "the best fighting soldiers I have ever seen." L. Wardlaw Miles—Plattsburger, Princeton professor, and Congressional Medal of Honor winner—called one Irish trooper "an ideal soldier and a splendid man."[19]

The nation, hailing this new symbol of patriotism and unity, praised the 77 Division as it once had celebrated the Rough Riders. Popular writers said that urban aliens, militarily "transformed from strangers into Americans," had become the country's best soldiers. Upper-class newspapers wrote that these doughboys had shown that the country is "no longer divided by place of birth." As nativistic sentiments against immigration grew, the division was used (albeit futilely) as an argument that America was a viable melting pot.[20]

The 77th even helped inspire a short-lived postwar Americanization program in the regular army. Although the military service usually shunned social uplift projects, it obtained temporary authorization to induct non-English-speaking soldiers into educational centers conducting patriotic lessons in civics, economics, and history. Using these techniques first developed at the home base of the 77th Division, the project transformed immigrants, likely to fall "under the influence of disloyal agitators," into "straight thinking American soldiers." But this lavishly praised program was meagerly financed. Both before and after the war, patriots used the threat of left-wing subversives, from the Wobblies to the Bolsheviks, to arouse the nation's lackadaisical efforts at Americanization. Consequently, once the postwar Red Scare ebbed, they found that they had lost their political justification. Then martial Americanization, like the whole military training movement, fell before the popular desire to reduce public (and increase private) expenditures. Hereafter, radios, movies, ready-made clothes, and the other standardized goods of mass-consumption capitalism overshadowed the 77th Division and its military "fires of patriotism aiding the

melting pot." These products, creating a common consumer consciousness and uniform purchase patterns, would assimilate more immigrants
than martial Americanization ever did.[21]

Without a Theodore Roosevelt ready to promote its deeds, the 77th
Division never became a lasting American legend. Nevertheless, its
own history permanently affected those officers who agreed that "living and suffering with these fellows has done more to get rid of [my]
race prejudice than anything else could have done." In the future, Delancy K. Jay, executive member of the MTCA and the Groton Alumni
Society, would solicit army camp enlistments from his prep school alma
mater by saying that this experience could teach young Grotonians
"that the son of our local butcher is perhaps as good" as they. Later, as
secretary of defense, Robert P. Patterson saved the common soldier
from draconian martial justice when he reduced legal penalties and enabled enlisted men to be tried by their peers. When Secretary Patterson visited an army post, it was observed that he preferred the GIs to
the generals. Finally, there was Henry Stimson. Before the war he
moved from New York City to "a typical New England village" on
Long Island where he could avoid the foreign-born residents of America's most cosmopolitan metropolis. When the war began neither Stimson nor the War Department thought very much of the 77th. Soon,
however, "joyfully astonished" at the resilience of "the little New York
Jew," he found himself boasting that army inspectors called his division
"the best disciplined and finest body of American troops in France."[22]

Stimson's prejudices did not completely disappear as if they were the
whims of a much younger man. He continued to support ethnically bi-
ased immigration quotas and opposed plans to build a special diplomatic institute at Columbia University. Because that particular program
was supposed to develop "American character, American ideals and
American viewpoints," he worried about "the tremendous Jewish influence there." These acts notwithstanding, the 77th Division left an indelible imprint on Stimson. Its lesson in "tolerance" not only influenced
his future stand against fascist "racial hatred," it helped sustain his
faith in the "gratifying task" of Americanization and, for that matter,
in the American people themselves. In the midst of neoisolationism and
the New Deal, his memory of the unit remained "one of the pillars upon
which I rest for hope": "When I get despondent or pessimistic, I like to
think of the young men who came to my regiment in 1917 and with
whom I thus came in contact under the strenuous test of war. There
had been much doubt and questions beforehand . . . as to whether our
country was getting soft, but the way these men in the Seventy-seventh
Division responded to the great test gave me a boost of encouragement
which was magnificent and which I have never gotten over. It has left

me with a faith that the same thing would happen again if such a test came." For the rest of his life Stimson told nearly everyone, from industrial union leaders to General George C. Marshall and the British ambassador, that the 77th Division was "my greatest lesson in democracy."[23]

As well as instructing the alien, the army trained the eminent when it assigned Arthur Woods, the former Groton master, to educate a new group of "thoroughbreds"—the mental, moral, and physical elites of the combat air corps. After Theodore Roosevelt's division aborted in 1917, the forty-seven-year-old Woods could only join the propaganda war waged by the government's Committee on Public Information. Then General George O. Squirer of the signal corps, the same man who saved ex-Mayor John Purroy Mitchel from a disgraceful desk job, offered Woods an army air force commission.[24]

Woods was needed because Mitchel was only one of many flight school fatalities. Between July, 1917, and May, 1918, the air corps suffered 108 deadly accidents, most of which were not really accidental. Washington, pressured by its allies to send emergency replacements to their infantries, imposed quick action on its own air corps, in part, to fend off the French. But no matter how dramatic its potential, no other service was less prepared for war. Its "flaming coffin" planes were "death traps" and its air fields were not much better built. Moreover, the corps's training schools were as obsolete as its equipment. Army Signal Corps regulars, who ran the program, knew nothing outside of reconnaissance and cared even less. Consequently, the instruction was at best disorganized, confused, and time-consuming. It was also quite hazardous. Inexperienced and insouciant cadets, given "the stick at the earliest moment," were colliding in mid-air. By 1918, recruits, no longer nonchalant, had lost all confidence in the instruction they received.[25]

Although the army (a political machine itself) had no love for reformers or outsiders, General Squirer asked Arthur Woods to help rectify this problem. Woods, in turn, did not need to ponder his reply. When still New York City's police commissioner in September, 1917, he saw a street urchin running between cars and said: "Wouldn't it be a great thing if [that boy] had that fine adventuresome disposition in an airplane, fighting for his country's life?" In mid-1918, Woods became the director of Military Aeronautics' Personnel Division. He knew nothing about aviation but, for some thirty years, he had been teaching the attributes of character which he deemed vital to this task. Above all else he would try "to turn out air fighters of courage, honor and reliability [for] if they have not these qualities they cannot fight well, no matter how skillfully they may be able to fly, or how straight they can shoot."[26]

Woods's training program, applying the principles that he once used at Groton, emphasized social discipline, "personal initiative," and to America's formal citation for "extraordinary executive ability, untir-mation throughout the day, complied with military regulations from dawn to dusk. Previously insensitive instructors, prone to "produce creatures out of a mold," now had to develop a student's "confidence as well as his understanding." The "initiative and aggressiveness" that flyers had to have were qualities which Woods always tried to instill. To foster their development, the former Groton coach required boxing and encouraged baseball on all air fields. Tradition and duty, the pillars of the prep school, were also nourished in the corps as Woods ordered compulsory instruction in the "obligations of an officer and pride in the Air Service."[27]

For planning and running this program which helped the air corps expand 150-fold during World War I, Woods's superiors, who originally resisted his suggestions, gave him a Distinguished Service Medal and their recommendation for promotion to brigadier general. In addition to America's formal citation for "extraordinary executive ability, untiring efforts and originality," he received England's informal commendation for having "more brains than the whole rest of the [Washington air force] crowd put together." Woods had earned the right to call himself "Colonel" for the rest of his life.[28]

While Arthur Woods was training his flyers, other Plattsburgers were also involved in military education. Secretary of War Newton Baker planned to turn his military camps into colleges; they wanted to make their colleges into military camps. The result was the Student Army Training Corps (SATC), which drafted the male student body into the service but assigned their training to the campus. This virtually made higher education into a big army post.[29]

Most university administrators greeted the corps as their financial salvation. Like other American industries from 1914 to 1917, the education business prospered from the European war. But instead of saving its endowments for a rainy day, it used its treasure to expand its already overbuilt capital plant. After America declared war, some 20 percent of the nation's prospective students joined the army or went into a booming industry, thereby depriving academia of some $2,000,000 in potential tuition. War taxes and charities, preempting donations, further reduced incoming assets, and wartime expenditures, in general, inflated operating costs. Then the SATC, called "the richest gift which the Government has ever made to higher education," rescued the universities from their liquidity crisis.[30]

At least as far as many Plattsburg enthusiasts were concerned, the SATC was more than a great federal subsidy paying room, board, and tuition for a national college class. To them, it was the reformation of the university education which they long had criticized. Princeton's Hibben, who already had built his own campus training program developing "self-control, sacrifice, punctuality and precision," felt that the corps was "a rare [educational] privilege." Cornell's Schurman, who recently put part of his school "under proper military discipline," called this innovation an "ennobling experience." Their students, obeying the army officers assigned to each campus and "subject to military discipline at all times," marched to their required classes, lived in barracks, and ate at a mess. This routine resurrected the ideal eighteenth- and early-nineteenth-century college in which the student body, housed with its instructors, proceeded through an "orderly" schedule of meals, prayers, and lessons. In loco parentis, garbed in army uniform, had returned to higher education with a vengeance. Any social institution, be it fraternity or eating club, which subverted this regime was suspended for the war. As one Princetonian put it: "The old college life is all shot to hell."[31]

Intercollegiate athletics, like fraternities, were casualties of war. High taxes crippled gate receipts and frivolities embarrassed a nation embattled in war. The army, moreover, demanded mass participation programs to prepare its citizen-soldiers for combat. Therefore, even before the SATC began in August, 1918, colleges started to develop intramural sports at the expense of those varsity teams now sacrificing their professional coaches and lavish training tables to help make the world safe for democracy. The SATC furthered this process by requiring exercise for all cadets. Henceforth, interplatoon competition became the big game on campus. To old critics of collegiate athletics this seemed "a priceless opportunity" to reconstruct sports. War had "wiped the slate clean" by minimizing commercialism everywhere. In addition, army statistics showed that 31 percent of its draftees were physically defective, partly because 75 percent of them never played any form of organized athletics. This documented a national health problem which SATC activities already were improving. Educators consequently approached the 1920s, the golden age of spectator sports, fatuously thinking the war had made the campus safe for "physical democracy."[32]

Besides compulsory athletics, the SATC required a nine-hour-a-week "War Issues Course"—an interdepartmental enterprise blending history, political science, philosophy, and literature into one class on the causes of the conflict and the problems of modern civilization. Actually, this ostensible attempt to contemporize the curricula functionally revived the defunct senior course in moral philosophy. That old class in character-building refined morality; this new one built "morale." Originally suggested by Woodrow Wilson, a former leader of the humanist reformation of university education, it allowed colleges to try once again to make their students "fit for citizenship." Because this attempt to "burn up much of the rubbish of electives" was a fundamental reform, not simply situational propaganda, several schools voluntarily incorporated the subject after the armistice. When the Bolsheviks threatened the social order, this class, once "a strange course imposed by the army," helped make the "citizen safe for democracy" and the social sciences safe for the college catalog.[33]

The total SATC program fulfilled many Plattsburg educational ideals. Camp organizer and Harvard philosophy professor Ralph Barton Perry, having "the time of his life" as the corps' executive secretary, said that its program would redirect university priorities towards "developing and perfecting a coveted type of American manhood." Harvard alumnus and chief Plattsburg leader Grenville Clark (1882–1967), having conceived and developed the SATC for the War Department, thought it was "a long step towards permanent military training." Buoyant but mistaken, they both believed that most colleges would never relinquish this "positive gain to the educational system of the country."[34]

Many schools certainly felt that the SATC had been good for business, providing "splendid publicity" for higher education and expanding its market through a military scholarship system. At least one ambitious president now believed that "if we can keep these young men for a year, many of them will go on with college . . . [even] without government aid." Other administrators, concerned with "furnishing a much needed discipline for a growing generation," thought that the corps had improved the "habits of courtesy" on campus. Several of them felt that the army's supervised study halls (another wartime revitalization of an old scholastic custom) should be permanently adopted as "a great improvement over the haphazard methods [of] ordinary college organization."[35]

Nonetheless, the SATC handed the universal military training movement "a most unfortunate setback from which it [was] hard to recover." The corps, as a brand new program, had numerous operational problems, the most severe being competition for authority between academics and the army. Because students were officially soldiers, noncoms could bust into a classroom barking out orders for privates to report to other duty. As one chancellor, who obviously wished to be first in command, put it: "If we could uniform our freshmen and sophomores, put the freshmen upon a barracks regime which we could control ourselves, give to both classes six hours a week of military drill . . . and maintain a summer camp, it would undoubtedly prove of benefit to our young men. . . . But I certainly hope not to live long enough to see our universities again turned into mere officer nurseries to help organize a great army." [36]

Students, after the armistice, also grew displeased with the SATC. The college cadet, like the doughboy overseas, then rebelled against military constraint. "General unrest, emotional dissatisfaction and mental dissipation" grew until, by February, 1919, Perry was writing Clark about "the utter disappearance from the undergraduate body of the spirit which has prevailed there since 1916." When the pursuit of tuition dollars revived as SATC subsidies declined, these students forced their schools to demand the end of compulsory drill. Meanwhile the War Department tried to save its ROTC from this reaction by claiming that the corps, demobilized before it was completely organized, "never really existed." To prevent anyone from recalling what never really happened, it censored Perry's favorable article on the SATC lest any publicity that kept "the subject fresh in [student] memory" proceed to "open wounds not fully healed." [37]

While some students went into the SATC, others served in the AEF (American Expeditionary Force). When the latter returned to school, Plattsburgers argued that their military service deserved adacemic recognition. Educational honorariums for military sacrifice had been given after other wars and army training advocates felt that they were also justified now. Because these men believed that combat had been a "great educational experience" and "the final, searching test" of collegiate life, academic credit was not some minor commendation—their scholastic equivalent of an army bonus. It was, instead, justifiable recognition of moral character and honor, two "of the many useful things learned during the war." General Leonard Wood and Plattsburg devotees Arthur Woods and Franklin Roosevelt had finished first, second, and third in the 1917 election to the Harvard College Board of (Alumni) Overseers. In 1919, along with other Crimson supporters of UMT, they tried to make their alma mater reward its veterans. However, Harvard President A. Lawrence Lowell believed that military training was a regrettable necessity which posed an impediment to all free thought. Agreeing with other scholastic organizations, he maintained that academic degrees should recognize only intellectual work, not patriotism. A heated debate between the Plattsburgers and the president resulted in a compromise: an honorary degree bearing the words "Military service." This symbolic decision indicated that university education would survive its short-lived martial reformation. [38]

Repression: An Alternative to Uplift

Military activities waged at home and abroad may have been a great educational experience, but many preparedness leaders made use of repression when confronting uneducable members of the body politic. Within the army, Leonard Wood, that "strange combination of kindness and severity," uplifted the corrigible and oppressed the obstinate. This general, who discouraged courts-martial by blaming desertions on the army not on the soldier, was the same man who castigated conscientious objectors as the social "type that we must suppress or go under as a people."[39]

The War Department assigned Wood to train draftees from the Plains States, physically excellent men from an isolationist area. He found inexperienced enlisted men and junior officers standing "around with their hands in their pockets and cigars in the corners of their mouths." Wood professed that he had "never seen troops more lax in appearance, military courtesies and obligations." But training men, whether from Harvard or Missouri, was his specialty and, hence, his pleasure. While performing this task his physical health, which generally reflected his emotional state, was "never in better condition." By the time Wood finished, his troops were also in shape. Even his critics considered them the best disciplined American soldiers sent to France.[40]

The draft, assembling the able-bodied, was a social sieve excluding the deficient. It consequently gave Wood, the former "headmaster" of Plattsburg, the raw material from which to construct another community of virtue, this time in the midst of Kansas. Obviously pleased with himself and the little world he created, he wrote Endicott Peabody of Groton, his colleague in uplift: "We have a fine Division here. . . . They are the American people—less the physically, morally, and mentally unfit. We have no disciplinary troubles . . . almost no profanity and vulgarity." Although President Wilson denied Wood's request for duty overseas, the general could still take "great pride" in his 89th Division for it had "the right kind of character which counts in an organization as in the individual."[41]

To develop that character, Wood utilized skills which he acquired from his medical experience. Committing "himself to learn how to understand his men," he applied, said one observer, "a psychological element in his judgments and decisions." While he enforced "strict military discipline," he nonetheless warned officers to preserve the self-respect of soldiers who, "under no circumstances," were to be ridiculed. He also continued to think that desertions were human responses to dehumanizing orders and sheer boredom. Courts-martial for that offense were, in his mind, prima facie proof of incompetent command. His maxim for desertion still read: "In handling men, the idea of reform should be made superior to that of punishment."[42]

But the enlightened physician, who could empathize with stateside deserters, could not control his hatred for conscientious objectors. To him, they were not protestors or even opponents; they were simply "degenerates." In time of war, when Wood was convinced that the country could create "a better spirit and greater solidarity," he believed that pacifists preached the most treasonous principle: "individualism as against nationalism." Although he would not let others ridicule a private, Wood himself scorned the major general who kindly asked objectors to serve. "There is," he said, "only one thing to do and that is to punch them and punch them hard, for they are preaching a doctrine which means our degradation and ruin."[43]

Most of the objectors whom Wood confronted were extreme and isolated Mennonites and Hutterians. Politically, this "sad and unshave[n] lot" of men, comprising about .007 percent of the draft, were hardly worth his worry. Yet when these devout Christian communitarians refused military service, Wood erroneously viewed them as representatives of the "unrestrained individualism" he deplored. Thus, in his mind, an insignificant sect bloomed into a "widespread and well-organized" threat to his noble 89th Division and all the rest of America. Never a military bureaucrat, Wood had bent regulations to be lenient to deserters. Now he disobeyed Washington's directives and was brutal to pacifists, sanctioning physical and mental persecution within his command.[44]

Civilians could also educate or repress, Americanize or exclude. Theodore Roosevelt, hailing the army's ethnic diversity, called one dogmatic nativist an "addlepated ass." Yet he and the Military Training Camps Association, which believed that aliens should be drafted or deported, felt that all residents must now be assimilated or expelled.[45]

In politics, as in civic education, the preparedness movement used coercion as well as persuasion. Located in New York but harboring an antiurban bias, it was determined to eliminate that city's dissidents. The American Defense Society (ADS) organized a vigilante patrol to roam the city's streets making citizens' arrests on suspicion of sedition. In addition, it used loyalty oaths to elevate the moral condition of the metropolitan schools. Proponents of the Gary school system had earlier proclaimed the patriotism of their program and the disloyalty of its critics. Now, with John Purroy Mitchel off in the air corps, William Temple Hornaday left the Bronx Zoo to lead the fight for a "new Americanism" in New York's public schools. This man, who believed that the classroom was a "powerful machine for good or evil," wanted to create a forum of "pure patriotism" safe from "the poisonous doctrines [of] socialistic snakes." Having once purged the Boy Scouts of pacifists, he now mobilized Theodore Roosevelt and the whole ADS to "clean out the Augean stable" of the city's schools. In what teachers called an "intellectual reign of terror," they demanded the dismissal of faculty less "loyal" than "officers of the army." Their criteria for judgment was the willingness to teach "instinctive respect" to the "ignorant Jews of New York."[46]

The National Security League also planned to prepare the East Side of Manhattan "for good citizenship during and after the war." It not only presented sidewalk patriotic speeches in native languages, it organized a fusion political ticket to oppose left-wing candidates for Congress. In the 1918 election, its actions helped defeat incumbent Socialist Meyer London who, by just 827 votes, lost a third term from his Lower East Side district.[47]

Preparedness organizations, not confined to Eastern cities, also attacked the western-bred Industrial Workers of the World. The destruction of the Wobblies by vigilantes and the government was largely a local affair in which national patriotic societies promoted and supported branch chapters thoroughly involved in this suppression. The American Defense Society, fulfilling its pledge "to urge lawful authorities to repress treasonable orations," organized 276 surveillance units, which pressured U.S. attorneys to prosecute dissidents. In Montana, the Missoula branch took credit for eliminating the area's Wobbly threat. In Arizona, after John Greenway could not ship overseas as a colonel in Theodore Roosevelt's abortive division, this ADS member and former Rough Rider went to war on the homefront. He personally led the vigilantes who forceably deported 1,186 Wobblies from the state.[48]

This patriotic repression was not just an emotional adjunct of total war, an event that mobilizes passions as well as industries. At least some Wilson administration officials, subject to the same psychological pressures in the same milieu, were able to remain relatively liberal. Labor Department mediators warned state authorities to prevent mob action and staffed a commission investigating the deportation of the Wobblies. When their report chastised the vigilantes and recommended federal laws prohibiting such acts, Theodore Roosevelt called its authors Bolsheviks. Other militant preparedness leaders called Wilson a dangerous pacifist or a German sympathizer. Wilson's own propaganda chief, George Creel, whom they termed a security risk, later said that the Security League and Defense Society "were easily the most active and obnoxious" organizations in America. Their "patriotism was a thing of screams, violence and extremes, and their savage intolerances had the burn of acid."[49]

Suppression was more than a necessity of war and much more than self-seeking pocketbook politics. Some people certainly believed that the NSL was "merely a commercial proposition" opposing any "raid on the [business] interests." However, a hostile congressional subcommittee, trying to prove that the organization was an economic pressure group, took over 2,000 pages of testimony and found that only one league branch asked just one political candidate for his opinion on economic issues such as labor unions and the public ownership of railroads. Since financial profit was not the primary motive for their use of political repression, it seems that coercion often arose from the desire to eliminate human obstructions to the moral reformation of America.[50]

As an example, one may take the case of Lyman Abbott (1835–1922), the Congregational minister and magazine publisher who was once a pacifist. Abbott always believed in national uplift through moral revival, saying that "if we can get rid of sin in the individual we shall get rid of evil in the state." Nonetheless, before the Spanish-American War, he was convinced that combat left legacies of "moral pestilence" by upsetting Christian institutions like the family. Because he hoped to reform America by spreading the gospel and reducing the army, he supported conciliatory negotiations with Spain. But once that failed in early 1898, Abbott began to glorify the warfare which he had condemned. Becoming in this way indistinguishable from Theodore Roosevelt, he now claimed that these hostilities elicited "the noblest traits of human nature," awoke America "from its preoccupation with money," and summoned it forth "to heroic self-sacrifice." It not only closed the East versus West political "chasm" of 1896, it buried the Civil War, reestablished national "discipline," and terminated the "breach between rich and poor." In summary, he said, "the floodtide of patriotism" united and uplifted the entire country.[51]

After the Spanish-American War ended, Abbott returned to peace movement activities but not without some permanent change in his demeanor. Despite his support for international law, his *Outlook* magazine continued to praise military morality for embodying virtues all too rare in America: honor and the "spirit of obedience." Such beliefs ensured that Abbott would not have to be dragged into the next conflict. When World War I began, he was ready to identify it as America's great opportunity to transform itself from a "money changers' cave to a great cathedral." This prospect inspired him to support the firm enforcement of sedition laws, Columbia University's dismissal of pacifist professors, and the government's refusal to mail *The Masses,* a radical magazine which he deemed injurious "to public safety and morals." Prompted by hope as well as hate, Abbott and his sons, once civil libertarians, allied themselves with William Temple Hornaday, a man who for two decades ardently preferred a swift and severe tribal justice to "legal precedents and technicalities." To them, America's opportunity for righteousness justified their own use of repression.[58]

NOTES

1. Wilson and Roosevelt quoted in Arthur S. Link, *Wilson: Campaigns For Progressivism and Peace, 1916–917* (Princeton: Princeton University Press, 1965), pp. 7, 187. Speech by Root in *Proceedings of the Congress of Constructive Patriotism*, p. 23.

2. For Wilson's decision for war, see Link, *Wilson: Campaigns For Progressivism and Peace*, pp. 411, 415–19; Ernest May, *The World War and American Isolation, 1914–1917* (Chicago: Quadrangle Books, 1966), pp. 422–23. Statement of Edgar Bancroft in House, *Hearings on National Security League*, 65th Cong., 3rd Sess., 1919, p. 1552.

3. Scott, ed., *Robert Bacon*, p. 287; *National Security League Bulletin* 1 (June, 1918): 5; Roosevelt, Jr., to Roosevelt, Sr., Jan., 1918, Roosevelt, Jr., MSS, Box 7; Theodore Roosevelt, *The Great Adventure: Works of Theodore Roosevelt*, 19: 261, 279, 326, 394; Morison, ed., *Letters of Theodore Roosevelt*, 8:826, 857.

4. For Roosevelt's presidential diplomacy, see Howard K. Beale, *Theodore Roosevelt and the Rise of America to World Power* (New York: Collier-Macmillan, 1965), passim; Theodore Roosevelt, "The World War: Its Tragedies and Its Lessons," *Outlook* 108 (Sept. 23. 1914):173; Morison, ed., *Letters of Theodore Roosevelt*, 8:824.

5. Blum, *Republican Roosevelt*, p. 23. For Roosevelt on race relations and trust-busting, see Morison, ed., *Letters of Theodore Roosevelt*, 2:1351, 1385; George Mowry, *Theodore Roosevelt and the Progressive Movement* (New York: Hill & Wang, 1960), pp. 267–72, 294–99. The final quotation on politics is in Harbaugh, *Life and Times of Theodore Roosevelt*, p. 211.

6. Morison, ed., *Letters of Theodore Roosevelt*, 8:836; Roosevelt quoted in Hermann Hagedorn, *The Bugle That Awoke America* (New York: John Day, 1940), pp. 14, 44.

7. Roosevelt and Leonard Wood quoted on the war in Morison, ed., *Letters of Theodore Roosevelt*, 8:831, 890, 961; Hagedorn, *Leonard Wood*, 2:202. Mark Anthony DeWolfe Howe, *The Harvard Volunteers in Europe* (Cambridge, Mass.: Harvard University Press, 1916), pp. 15–45. Bacon quoted in Scott, ed., *Robert Bacon*, p. 310.

8. J. G. Harbord to Frank McCoy, July 9, 1916, McCoy MSS, Box 14; Roosevelt to Halbert P. Garner, Mar. 5, 1917, Roosevelt to R. R. Rosen, Aug. 7, 1915, both in Roosevelt MSS, Reel 388; Morison, ed., *Letters of Theodore Roosevelt*, 8:845, 1085–86.

9. Ibid., 8:1028; Theodore Roosevelt, Jr. (a leading organizer of the division) to Mrs. Luis Muñoz Marin, Apr. 30, 1931, Roosevelt, Jr., MSS, Box 50; Roosevelt, *The Great Adventure*, pp. 352–53; W. E. Dame to Roosevelt, memorandum and report of June 23, 1917, Roosevelt to E. A. Koehr, Apr. 10, 1917, Roosevelt to Emmett J. Scott, May 17, 1917: all in Roosevelt MSS, Reels 238, 389, 391.

10. Frank McCoy to Henry Stimson, Aug. 4, 1916, McCoy MSS, Box 14; Roosevelt to Irvine L. Lenroot, Mar. 5, 1917, Roosevelt MSS, Reel 388. This last letter is not about the division per se, but it represents Roosevelt's point of view about the war. For T.R. on assimilation, see Dyer, *Theodore Roosevelt and the Idea of Race,* pp. 97, 109.

11. Coffman, *War to End All Wars,* pp. 54, 152; Pershing quoted in Harbaugh, *Life and Times of Theodore Roosevelt,* p. 472; Morison, ed., *Letters of Theodore Roosevelt,* 8:1187; Hugh L. Scott, *Some Memories of a Soldier* (New York: Century, 1928), pp. 561–62.

12. For Roosevelt's illness, see Morison, ed., *Letters of Theodore Roosevelt,* 8:903. For Roosevelt's wish to be a martyr, like Lincoln, in a great national crisis, see Richard T. Fry, "Community Through War: A Study of Theodore Roosevelt's Rise and Fall as a Prophet and Hero in Modern America" (Ph.D. diss., University of Minnesota, 1969), pp. 195–208, 236, 249. The quotations on Roosevelt's death and dying in battle are in Roosevelt, "The Cuban Dead." *Works of Theodore Roosevelt,* 9:343; Morison, ed., *Letters of Theodore Roosevelt,* 8:1152–53, 1234; Eleanor Roosevelt quoted in Kenneth S. Davis, *F. D. R.: The Beckoning of Destiny* (New York: Capricorn, 1974), p. 460.

13. Shailer Mathews (member of the Security League's Committee on Patriotism through Education) to William Orr, July 31, 1917, Mathews MSS, University of Chicago; William Franklin Willoughby, *Address* (New York: National Security League, 1919), p. 19; Westel W. Willoughby, *Some Fundamentals of the American Political System* (New York: National Security League, 1919), p. 10.

14. Moses Rischin, *The Promised City, New York City's Jews, 1870–1914* (Cambridge, Mass.: Harvard University Press, 1962), pp. 81–90; *New York Times,* Jan. 14, 1918; Menken quoted in *National Security League Bulletin* 1 (June, 1918):2.

15. Stallings, *Doughboys,* p. 198; L. Wardlaw Miles, *History of the 308th Infantry* (New York: Putnam's, 1927), p. 21; Theodore Roosevelt, *Roosevelt in the Kansas City Star* (Boston: Houghton, Mifflin, 1921), p. 14.

16. Frederick R. Palmer, *America in France* (New York: Dodd & Mead, 1918), pp. 280–82; Miles, *History of 308th Infantry,* pp. xii, 7, 45, 67–68; W. Kerr Rainsford, *From Upton to the Meuse: With the 307th Infantry* (New York: D. Appleton, 1920), pp. 7, 10–11, 48, 98; Julius Ochs Adler, ed., *History of the 306th Infantry* (New York: 306th Infantry Association, 1935), pp. 8, 10: Delancey K. Jay to Endicott Peabody, Aug. 30, 1917, Peabody MSS, Box 53; Henry L. Stimson Diary, Nov. 30, 1943, Stimson MSS.

17. Julius Ochs Adler, ed., *History of the Seventy-Seventh Division* (New York: Seventy-Seventh Division Association, 1919), p. 13: Newton Baker quoted in Frederick Palmer, *Newton Baker: America At War* (New York: Dodd & Mead, 1931), 2:247; Pershing, *My Experiences in the World War,* 2:3, 60, 113; "Memorandum of General Robert Alexander," Oct. 17, 1918, 77th Division Records, Box 18, National Archives.

18. For Pershing's quote and the Argonne, see Beaver, *Newton Baker and the American War Effort,* pp. 191, 195, 198. Henry Stimson Diary, Mar. 30, 1919, Stimson MSS; "Memorandum of General Robert Alexander," Dec. 1, 1918,

77th Division MSS, Box 11; Adler, ed., *History of the 306th Infantry,* p. 23.

19. Ibid., p. 5; Rainsford, *From Upton to the Meuse,* p. 165; Robert Patterson to W. F. Lent, Dec. 13, 1922; Patterson to Maj. Leon Fraiser, May 3, 1922, Patterson MSS, Box 3, Library of Congress; Miles, *History of 308th Infantry,* pp. 59, 131.

20. Irvin S. Cobb, *The Glory of the Coming* (New York: George H. Doran, 1918), pp. 462–63; *Boston Evening Transcript,* Oct. 4, 1918; New York State Legislature, *Revolutionary Radicalism,* 1920, pp. 3271–72.

21. White, "American Military and Melting Pot in World War I," pp. 44–46; Willis Fletcher Johnson, "Students at Camp Upton," *North American Review* 211 (Jan., 1920):47–50. The quotations are from Bernard Lentz to Theodore Roosevelt, Jr., Aug. 2, 1920, Roosevelt, Jr., MSS, Box 6; Peyton C. March, "1919 Annual War Report of Army Chief of Staff Peyton C. March," in *American Military Thought,* ed. Walter Millis (Indianapolis: Bobbs-Merrill, 1966), p. 362. For Americanization through mass consumption, see Boorstin, *Americans: Democratic Experience,* pp. 100, 121, 147.

22. Charles Minder quoted in Dixon Wecter, *When Johnny Comes Marching Home* (Boston: Houghton, Mifflin, 1944), p. 419. Jay to Endicott Peabody, May 25, 1922, Peabody MSS, Box 73; Julius Klein, "Judge Robert P. Patterson as I Knew Him," *U.S. Congressional Record,* 82 Cong., 2d Sess., 1952, 98:417; Stimson to Rev. E. J. Juneston, Dec. 17, 1937, Stimson conversation with McGeorge Bundy, July 8, 1946, Stimson Diary, Mar. 14, 1918, May 1, May 12, 1918: all in Stimson MSS, Reels 4, 94, 136; Stimson to Theodore Roosevelt, May 13, 1918, Roosevelt MSS, Reel 276,

23. Stimson Diary Sept. 16, 1930, Mar. 19, Apr. 8, May 26, 1931, Stimson to Felix Frankfurter, Mar. 31, 1943, Stimson to Mrs. Howard Tracey, May 24, 1938, Stimson to Frederic Rene Coudert, Jan. 5, 1938, Stimson Diary, Dec. 18, 1942, Nov. 10, 1944: all in Stimson MSS, Reels 4, 94, 95.

24. Arthur Woods to Director of Military Aeronautics, July 15, 1918, Woods MSS; *New York Times,* Feb. 18, Feb. 20, 1918.

25. Unsigned memorandum to Gen. Kenley, May 15, 1918, memorandum from Maj. Gen. J. L. Chambertain to Adjutant General, Nov. 13, 1917, Subject: Memorandum for Chief of Staff Aviation Schools, unsigned memorandum of Apr., 1918: all in American Air Force MSS, Record Group 18, Boxes 587, 620, National Archives. For the Wilson administration's demands for quick use of the air corps, see Beaver, *Newton Baker and the American War Effort,* pp. 57–58.

26. Samuel Martin to John Purroy Mitchel, June 21, 1918, Mitchel MSS, Box 19; Woods quoted in *New York Mail,* Sept. 22, 1917; Woods to Director of Military Aeronautics, Subject: Discipline, July 15, 1918, Woods MSS.

27. Ibid.; Woods, "Notes Made on My Trip to the South and South-West Flying Fields in March, 1918," Woods MSS.

28. Samuel Martin to John Purroy Mitchel, June 21, 1918, Mitchel MSS, Box 19; Maj. Gen. Kenley to Director of Air Service, Nov. 8, 1918, Maj. Gen. Menoher to Woods, Apr. 28, 1919, Lt. Col. Charles Lee to Lord Weir, Sept. 16, 1918: all in Woods MSS.

29. Beaver, *Newton Baker and the American War Effort,* p. 200; Clifford, *Citizen Soldiers,* pp. 255–60.

30. Parke Rexford Kolbe, *The Colleges in Wartime and After* (New York: D. Appleton, 1919), pp. 171, 177; Charles F. Thwing, *The American Colleges and Universities in the Great War* (New York: Macmillan, 1920), pp. 46, 48. The quotation is from Charles Thwing, "The Colleges As War Camps," *Independent* 96 (Oct. 5, 1918):12.

31. Hibben to Theodore Roosevelt, May 25, 1918, Roosevelt MSS, Reel 277; John G. Hibben, "The University Cantonment: Princeton," *Bookman* 48 (Nov., 1918):288; Jacob G. Schurman to Chief Signal Officer, U.S. Army, May 14, 1917, American Air Force MSS, Record Group 18, Box 586, National Archives; Jacob Gould Schurman, "The University Cantonment: Cornell," *Bookman* 48 (Nov., 1918):294–95; unnamed student quoted in Edmund Wilson, *A Prelude* (New York: Farrar Straus & Giroux, 1967), p. 162.

32. National Collegiate Athletic Association: *Proceedings of the 12th Annual Convention,* Dec. 28, 1917, pp. 20, 25, 55; *Proceedings of the 13th Annual Convention,* Dec. 27, 1918, pp. 16, 18–19, 20, 48, 69. Briggs, "Intercollegiate Athletics and the War," pp. 304, 309. The army's statistics on athletics are in Millett, *The General,* p. 449. The final quotation is from Kolbe, *Colleges in Wartime and After,* p. 58.

33. Ralph Barton Perry, "The Student Army Training Corps," manuscript copy in Perry MSS; William E. Hocking and Dean Hawkes of Columbia University quoted in Carol S. Gruber, "Mars and Minerva: World War I and the American Academic Man" (Ph.D. diss., Columbia University, 1968), p. 302; Perry to R. F. A. Hoernle, Nov. 21, 1918, Perry MSS; Canby, *American Memoir,* p. 261; Thwing, *American Colleges and Universities in the Great War,* p. 257.

34. Perry quoted in Gruber, "Mars and Minerva," pp. 124–25; Grenville Clark to Leonard Wood, Aug. 5, 1918, Wood MSS, Box 112; Ralph Barton Perry: "The Student Army Training Corps," *National Service with the International Military Digest* 4 (Aug., 1919):84; "The Colleges and the New Age," *Harvard Alumni Bulletin* (Feb., 1919):490.

35. President B. H. Kroezer of Jamestown College to Dean E. E. Nicholson, Nov. 27, 1918; President R. Ames Montgomery to Nicholson, Nov. 24, 1918; Dean S. W. Stookey to Nicholson, Nov. 29, 1918; illegible, Assistant to the President of Doane College, to Nicholson, Nov. 30, 1918: all in Nicholson MSS, University of Minnesota; Thwing, *American Colleges and Universities in the Great War,* pp. 72–73, 76.

36. President Arthur T. Hadley of Yale quoted in Gruber, "Mars and Minerva," p. 315; Clifford, *Citizen Soldiers,* p. 258 n. 112; President W. G. Hastings of the University of Nebraska to Dean E. E. Nicholson, Nov. 27, 1918, Nicholson MSS.

37. Perry to Clark, Feb. 17, 1919; Perry to Thompkins McIlvaine, Mar. 18, 1919; E. S. Hartshorn, "Memorandum for the Assistant Chief of Staff, Subject: Permission to publish article on the Student Army Training Camps," May 10, 1919; W. F. Clark, "Memorandum for the Chairman, Committee on Education and Special Training, Subject: Permission to publish article on Student Army Training Corps," May 19, 1919: all in Perry MSS.

38. Thwing, *American Colleges and Universities in the Great War,* p. 243. The quotations are from Frederic Rene Coudert to Nicholas Murray Butler, Dec. 18, 1918, Butler MSS; Leonard Wood to Mrs. William Wood, Mar. 20, 1917, Wood MSS, Box 89; Henry Stimson quoted in *New York Times,* Nov. 22, 1920. Arthur Woods to A. Lawrence Lowell, Dec. 7, 1918; Lowell to Woods, Dec. 9, 1918, Lowell MSS, File 1715.

39. Wood described in Thomas F. Logan to Hermann Hagedorn, Mar. 27, 1919, Hagedorn MSS, Box 21. Wood to Frank Vanderlip, Mar. 20, 1917, Wood MSS, Box 98.

40. Wood Diary, Aug. 28, 1917; Sept. 8, 1917, Wood MSS, Box 4; Col. J. C. Lee, "Recollection of Service with General Leonard Wood," n.d.; statement of Heinzman, Nov. 6, 1928: both in Hermann Hagedorn MSS, Boxes 20, 21; Villard, *Fighting Years,* p. 268.

41. Wood to Endicott Peabody, Nov. 6, 1918, Peabody MSS, Box 99; Wood to Colonel James Reeves, Mar. 6, 1921, Wood MSS, Box 157.

42. Paul Azan, "Anecdotes of General Leonard Wood," n.d., Hermann Hagedorn MSS, Box 20; Wood Diary, May 2, 1918, Apr. 16, 1919; Wood to adjutant general, Dec. 13, 1920, Wood MSS, Box 4, 161.

43. Wood to S. H. Wolfe, Mar. 19, 1917; Wood to Frank Vanderlip, Mar. 20, 1917; Wood Diary, Oct. 16, 1917, Wood MSS, Boxes 4, 98, 100.

44. The first quotation on conscientious objectors is from Secretary of War Newton Baker as cited in Harvey DeWeerd, *President Wilson Fights His War: World War I and the American Intervention* (New York: Macmillan, 1968), p. 242. Wood Diary, Oct. 26, 1917, Sept. 1, Sept. 2, 1918; Oct. 13, 1918, Wood MSS, Box 4.

45. Morison, ed., *Letters of Theodore Roosevelt,* 8:1419; statement of Thomas McIlvaine in U.S. Congress, Senate, Committee on Military Affiars, *Hearings on Army Reorganization,* 66th Cong., 1st. Sess., 1919, pp. 826–27.

46. H. C. Peterson and Gilbert Fite, *Opponents of the War, 1917–1918* (Seattle: University of Washington Press, 1968), pp. 18, 109; *American Defense Society: History, Purpose and Accomplishments,* (n.p., n.d.) p. 13; Hornaday, *Awake! America,* pp. 80, 118, 185–88; Hornaday to J. M. Stricker, Nov. 27, 1917, Theodore Roosevelt MSS, Reel 235; Morison, ed., *Letters of Theodore Roosevelt,* 8: 1252.

47. Statement of Albert Parker in House, *Hearings on National Security League,* 65th Cong., 3rd Sess., 1919, pp. 1830, 1834; *National Security League Bulletin* 1 (Nov., 1918):4.

48. *American Defense Society,* pp. 9–16; Morison, ed., *Letters of Theodore Roosevelt,* 8:1182, 1262–65.

49. Peterson and Fite, *Opponents of the War,* p. 54; House, *Hearings on National Security League,* 65th Cong., 3rd Sess., 1919, pp. 1899, 1981–83; George Creel, *Rebel at Large: Recollections of 50 Crowded Years* (New York: Putnam's, 1947), p. 196.

50. Milton Fairchild to John G. Hibben, Nov. 21, 1918, Hibben MSS, Box 1; House, *Hearings on National Security League,* 65th Cong., 3rd Sess., 1919, p. 1842.

51. Lyman Abbott, *Christianity and Social Problems* (Boston: Houghton, Mif-

flin, 1896), pp. 131–34, 248–49, 293, 363; Abbott to William McKinley, Mar. 6, 1898, McKinley MSS, Library of Congress; "A Moral Miracle"; "Some Advantages of War," *Outlook* 59 (June 11, 1898):362; (June 25, 1898):461–62.

52. "The American Army," *Outlook* 74 (July 1, 1903):645; Lyman Abbott, *The Twentieth Century Crusade* (New York: Macmillan, 1918), pp. vi–ix, 21, 54–55, 182; "Sedition," *Outlook* 116 (May 1, 1917):10–11; "Free Speech," ibid. 117 (Oct. 17, 1917):239; "Free Press But Not Free Mails," ibid. 117 (Sept. 12, 1917):43–44; Hornaday: *Man Who Became a Savage,* pp. 31–32, 333–34, 337; *Awake! America,* pp. 139–40.

Henry Sturgis Drinker of Lehigh, executive secretary of Plattsburgh's Advisory Committee of College Presidents: promoting a "hard disciplinary experience." (from Catherine Drinker Brown, *Family Portrait*, 1970)

John G. Hibben of Princeton, chairman of the Advisory Committee of College Presidents: emerging from the battlefield "chastened and purified." (courtesy Princeton University Archives)

Episcopal Bishop Charles Brent (left) and Dr. Samuel Drury of St. Paul's School: "Beat me into a comely form upon thy anvil." (courtesy Roger W. Drury, Sheffield, Mass.)

Arthur Woods: a "hard-boiled sentimentalist." (from *Harper's Weekly*, Oct. 30, 1915)

Arthur Woods's New York City Junior Police: "instilling law and order into the minds and hearts of children." (from *The Modern City*, Jan. 1918)

William Temple Hornaday: "too much liberty and too much personal sovereignty." (from W. T. Hornaday, *Thirty Years War for Wildlife*, 1931)

William Temple Hornaday's Junior Naval Reserve on maneuvers in Central Park: learning "the enormous value of discipline." (courtesy National Archives, Washington, D.C.)

Henry Alexander Wise Word: the pariah's son as patrician. (from *Everybody's Magazine*, Sept. 1915)

John Purroy Mitchell: "a dauntless fighting spirit." (courtesy New York Historical Society, New York City)

S. Stanwood Menken, founder and president of the National Security League: "to make democracy safe for the world." (from *Outlook*, Feb. 16, 1916)

Theodore Roosevelt, Jr., in World War II: he "sinned by loving his men too much." (courtesy Eliot Elisofon, *Time* Inc.)

General Clarence Huebner (left) replacing Terry Allen in World War II: the First Infantry Division rejoins the United States Army. (courtesy U.S. Army Office of Military History, Washington, D.C.)

CHAPTER 8

Postwar America: Fears, Hopes and Disappointments

WHEN WORLD WAR I ended, the military preparedness movement buoyantly assessed itself and the national condition. The National Security League, the self-proclaimed catalyst of the wartime revival of patriotism, predicted that its 85,000-man membership would soon triple, thereby making the organization a permanent force in American politics.[1] This euphoria, however, proved ephemeral, for the postwar decade soon became a bitter disappointment. It first presented a false political danger: populism thought to be Bolshevism. Later, in the mid-1920s, it revealed a real cultural hazard: mass consumption capitalism said to be moral decay. While the former problem was manageable, the latter relegated the movement for military training to virtual oblivion.

The Red Scare and the Fear of Radical Democracy

Immediately after the armistice the preparedness movement confronted the challenge of Bolshevism. Although Soviet revolutionists surrendered to the Germans and preached class conflict to the world, that alone does not completely explain the fervid reaction to communism. Russia, then in utter chaos, was a political Rorschach test reflecting hopes and fears. Like naive liberals, apprehensive preparedness leaders erroneously thought that Bolshevism, a yet incipient instrument for social control, was a new form of radical democracy. William Temple Hornaday said it was "the people's Majority" while Robert Bacon called it "the great movement of the organized masses." Speaking for Theodore Roosevelt, the Abbots, and others who thought that revolutionary Russia exemplified popular government without discipline, Henry Alexander Wise Wood graphically described it as "democracy pure and undefiled. . . . None high, none low. An all-on-a-level, obey if you wish people."[2]

If these preparedness patriots had had a better comprehension of communism, they might have been less hostile to it. Once S. Stanwood Menken acquired a more accurate perspective, this former admirer of Imperial Germany found much to praise in the "stoic" Soviet system. Even if it lacked God and property, it "created a revivalist spirit of patriotism and a willingness to give 'until it hurts' [in] two million highly organized Communists [who] are dedicating their lives to the single purpose of upbuilding their country, regardless of individual sacrifice."[3]

Menken's membership in the pro-Stalin right (as opposed to the anti-Stalin left) was nonetheless atypical of the preparedness movement. Most leaders of this attempt "to make democracy safe for the world" considered Bolshevism, defined as radical populism, the social revolution they long had feared. Thus the postwar National Security League, making a transition from military training to Red Scare politics, resolved to "create a greater regard for representative government as distinguished from mass administration [which is] the present curse of Russia."[4]

David Jayne Hill (1850–1932), a veteran of prior constitutional battles, directed the league's new propaganda campaign. A prototypical preparedness leader, he descended from Puritan stock and ascended to the presidencies of Bucknell and Rochester at the time in which both schools were being transformed from nineteenth-century colleges to twentieth-century universities. This transition, according to President Hill, was economically imperative but educationally dangerous for "indolent and inexperienced" students pursuing their own "inclinations." Like other university administrators in the future preparedness movement, he consequently preserved "disciplinarian" courses within a "utilitarian" curriculum and promoted athletics when he stopped teaching moral philosophy.[5]

In 1896 Hill left academic life to pursue a diplomatic career but, in both war and peace, he remained active in movements for social control. As the assistant secretary of state in 1898, he believed that the Spanish-American War developed an unprecedented "consciousness of national solidarity." Later at The Hague Conference and the Carnegie Endowment for International Peace, he promoted an international judiciary whose decrees might provide elitist restraints on democratic diplomacy. During the Progressive Era, he fought against "the rising tide of radicalism" by organizing, in April, 1914, the National Association for Constitutional Government. Thereafter Hill was a leading conservative opponent of direct democracy, the redistribution of income, and "unlimited experimentation in social legislation." His books went through four printings in one year, his pamphlets were distributed by the thousands, and his political society began its own propaganda organ: the *Constitutional Review.*[6]

After World War I erupted, Hill projected domestic issues onto the battle for the seas. He interpreted the struggle as a fight between the forces he supported and resisted in the United States. In his political passion play, the Allies embodied the legal principles ensuring "peace and order" at home. As to the Germans, he disagreed with progressives who saw in them the image of their own enemies. To many liberals, U-boat captains were pirates resembling America's robber-barron class. Hill, on the other hand, saw them as typical agents of a government bureaucracy. Besides these foreign forces, American neutrality also had domestic significance. According to Hill, that policy sacrificed private prerogatives and property on the high seas to the public's general tendency to "deny that any person possesses any rights except those a majority chooses to grant." Yet World War I could be functional as well as symbolic. For Hill, it was an instrument to rectify "the undisciplined state of mind" which predisposed America towards left-wing legislation. Taking a "very active part" in the preparedness movement, he believed that a citizen-soldier army raised by UMT would develop character and discipline, the lack of which plagued his country.[7]

Following the armistice, Hill readily transferred his energy from the war with Germany to the fight against communism. Both enemies, in his mind, represented the limitless use of state power. Because his own National Association for Constitutional Government was "far too academic" to have any "popular influence," he joined the NSL's propaganda campaign. In 1919, this effort, culminating in 20,000 local Constitution Day celebrations, gave Hill a public forum during an "opportune and imperative" period of American history—a time when so-called radicalism seemed to culminate the country's "drift in recent years distinctly away from restraint on the powers of government."[8]

The American Legion: To Make the Doughboys Safe for Democracy

While David Jayne Hill and the National Security League were organizing an anti-Bolshevik campaign at home, other preparedness leaders were planning a similar program in the AEF abroad. A post-armistice diminution in military discipline is traditional, predictable, and probably unavoidable, but in 1919, it was nonetheless upsetting. In Paris, Robert Bacon, having hoped that civilization could be purified by its own pain, witnessed a resurrected night life and repined: "Human nature is weak, oh so weak and returns easily to its excesses and selfish amusements." Back in New York, Archibald Thatcher, a Plattsburg leader recently demobilized from the 77th Division, concluded that democracy is anarchic everywhere "except on the front lines," where "men have come to learn that discipline is really life insurance." In transit from France to America, Dr. Harvey Cushing, who once believed in the medicinal worth of military life, now exclaimed: "I've confessed before that we were a blasphemous and a thieving army but this gambling business never came home to me so acutely as on this voyage home. . . . I'm not sure but that wine and women are less serious evils. War, after all, isn't Hell—its demoralization, which is far worse. Hell, for all one knows, may be very well governed."[9]

However inevitable, this postwar decline in morale was exacerbated by misconceived army policies that "roused the ire of the rank and file." Troops who anticipated immediate rest and an early trip home faced a cold, wet winter, often in the war-wrecked billets of "some God forsaken little village" where they lived, ate, and slept in mud and manure. When not down with influenza or pneumonia, they also faced fifty-one new companies of military police. Those MPs were organized to enforce General Pershing's orders against any "relaxation in discipline, conduct, appearance [and] everything else that marks a soldier." He and the AEF general staff, having learned new lessons in the Meuse-Argonne offensive, wished to retrain their troops for possible operations against a recalcitrant Germany, a communist Russia, or any unforeseen enemy. Even the onset of a secure peace did not affect "regular officers who, by their habits, knew practically but one way of securing discipline, namely, by force." Those devotees of "drill 'em till they drop" continued to work their soldiers, lest enlisted men, "hunting for trouble," work these officers instead. Therefore, regardless of bad weather and a veritable sea of mud, men who no longer felt any need for training were marched in close-order up to six hours a day. Staff officers, who had not undergone the democratizing experience of common deprivation, replaced line officers who would not enforce "the most stringent and unrelenting discipline." Combat soldiers, even decorated heroes, who could not abide these officers, deserted or went AWOL. By mid-1919, as courts-martial increased threefold their wartime rate in the U.S. Second Army, numerous observers, from Leonard Wood to Newton Baker, were commenting on the "bitterness" openly expressed "toward the AEF."[10]

The demoralization of the doughboys had revolutionary implications after the nature of the peace movement changed in World War I. Antiwar activities, formerly the cause of conservative financiers and lawyers, now became linked with a radical indictment of "mechanized slaughter" by the military elite. By 1919, with recent European revolutions in mind, both leftists and rightists felt that embittered American veterans were ripe for rebellion. The belief that ditch-digger life in the trenches had ground combatants into "day laborers of death" inspired proletariat groups like the Wobblies to organize soldiers' and sailors' councils. A similar conviction caused Herbert Hoover to fear whether any anti-Soviet expeditionary force "could resist infection with Bolshevik ideas." While Ralph Easley, the president of the National Civic Federation, worried that "our boys [will] get into the hands of radicals," Archibald Thatcher mused that a veterans' society, sustaining "a disciplinary attitude in economic life," could become a "bulwark against Bolshevism and kindred perils" affecting former soldiers once demobilized.[11]

For nearly a year before the armistice, Theodore Roosevelt, Jr., had envisioned a World War I veterans' society attentive to broad patriotic programs, not provincial doughboy problems. Now, in these "troublous times" when "proper hands" were needed to direct "restless energies in the right direction," he asked the expeditionary force's high command to support an organizational meeting that he had recently planned. The army, imputing waning discipline to a diffuse communist influence, was already trying to rebuild morale through athletics, entertainment, and tradition. Doughboys, however, dismissed all efforts under Pershing's auspices as "headquarters propaganda." Conversely, Roosevelt's own citizen-soldier project bore no such burden. In fact, he seemed to be the ideal sponsor for this kind of program. His name itself evoked patriotic emotions; the man himself held the respect of both the generals and the privates. Hence, when Roosevelt selected the proper men, the army ordered their prompt meeting. Convened to discuss morale, the American Legion was born. Although it was called "the successor of the Grand Army of the Republic," this new veterans' society did not repeat its predecessor's pledge "to inculcate a proper appreciation of their [own] service." The legion, eschewing such lobbyist motives, simply vowed "to inculcate the duty and obligation of the citizen to the State; to preserve the history and incidents of our participation in the war and to cement the ties of comradeship formed in the service."[12]

To build an organization around this declaration, Roosevelt sought immediate help from preparedness movement patriots, especially Rough Riders David Goodrich and John Greenway, and Plattsburgers Grenville Clark, Ralph Barton Perry, Eric Fisher Wood, Henry Stimson, and Charles Henry Brent. Unlike the civic groups, newspapers, and employers who supported the legion out of fear of communism, many of these individuals were more optimistic than apprehensive. The army had trained nearly five million men who had served, they be-

American Legion

lieved, "not for pay but from a sense of duty and obligation." If reorganized, these veterans would present an unprecedented power for immense social improvement. Leonard Wood, the midwife of the Illinois State Legion, maintained that demobilized soldiers could "rule the country for the next fifty years," thereby giving him a "weapon with which to control the present tendency to loot [America]." Similarly, Bishop Charles Henry Brent, the legion's first chaplain and a member of its original governing committee, believed that the organized veterans would "change the character of the whole country, lifting it up to a higher plane of political, industrial and religious life."[13]

Brent, like other preparedness advocates who worried about America's viability, had hoped that war would "make democracy safe for the world." Bolshevism, however, did not frighten this former Plattsburg chaplain who recognized that the word "Red" had become the battle cry of "intrenched interests" everywhere. He not only believed that American society should reconstruct itself along British Labour Party lines, he felt that the Red Scare "dangerously" infringed civil liberties, that New York State's repressive Lusk Laws were a legal abomination, and that all political prisoners should be unconditionally pardoned. No paranoid reactionary searching for protection, Brent joined the American Legion because of the recent confirmation of his faith in battlefield purgatory. In his wartime position as senior chaplain at the AEF's General Headquarters, the bishop believed he had performed the best "piece of work" in his life. Soldiers, "hungry" for moral inspiration and religious information, followed his sermons with "breathless attention." This convinced him that these men, "wonderfully susceptible to [his] influence," were truly preparing themselves for "a new outlook on life."[14]

However naive Brent now appears to have been, he was almost always humble and rarely obtuse. Quick to recognize his own shortcomings, he admitted that his wartime effort to control venereal disease was a fight in which "we have had our sad failures." Its happy successes he frankly attributed to prophylactic treatments, not purity. But while some 71 percent of the AEF had illicit intercourse, many of its soldiers were nonetheless religious, and not just because they had to face death. Troopers offtimes cherish the clergy to compensate for their own profanity, just as soldiers, satiated with killing, will nurture the life of some pet or waif. Sensing this phenomenon, the physically frail Brent disobeyed Pershing's instructions to the contrary and went directly to the front. There, addressing the "most enthusiastic [of all] audiences," he did "heavy and wonderful work" among combatants who had a "real desire for personal attention from chaplains with a religious message."[15]

Brent's audiences were devout and he hoped that the legion—"A-1 men, young, clean and able"—could preserve their faith from the tendency towards postwar hedonism. Soon enough he would see the Jazz Age seduce his foxhole converts with sex made safe by the prophylactics popularized in the war.[16]

Other Plattsburgers were also dazzled by the American Legion's potential to "control the U.S." Ralph Barton Perry, convinced that the army had produced five million men "with a similar point of view," thought that the legion had "overwhelming possibilities," whose fulfillment he hoped to ensure as its executive secretary. His colleagues in the Military Training Camps Association already had paid twenty-five thousand dollars for a national army officers index, the first step towards organizing a veteran's society which would incorporate enlisted men after it established its economic solvency, political conservatism, and public commitment to UMT.[17]

The legion could easily have become this type of officer-dominated organization since its initial leadership was necessarily composed of the elite few with the "time and the means to devote to the work." Typical of the infant legion, its Chicago planning council, led by Colonel Robert McCormick, publisher of the *Tribune,* described itself as "three-fifths money and influence." But despite their upper-class origins, certain key legionnaires, especially Theodore Roosevelt, Jr., worked for a democratic admissions policy. In 1919, he was an indispensible source of money, "service and support" to the organizing committee at the legion's national headquarters. As its chairman, he always "talked about the necessity for an association that could contain *all* of the people in the Army" [italics mine]. To attract an otherwise indifferent rank and file "not falling over themselves to join" the legion, Roosevelt devised an affirmative quota system giving enlisted men a majority in his own committee, 60 percent of the first national convention, and another 60 percent of that meeting's committee assignments. Pragmatically, he realized that the society had to incorporate the "average man" or alienate his loyalty. Personally, he did not fear a doughboy democracy. Like his father before him, he thought that combat veterans were America's natural elite. Although professional soldiers from sergeant to four-star general felt that Roosevelt was an incurable romantic, his own limited experience with infantrymen seemed to support his sentiments.[18]

In 1916 Roosevelt's subordinates in the 26th Infantry Regiment prepared for World War I in the Mexican border campaign. There, while many of their officers were absent on separate assignments, enlisted men were scattered in small detachments over 15,000 square miles. Soldiers, under these conditions, never had "a better chance or a greater need to learn [the] self-reliance" that later proved invaluable in European combat. Armies never seem to learn from one another, least of all when lukewarm allies speak different languages and harbor conflicting desires. In 1917, French strategists under Marshal Pétain vowed to "be lavish with steel but stingy with blood." American generals, then suspicious of French schemes to use Yankee doughboys within their own commands, accused these "Frogs" of having lost "the spirit of the offensive." Carrying out Pershing's call for "no trench nonsense" and a "sound fighting doctrine of our own," the 26th Regiment, one of the first U.S. units in action, learned the cost of "American methods" the hard way. With Roosevelt "the farthest man forward," its line officers were cut down "like fallen bean poles," leading open field assaults frontally upon fortified machine gun positions. Soon, "only enlisted men were left." By the last battle of the war, former orderlies had become the field and company commanders who, in just two days, marched men carrying sixty-pound packs, seventy-two kilometers to fight at Sedan. According to Lt. Gen. Robert Bullard, the rank and file "made this [regiment] the finest fighting machine that I have ever seen."[19]

Roosevelt, Jr., who "always thought that the essence of leadership lay in being genuinely fond of your soldiers," concurred with Bullard. He believed that he knew his men better, and he certainly trusted them more, than he did "anyone else." Of all their traits, he particularly praised the individual initiative that enabled them to carry on without their officers. When the high command later said that subversives caused their post-armistice problems, Roosevelt maintained that a "plague of [staff] officers" undermined "the morale of the men." While Grenville Clark, Perry, and other elitists thought that only "careful leadership" could prevent the legion from degenerating into a veterans' lobby group, Roosevelt worried that the organization might not represent the army's enlisted men who, he believed, exemplified service, loyalty, and idealism. Accurate or not, his position triumphed because elitism would have cost the legion its chance for numerical strength while simultaneously nourishing the "class hatred" it opposed.[20]

When Roosevelt, Brent, Stimson, and other men of high social standing controlled the legion, they were able to squelch demands for the cash bonus. These men, who called that payment a "vicious" proposal, did not reject expenditures for veterans per se. Unlike the "pocketbook hypocrites" whom Roosevelt abhorred, they worked to expand care and compensation for the wounded and disabled. They also advocated a precursor of the GI Bill in the form of scholarships, home loans, public lands, and other grants that required "work on [a veteran's] part." They maintained that this scheme would make the former doughboy of "greater value to both himself and the nation." These Plattsburgers, not opposed to all forms of compensation, sincerely felt that the cash bonus put a "price on patriotism." Thus the issue became their symbolic test of whether the legion would "exist to inculcate individual obligation to the community" or community obligation to the soldier. Its initial defeat in May, 1919, caused a jubilant Roosevelt to declare that his comrades had proved that they really did reorganize "to put something into Government, not take something away." Even men who confessed they once feared that the legion's founders could not "swing the sentiment of the organization," now predicted that the association "will be the biggest [patriotic] thing this country has ever known."[21]

While Roosevelt and his friends rejoiced, perspicacious newspapermen already were reporting that the legion's "rank and file" was sorely tempted to renounce "the higher ideals" of its leadership. Three months later, in August, 1919, a newly democratized legion, demanding the cash bonus, was fulfilling Clark's original prediction by "degenerating into a protective league [and] a merely social organization." The preparedness movement, ironically like the Wobblies, had hoped that veterans would overturn the capitalist code which emphasized material self-interest. In retrospect, both groups were wrong. Army life, making civilian society appear idyllic in comparison to military discipline, had reinforced the real status quo. Unlike Plattsburgers who wished to disseminate their Spartan values, the average veteran aspired to more conventional goals. Pursuing the American dream of greater consumption, he joined a democratic legion that solicited new members with the slogan: "Do you know what you've got coming to you? " Then the average congressman, courting the same veteran bloc that once enticed Plattsburgers, was happy to support the bonus demands of legion posts with 8,000 voters per legislative district.[22]

Once democratized, the American Legion did not completely abandon its old ideals. Yet it certainly reordered its priorities. Plattsburgers had hoped that the organization would become a powerful public lobby for UMT but, as Roosevelt, Jr., admitted, most legionnaires "were not really interested one way or the other." They first ignored the proposal. Then, deferring to those founding fathers who remained particularly "keen on the matter," they gave it a halfhearted endorsement. After that, they took "practically no steps toward furthering the issue."[23]

Military training, however, was only one of the legion's anticipated civic projects. Its first Americanization committee, chaired by Arthur Woods, distributed patriotic history texts and inspirational speakers "to stimulate and promote the real American influence of the public schools." At the same time, Woods's former Groton pupils, Franklin and Ted Roosevelt, were asking individual legionnaires to assume more educational responsibilities. Before the war they and their allies had driven pacifists out of the Boy Scouts and recruited Plattsburgers to take their place. Now, for scoutmasters and coaches, they turned to legion members as "the logical leaders of the youth of the country."[24]

Throughout the 1920s the legion did participate in educational projects with at least enough relish to outrank the Ku Klux Klan on the American Civil Liberties Union's dangerous enemies list. Yet its civic commitment remained relatively weak; its Americanization committee used only 2 to 5 percent of the legion's annual budget. The rest, earmarked for administration and public relations, became a cash bonus for the association's new elite, the professional legionnaires who came to run the organization. In fact, the civic affairs allotment was only part of the public relations program, since it was explicitly used to promote a benign public image. That strategy, furthering the legion's political strength, enabled it to sponsor 473 different bills on Capitol Hill by the end of 1920. This, in turn, allowed the leadership to tell prospective members that, in just one year, it "has extracted from Congress ... more than the Yanks of '61–'65 were able to get in thirty." That, in turn, helped discredit the entire military experience for civic-minded young men who came to feel that the veterans were just another "selfish lobby."[25]

Only two years after Theodore Roosevelt, Jr., began the legion, he found himself "very much out of touch with [its] line of thought." He frequently warned its members that they would be civilian slackers, "false to their actions in war unless they prove themselves self-sacrificing and earnest patriots in peace." But, like other founding fathers, he too was honored, cheered, and then ignored.[26]

The 1920s: Economic Expansion and Patriotic Contraction

In the months immediately after the armistice, moderate labor unions striking for equity, juxtaposed with verbose radicals yelling "revolution," created an illusion of institutional instability. By 1921–22, however, the nation had embarked on a peacetime productivity that decreased inflation but increased spending. The recovery of capitalism subsequently forged an economic consensus that largely destroyed the political left. Henceforth, advertising and installment-buying were rarely said to be "the vilest system yet devised to create trouble." Indeed, they stimulated intraclass competition ("keeping up with the Joneses") rather than working-class resentment and revolt. Even laborers who lacked an adequate paycheck participated in the consumption culture, through financial credit or the mass media.[27]

The economic conditions which helped stabilize politics nonetheless accelerated cultural change. Advanced technology, routinizing many aspects of production, enabled entrepreneurs to concentrate on marketing, now the major problem of American business. To create a constant demand for the consumer goods that continuously flowed off the conveyer belts, their advertising agents had to challenge the "customs of ages." But before they could do this, politicians would have to provide five million dollars worth of copy space that proved the enormous power of "salesmanship." As late as 1914, mass consumption could still be said to be "distinctly Utopian," if not immoral. ("Any man whose wife wants more than two calico dresses a week is married to an indecent woman.") Now in the 1920s, after copywriters for the government successfully launched wartime propaganda which was called "the world's greatest adventure in advertising," the two billion-dollar-a-year commercial advertisement business had the prestige and confidence to attempt to market new products by selling "a new philosophy of life." It thereupon adopted a cult of youth favoring originality, inclination, style, and consumption at the expense of tradition, maturity, durability, and thrift. This cultural change profoundly distressed those patriotic societies actively involved in the recent Red Scare panic. If the National Security League, the American Defense Society, and the National Civic Federation were solely concerned with political stability, they might have declared victory and voluntarily dissolved. However, their leaders emotionally required certainty, familiar social standards, and the sense of permanence on which "character" is built. America's philosophic change thus kept them politically active. Opposing the youth culture as a "barbaric" denial of the "wisdom of the past," they became spokesmen for those who still hoped to apply the old moral code of limited wants to "the gravest of all responsibilities in life—namely, the training and character molding of the growing generation."[28]

While most of the nation wished to be left alone to enjoy consumer goods and mass entertainment, preparedness organizations urged their fellow citizens to concentrate on the repression of subversives. With few subversives left to repress, their political fear seems to have been based on their belief that the revolt against "decent restraints of print, speech and dress" foretold class revolution. ("It is the breaking away from the old faiths. When one of these goes, the rest is likely to follow.") From their premise that "socialism means the destruction of the family, home, religion, and the extinction of the greatest government on earth, that of the parent over the offspring," many patriots concluded that the decline of parental authority and traditional customs

Modernist youth culture

adults now imitate youth!

meant socialism. In fact, it only meant consumer capitalism, whose cult of youth produced immature parents and independent adolescents. After advertising encouraged adults to seek youth and self-expression for themselves, children had less reason to defer to elders who were often emulating them.[29]

This generational role-reversal was facilitated by technology's premier consumer innovation, the automobile, which every other family owned by 1927. As a major purchase by parents and a place for teenage privacy, it enhanced adult demands for extended credit and hid adolescents from parental oversight. Nonetheless the NSL, overlooking Henry Ford, blamed radical agitators for subverting family controls, mid-Victorian morals, and Christian self-restraint. These critics consequently encountered imaginary political dangers throughout this apolitical decade. In 1927, three years after radicalism died with a whimper in Robert La Follette's presidential campaign, the league was still complaining about unprecedented "revolts against authority, political turmoil and social chaos." The *New Republic* investigated the organization and noted its paranoia but, overlooking cultural issues, could not understand its fears. The magazine remarked that after the Bolshevik issue "petered out" in 1921, the patriots began to fight an "inexplicably catholic" enemy. Neither its writer nor his subjects fully understood that prosperity (not poverty) could be the subversive force and that the real adversary was a cultural process, not a political cabal.[30]

Mistaking cultural change for political revolution was only one root of the patriots' paranoia. A nostalgia for arms was its other source. In retrospect, the Great War seemed to have displayed "the highest heights of self-sacrifice." Indeed, it was barely over before the Security League resolved that "the natural [postwar] let down" must not "have more than a temporary sway." Its officers, hoping to replace peacetime individualism with wartime unity and resolve, used internal subversives as functional equivalents of the German Hun, an enemy whose presence had supposedly created moral uniformity within the United States. Yet all this only bored the rest of the country, as the NSL admitted. "The smug, self-confident American citizen" dismissed its assertions by saying: "'I am through with war.'" Patriotic paranoia, ignored by others, served only personal needs. Imaginary enemies, saving preparedness organizations from total dissolution, provided its members with the compensation of indignation, a target for hostility, a purpose to justify their lives, and a small community of support in a morally alien world. This outlook, however, cost the patriots whatever political influence they had. United by their common principles, not by the mass media or the chain store, they became irrelevant to many of their countrymen, who seemed to care most for what they bought and where they bought it. Because those Americans enjoyed the mass-produced goods that tend to create classless consumption patterns, they were as oblivious to appeals from the reactionary right as from the radical left.[31]

During World War I, the *New Republic* thought that the preparedness societies were serious threats to civil liberties. Now in the 1920s, as Security League membership plunged from 85,000 in 1919 to 15,000 in 1927, the magazine paid its old adversaries the ultimate insult of pity. They were, it said, "old fashioned and sadly, too... ridiculous."[32]

The NSL, as an outcast from the cultural consensus for consumer goods, went through the 1920s fruitlessly "begging" apathetic businessmen for memberships and money. Repeatedly spurned, it wondered why other "people somehow do not feel the need of its work in the cause of constitutional teaching, national defense, and [the campaign] against radicalism." Actually, it was estranged from the capitalists it claimed to represent. While these two groups shared a common concern for private property, they nonetheless possessed irreconcilable conceptions of life. Preparedness leaders were often reactionaries alienated from urbanization, technology, economic growth, and modernity itself. Capitalists, on the other hand, were conservatives content with material progress and economic individualism. Once political radicalism showed its real weakness, businessmen would not sustain the Red Scare, which consequently waned. They certainly filed no brief against their times. Historically, merchants and manufacturers have been America's postwar heroes. Promising material pleasure in peace, they upstage politicians and soldiers who recently imposed sacrifice in war. The business community, gratified with their preeminence, abandoned the patriotic Jeremiahs who subsequently cursed the indifference they consistently encountered. Ironically, these patriots were the real subversives of the age, for the apathy and affluence which they denounced created the consensus that destroyed the political rebels they feared.[33]

James Montgomery Beck (1861–1936)—constitutional scholar and President Harding's solicitor general—formulated reactionary patriotism into a systematic philosophy. As the Security League's unofficial theoretician through the 1920s, he wrote that this period witnessed a general "revolt against the past in all departments of human life," whether "literature, art, music, sociology [or] government." Less sophisticated patriots blamed radicalism, evolution, or the closed shop for the disconcerting developments they could not comprehend. Beck, however, recognized the more substantive, technological cause. A patrician Luddite in the John Ruskin-Thomas Carlyle tradition, he blamed a "mechanical civilization" for "destroying the spiritual element in man." By minimizing "real physical exertion" and the incentives for craftsmanship, industrialization caused an "excessive elimination of work"—"the greatest moral force in the world." This Beck insisted, "was the root cause of the steady deterioration in human character," symptomatically expressed in America's "excessive thirst for pleasure" and its diminished "spirit of discipline." Before 1917, that type of social criticism would have found its home in the movement for universal military training: a self-identified renaissance of work, obedience, and character. Now, after soldiers in the Great War were said to have been victims of the "tyranny of [army] technology," Beck's indictment lacked a conceivable solution. In this predicament he could only rant away at the traditional bogeymen of reactionaries: obsequious Jews, pluralistic cities, "smoke belching factories," sexual equality, and the mass media.[34]

Like Ruskin, his mentor, Beck still maintained that war was an emotional experience requiring a spiritual preparedness. Surveying America's alleged moral decline, he must have doubted its military capability. He would not live until the next world war, when romantic reactionaries in Germany, Italy, and Japan staked their empires on their own belief that machine-age Americans, having "materialistic conceptions of happiness," were a weak-willed people "spoiled by luxuries." Contrary to their prediction, America's "Ford-minded young men" provided their country with a distinct combat advantage. As an army of amateur mechanics, able to repair their own equipment while steering huge convoys across vast continents, they substantially increased military mobility. General issue "GIs," nicknamed for production off the assembly line, may not have had the puritan spirit implied by the "Yanks" of World War I. No matter, they had the machine.[35]

In the 1940s, ideological reaction proved a military miscalculation; in the 1920s it was a major political mistake. Then the National Security League "drifted into obscurity" along with the American Defense Society. It subsequently struggled through the 1930s without making the *New York Times' Index* let alone the nation's policy. The Communist Party's National Students' League, apparently oblivious to any rival claim, would adopt the NSL insignia without fear of confusion or laughter. When, in 1940, the once powerful preparedness society finally died, the people who closed its dilapidated, walk-up office found a vast quantity of "old records, letters, etc. that certainly ceased to be of consequence 16 to 20 years ago." They observed that the fact that this literature was kept "seemed to show a strong thought in the Officers and Directors that the League [would] be of great importance for a very long time." Then, ceasing their reflections, they burned the files.[36]

NOTES

1. S. Stanwood Menken cited in *National Security League Bulletin* 1 (June, 1918):3.

2. For Bolshevism and American public opinion in general, see Christopher Lasch, *The American Liberals and the Russian Revolution* (New York: McGraw, Hill, 1972), pp. 68–69, 76–77, 95–100, 105–6. Hornaday, *Awake! America*, p. 129; Scott, ed., *Robert Bacon*, p. 435; Roosevelt, *Great Adventure*, pp. 338, 342–44; "Russia's Catastrophe," *Outlook* 120 (Dec. 22, 1919):551; Henry Alexander Wise Wood's letter in the *New York Tribune*, May 31, 1917.

3. S. Stanwood Menken, "The Russian Dilemma: Why I Favor Recognition," *North American Review* 230 (Dec., 1930):660, 662.

4. *National Security League Future Work* (New York: National Security League, 1919), p. 3; statement of Security League President Charles Lydecker in House, *Hearings on National Security League*, 65th Cong., 3rd Sess., 1919, p. 143.

5. *New York Times*, Mar. 9, 1919, June 23, 1919; Aubrey L. Parkman, "David Jayne Hill" (Ph.D. diss., University of Rochester, 1961), pp. 1, 42, 49.

6. David Jayne Hill: *Our National Development* (Philadelphia: Anvil Printing, 1902), p. 7; *Americanism, What It is* (New York: D. Appleton, 1916), pp. 229–30; *The National Association for Constitutional Government: A Statement of its Aims and Purposes* (Washington: n.p., n.d.), passim. Parkman, "David Jayne Hill," pp. 234–38, 361–63, 412–23, 451–53.

7. Hill, *Americanism*, pp. 38, 90–93, 190–91, 201–2; speech by Hill in *Proceedings of National Security Congress*, p. 25; Hill quoted in Parkman, "David Jayne Hill," p. 489. For perceptions by progressives, see Robert Dalleck, *The American Style of Foreign Policy: Cultural Politics and Foreign Affairs* (New York: Knopf, 1983), pp. 78–83.

8. Hill to Nicholas Murray Butler, Sept. 14, 1918; Nov. 29, 1918, Butler MSS; David Jayne Hill, *Washington As A Citizen*, (n.p., n.d.), p. 18.

9. Scott, ed., *Robert Bacon*, pp. 418–19; Archibald Thacher to George Van Horn Mosley, Jan. 15, 1919, Mosley Letterbooks MSS, Library of Congress; Cushing, *From A Surgeon's Journal*, p. 508.

10. The quotations are from : ibid., p. 509; George Marshall in Pogue, *George C. Marshall: Education of a General*, p. 194; Pershing and Gen. David Shanks in Wecter, *When Johnny Comes Marching Home*, pp. 273; Gen. Robert Bullard in Millet, *The General*, p. 429; Leonard Wood to Frank McCoy, May 31, 1919, McCoy MSS, Box 15; Vandiver, *Black Jack*, 2:1011. Also see Fosdick, *Chronicle of a Generation*, pp. 165, 177–81; Fred Davis Baldwin, "The American Enlisted Man in World War I" (Ph.D. diss., Princeton University, 1964), pp. 186, 221.

11. Marchand, *American Peace Movement and Social Reform*, passim. Leftists and then Hoover quoted in Leed, *No Man's Land*, pp. 91, 138, 206; Joan Hoff Wilson, *Herbert Hoover: Forgotten Progressive* (Boston: Little, Brown and Company, 1975), pp. 54–55. Ralph Easley to Theodore Roosevelt, Nov. 6, 1918, Dec. 17, 1918, Roosevelt MSS, Reel 300; Archibald Thacher to Kenneth Budd, Jan. 27, 1919, Grenville Clark MSS.

12. Richard Seeley Jones, *A History of the American Legion* (Indianapolis: Bobbs-Merrill, 1946), pp. 25-26, 29. Roosevelt, Jr., quoted in *New York Times,* Mar. 21, 1919; Raymond Moley, Jr., *The American Legion Story* (New York: Duel, Sloan & Pearce, 1966), p. 63. Roosevelt, Jr., to Eleanor B. Roosevelt, Jan. 21, 1919; Roosevelt, Jr., to Frederick Palmer, Jan. 9, 1931; Roosevelt, Jr., "The Founding of the American Legion," 1937: all in Roosevelt, Jr., MSS, Boxes 7, 50, 52. For the rank and file's esteem for Roosevelt, Jr., see David L. Shillinglaw, *An American in the Army and YMCA, 1917-1920: The Diary of David L. Shillinglaw,* ed. Glen Holt (Chicago: University of Chicago Press, 1971), p. 111.

13. Roosevelt, Jr., to Henry Stimson, Apr. 9, 1919, Stimson MSS; Grenville Clark to Roosevelt, Jr., Feb. 11, 1919, Clark MSS. The first two quotations are from Leonard Wood to Theodore Roosevelt, Sept. 19, 1918, Roosevelt MSS, Reel 292. Brent quoted in George S. Wheat, *The Story of the American Legion* (New York: Putnam's, 1919), pp. 21-22.

14. Brent, untitled statement, Feb. 15, 1918; Brent to John Markol, Feb. 9, 1920; Brent to Bishop Lawrence, Mar. 31, 1919, Good Friday, 1919, Dec. 20, 1919; Brent to Mrs. W. C. Rivers, Oct. 4, 1918: all in Brent MSS, Boxes 14, 16.

15. Zabrinski, *Bishop Brent,* p. 121, 127-28; Brent to E. C. Carter, Jan. 27, 1918; Brent to R. Oglivy, Feb. 2, 1918; Brent to Endicott Peabody, Feb. 15, 1918: all in Brent MSS, Boxes 14, 16. The statistic is from George Walker, *Venereal Disease in the American Expeditionary Forces* (Baltimore: Medical Standard Book Co., 1922), p. 101.

16. Brent Diary, June 6, 9, 1919, Brent MSS, Box 2; Davis, "American Enlisted Man in World War I," p. 45.

17. Ralph Barton Perry, "The American Legion in Politics," *Outlook* 124 (Jan. 14, 1920): 63; Perry to Grenville Clark, Apr. 12, 1919; Clark to Perry, Feb. 8, 1919, May 1, 1919, Clark MSS; Delancey K. Jay to George Van Horn Mosley, Jan. 10, 1919, Feb. 4, 1919, Mosley Letterbooks MSS.

18. Milton Foreman (Chairman of the American Legion's Executive Committee) to George Van Horn Mosley, Apr. 12, 1919, Mosley Letterbooks MSS; John S. Miller to Col. G. C. Seaman, May 15, 1919; Thomas F. Harwood to John S. Miller, June 25, 1919: both in American Legion MSS, Chicago Historical Association; Roosevelt, Jr., to Eleanor B. Roosevelt, Jan. 21, 1919, Roosevelt, Jr., MSS, Box 7; *Boston Evening Transcript,* May 7, 1919, 3:3. My statement on Roosevelt's romanticism is based on personal interviews with Gen. Robert Porter, Sept. 26, 1972; Sgt. Henry Kelty, Oct. 10, 1971. The first thing Porter said to me was: "So you're studying Ted Roosevelt. He thought GIs were the finest people in the world. What a romanticist he was."

19. The first quotations are from Gen. Robert Bullard, *Personalities and Reminiscences of the War* (Garden City: Doubleday & Page, 1925), p. 222; Marshal Pétain quoted in DeWeerd, *President Wilson Fights His War,* pp. 184-85. For American tactics and contemporary quotations about it, see Millet, *The General,* pp. 318, 322, 405; Baldwin, "American Enlisted Man in World War I," pp. 97-98, 104, 170; Vandiver, *Black Jack,* 2:772. The quotation on Roosevelt, Jr., is from George Van Horn Mosley to Roosevelt, Jr., Aug. 11, 1918, Mosley Let-

terbooks MSS. Robert Bullard Diary, Oct. 18, 1919, Bullard MSS, Library of Congress.

20. Roosevelt, Jr.: to Maj. Philipps, June 1, 1939; "Graduating Address to United States Naval Academy, June 2, 1922; "Sergeant Rose," 1927: all in Roosevelt, Jr., MSS, Boxes 22, 7, 41; Grenville Clark to Ralph Barton Perry, Apr. 10, 1919, Clark MSS; Clark to Perry, Apr. 16, 1919, Perry MSS.

21. Charles Nagel to Henry Stimson, July 7, 1923; Stimson to Nagel, July 9, 1923, Stimson MSS; Bishop Charles Henry Brent Diary, Aug. 23, 1919, Brent MSS, Box 2: Roosevelt, Jr., to R. J. Caldwell, May 11, 1920, Roosevelt, Jr., MSS, Box 20; Stimson quoted in *New York Times,* Oct. 26, 1920; Roosevelt, Jr., quoted in George Palmer Putnam, "The Birth of the American Legion," *Outlook* 122 (May 21, 1919):104. The final quotation is from illegible to Eric Fischer Wood, July 19, 1919, Fischer Wood MSS, Series 2, Box 1, Syracuse University.

22. *Brooklyn Eagle,* Apr. 11, 1919; Clark to Roosevelt, Jr., Feb. 11, 1919, Clark MSS. For veterans in general, see Stouffer, *American Soldier,* 2:596–97, 620–23. *American Legion Weekly,* July, 1919 through Dec., 1919; Henry Stimson Diary, Feb. 17, 1931, Stimson MSS.

23. Roosevelt, Jr., to Gen. F. C. Marshall, Jan. 3, 1920, Roosevelt, Jr., MSS, Box 68; Henry Stimson Diary, Dec. 10, 1919, Stimson MSS; Horace Stebbins to Grenville Clark, July 7, 1920, Clark MSS.

24. Statement of Arthur Woods in "Minutes of the Meeting of the National Americanization Committee," Jan. 19, 1920, p. 5, copy in the American Legion National Library, Indianapolis, Ind.; *American Legion Weekly,* Feb. 3, 1920, p. 18; Roosevelt, Jr., quoted in *New York Times,* Sept. 6, 1924; Franklin Roosevelt to A. L. Boyce, Mar. 8, 1922, Group 14, Box 1, Roosevelt Presidential Library.

25. Rodney G. Minot, "The Organized Veterans and the Spirit of Americanism, 1898–1959" (Ph.D. diss., Stanford University, 1960), pp. 104, 132–36; American Legion quoted in Wecter, *When Johnny Comes Marching Home,* p. 446: Eric Sevareid, *Not So Wild a Dream* (New York: Knopf, 1946), pp. 63, 66.

26. Roosevelt, Jr., Diary, Oct. 27, 1921, Roosevelt, Jr., MSS, Box 1; Roosevelt, Jr., quoted in *New York Times,* Sept. 16, 1921, Feb. 24, 1925.

27. Robert Murray, *Red Scare: A Study in National Hysteria, 1919–1920* (New York: McGraw-Hill, 1964), pp. 240–47, 253–62. Traditional nineteenth-century businessman quoted in Mark Hanan, "Corporate Growth through Venture Management," *Harvard Business Review* 47 (Jan.–Feb., 1969):44; Robert S. Lynd and Helen Merrill Lynd, *Middletown: A Study in Modern American Culture* (New York: Harcourt, Brace & World, 1929), pp. 80–88, 98, 158.

28. Cochran, *200 Years of American Business,* pp. 89, 126. The quotations against mass consumption are from Henry Ford as cited in Keith Sward, *The Legend of Henry Ford* (New York: Atheneum, 1968), pp. 54–55. For quotations from advertising executives and their activities in WWI, see Stuart Ewen, *Captains of Consciousness: Advertising and the Social Roots of the Consumer Culture* (New York: McGraw-Hill, 1976), pp. 19, 54, 201; Stephen Vaugh, *Holding Fast the Inner Lines: Democracy, Nationalism, and the Committee on Public Information* (Chapel Hill: University of North Carolina Press, 1980), pp. 141–42, 191.

For the patriots, see *National Security League Quarterly* 4 (Dec., 1930):4; Sidney Howard, "Our Professional Patriots," *New Republic* 40 (Sept. 10, 1924):38. The final quotation is from Ralph Easley, *The Youth Movement: Do We Want It Here?* (n.p.: n.d.), pp. 26–27, 45.

29. *National Security League Bulletin* 2 (Dec., 1919):4. The second and third quotations are from James M. Beck, "The Age of Lawlessness," *Current History* 25 (Oct., 1921):62.

30. Joseph Cashman, *Give the Constitution a Chance* New York: National Security League, 1927), p. 2. Howard, "Our Professional Patriots," 39 (Aug. 20, 1924):347. For general role-reversal, see Canby, *American Memoir,* pp. 37–42.

31. Beck, "Age of Lawlessness," p. 66; *National Security League Future Work* (New York: National Security League, 1919), pp. 3, 6. Security League quoted in Howard, "Our Professional Patriots," 40 (Sept. 10, 1924): 38. For general ideas on political paranoia, mass consumption, and politics, see David Bryon Davis, ed., *The Fear of Conspiracy: Images of Un-American Subversion from the Revolution to the Present* (Ithaca: Cornell University Press, 1971), pp. 13–16; Boorstin, *Americans,* pp. 89–165; Seymour Martin Lipset, *Political Man: The Social Basis of Politics* (Garden City: Doubleday Anchor, 1963), pp. 50–51, 268–69.

32. Peterson and Fite, *Opponents of War,* p. 120; Howard, "Our Professional Patriots," *New Republic* (Sept. 17, 1924):73.

33. The first quotations are from Robert Bullard Diary, Mar. 1, 1926, Dec. 27, 1926, Bullard MSS. Sward, *Legend of Henry Ford,* p. 279; Murray, *Red Scare,* p. 253.

34. Morton Keller, *In Defense of Yesterday: James Beck and the Politics of Conservatism, 1861–1936* (New York: Coward-McCann, 1958), passim; James Beck: *The Six Fundamental Principles of the Constitution* (New York: George H. Doran, 1924), pp. 296, 314; "Age of Lawlessness," pp. 64–65; to Henry Fairchild Osborn, Feb. 15, 1926, Mar. 4, 1926, Beck MSS, Princeton University; "America's Need of Youth," *Saturday Evening Post* 193 (May 14, 1921):8. For Luddite attacks on WWI, see Leed, *No Man's Land,* pp. 31–32, 96.

35. James Beck, "A Yearning for World Peace," *Annals of the American Academy of Political and Social Science* 72 (July, 1917):214–16; Fujiwara Akra, "The Role of the Japanese Army," *Pearl Harbor as History: Japanese-American Relations, 1931–1941,* ed., Dorothy Borg and Shumpei Okamoto (New York: Columbia University Press, 1973), p. 194; Mussolini quoted in John P. Diggins, *Mussolini and Fascism: The View from America* (Princeton: Princeton University Press, 1972), p. 458; George Patton quoted in Blumenson, ed., *Patton Papers, 1940–1945,* p. 728; Weigley, *History of the United States Army,* p. 477.

36. Charles Davison to William T. Hornaday, Apr. 18, 1934, Hornaday MSS, Box 11; Millet, *The General,* p. 468; Robert Bullard Diary, Aug. 27, 1942, Bullard MSS.

CHAPTER 9

The 1920s: Prosperity, Defeat, and Retreat

THE GROWTH of national prosperity produced an out-growth of public apathy which enfeebled the National Security Leaque throughout the 1920s. The same factors also crippled the universal military training movement, which lacked financial and political support from government officials, the electorate, and army officers alike. Pre-paredness leaders, failing to enact this major goal, promoted mass athletics, outdoor camping, classical education, and heroic literature. But subject to the same public indifference arising from commercial concerns, these moral substitutes for the army fared no better than UMT. Sports were often entertainment spectacles and a day in the woods meant a drive in the country. Classical education was not economically expedient and heroic literature was artistically passé. Their hopes shattered, some preparedness patriots fled the nation they had failed to reform. Leonard Wood, setting an example for Henry Stimson and Theodore Roosevelt, Jr., went off to the Philippine Islands. Toiling away at the now thankless task of colonial administration, he died in relative obscurity. Others, specifically George Wharton Pepper and William Temple Hornaday, took sojourns to the church or the zoo. In these quarters, accompanied by God or the gorilla, they found pesonal asylums of their own.

The Decline and Fall of the Universal Military Training Movement

Citizen-soldier training prospered in war and then failed in peace. The national army, turning raw recruits into seasoned soldiers, seemed to have sustained the military argument for modern militiamen. In one year of war, with three months of intense instruction, the service produced ten times more officers than West Point had graduated in its history. From a bare 6,000 regulars, that corps grew into 180,000 men whose performance in battle sustained America's demand for an auton-

omous army free from the French and English high commands. This
lesson was not lost on AEF headquarters, whose major task had been
one of training. During the war, General Pershing and his demanding
staff showed little sympathy for draftees, whom they purposely treated
as if they were Academy cadets. Nonetheless, after the armistice, they
were apt to proclaim "that soldiers should come from the people, the
whole people and nothing but the people"—certainly not from a professional caste. Even that fortress of professionalism, the War Department
in Washington, moved to add an auxiliary citizen-soldier component to
its postwar plans. It too agreed that "modern war is a war of nations
rather than of armies." Understandably optimistic, preparedness leaders felt ready to reorganize the whole defense force so as to make the
army "part of National life instead of a little trade union performance."[1]

Their hopes, however, proved premature. Americans, once fearing
that a professional army might endanger their political liberties, now
worried that a citizen force, raised by universal military training, would
endanger their pursuit of personal pleasure. The preparedness leaders,
school officials, and penal officers who proposed UMT wanted more
"social discipline"; the general public—producers and consumers alike
—preferred less public expense. Congressman Frank Mondell (R.-Wy.),
"*the* man who killed Universal Training," grasped the popular will
when he buried this proposal in a billion-dollar-a-year cost-estimate prediction. Mondell's financial calculations may have been wrong, but his
political instinct surely was right when he tapped the national aspira-
tion to end military spending and resume consumer-goods capitalism.[2]

Along with taxes, UMT itself aroused "widespread opposition
throughout the country." In fact, the policy was inherently unpopular
since it aimed to curtail popular appetites. Americans, fighting a war to
end all wars, joined an army to end all armies, not the army to sustain
Leonard Wood. When they got out, they usually rejected the training
that their victories confirmed and dismissed this general as "a bag of
wind." Consequently Wood, as a presidential candidate in 1920, had to
camouflage his principles behind "universal training for National Service": a slogan that denied legal "liability for military duty."[3]

While Wood, in this presidential year, equivocated on his own creation, others completely dodged the "political folly" of mandatory training. In caucus, House Democrats, disregarding President Wilson's recent conversion to UMT, voted 6 to 1 to protect their jobs by opposing
this program. Then Republicans, "overwhelmed by a flood of letters
and telegrams from agitated constituents," decided to kill the issue in
committee before it killed them in the upcoming election. As George
Wharton Pepper observed: "Neither party is likely to prescribe a course
of treatment which makes people uncomfortable. It is like recommend-

ing compulsory exercise at a meeting of the fat man's club." Hereafter, Plattsburgers always tried to see that Congress voted on military training only *after* elections.[4]

Although UMT failed politically, the 1920 Army Reorganization Act did include a voluntary program for Citizen Military Training Camps (CMTC). By using them to provide "a big time demonstration of camp life and training," preparedness leaders still hoped to "convince the country [to enact their] comprehensive obligatory system" of militiaman conscription. However, Plattsburg had existed since 1913 without inspiring great emulation in the past. Now, when conventional wisdom held that disarmament ensured peace, it was naive to think that these camps could "flank attack" public opinion in a future devoid of specific threats of war.[5]

Peace between nations did not preclude a bloodless combat at home. The (Plattsburg) Military Training Camps Association and the regular army establishment annually fought for the lion's share of a retrenched defense budget. In retrospect, by the early 1920s, the tactical futility of World War I seemed to show that citizen-armies ("the Nations in Arms") were ponderous creatures likely to sink into a "butting match" that bled every one white, victor and vanquished alike. Therefore, a new strategic emphasis on airplanes, artillery, and armor favored funding a "small, professional and highly mobile" army that promised to win a quick victory. In these hard times for the infantry, most of its officers naturally favored themselves over their citizen-soldier competition. Chief of Staff Pershing remained "sympathetic" to the arguments of the MTCA. A former school teacher always worried about degradation in democracy, he endorsed the Plattsburg program with the standard litany stating its "physical, moral and mental benefits." Yet even he, an advocate of UMT since 1916, could not restrain the War Department's consensus decision to emphasize conventional army divisions with regular command and staff positions. According to one bitter critic, a "lifer" himself, the general staff did "all they could to kill the whole citizen army program."[6]

Although an enlarged military budget might have revived the MTCA's project, its members rejected the army's advice to lobby for an overall increase in defense appropriations. Plattsburgers, as traditionalists who sustained their organization with their own time and money, faithfully believed in the small and balanced budgets that defeated their plans. Convinced that a viable citizen-training system was "purely a question of priorities," they tried "to persuade" the regulars "to cut down their own items." The professionals, adding irony to injury, used the MTCA's own argument to dismiss its appeal. The War Department said that "under budgetary restrictions" it had to subordinate educational camps "molding better citizens" to other activities "of greater value from a strictly military viewpoint."[7]

The rage for public economy severed the army's wartime rapprochement with society. Once again proud and glad to be an insular institution separate from the world of civilians, the service was reassuming the "professional" stance it held before the appearance of Plattsburg, the AEF, and the movement for UMT. "The code of the soldier," wrote one officer, "can never be the same as that of the civilian; why try to mix them?" "In method and way," said another, they "are as far apart as the antipodes." Civilian preparedness leaders, who opposed the army's policy of "monastic seclusion," should have understood the military's point of view. Many of them would soon seek isolation for themselves.[8]

In the meantime, unable to budge the armed forces, Plattsburgers appealed directly to Congress, the President, and the public. To appropriations committees they claimed that their summer instruction camps provided an inexpensive "dose of moral tonic" and the "least military form of [military] training." Although Congress seemed "fully sympathetic," the MTCA lobby, which began the decade planning universal training, expended all its energy fighting reductions in an admittedly inadequate program.[9]

When those appeals to Congress failed, Plattsburgers personally brought their case before President Calvin Coolidge, a man who handled most petitioners by staring out the window and smoking a smelly cigar. He had already told the American Legion that "our people have had all the war, all the taxation, and all the military service that they want." Nonetheless, he was now unusually "cordial and sympathetic" to the MTCA delegation. His own son once enrolled in their program and Coolidge, "thoroughly conversant with the CMTC," praised it for building patriotism, along with physical and mental health. But, "obsessed with the idea of economy," this businessman's president in a businessman's era felt that the military budget was "a business proposition." Although Coolidge supported UMT in principle, it proved "merely a question of money with him."[10]

Having failed in their appeal for public funds, Plattsburgers asked private philanthropists to support the training camps as schools "of clean living and true patriotism." In 1916, John Rockefeller, Jr., who thought UMT would "do away with class spirit," had lent his public relations expert to the MTCA. Postwar advocates of military training therefore solicited funds from the Rockefeller Foundation, whose trustees now included Arthur Woods and Bishop Charles Henry Brent. The former already favored their program, but another trustee, Raymond Fosdick, remained wary of what he had called the "blundering, chaotic, stupid business" of battle. During the war, to the bemusement of professional soldiers who thought his efforts "hopeless," he fought venereal disease and alcoholism in the army. Now obstructing a grant to the MTCA, Fosdick helped ensure that this foundation, primarily funding scientific research, continued to belittle "mere patriotism."[11]

Plattsburgers, still searching for support, appealed to private industry by presenting their camps as a form of "business insurance for social stability." Tactically, they may have remembered the arguments successfully used by naval expansionists in the late nineteenth century. Then, admirals appealed to the public's "dollar and cents point of view" by declaring bigger fleets would provide defense contracts and protect foreign trade. Although the army might not create similar markets at home or abroad, some employers were now led to believe that its training could ensure industrial tranquility. Those businessmen sent their employees to camp and, at times, requested their workers' military records for their own information. More often, however, industrialists either contributed a few hundred dollars or, like Andrew Mellon, Elbert Gary, and Charles Schwab, completely ignored even direct appeals. Apparently most of these men felt that advertising (not UMT) was the best way to provide a "conscious and intelligent manipulation of the organized habits and opinions of the masses."[12]

The Military Training Camps Association, like the National Security League, could not thrive in peace and prosperity. Between the two world wars, the appropriations voted for their army camps accommodated only one-fourth of the applicants, some 2.5 percent of a *universal* military training program. From Pershing to Congress to Coolidge, "sympathetic" Americans verbally endorsed a policy for which they would not pay. A small public budget took priority and, George Wharton Pepper to the contrary, Americans felt that military training was an expensive "dose of moral tonic."[13]

Moral Equivalents of War: Athletics, Camping, Classics, and Literature

With the universal military training movement in decline, some of its supporters became advocates of compulsory athletics. Harvard's student body after the war rapidly lost "interest in all military things" and its president forbade its ROTC to drill on campus. There and elsewhere, club rites became the new collegiate equivalent to combat as "fraternity patriots," who weathered "Hell week," displayed their house pins as medals of honor. Plattsburgers, unimpressed with this type of analogue to war, tried to rebuild "health, morale and discipline" by staging a "thorough revolution" in physical education at Harvard. Influenced by wartime Student Army Training Corps activities, Grenville Clark, Ralph Barton Perry, Arthur Woods, and others planned a compulsory "mass athletics" program as a physical, ethical, and spiritual education in "loyalty, readiness, leadership and courage." They felt that their physical drill policy did not belong in the Physical Education Department. To succeed, it should be placed in the Department of Military Science and Tactics in order to accomplish a clean break from "the old form of competitive sports, where group training is relegated to a few despised gymnasium classes." Their plans, however, were not fulfilled. Harvard College, like the American Legion, made a token commitment that proved a substantive disappointment. Although physical education for freshmen became a requirement, traditional instructors directed traditional programs within those traditionally "despised gymnasium classes."[14]

Moreover, at Ivy League and most other schools, physical education remained a side show to the main event—the intercollegiate athletic spectaculars that stimulated drinking and gambling while hindering mass exercise. During the SATC period, optimists predicted the demise of these events after numerous colleges pledged never to resume furnishing "the general public with substitutes for the circus." Nevertheless, athletic reform aborted in 1919 when, for example, Harvard's Student Council and its "most vociferous alumni" immediately resolved to resume football on "a basis identical to that of former years." By the end of the first postwar season, leading critics were already expressing their "sense of depression and disappointment at a marked reaction in athletic matters, particularly football, away from the relatively high [wartime] standards."[15]

Contrary to the expectations of military preparedness leaders, war reinforced the commercialization it was supposed to undercut. Combat had not only exhausted the will to sacrifice amusements, it had depleted athletic treasuries which had upkeep expenses without box office incomes. Grenville Clark and his associates did not want "big game receipts" to pay for mass training, but these reformers, who preached more programs for more students, could not suggest alternative financing. The parsimonious Congress, which rejected UMT, "killed by neglect" the National Collegiate Athletic Association's proposals for organized exercise. Proud Harvard's proud President A. Lawrence Lowell, insisting that "profit" was no "consideration," claimed that he would "never use any athletic team as gladiators performing to earn money." Yet despite his school's unequalled endowment, even its general athletic program fed off those big football games that, according to one academic, made America's colleges "for several days nothing less than a great carnival."[16]

Athletic participation may have increased in the 1920s but, put into proper perspective, it provided no moral substitute for war. Golf, easily the most popular sport, was the quintessential game of those suburbs that provided urban pleasures without urban irritants. As such, it was a leisure pastime, not a strenuous ordeal. Moreover, the entire sporting goods industry constituted a relatively minor part of a national budget spending approximately 250 percent more money on alternative entertainment through movies, cosmetics, chewing gum, or soda pop and ice cream. Preparedness leaders, being heirs of a puritan ethic that forbade seductive diversions, denounced these priorities. As "time out for mass consumption became as [economically important] as time for production," fear of a "degenerating idleness" became evermore pronounced in their social thought. Philosophic men, like George Alger and James Beck, rued the machine age, while Theodore Roosevelt, Jr., and Arthur Woods tried to develop an unleisurely leisure for American society.[17]

Roosevelt, Jr., as a social traditionalist, disliked the consumer culture of big machines, big cities, flappers, night clubs, and society life. But able to differentiate cultural change from political revolution, he eschewed the anticommunist obsession that saw "Bolsheviks behind every bush." In fact, he favored seating the expelled Socialist delegation to the 1919 New York State legislature, advocated the diplomatic recognition of Russia, and opposed the Harding-Coolidge tendency to confuse union strikes with rebellions. Roosevelt, criticizing contemporary culture without scapegoating subversives, once said that opulence was enough to make him "a confirmed Bolshevik."[18]

Leftists, when alienated from capitalist culture, tend to look towards the future. Rightists, disliking machinery itself, often idolized the past. European elites who fondly remembered sacrifices made on the battlefield generally praised the Middle Ages; Roosevelt invoked the frontier. According to him, "physical discomfort and danger" in the West had provided a "hardening and purifying force" that "left a heritage of character more valuable than any material legacy." To ensure that the wilderness could continue to "offset the detrimental effects of great [economic] development," he led an effort on behalf of what he called "conservation in terms of humanity."[19]

In 1924, Roosevelt, then assistant secretary of the navy, organized the National Outdoor Recreation Conference to bestow on "every citizen" the "physical and moral" benefits of life on the frontier. Hundreds of delegates accepted his invitation to exchange ideas, plans, and programs. Roosevelt, who "rarely enjoyed anything" more than this meeting, said it contained "every sincere outdoor lunatic from the 'Icy Capes of Labrador to the Spanish land of flowers.'" When the confer-

ence adjourned, he continued its work in an executive committee for-
mulating guidelines for federal recreation facilities. In addition, he
successfully petitioned Arthur Woods, now the acting president of the
Laura Spellman Rockefeller Memorial Foundation, to commission a
survey of the recreational needs and capabilities of American society.[20]

Roosevelt's efforts identified problems, planned their solution, and
"ended in general futility," for no real commitment existed "to go
ahead and do the things that the conference showed needed to be done."
Thus did virtue fail and liberty triumph. The common people, as the
sovereign playboys of their own weekend world, would not sanction
the "attempt to control what a person does when he does not need to
do anything." Despite the pleas of alienated moralists, they spent their
free time and money as they themselves saw fit. This meant more demand for private goods and less support for the wild frontier. Because
Detroit democratized the automobile and Roosevelt could not popula-
rize the wilderness, most citizens seemed to accept Henry Ford's program for taking one's "pleasure in God's open spaces." Outdoor life in
the United States now emphasized a Sunday drive in the country to
someone's new home in the suburbs, where the masses received the
media's message that store-bought toiletries, not strenuosity, ensured
their health. Advertising executives, who claimed to be the greatest
"force at work against puritanism in consumption," had turned the
Calvinist sense of sin into a "self-conscious [concern for] enlarged nose
pores and bad breath." Hence Americans, in the '20s, not only increased
eightfold the money they spent on cosmetics, they often adopted
Coueism or other creeds which told them to enjoy prosperity and self-
indulgence. Rather than adhere to regimen and discipline, these doctrines preached what William James once called a "systematic exercise
in passive relaxation."[21]

Technological growth even changed the nature of living in nature. A
strenuous struggle in the great outdoors made more sense in a pre-
industrial society which had to conquer the wilderness. In advanced
economies, however, most citizens work with one another—not directly
with the land or the machine. Adolescent camping, reflecting this development of personal service industries, came to emphasize the coop-
erative play which develops social poise, not the hardening ordeal that
builds character. While pacifists never subverted the Boy Scouts, the
Babbitts certainly did. Although the Roosevelts continued to appeal to
combat veterans, publicity-seeking salesmen made up some 40 percent
of the scoutmaster corps. Most days in the wilderness now resembled a
"Sunday school picnic," complete with chicken salad sandwiches and
ladyfingers for dessert. Even the defenders of scouting had to admit
that they too longed "for the old days when there was more hiking

[and] less blah." Universal comprehensive physical exercise, like universal compulsive military training, was an idea whose time had not yet come.[22]

Academic subject matter, as did physical education, failed to fulfilll many postwar expectations. Reminiscent of the Plattsburg belief that war sustained the concept of the citizen-soldier, Andrew West, dean of Princeton's graduate school, felt that combat validated the humanist studies that had taught patrician heroes "how to die" in battle. Thus inspired, West vowed to spread the lessons of "civitas" which deprecated the pursuit of private pleasure. In 1919 he organized the American Classical League, whose program attracted Theodore Roosevelt, Sr., Elihu Root, Henry Stimson, and others searching for a desperately needed "renaissance of discipline in education."[23]

The classics had been the staples of Stimson's own schooling at Phillips Academy (Andover). Whenever Trustee Stimson returned to visit his alma mater, he inspected its Latin classes because he believed that student translations of Caesar, Cicero, and Horace gave him a "feeling for the character work of the Academy." Always excellent preparation to meet "the vicissitudes of American life," these painstaking academic exercises were particularly important to him in the 1920s—a decade when indulgent "modern parents" failed to teach their children that "life is a serious business in which self-control, endurance, patience and discipline are the most essential factors." This oversight, he said, "is one of our great national shortcomings" and a valid cause of "very grave apprehension." His solution for juvenile degeneration in an affluent environment lay in military training, which was not feasible after the war, and in Greek and Latin: "my joy and my guide." Consequently Stimson gave the American Classical League a thousand dollars, the prestige associated with his name, and whatever influence derived from the pedagogic arguments he made.[24]

But however hard Stimson worked for the restoration of the classics, said to give eternal standards for mankind, he never could undo the damage done by America's intervention in World Wars I and II. Whatever enthusiasts like him may have thought, war proved to be the Greek tragedy of classical education: an episode in which true failure arose from apparent success. Most military and political leaders, planning to wield high technology, felt that the humanities were irrelevant to power. During World War I, when the War Department's Student Army Training Corps administered most universities, classes in the classics were temporarily dissolved. As prescient academics then predicted, the subject never recovered fully from this blow. In the 1920s, when "the business of America was business," educators who tried to "meet industrial specifications" helped reduce student enrollment in Latin by some 50 percent. Later, in World War II, when scientific capability replaced steel capacity as the key ingredient of military strength, Stimson himself (reappointed secretary of war in 1940) had to augment the investment in research and development.[25]

This military expansion of science and industry contracted both the classics and support for UMT. Stimson always hoped that a citizen-soldiery would help America overcome the charge that it was a "frivolous, selfish, pleasure-loving country" demoralized by its comfort and wealth. In the 1940s he found that a "diabolical" military technology was producing a push-botton devastation that not only antiquated plans for UMT. This "Frankenstein," personified in the atomic bomb he helped construct, created a "civilization so fragile and weapons so destructive" that the very future of humanity was hostage to "the race between man's growing technical power for destructiveness and his psychological power of self and group control." When World War II came home to Andover Academy, Secretary Stimson, whose War Department was encouraging even secondary schools to commit themselves to physics, wrote his beloved alma mater:

> I hope that your [curriculum] changes do not involve any further reduction in the time spent on the classics. I am an old man and my views are certainly out of the current of the past quarter of a century of educational thought. But, unless I am greatly mistaken, we are in the immediate future going to feel the want of that poise of knowledge and character which the classics give more heavily than ever before. I find myself that in the strain which I am carrying under the pressure of this mechanized world, I am turning more and more in my reading to the lessons of the classics for comfort, relaxation and hope. I trust that Phillips Academy is not going to join the bandwagon in changes which are more shortsightedly opportunistic than farsightedly essential for character building.[26]

The colonel could "hope" and "trust" in the classics but he could not alter the academic priorities determined by his own foreign policy. As he once told a despondent old cavalryman: "Don't get too bitter. Nearly all of us have to see some of the things we love remorselessly replaced in the modern mechanized world—a world that is just as repellent to me as I think it is to you." To his regret, Greek and Latin were inexorably becoming the dead languages of a dead culture.[27]

The classics were one traditional form of moral instruction; heroic biography was another. Theodore Roosevelt once employed it; now his disciples in the Roosevelt Memorial Association (RMA) combined his life with his genre in their attempt to make him "the hero of every

American school boy." Most of these hagiographers had roots in the old preparedness movement, especially the association's director: Hermann Hagedorn (1882–1964). In 1916, some fifteen years after being taught the prep school principle that an elite could yet "redeem" the moral stature of America, he founded and directed the literary Vigilantes, in which 400 writers, with access to 15,000 newspapers, joined forces to "send thrills down the spines" of the country's adolescents. Their readers, it was hoped, would be inspired to attack "materialism, selfishness and disloyalty" in themselves. Although the armistice curtailed this great "war within," Hagedorn continued to publish inspirational prose through the 1920s. As an alternative to the "greed and materialism" that he found pervasive, he collected biographical quotations such as this: "Theodore moved about in the midst of shrapnel explosions like Shadrach, Meshack and Co. in the midst of the fiery furnace." Hagedorn was often, as Newton Baker said, "more of a poet than a historian," but whatever he was, he never lacked insight or information. Unlike his RMA editions, the interview notes and comments that he buried deep in his own manuscript collection illustrate the human shortcomings of his superhuman subjects. Hagedorn had the analytical means; he simply lacked a critical purpose.[28]

Several other organizations, allied with Hagedorn, helped promulgate the "Roosevelt cult" of the 1920s. By all accounts the most messianic was the Women's Roosevelt Memorial Association. Using phraseology from *Pilgrim's Progress,* the book on which all young Roosevelts were raised, this group pledged to make TR "the Good Fairy, Greatheart guardian" of the young. The wife of Henry Alexander Wise Wood founded this society, chaired its key committees, and edited its newsletter. Other members included Mrs. Robert Bacon, Mrs. Henry Stimson, Etta Leighton of the National Security League, and Corrine Roosevelt Robinson, president of the Women's League for Universal Military Training. Mrs. Robinson (the deceased hero's sister) and her colleagues published more adventure tales about TR, promoted "training camps for good citizenship" in the public schools, and preserved the late president's New York City birthplace. That house, which took more than five years and $500,000 to restore, was a "permanent Mecca" for Roosevelt's ideals and a chronic deficit on the association's ledger. Financially impractical though it was, the undertaking had an emotional justification. These women, supposedly "true to their womanly instincts," resurrected a "Victorian Home and Setting" when such institutions were most visibly in decline. Like the genteel literature the organization published, the Victorian home it reconstructed was a moral "museum" preserving what was yesterday to influence tomorrow.[29]

Ironically, however, the Roosevelt worshippers helped overthrow their own idol. By building a superheroic strawman, they created an ideal target for Henry Pringle's debunking biography, *Theodore Roosevelt*. That book portrayed Roosevelt, the soldier, as an expression of the principles the President despised. Whereas the RMA's hero suffered combat to strengthen his moral character, Pringle's own protagonist embraced war to gratify his adolescent urges. Thus, in the Freudian terms intellectually popular in the '20s, Roosevelt became a hero of the id whose self-indulgence sanctioned the culture of consumption. But no matter how one-sided Pringle's picture was, Roosevelt's supporters could not offset that image. In fact, when this biography went on sale in 1931, the Women's Memorial Association advertised the book. Its own publications needed the revenue to help climb out of debt.[30]

While some Americans were deifying and others later deflating Theodore Roosevelt, Sr., his eldest son and namesake was writing his own historic "hero tales" about the Great War for "boys and girls from twelve to twenty." Unlike the deceased President, who enjoyed a pre-Pringle decade of literary grace, the war was scarcely over before the cultural avant-garde assailed it as a character-destroying calamity that left its soldiers sapped of human will, submerged in anonymity, and dying in disgust. Writers, when serving in this conflict themselves, felt "enslaved," like "castrated sheep," hiding behind their barbed wire trenches. Yet this "great weight of self-subordination," that made soldiers feel as if they were buried alive, affected different types of writing to different degrees. Magazines for the general public, rather sick of sacrifice, deemphasized the themes of "self-discipline" and "service" prevalent in articles before the war. Avant-garde artists, however, taking this tendency to its extreme, loudly announced a robust urge for unencumbered self-expression. In reaction to military restriction, they used their talents to attack the fetters of authority, country, and custom. According to rebels who employed the aesthetic weapons of shock and sensation to achieve a hedonistic liberation, to have died in combat for one's nation was to have been slaughtered in the "stockyards" for "an old bitch gone in the teeth." This revolt against the very ideal of heroic self-sacrifice sickened Roosevelt, Jr., who deprecated such works as a slander of the past that endangered virtue in the present. If American society, now "obsessed" with material prosperity and divided by ethnoracial conflict, were to reform, he felt it would have to revive "the ideals engendered in the war." Thus the man who had motivated his soldiers with regimental tradition now tried to save the country by making "the rank and file of the people proud of our past history and notable accomplishments." His own book, entitled *Rank and File*, presented nine biographical vignettes celebrating wartime "comrade-ship, honor, loyalty and courage."[31]

Although Roosevelt admittedly censored "the rough stuff" empha-sized in what he called "the soul searching obscenities of many modern novels," he honestly felt that vice and degradation played a "very small part" in the war which he fought. But Roosevelt's stories, no matter how sincere, were provincial products of his insular experience. Just as his regiment shaped his political faith in the average American Legion-naire, his particular division furrowed his vision of the entire conflict. Roosevelt and the debunkers, serving in different capacities, observed different types of casualties. "Lost Generation" writers, like Ernest Hemingway, were often ambulance drivers who saw both the physi-cally and the psychologically wounded. At the Battle of Caporetto, described in *A Farewell to Arms,* morale was so low that ten Allied sol-diers surrendered and twenty more deserted for each man shot. Roose-velt, as a 1st Infantry Division officer, witnessed many casualties but few breakdowns. This body of volunteers and its select officer corps initially contained no disgruntled draftees. Moreover, as the first divi-sion organized in America's expeditionary force, "Pershing's Pets" went through an exceptionally long and rigorous training period, one in which all "weaklings were eliminated." After that, despite 22,230 casualties, 67 percent more dead and wounded than in any other American divi-sion, its leadership, spirit, and cohesion fortified its men against emo-tional collapse. One French officer said of them at Soissons, where their 5,500 casualties went without medical care: "I don't believe I've ever seen such pride and dignity in suffering." By the battle of Sedan, drafted replacements and sheer fatigue had weakened the division's vaunted esprit. Yet this came too late to affect Roosevelt's memory of combat. It was, after all, the last engagement of the war.[32]

Besides self-denial, Roosevelt's soldiers embodied the national unity which he called "a community of service to the United States." Unlike most divisions, which mobilized citizens from one specific area, the 1st took recruits from across the country. Of the 870 men killed in Roose-velt's own regiment, 234 had Irish, Latin, Slavic, Jewish, and other un-questionably ethnic names. That casualty list, Roosevelt's honor roll, comprised a national lesson which he felt must be taught.[33]

Roosevelt, as an inconsistent champion of ethnic and racial equality, endorsed immigration quotas, racist books about *The Rising Tide of Color* and the belief that blacks were primitive, Italians dirty, and "kikes" a vulgar lot of "sweating humanity." Nonetheless, he made a series of strong, politically disadvantageous attacks on "bigotry" per-sonified in the Ku Klux Klan.[34]

When Roosevelt opposed Al Smith in the 1924 New York State gubernatorial election, his only chance to win lay in an overwhelming up-state vote. That, in turn, could depend on the Klan, which was strong in the Hudson Valley and a power on Long Island. While many politicians courted its members or joined it themselves, Roosevelt, facing a Catholic, "wet," and urban opponent, had the Klan vote by default. He only had to stop the special efforts he made to repudiate their "un-American" support. When campaign workers tried to mollify the KKK's anger, he repudiated them. The Klan could not turn to Smith but they could sit out the election. While President Coolidge, who dodged the Klan issue, carried New York by a million votes, Roosevelt lost by 140,000. His political career never recovered from this defeat. Hereafter, some other Roosevelt would have to retrace his father's ascent to power.[35]

Except for his attack on the KKK, Roosevelt was not a particularly courageous politician. In 1926 his slanderous attempts to link Al Smith to vice traffic in Albany embarrassed other Republicans, some of whom came to think that Roosevelt was "a strict liability to the party." In his own campaign he solicited support from "the bigoted" Anti-Saloon League by publicly pledging to enforce the prohibition laws he privately ignored. Roosevelt, like all politicians, would stoop for some votes. Yet he would not accept, let alone court, the Klan. Explaining his position to his diary, his friends, or his audiences, he usually mentioned soldiers in his regiment such as Fennessy, an Irish Catholic, or Fleishman, the Jew who won the first Distinguished Service Cross in the war. "I couldn't help but reflect that these were people whom the Ku Klux Klan is endeavoring to discriminate against." If they succeed, the country will "betray memories of those who fell thinking only of America." Because Roosevelt's memory tempered his own prejudice, he seemed to feel that history, a national memory in narrative form, could allay the country's bigotry.[36]

Roosevelt's racial stereotypes were always abstract. On a personal basis, he judged individuals according to their individual merits. His war stories also emphasized personal character. Whether black porter, Princeton professor, or Slovakian immigrant, none of Roosevelt's nine protagonists in *Rank and File* were "pale, unsubstantial creatures trailing behind them a string of events." True heroes, their exploits personified self-sacrifice and national unity. History that "lived" through their drama could have, he reasoned, a maximum impact on the consciousness of the young.[37]

Roosevelt's motives were noble, his plan thorough, and his writing sincere. Yet his heroic history, like his recreation projects, was publicly ignored. Both he and his father had hoped that war would solidify society but, in the final analysis, it widened the generation gap. Many combat veterans felt, as survivors generally do, that they would betray comrades who died that they might live if they did not perpetuate the glory of their deeds. When adolescents were not enthralled with those exploits, they concluded that the young were simply shallow ingrates. The youngsters, in turn, not having experienced the war, could not understand the veterans' point of view. They assumed that their elders were artless antiquarians unable to adapt to the postwar world. As one of Roosevelt's World War II comrades later said about the Normandy invasion: We were told that "we'd be bragging to our grandchildren about D-Day, and I have and I do, but they don't pay any attention."[38]

While Theodore Roosevelt, Jr., was writing *Rank and File,* a young man approached him for letters of introduction abroad. Apparently, Charles Lindbergh did not know anyone in Paris. When he arrived, several frustrated patriots saw in him the hero America desperately needed.

Lindbergh galvanized most of the country and much of the world but he, the son of a leading isolationist who had called World War I the "maelstrom of hell," particularly affected former preparedness leaders. Roosevelt, Jr., then hoping that his own recreational conferences and war stories could develop virtue in the young, said that this heroic flyer, "by right of achievement," was the lineal descendant of the noble Daniel Boone. Owen Wister, concurring, recommended that Lindbergh receive the Roosevelt Memorial Medal for the leadership of youth and the development of American character. His flight made Wister feel better than he had felt at any time since the Great War.[39]

For a moment it seemed that Lindbergh might revive the nation's idealism. According to the army, he inspired a Citizen Military Training Camp enrollment which exceeded its quota in every corps area for the first time in its history. But in the midst of initial celebration, George Wharton Pepper called his comrades back to their senses by saying that "we" also thought "the war would transform the world." "Today," he continued, "multitudes of people are congratulating themselves that Lindbergh's example will regenerate the young, but of course it will do nothing of the sort. Ninety-nine percent of those who shout and cheer are absolutely unaffected by the incident as far as their course of life is concerned."[40]

Lindbergh's influence was short-lived indeed. Preparedness leaders tried to make him, along with Theodore Roosevelt and Sergeant Alvin York, the paragon of adolescent values. But gangsters, hustlers, and hucksters, spawned by prohibition, seem to have had as much impact on the young. These criminals, who used illegal means to achieve conventional goals, aggressively aspired to material success. Nonetheless, many juveniles saw them as urban America's new adventure heroes.

Preparedness leaders admitted as much when they tried to censor the media which perpetuated that myth. Henry Stimson not only advocated the governmental regulation of movies and the "sensational press." He joined other moralists, who also once hoped combat would cleanse the country, to support a "Clean Books Bill" which Stimson now called the "most effective [means] yet devised to protect and keep from debasement the youth of our community." North of New York State, headmasters Endicott Peabody of Groton and Samuel Drury of St. Paul's defended virtue in their flocks by destroying the subversive literature that infiltrated their compounds. But since no prep school is an island entire to itself, their censorship was self-defeating. Once a student left protective custody at Groton, he found within society new authorities with a different moral code. When the voice of convention often preached a money-making hedonism, many Grotonians, trained to obey, deferred to this new orthodoxy.[41]

At Princeton University, now said to be a "glorified playground," President John G. Hibben performed the ethical oversight duties. Like his fellow censors, he wistfully compared the "moral and spiritual exhilaration" of the Great War with the "crude materialism" of the present peace. Yearning for the martial past, he suppressed "obscene" literature, closed neighborhood roadhouses, and then set out to conquer the car. Those vehicles for "promiscuous 'joy-riding' and dawn parties at distant points" facilitated vice as could no stationary object. Lest young men be led "to places of dissipation," Hibben braved the resignation of the whole student council when he banished the automobile from his campus. He was about to begin movie censorship in 1933 when he himself was killed in a car accident.[42]

In the final analysis, popular indifference, not the Bill of Rights, prevented censorship in the 1920s. Most Americans might have called youth degenerate but, sensing their behavior was apolitical, the country rarely took direct action. In the 1930s, when politically oriented youth, now less obsessed with sex and liquor, threatened to become "a dangerous addition to the radical-minded elements" of society, politicians and the public were finally willing to fund special programs like the Civilian Conservation Corps. Stimson and Peabody, taking their ethics seriously, had different priorities. They practiced political libertarianism and moral censorship.[43]

Exiles Abroad: Leonard Wood, Henry Stimson, and Theodore Roosevelt, Jr.

In the 1920s several military training leaders, like defeated church militants retreating to a monastery, went into physical or psychological exile. One of the first of these patriotic expatriates was General Leonard Wood. When he sought the 1920 Republican presidential nomination, the Plattsburg movement, reorganized in the Leonard Wood League, appropriately staffed his new crusade. This "inner sect of the [country's] war party" struck Walter Lippmann as a body of "mystical" American Junkers who ignored "capitalistic" (interest-group) politics to exalt the glory of the state.[44]

"Truly convinced that they have a cause and a prophet," the general and his entourage repeated the tactics they used in the prewar movement for UMT. Then, from 1913 to 1917, they countered the apathy of the executive branch of government by extensively publicizing their model military camp at Plattsburg Barracks, New York. Now, in the 1920 Republican primary, they again circumvented the political establishment by appealing directly to the public. As if he were selling more soap, campaign manager William Cooper Proctor of Proctor and Gamble directed a $1,500,000 media blitz for Leonard Wood—that 99 and 44/100 percent pure American who, according to Henry Alexander Wise Wood, "possessed in extraordinary degree the wise and virile qualities which have brought about and [will] preserve the ascendency of our great [and] dominant race." In retrospect, some of Wood's friends admitted that the general should have spent that money in a way which he refused: bribing delegates to the Republican Convention. When the primaries were over, Senator Hiram Johnson, Wood's underfinanced but antimilitary opponent, received more votes. Wood's backers, unable to sell a candidate that the country would not buy, had failed to take the nomination "by assault." Once his campaign lacked the public mandate which it sought, it could not hope to carry a normal political convention. In 1920, a "loose fraternity of average men" nominated the affable and agreeable Warren G. Harding, a candidate who would not ask anyone to make any substantial sacrifice. Unlike the heroic Leonard Wood, that man who called himself "an ordinary citizen . . . no different than anyone of you" was the true spokesman for his party and symbol of his age.[45]

To keep Wood from bolting the Republican Party as his friend Theodore Roosevelt had done in 1912, Harding dangled the Department of War in front of his face. This chance to practice in the cabinet the citizen-soldier policies he preached enticed Wood to stay in the Republican camp. However, his support for UMT in war and peace made him a controversial figure with more than his share of enemies. Harding's bait therefore was only a ploy. When appointments were to be made, as Colonel Frank McCoy predicted, "harmonious Mr. Harding will seek peace." The President-elect, admittedly worried that the old soldier "would make trouble," made a former politician, turned stockbroker, his secretary of war. Then Leonard Wood, who sought the presidency of the United States of America, was asked by trustees to preside at the University of Pennsylvania.[46]

"Penn," lacking capital and student customers, was in grave financial trouble. Because Philadelphia's academic dollars were often invested abroad at Harvard, Yale, or Princeton, the school had a meager endowment. Because the war and the draft recently preempted 3,000 potential undergraduates, it also lacked adequate consumer demand. Some trustees reasoned that General Wood's prestige could raise enough money to prevent their debt-ridden private school from falling into state university status. Nonetheless, his academic inexperience and the school's Quaker tradition created doubts which George Wharton Pepper, chairman of the trustees' search committee, worked hard to allay. For years Pepper had opposed the utilitarian emphasis in modern collegiate instruction. Because he felt that Wood's total commitment to increased discipline would have a beneficial "influence on American education," he begged his old Plattsburg commander to come to Philadelphia where he could fulfill his "duty to the youth of America."[47]

Wood initially questioned his selection but then, upon reflection, reconsidered the appointment. The contract he was offered, doubling the previous emoluments, included a $25,000 salary, a large expense account, and rent-free occupation of the president's home. It thus provided an opportunity to recoup the personal savings that Wood had depleted in his recent primary election campaign. It also offered a politically opportune "field for widespread activities at home." Thoroughly enjoying public speaking but heretofore restrained by military service, he could now express his opinions on what he felt was a "rapidly approaching" social crisis from the heights of a prestigious university platform. Hence he could remain a viable candidate for the 1924 presidential nomination that was every bit as open as Harding was weak. Financial interest, political ambitions, patriotic principles, and personal friends were leading Wood towards Philadelphia when Harding asked him to become the governor-general of the Philippines.[48]

Since Manila lacked nearly everything that Philadelphia offered, that proposition seemed to be, in Elihu Root's words, "a damned insult." Physically, the position not only would discomfort Wood's wife and daughter, never happy in the tropics, it could aggravate the general's neurological injury recently inflamed in his political defeat. Financially, the governor's salary might just pay his expenses. Politically, the benefits were also minimal. The islands were, as Wood himself once said, "the burial ground of [one's] reputation." Even if the governor-general could cope with a morass of postwar problems, he could only win a place in public oblivion. Most Americans, preoccupied with the new consumer markets developing at home, had lost all interest in this profitless piece of colonial territory.[49]

Although a diminishing band of expansionists still touted the riches of the Philippines, the colony remained economically marginal to America. This superfluous port of call on the way to a mythical market lay further from the United States than Hong Kong or Shanghai, the primary entrepôts to a China trade which had never passed the acid test of national interest by being judged worthy of war. In direct trade, America's imports from and exports to the Philippines were meager and easily replaced. Balancing income gained against tariff revenue lost and government expenses, the islands cost America some $3,000,000 a year. Moreover, the U.S. investment, great or small, did not need imperial protection. Anxious to calm the political uncertainties that hindered economic growth, members of the American-Philippine business community had long been willing to grant dominion status, if not independence. Confident that market ties would survive, they were ready to give up their own empire.[50]

A minor economic deficit, the Philippines were a major strategic liability: their lines of communication to America stretched over 6,000 dangerous miles. Wood himself for the last fifteen years acknowledged that the islands were an indefensible commitment that weakened America's international posture. After the Washington Conference and other naval reductions in the '20s effectively disarmed the United States west of Hawaii, the Philippines were more vulnerable than ever.[51]

All things considered, Wood had numerous reasons to fulfill his pledge to become the president of the University of Pennsylvania. Nonetheless, he reluctantly agreed to inspect the Philippines for a government report. It was on that trip that he chose to stay. The general's decision appeared irrational to his friends but it suited the man and the decade. With rare and penetrating insight, Wood sensed that he might as well leave the mainland since he, like the Philippines themselves, had become irrelevant to America. As he confided to a friend: "I am afraid my doctrines and principles—honesty and courage among men, virtue among women and a keen sense of citizenship obligation—may be regarded as primitive in the onrush of modern so-called liberal ideas."[52]

Although the great days of empire were now past, colonialism could still provide a personal escape from postwar disappointments. Charles Nordhoff and James Hall, two pilots from the Lafayette Escadrille, migrated to the South Seas where they wrote *Mutiny on the Bounty* and other romances. Senator Henry Cabot Lodge and Solicitor-General James Montgomery Beck, vicarious imperialists, exchanged letters and essays on Shakespeare's *The Tempest*—a play about "a beautiful land where we can escape from the cares that are the day." But these two men, Wood's friends, only thought about Prospero. Wood himself played the part. His country had spurned his social reform efforts, and his once magnificent body, the source of a "childish pride," was now deteriorating. Unlike the Americans who ignored him, the "docile, patient, quiet" Filipinos might give Wood the homage that would appease his damaged ego. When they begged him "like children" to stay in the Philippines, he "became thoroughly interested" in the job.[53]

Wood's closest aide Frank McCoy, once said that "in the face of the evidence [the general] had infinite capacity for believing in himself." As proconsul in the Philippines, Wood's talent for self-deception was particularly evident. To play the role of the imperial ruler, he concocted a scenario in which the governor-general of the Philippines ran the islands which, controlling the Pacific, ruled the world. Notwithstanding the facts, Wood told himself and his country that America's Far East colony was invaluable to its foreign trade, military security, international credibility, and moral honor. He also told America that its colonialism would cost an expanded Pacific fleet, a fortified Hawaii, at least two major repair ports on the West Coast and, in violation of the Washington Conference Treaty, increased ground, air, and sea power on Guam and the Philippines themselves. Yet he seemed to have known that the country would not pay this price. (In his own administration the manpower of the island's garrison actually decreased some 65 percent.) Therefore, doing precisely what he once condemned, Wood encouraged a diplomatic commitment without suitable military support.[54]

Were it not for men like Wood, the island's meager assets might have been enjoyed without major liability. In 1898, the secretaries of state, the navy, and the treasury originally suggested that the United States do what it eventually did in 1946: grant the natives official sovereignty but still retain commercial and military bases. Wood, in 1923, did all he could to prevent a similar diplomatic solution then supported by many Americans and Filipinos. Although the general may not have understood his own motives, he opposed home rule in order to maintain the personal gratification of his own reign. As aides observed, Wood was conscious of a last "great job to be done and the power to do it." For that he sacrificed Philadelphia's more tangible rewards.[55]

There certainly was "a great job to be done." Epidemics, bankruptcy, corruption, exploitation, illiteracy, and the demoralization of character caused by excessive poverty were all very real Philippine problems. Wood's power, however, to develop a "strong, well-trained, well-disciplined people" was largely an illusion. As he once acknowledged: "The benevolent despotism" days were over. Woodrow Wilson's colonial reforms, codified in the Jones Act of 1916, shifted the locus of power from the imperialists to the Filipinos. A native legislature now confirmed the governor-general's appointments, voted most appropriations, and passed all internal statutes. A native judiciary interpreted the laws which a native bureaucracy enforced. The governor-general, representing a foreign race and lacking indigenous partisan support, could not effectively ask the electorate for help against the legislature. Nor could he expect Washington to increase his authority. An imperial counterrevolution could provoke a native insurrection, and rather than fight another war against Philippine guerrillas, as America had done in 1899, the United States might completely withdraw. In fact, many Americans would have welcomed such a revolt as an excuse to abandon their Achilles heel. For them, granting independence to rebel Filipinos would be an Occidental face-saving incident.[56]

When Wood landed in the Philippines in 1921, he recognized that political conditions had changed there since 1908, "the good old days when we had a difficult problem but a free hand." Then, as the ranking officer in the regular army, he had lived "like a prophet" and left in a "blaze of glory." Now, since the governor-general had "responsibility without authority," Wood initially consented to make just an inspection report. The jubilant reception he first received must have been an encouraging surprise. The islands, after World War I, were suffering from an economic crisis that left their products without markets and their banks without liquidity. Desperate natives, reverting to tradition, greeted Wood like some all-powerful Oriental despot. This encouraged his entourage to imagine, erroneously, that the general possessed a unique power. When Wood asked one of his closest advisors, former Governor-General W. Cameron Forbes, for his assessment, Forbes replied: "I am inclined to think you will find the Filipinos scared to death and that they will be pitiably and almost cringingly anxious to do as they are told. . . . This, together with your prestige, reputation and force will make it much easier for you to make them do things that you want than anybody else. They are tremendous respecters of authority and the name 'Governor-General' has tremendous weight with them. . . . I look for little opposition, at least at first, to your desires." Taking advice from Forbes, a devotee of Rudyard Kipling, the great poetic proponent of the white man's rule, Wood accepted Harding's offer of proconsulship.[57]

As the postwar crisis subsided, Filipino legislators began to reassert themselves against the general's rule. In 1923, for example, Wood, the martial benefactor, proposed a system of military training on the islands to strengthen the natives physically, "to make them better citizens, to build up a spirit of service, and to create respect for the constituted authorities." Yet many of the legislators to whom the governor-general appealed called him a would-be tyrant. Their recalcitrance appears to have produced political schizophrenia in Wood. On the one hand, he imagined himself a great colonial governor upholding "the White Man's Burden" by protecting child-like peasants from a rapacious native ruling class. At the same time, Wood cajoled and deferred to that ruling class when it met as the legislature. Thus people on the islands criticized him on two counts. Some thought he acted like a "Roman consul" full of "personal puffing." Others felt he was a weakling who would not stand up to the native politicians. Ostensibly conflicting, both assessments were correct. When Wood was really sovereign, as he was in 1900 while military governor of occupied Cuba, he was noted for his informality. Now lacking the substance of power, he grasped at the pomp and circumstance of office. Those ancient (but now misleading) colonial conventions were rituals, if not fantasies, that saved him from despair about his true insignificance. And to keep the largely ceremonial position that supported his ego, Wood usually complied with the native elite—those "unruly children" who really ruled America's nominal colony. Wood's self-delusion was his reward and whether absurd or authentic, it was invaluable to him. When Harding's death left the 1924 Republican Convention temporarily wide open, Wood's old supporters hoped he would return to seek the nomination. However, the governor-general, now "prepared to die in the harness," would not even submit the perfunctory resignation customarily given to a new administration. He obviously feared that it just might be accepted.[58]

In Wood's self-written role as the imperial protector he paid special attention to Moros and lepers. The former were an ethnic minority of primitive tribesmen who had "a keen sense of honor" and were "faithful unto death to those they loved." Unfamiliar with bureaucracies and constitutions, they were accustomed to the personal rule of men to whom they attributed God-like traits, as they did the governor-general who was their sole protection from Filipino domination. Aside from the Moros who gave him their "pathetic devotion," Wood served the sick. Having failed to save America from self-indulgence, he "displaced" his missionary impulse onto the effort to rid the Philippines of leprosy. For him, that project "alone has been worth many times all the work and trouble we have had" on the islands. At least once a month, the doctor-soldier visited a leper colony where he received the well-earned homage of his patient-subjects. But to really comfort his charges the general had to emerge from his self-imposed exile in order to ask the American public for a $2,000,000 hospital-research center grant. This man, who once said that it was his "duty to remain [in the Philippines] not because our people are interested but because they are not," might have known what would happen. His appeal, published in newspapers and magazines across the country, raised a few hundred dollars. A little later Wood pondered the Jack Dempsey-Jack Sharkey prize-fight and wrote: "It is a sad commentary on the American people when two pugs can get a purse of $650,000 for a seven round fight and it is so difficult to raise $2,000,000 throughout the country for a great cause like the leper drive."[59]

Shortly thereafter, in mid-1927, Wood "died as he would have liked to have died, in harness and facing the foe." He was fortunate to have perished when he did. President Calvin Coolidge, running a staid administration shunning controversy, was about to dismiss this outspoken soldier from his colonial post.[60]

Leonard Wood's good friend Henry Stimson took his place in Manila. Another self-confessed "lone Indian in the midst of a different world," Stimson appears to have considered the Philippines to be his therapeutic reservation free from corrupting contact with Western materialism. His life in postwar America seemed "trivial and unsatisfying." Only half in jest he called his law practice "the harness," "a Frankenstein," and the "hunt for 'filthy lucre.'" A "fear of uselessness" alone kept him at work since there was "nothing," he confessed, "more miserable than a zealous man without a job." At this time public life provided no alternative to the bar, for Stimson was proud to be isolated from the "political deserts of today." Government office, which "seemed to be going out of the way to spit in the faces of the things and people I believe in," was "not worth anything if it ... sacrifices self-respect. And in these days," he said, "it rarely comes on any other terms."[61]

When frustrated emotionally, Stimson tended to become physically ill. If insomnia and stomach pains did nothing else, they justified the temporary exiles that lightened his life. He was thereby able to spend "a great deal of time at the farm," his "solace [for] strain and fatigue." Taking other medicinal vacations, he became "childishly elated" on a successful hunting trip and energized by a tour of the Great War's battlefields. Two prominent psychiatrists, O. Mannoni and Frantz Fanon, have observed that the imperial colony, where disenfranchised natives lack political rights, represents symbolically "a world without men." Psychological similarities therefore exist between the uninhabited wilderness and "no man's land" at the front, the places where Stimson sojourned, and the colonial "frontier" to which he later went.[62]

In 1898, America's imperial adventure in the Philippines "scandalized" Stimson. By 1913, he changed his mind. Then, he grew convinced "that we owe it to our dignity" to stay because the annals of man contain "no nobler page of high ideals [more sincerely held] and difficult duty [more] worthily performed." In the 1920s, when America seemed to suffer a "relaxation in all kinds of moral efforts," the islands remained important to Stimson. "Down [there] in the front trenches," Proconsul Leonard Wood continued as "one of the few, strong, dutiful personalities who are shaping their course by service instead of interest." After Wood died on duty, Stimson appropriately was offered his post. However, the enervating tropical climate and his faltering vitality initially led him to reject the offer. Then, like Wood had done, he reconsidered. This self-identified soldier "never wished to turn a deaf ear to the call of service." And besides, he was simply glad to have "some possibilities of usefulness in the world."[63]

The new governor-general tried to help the islands and his "interlude of high adventure" there, most certainly helped him. Stimson, suddenly free from enervation and illness, felt "much better than I have been for several years in New York. . . . In fact I have become young again." His rehabilitation seems due in part to regular exercise, preeminent social status, and a relatively strong public regard. But the most important factor in his restoration was probably an emotional satisfaction reminiscent of his military action in World War I. "There is," he later said, "no thrill in life like feeling that you represent the interest of this wonderful country of ours out in the world, where you are face to face with other countries and with other systems and with other ideals than ours." He felt that those doing foreign service, inside or outside the government, "were great stalwart Americans" "as important and honorable as the army and the navy."[64]

Despite Stimson's efforts, or perhaps because of them, America began to abandon "one of the noblest colonial experiments in the world." As secretary of state (1929–33), he insisted that the United States must "not diminish its sovereignty in the Islands." This position undercut those Japanese moderates who, in 1930 at the Stimson-led London Naval Conference, dared to consider trading additional warship quotas for the future neutralization of the Philippines. They consequently became, as Stimson later admitted, too weak to restrain army militants who stormed Manchuria in 1931. The secretary, reacting to what he felt was a threat to America's "territorial possessions," then expressed his own martial code through his foreign policy. Determined "to keep up the firm front" and avoid "any sign of weakness," he argued that the United States should remain ensconced in the Philippines, where staging points could be mounted to stem further Japanese expansion. Actually, his repudiation of "yellow-bellied responses" to foreign militarism made it more likely that Japan might launch a preemptive attack against the islands, America's closest base to its home waters. Hence Stimson inadvertently helped ensure that the U.S. in 1932 and 1934, would grant the Philippines transitional autonomy and future independence largely to avoid armed conflict with Japan. Still, to the bitter end, the secretary was "not ready . . . to admit that all that magnificent work of thirty-five years will be thrown away." That, he said, was so "bad that it could not come true."[65]

Nevertheless, in the Tydings-McDuffie (Philippine independence) Act the United States wrote what Stimson called "the saddest chapter in American history": its political retreat from the archipelago. Later, as secretary of war (1940–45), he sought to redeem his nation's honor by using the army to "put our attitude towards the Philippines on a correct and elevated basis." Unfortunately, in the process, he contributed to the destruction of much of Manila and much of what he called the "other great group of English speaking peoples known as the British Empire." When the Japanese attacked south in 1941, all the English and many American strategists wanted Allied strength withdrawn from the Philippines so that Singapore, entry to four-fifths the world's rubber and two-thirds of its tin, could better be defended. This particular port was not only the strategic key to England's "life line." It was, according to Stimson, the State Department, and the chiefs of the Royal Armed Forces, a "symbol of power" crucial to "the prestige of the white race, the British Empire and the United States" in Asia. Moreover, as the world's greatest naval base east of Gibraltar, Singapore seemed relatively defensible. Manila, on the other hand, was long considered "a military liability" whose defense would be "futile," if not "an act of madness." Nonetheless, this soldierly secretary of war performed the cardinal strategic sin when he insisted on handing the "defenseless" Philippines a political commitment that exceeded his country's physical strength. In fact, he threatened to resign if those islands, then diverting scarce weaponry from Pearl Harbor as well as Singapore, were not given what Stimson later called a "glorious but hopeless defense." His irrational military tactics seem to have arisen from what his own aide called Stimson's "enormous emotional reaction in connection with the Philippines." Stimson himself confirmed this analysis the day before the Japanese attacked Hawaii. Still grateful for his reinvigorating term as proconsul, he then acknowledged that his efforts for the islands were "keenly spurred by the memory of the friendships which I received and enjoyed." Perhaps Stimson was also still ashamed of his country's retreat from colonialism—"the most irresponsible act of government [that he] had ever come in contact with." But whatever his motives, he never failed to demand an obdurate, however inadequate, defense of the Philippines. When confirmed by the President this policy foreclosed the neutralization Stimson scorned. Thus perished the only possibility to forestall a full-scale attack. The rejection of last-minute demilitarization, suggested by Philippine and American leaders in the field, helped ensure that the following sequence would occur: invasion, American humiliation, occupation, widespread collaboration, and some of the most destructive fighting seen in World War II. By 1945 even Douglas MacArthur would say that Manila had undergone "a physical and moral disaster."[66]

Manila, however, was not the West's only casualty. When a theoretically defensible Singapore, the supreme symbol of imperial power, was not reinforced, "the only prize" that could uphold, in Winston Churchill's words, "British prestige" in India and the Far East precipitously crumbled. This, "the worst disaster and largest capitulation of British history," irrevocably damaged the reputation of colonialism, which Stimson had worked so hard to maintain. In the 1930s he told one friend: "Don't be too pessimistic about the demise of the British empire. My own impression, based upon careful study and long experience, is that the empire is a tough old bird and will outlast in the future as it has in the past many of its despairing friends."[67]

"Study" and "experience" to the contrary, this optimistic friend of empire proved to be wrong. The bulk of Britain's Pacific colonies could not outlive Henry Stimson when hindered by the misconceived military strategy he helped create. Once again, as he had done with classical education, the secretary of war helped subvert his own objectives.

Theodore Roosevelt, Jr., was also an exile abroad. In 1932 he replaced Henry Stimson's successor as governor-general of the Philippines. This was, however, Roosevelt's third migration. His first came in 1924 after his political loss to Governor Al Smith.

Whether playing Rough Rider with his neighborhood gang or making gold-standard speeches to the hired help, Roosevelt, Jr., as a child, imitated his father. Twenty-six years later, as assistant secretary of the navy in 1922, he was still emulating his parent's career. But now an adult, he paid a price for his ambition.[68]

Roosevelt found the policies, politics, and protocol of the Navy Department fundamentally unpleasant. This big fleet man had the bad luck to hold office during "the invariable backwash which follows stirring events of self-sacrifice and patriotism." Reorganization and economy excited hardly anyone, least of all the former warrior now assigned to direct "tactics" during the annual fight for congressional funds. Those "bitter" battles for naval appropriations were a far cry from Soissons since legislators, who seemed "petty" and contemptuous, were appeased instead of attacked. Roosevelt, "sick to death of the budget," exclaimed that he "would like to kill [Congressmen] good and plenty in a brutal fashion." Then, staying on duty, he courted the people he despised, even campaigning for the "thoroughly useless" chairman of "that mad house" Naval Affairs Committee.[69]

"Penance" for his "sins," the political speeches Roosevelt made were "dreary affairs." The audiences whom he addressed were uninterested in moral exhortation, his natural genre. Wanting instead "pleasing platitudes" and "pointless jokes," they made him feel like a "dodo" or a "two-headed calf in a side show." He would finish a painful speech as soon as he could to pursue a satisfying game of squash. Repressed in his work, he could vent himself in play. Submissive to his job, he could dominate a ball.[70]

Roosevelt's protocol responsibilities at navy dances, dinners, and reviews were equally unpleasant. Whenever he could, he made a quick appearance, disguised his irritation ("that is all important"), then "drearily paddled home." One event that he could not avoid was particularly distasteful. Escorting congressmen to the Quantico naval base, he and his party reviewed marines on parade through ankle-deep mud. It was the same type of "farce" that plagued his own regiment after the armistice. "I know just how they felt," he wrote. "I have done it so often myself."[71]

Roosevelt, "yoked to" his Navy Department desk, experienced "one bright spot in [his] day" whenever a 1st Infantry Division veteran came to visit. He then "longed to be in command of troops again." Unlike his daily routine of committees, speeches, and dinners, that was "essentially and utterly a man's job." Since peacetime army life, however, meant that Roosevelt would march in parades instead of reviewing them, he also dreamed about hunting trips—not some "semi-camp with a lot of women and children" but a struggle with nature "hard and alone." Yet, like Henry Stimson trapped in his own law firm, Roosevelt rejected retirement. "The Lord knows that drudgery is an awful thing, but the idea that work is something to be avoided is even more disastrous than drudgery." His hunt therefore had to await his political defeat. "Just as soon as they beat me," he said, he was ready to go. Al Smith, always considerate, gave him his chance.[72]

Roosevelt knew that he received the 1924 Republican gubernatorial nomination because no one else wished to challenge Smith. His friends advised him to let the party find another human "sacrifice" lest he sustain a "permanent" political injury. Roosevelt, however, disagreed with their assessment. If he somehow took the New York governor's mansion, step three on his father's ladder of ascent, he would have a salient pointed towards the White House. By 1928, he calculated, America should be about ready for another President Roosevelt.[73]

Waging unrelenting attack, Roosevelt campaigned against Smith as he had fought at the front. He attended 185 meetings in just eighteen days and, for a while, it even looked as if he could win. Then he made the blunder Smith was looking for. In Hampton, Roosevelt congratulated Colgate University for winning the big football game it had lost. Informed that he was wrong, he turned to his entourage and asked: "I wonder who told me that?" Smith, repeating that phrase through the rest of the campaign, ridiculed him into obscurity.[74]

To challenge the governor at all, Roosevelt had to meet thousands of people in an effort so demanding that it left even him worn and hoarse. If he had not had a photographic memory, his error would be understandable. As it was, his lapse was unique. In war, although suffering a fatigue that eventually killed hm, his remarkable memory retained total recall. For example, comrades said that he knew thousands of soldiers by name and hometown. Yet, in 1924, he could not remember who told him who won a football game. Perhaps on that occasion, he did not want to win himself.[75]

Roosevelt was hurt by this political defeat that labeled him "dead and buried for good and all." But painful though it was, losing had its compensations. Once he took his "knocks like a good soldier," going "down fighting" in "true 1st Division style," he was finally free do to what he really wanted. Even before the election, a man who came to discuss campaign strategy found Roosevelt completely absorbed in Himalayan big game talk. After the defeat, he could do more than fantasize.[76]

Roosevelt took no motor car vacation. With his brother Kermit, he made one of the most difficult of all possible excursions, chasing ferocious Himalayan animals in unexplored territory. Compared with the weather, terrain, altitude, and avalanches, the wild beasts themselves were relatively harmless. No matter; hunting all day and skinning game in the freezing night was a task of "toil and achievement" that Roosevelt relished. An insomniac in America, he "slept like a log" in those austere mountains. In fact, "the harder the work, the healthier [he] got." According to his wife, after nine months out there Roosevelt looked "better than he [had] at anytime since the war"—that is "during the war, not afterwards."[77]

Exiles at Home: George Wharton Pepper and William Temple Hornaday

Roosevelt, Jr., Leonard Wood, and others sought refuge abroad; George Wharton Pepper found asylum at home. When Senator Boise Penrose died in office in 1922, the fifty-five-year old Pepper (R.-Pa.) began his political career with an interim appointment to the U.S. Senate. Although active in public policy debates, he had never sought office

before—and he did not seek it now. Legislative lobby groups fighting
for self-interest not only repelled him aesthetically, he was simply unprepared for that type of combat. Contemplating a future of "inevitable
mistakes" and disappointments, Pepper felt "as if I had enlisted for
war with as little knowledge as I had when [I] first went to Plattsburg."
Yet he was trapped in the moral code that previously led him to military
training and Muldoon. The upper-class self-indulgence that he always
loathed seemed particularly acute in the 1920s, when the "sons of privilege" appeared to have "degenerated into little snobs who think themselves too good for politics." For Pepper, long critical of patrician Philadelphia's refusal to compete against plebian pols, Capitol Hill was a
new Spartan test of his commitment to his professed values. If he could
not become an army private, at least he could be a U.S. senator.[78]

Pepper's duty in Washington proved to be the unpleasant experience
he expected. In an age of interest-group democracy, when question-
naires, referendums, and lobbyists made representation "a mere weather vane," he tried to uphold classic Whig principles of legislative independence. He wished to make his senate office into a study but found it
a "hotel"; he tried to be a philosopher-king and found himself a "bell
hop." He had hoped that war would unify his country but discovered,
amidst the clashing blocs of Congress, that the nation remained "a
loosely bound group of divergent economic [ties], sectional interests
and political factions." Americans, lacking faith in a common public
good, would not politically defer to a patrician elite. Because a conflict
therefore existed between Pepper's philosophy and social reality, he inclined towards "nervous strain" and electoral defeat. More concerned
with honor than with office, his voting record alienated veterans, immigrants, labor unions, "wets," and "drys." He consequently got the res-
pite he craved. In the 1926 election, Pepper went down to a "glorious
defeat," cherishing the belief that he had "fought to the finish" and did
his "damndest." Since he reasoned that the public had deserted him,
he felt he had earned an "honorable" discharge.[79]

In subsequent years Pepper rejected all suggestions that he run again
for office. Instead, he devoted himself to religious philanthropy. Universal military training now a lost cause, he placed his faith in the Episcopal Church—a civilian expression of authority, devotion, and hierarchy. Perhaps this institution, whose catechism taught one to be "low
and reverent to all [his] betters," might yet be the agency that could
integrate society by creating a corporate consciousness. Thus, in the
mid-1920s, when Pepper concluded that "nations are incorporated
differences," he became the greatest lay supporter of the Episcopal
Church's Washington Cathedral. Gothic architecture had long attracted
men of patrician principles. In early Victorian England they financed

it to inspire political resistance to "Godless" democracy. Now, after
radicalism in America had waned, Whig idealists like Pepper con-
structed cathedrals for their cultural impact. According to President
Coolidge, an evangelist for commerce, "the man who builds a factory
builds a temple . . . and it is there, in the shadow of the industrial altar,
that worship must shift." According to citizen Pepper, no high priest
for great profits, the skyscrapers that dwarfed his Philadelphia church
cast God's "eternal verities into [their] shadows." America therefore
needed its own Notre Dame, a majestic shrine that could tower over all
secular monuments. Reminiscent of the medieval churches that dominated cities before bankers and merchants formed their downtown
business districts, the Washington Cathedral might become a great
"centripetal force" balancing modernity's centrifugal effects. But
whatever the cathedral did for America, it never disappointed Pepper.
This magnificent physical structure ironically became the spiritual sanc-
tuary in which he escaped the "chaos and madness of modern life."[80]

Senator Pepper took asylum in God's great cathedral. William Temple Hornaday, lamenting the "destruction" of "Victorian moral standards," returned to the zoo. Now that his preparedness preachings had
become "sarcophagi of murdered and buried ideals," Hornaday once
again hoped that man could learn parental responsibility, filial piety,
general "intelligence and honest industry" from "sane and natural wild
beasts." With this in mind he wrote his favorite book, *The Minds and
Manners of Wild Animals* (1922). However, "the osscophalic American
people," cursed by screen, radio, and tabloid press, read *Tarzan of the
Apes* instead. Hornaday's book, nonetheless, provided its author some
private consolation. When he "tired of men," he opened the volume
and found "real solace in a stolen interview with the white goat or even
a heart to heart talk with a skunk." Crushed but not compliant, Hornaday fought on for wildlife preservation and military preparedness until
his death in 1937. At his funeral, in accordance with his wishes, the
chorus sang "Home on the Range" and the Boy Scouts blew taps.[81]

NOTES

1. Tuchman, *Stilwell and the American Experience in China,* p. 54–55; George
Patton quoted in Blumenson, ed., *Patton Papers: 1885–1940,* p. 673; Army
Chief of Staff Peyton C. March quoted in Millis, ed., *American Military Thought,*
p. 351. The last quotation is Frank McCoy to James Wadsworth, Apr. 22, 1919,
McCoy MSS, Box 15.

2. U.S. Congress, Senate, Committee on Military Affairs, *Hearings on Army
Reorganization,* 66th Cong., 1st Sess., 1919, esp. p. 1061. The description of

Congressman Mondell is from Gen. S. M. B. Young to H. H. Sheets, Apr. 15, 1920, National Association for Universal Military Training MSS, Box 13.

3. John McAuley Palmer (military advisor to the 1920 Senate Military Affairs Committee), *America in Arms: The Experience of the United States with Military Organization* (New Haven: Yale University Press, 1941), p. 178. The opinions of veterans on Wood are from Wecter, *When Johnny Comes Marching Home*, p. 371. Leonard Wood to Governor H. T. Allen, Feb. 24, 1920; Wood to George Thompson, Mar. 6, 1920: both in Wood MSS, Box 138.

4. Palmer, *America in Arms*, p. 178; James W. Wadsworth, "The Reminiscences of James W. Wadsworth," pp. 313-15, Oral History Project, Columbia University; George Wharton Pepper, "The Opportunities of the Republican Party," June 3, 1920, Pepper MSS, Box 13; John McAuley Palmer to Clarence Penfield, June 21, 1944, Grenville Clark MSS.

5. DeLancey Kountze to Grenville Clark, Dec. 7, 1920; Clark to Col. F. D. Morrow, June 10, 1920, Clark MSS.

6. The quotations are from George Patton in Blumenson, ed., *Patton Papers: 1885-1940*, pp. 855, 878, 904; Horace Stebbins to Archibald Thacher, Aug. 11, 1921, Grenville Clark MSS; John J. Pershing Diary, Nov. 8, 1921, Pershing MSS, Library of Congress; Vandiver, *Black Jack*, 1:15, 2:603, 1055, 1061. The last quotation is from John McAuley Palmer to Archibald Thacher, Oct. 24, 1944, Palmer MSS, Box 10.

7. Grenville Clark to Charles Pike, Dec. 12, Dec. 22, 1924; Nathan Lord to Clark, Dec. 15, 1924; Clark to Horace Stebbins, Feb. 21, 1922, Mar. 17, 1922: all in Clark MSS. Dwight Davis to Charles Pike, Jan. 8, 1919, Military Training Camps Association MSS.

8. The quotations from professional soldiers are in Huntington, *Soldier and the State*, pp. 303-12; Millet, *The General*, p. 461. The third quotation is from Maj. Gen. F. H. Osborn as cited in Menninger, *Psychiatry in a Troubled World*, p. 530.

9. Statement of George Wharton Pepper in U.S. Congress, House, Committee on Appropriations, *Hearings on War Department Appropriations Bill for 1929*, 70th Cong., 1st. Sess., 1928, p. 939; statement of Grenville Clark in U.S. Congress, House, *Hearings on War Department Appropriations Bill for 1923*, 67th Cong., 2nd Sess., 1922, p. 1426; Nathan Lord to Grenville Clark, Dec. 15, 1924, Clark MSS.

10. Archibald Thacher to George James, July 20, 1926; Thacher to Grenville Clark, May 25, May 26, 1926: all in Clark MSS. Coolidge quoted in Ekrich, *The Civilian and the Military*, p. 212.

11. Archibald Thacher quoted in *New York Times*, June 19, 1921, 7:2, 5; Rockefeller, Jr., quoted in *New York Herald*, Feb. 6, 1917; Arthur Woods to Grenville Clark, Nov. 16, 1923, Clark MSS; Fosdick, *Chronicle of a Generation*, pp. 137-38, 146, 150, 168, 227, 255.

12. Charles Pike to Grenville Clark, Feb. 2, 1925; Clark to George F. James, July 2, 1923: both in Clark MSS. For the quote, from Rear Admiral Bradley Fiske, and the expansion of the navy, see Peter Karsten, *The Naval Aristocracy: The Golden Age of Annapolis and the Emergence of Modern American Navalism* (New York: Free Press, 1972), pp. 301-3. Leonard Wood to Andrew Mellon,

Mar. 4, 1921, Wood MSS, Box 157; Charles Schwab to Nicholas Murray Butler, Feb. 25, 1920, Butler MSS. Advertising executive Edward Bernays quoted
in Ewen, *Captains of Consciousness,* pp. 93–94.

13. Tom Wyrles to Alfred Roelker, Mar. 30, 1944; "Attendance at Citizens'
Military Training Camp," Chart, MTCA MSS, Box 12.

14. A. Lawrence Lowell to Killis Campbell, May 1, 1919, Lowell MSS, File
519; Ralph Barton Perry to Roger Merrian, Jan. 30, 1919; Perry to Arthur
Woods, Jan. 30, 1919, Mar. 5, 1919; Perry to Grenville Clark, Jan. 29, 1919: all
in Perry MSS; Perry, "College and the New Age," p. 491; Perry to A. Lawrence Lowell, Jan. 31, 1919; Lowell to Perry, Feb. 4, 1919, Lowell MSS, File 51.

15. National Collegiate Athletic Association, *Proceedings of the 13th Annual
Convention,* Dec. 27, 1919, pp. 10–12, 48–50; *New York Post,* Mar. 6, 1919;
James R. Angell to T. A. Storey, Dec. 23, 1920, Angell MSS, Yale University.

16. Grenville Clark to Ralph Barton Perry, Apr. 10, 1919, Clark MSS; Com-
mittee on the Regulation of Athletic Sports, "Statement of Policy," n.d., A.
Lawrence Lowell MSS, File 72; Yeomans, *Abbott Lawrence Lowell,* pp. 170,
230; Lowell to L. B. R. Briggs, Jan. 23, 1924, Lowell MSS, File 6: James R.
Angell to Henry Pratt Judson, Jan. 2, 1923, Judson Presidential MSS, Box 15,
University of Chicago.

17. Jessie F. Steiner, "Recreation and Leisure Time Activities," *Recent Social Trends in the United States* (New York: McGraw-Hill, 1933), pp. 926–27;
"Memorandum from John L. Griffith," Dec. 7, 1926, David Kinley MSS, Box
139, University of Illinois. The quotation on mass consumption is from economist Norman Ware as cited in Ewen, *Captains of Consciousness,* p. 29. For
fears of leisure, see George W. Alger, "Leisure—For What?" *Atlantic Monthly*
135 (Apr., 1925):483–92; George Wharton Pepper, "Master Spirits," May 9,
1925, Pepper MSS, Box 12.

18. Roosevelt, Jr., Diary, Apr. 7, 1922, Jan. 13, 1923, Dec. 6. 1923, Aug. 6,
1924, Roosevelt, Jr., MSS, Box 1.

19. For the European elites, see Wohl, *The Generation of 1914,* pp. 231–32.
Roosevelt, Jr., "YMCA Speech," Mar. 16, 1923; "Conference on Outdoor Recreation," May 22, 1924; Roosevelt, Jr., to William Temple Hornaday, Dec. 11,
1926: all in Roosevelt, Jr., MSS, Boxes 25, 61.

20. *New York Times,* Apr. 12, 1924, May 4, 1924, 8:14; Roosevelt, Jr., to
Mrs. Richard Derby, July 28, 1924; Gustavus Kirby to Arthur Woods, Mar. 19,
1925; Roosevelt, Jr., to Murray Halbert, Mar. 20, 1925: all in Roosevelt, Jr.,
MSS, Family Papers, vol. 4, Box 24; *The Laura Spellman Rockefeller Memorial
Final Report* (New York: n.p., 1933), pp. 21–23.

21. French Strother to Julius Rosenwald, Juy 9, 1929, President's Personal
File, Box 85, Herbert Hoover Presidential Library. The second quotation is
from B. F. Skinner, *Beyond Freedom and Dignity* (New York: Knopf, 1971), p.
171. Steiner, "Recreation and Leisure Time Activities," p. 919. Advertising
executives quoted in Ewen, *Captains of Consciousness,* pp. 39, 57. Consumer
statistics on cosmetics are in Larry May, *Screening Out The Past: The Birth of
Mass Culture and the Motion Picture Industry* (New York: Oxford University
Press, 1980), p. 202. William James, *The Varieties of Religious Experience* (New
York: New American Library, 1958), pp. 97–99, 102.

22. Floyd Tillery, "Little Babbitts," *Forum* 84 (Dec., 1930):340–1; Horace C. Woodward, "Sneering at the Boy Scouts," *Forum* 85 (Feb., 1931):xxii; Kett, *Rites of Passage,* p. 308.

23. Andrew West, "The Humanities After the War," in the Association of American Universities, *Journal of Proceedings and Addresses of the 20th Annual Convention,* Dec. 4, Dec. 5, 1918, pp. 83–85; Morison, ed., *Letters of Theodore Roosevelt,* 8:1418–19; Andrew West to Henry Stimson, July 25, 1925, Stimson MSS; Root quoted in untitled pamphlet attached to West to Stimson, July 25, 1925.

24. Stimson and Bundy, *On Active Service in Peace and War,* p. xviii; Fuess, "Reminiscences of Claude Feuss," p. 87; Stimson to Alfred Stearns, Apr. 16, 1924; Stimson to A. Phimsister Proctor, Dec. 11, 1924; Stimson to Andrew West, June 22, 1925: all in Stimson MSS.

25. Thwing, *American Colleges and Universities in the Great War,* p. 51. Professor Charles Mass quoted in David F. Noble, *America by Design: Science, Technology and the Rise of Corporate Capitalism* (New York: Oxford University Press, 1979), p. 147. Statistics on Latin are from Charles H. Judd, "Education," in *Recent Social Trends in the United States,* pp. 331, 339. For Secretary Stimson's commitment to research and development, see Kevles, *The Physicists,* pp. 309, 312–13.

26. Stimson quoted in Cunningham, "The Army and Universal Military Training," p. 329; Morison, *Turmoil and Tradition,* p. 512; Charles L. Mee, Jr., *Meeting at Potsdam* (New York: Dell, 1976), p. 205; Stimson, *The Far Eastern Crisis* (New York: Harper & Brothers, 1936), p. 247. On education in World War II, see Kevles, *The Physicists,* p. 320. Stimson to Claude Fuess, Jan. 5, 1942, Stimson MSS.

27, Stimson to John K. Herr, July 11, 1942, Stimson MSS.

28. Elizabeth Ogden Wood (Mrs. Henry Alexander Wise Wood) quoted in *Roosevelt Quarterly* (Spring, 1923), p. 1. Hermann Hagedorn, *The Hyphenated Family* (New York: Macmillan, 1960), p. 133, 170–74; Hagedorn quoted in "You Are the Hope of the World," *Outlook* 117 (Sept. 12, 1917):43; Hagedorn to Theodore Roosevelt, Mar. 1, 1918, Roosevelt MSS, Reel 266; Newton Baker to James G. Harbord, Mar. 9, 1931, Harbord MSS, Library of Congress.

29. Richard Collin, "The Image of Theodore Roosevelt in American History and Thought, 1885–1965" (Ph.D. diss., New York University, 1966), pp. 296, 303; *Roosevelt House Bulletin* (June, 1920):3, 5; (Fall, 1925):7; (Spring, 1926):2; (Spring, 1928):4; *Roosevelt Quarterly* (Spring, 1923):1; (Summer, 1924):4.

30. Collin, "Image of Theodore Roosevelt in American History and Thought," pp. 302–3; Henry Pringle, *Theodore Roosevelt: An Autobiography* (New York: Harcourt, Brace, 1931), p. 592; *Roosevelt House Bulletin* (Spring, 1929):2–5; (Fall, 1931):10.

31. Roosevelt, Jr., to Hanford McNeider, July 8, 1926, McNeider MSS, Hoover Presidential Library; Roosevelt, Jr., to Col. A. V. P. Anderson, Jan. 9, 1927; Roosevelt, Jr., to [?] Bache, Dec. 6, 1926, Roosevelt, Jr., MSS, Boxes 28, 29. For the trauma of war and its hedonistic effects, see Leed, *No Man's Land,* pp. 22–23; Frank Tannenbaum, "The Moral Devastation of War," *Dial* 65 (Apr. 5, 1919): 333; Ference Szasz, "The Stress on 'Character and Service' in

Progressive America," *Mid-America: An Historical Review* 63 (Oct., 1971):145–54. The following avant-garde writers were quoted: Edward Blunden, William March, Ernest Hemingway, and Ezra Pound. Roosevelt, Jr., quoted in *New York Times,* May 31, 1926. Roosevelt, Jr., to Monsignor Delaney, Dec. 11, 1926; Roosevelt, Jr., to London *Times,* Jan. 31, 1930, Roosevelt, Jr., MSS, Boxes 27, 50.

32. Rooosevelt, Jr., to Hanford McNeider, May 9, 1927, McNeider MSS; Roosevelt, Jr., to Richard Tobin, Sept. 27, 1923, Roosevelt, Jr., MSS, Box 50. For the absence of emotional breakdowns in the 1st Division, see personal interview with Gen. Clarence Huebner, July 23, 1971, The quotations on the division's training period are from Marshall, *Memoirs of My Service in the World War,* pp. 8, 50, 80. The quotation from the French officer and the description at Sedan are from Coffman, *War to End All Wars,* pp. 246, 350.

33. Roosevelt, Jr., quoted in *New York Times,* May 31, 1926; Society of the First Division, *History of the First Division During the World War* (Philadelphia: John C. Winston, 1922), pp. 301–12.

34. Lothrop Stoddard to Roosevelt, Jr., Aug. 1, 1921; Roosevelt, Jr., to Stoddard, Aug. 9, 1921; Roosevelt, Jr., Diary, Mar. 11, 1922, Apr. 29, 1922, Aug. 29, 1923, July 12, 1924: all in Roosevelt, Jr., MSS, Boxes 1, 22.

35. David Chalmers, *Hooded Americanism: The First Century of the Ku Klux Klan, 1865–1965* (Garden City: Doubleday, 1965), pp. 255–57, 259–61; Roosevelt, Jr., "Lincoln Day Speech," Feb. 12, 1923; Howard Cole Townsend to Roosevelt Jr., Jan. 7, 1924; Roosevelt, Jr., to Townsend, Jan. 16, 1924; Roosevelt, Jr., to Curtis Wilbur, Aug. 26, 1924: all in Roosevelt, Jr., MSS, Boxes 24, 25, 61.

36. *New York Times,* Oct. 1, 1927; Oct. 7, 1927; Edwin Mordant quoted in unsigned memorandum, Oct. 21, 1927, Calvin Coolidge MSS, Reel 183, Library of Congress; Roosevelt, Jr., Diary, May 7, 1922; Roosevelt, Jr., to Richard Tobin, Dec. 4, 1923; Roosevelt, Jr., untitled speech of Jan. 28, 1938: all in Roosevelt, Jr., MSS, Boxes 1, 18, 50; Roosevelt, Jr., quoted in *New York Times,* May 18, 1923, May 31, 1926.

37. Roosevelt, Jr., *Rank and File,* passim; Roosevelt, Jr., to Col. A. V. P. Anderson, Jan. 8, 1927; Roosevelt, Jr., to John W. Thomason, Apr. 21, 1927: both in Roosevelt, Jr., MSS, Box 50.

38. For general discussions of survivors, guilt, and the generation gap, see Robert Jay Lifton, *History and Human Survival: Essays on the Young and Old, Survivors and the Dead* (New York: Random House, 1970), pp. 169, 171, 204; Fussell, *Great War and Modern Memory,* pp. 109–10. Red Reeder quoted in Robert Kotlowitz, "Taps at Utah Beach," *Harper's* 239 (Oct., 1969):112.

39. Lindbergh, Sr., quoted in John Milton Cooper, *The Vanity of Power: American Isolationism and the First World War, 1914–1917* (New York: Greenwood, 1969), p. 174. Roosevelt, Jr., quoted in *New York Times,* May 23, 1927; *Roosevelt House Bulletin* (Fall, 1928):4; Owen Wister, "Safe in the Arms of Croesus," *Harper's* 155 (Oct., 1927):546.

40. Statement of Gen. Lutz Walht in U.S. Congress, House, Committee on Appropriations, *Hearings on War Department Bill for 1929,* 70th Cong., 1st.

Sess., p. 922; George Wharton Pepper, "Tribute to Lindbergh," June 15, 1927, Pepper MSS, Box 10.

41. For the moral link between the war and censorship, see Paul Boyer, *Purity in Print: The Vice-Society Movement and Book Censorship in America* (New York: Scribner's, 1968), pp. 56–63. Henry Stimson to Ellwood Rabenwood, Mar. 5, 1924, Stimson MSS; Ashburn, *Peabody of Groton*, pp. 306–7, 338–39; Drury, *Drury of St. Paul's*, pp. 204, 263; George W. Martin to Endicott Peabody, Apr. 15, 1926, Peabody MSS, Box 77.

42. Dean Gaus of Princeton quoted in Paula Fass, *The Damned and the Beautiful: American Youth in the 1920s* (New York: Oxford University Press, 1977), p. 46. John G. Hibben, "Baccalaurate Address," *Princeton Alumni Weekly* 20 (June 16, 1920):853–54; James R. Cowell, "The New Undergraduate: An Interview with John Grier Hibben," *Saturday Evening Post* 200 (Jan. 14, 1928):129–31; Buenning, "John Grier Hibben," pp. 35, 85; Hibben to "Dear Sir," Feb. 18, 1926, Hibben MSS, Box 1.

43. Senator Walsh of Massachusetts quoted in George R. Leighton and Richard Hellman, "Half Slave, Half Free: Unemployment, The Depression, and American Young People," *Harper's* 123 (Aug., 1935):342. Peabody allowed leftist speakers and literature into Groton; see Ashburn, *Peabody of Groton*, pp. 336–39. Secretary of State Stimson granted passports to communists because he felt that "if our country cannot withstand communistic dectrine through the inherent strength of the principles of freedom which we are devoted to, repression won't help it"; see Stimson Diary, May 4, 1931, Memorandum of Conversation with Signor Dino Grandi, July 9, 1931, Stimson MSS.

44. Grenville Clark to George Wharton Pepper, Oct. 6, 1919, Pepper MSS, Book 13; Walter Lippmann, "Leonard Wood," *New Republic* 23 (Mar. 17, 1920):78–79.

45. The first quote is from ibid. Statements of Frank McCoy, May 16, 1929; of E. H. Clark, Dec. 19, 1928; of Frank Steinhart, n.d.: all in Hermann Hagedorn MSS, Boxes 17, 21, 22. The long quotation is from Henry Alexander Wise Wood, "Foreword," in William H. Hobbs, *Leonard Wood: Administrator, Soldier and Citizen* (New York: Putnam's, 1920), p. 20. Mark Sullivan quoted in *New York Post*, June 15, 1920. Harding quoted in Paul A. Carter, *Another Part of the Twenties* (New York: Columbia University Press, 1977), p. 169.

46. Statement of Mrs. Corrine Roosevelt Robinson, n.d.; Arthur Dunn, "After the Convention," n.d.: both in Hermann Hagedorn MSS, Box 21. Frank McCoy to Basil Miles, Dec. 17, 1920, McCoy MSS, Box 16; Harding quoted in "Journal of W. Cameron Forbes," series 2, vol. 2. p. 320, Forbes MSS.

47. Edward Potts Cheyney, *History of the University of Pennsylvania* (Philadelphia: University of Pennsylvania Press, 1940), pp. 388–89; Albert Brunker, "The Presidency of the University of Pennsylvania," Mar. 26, 1929, Hermann Hagedorn MSS, Box 22; George Wharton Pepper to Frank McCoy, Sept. 25, 1922, McCoy MSS, Box 16; Pepper to Leonard Wood, Aug. 9, 1921, Wood MSS, Box 157.

48. Brunker, "Presidency of University of Pennsylvania," Mar. 26, 1929; Col. Chitty to Hermann Hagedorn, Sept., 1929; both in Hagedorn MSS, Box

22. Wood to Charles Ruggles, Mar. 25, 1921; Wood to Gen. F. C. Parker, Apr. 27, 1922, Aug. 1, 1922: all in Wood MSS, Boxes 157, 158.

49. Root quoted in Henry Stimson to Leonard Wood, Jan. 31, 1921, Wood MSS, Box 157. Statement of Frank McCoy, Feb. 14, 1929, Edward Bowditch to Hermann Hagedorn, Dec. 18, 1930, Hagedorn MSS, Boxes 22, 23; Wood to Mrs. Ogen Reid, Mar. 4, 1921; Wood to William Cooper Proctor, June 29, 1922, Wood MSS, Boxes 157, 161.

50. Rufus S. Tucker, "A Balance Sheet of the Philippines," *Harvard Business Review* 8 (1929):16–17, 22–23; Michael Onorato, *Leonard Wood as Governor General: A Calendar of Selected Correspondence* (n.p.: MCS Enterprises, 1969), pp. 92, 100, 106; Forbes to Secretary of War, Aug. 6, 1921, Nov. 12, 1921, in "Journal of W. Cameron Forbes," series 2, vol. 2, pp. 161, 341.

51. Richard D. Challener, *Admirals, Generals, and American Foreign Policy: 1898–1914* (Princeton: Princeton University Press, 1973), pp. 229, 237–38, 272.

52. Statement of Frank McCoy, May 19, 1929, Hagedorn MSS, Box 22; Leonard Wood to Rev. Henry Larson, Feb. 28, 1922, Wood MSS, Box 161.

53. Wecter, *When Johnny Comes Marching Home*, p. 322; James M. Beck to Henry Cabot Lodge, Feb. 5, 1920, Feb. 12, 1920; Lodge to Beck, Mar. 22, 1920: all in Henry Cabot Lodge MSS, Massachusetts Historical Society, Boston. Henry Cabot Lodge, "Introduction," to Edward Everett Hale, "Prospero's Island," in *Discussions of the Drama* (printed for the Dramatic Museum of Columbia University, 1919) 3:29–30; Leonard Wood Diary, June 19, 1921, Feb. 16, 1926, Wood MSS, Box 1. The final quotation is from the statement of Frank McCoy, May 19, 1929, Hagedorn MSS, Box 22.

54. Statement of Frank McCoy, May 16, 1929, Hagedorn MSS, Box 22; Gerald E. Wheeler, *Prelude to Pearl Harbor: The United States Navy and the Far East, 1921–1931* (Columbia: University of Missouri Press, n.d.), pp. 6, 14–15; Wood Diary, Sept. 23, 1921; Wood to Henry Stimson, Jan. 7, 1921, Wood MSS, Boxes 1, 162.

55. Millis, *Martial Spirit*, p. 339; Michael Onorato, *A Brief Review of American Interest in Philippine Development and Other Essays* (Berkeley: McCutchan, 1968), pp. 8, 57, 115; statements of Nicholas Roosevelt, Feb. 4, 1929; Gordon Johnston, Feb. 21, 1929, Hermann Hagedorn MSS, Box 22.

56. Onorato, *Brief Review of American Interest in Philippine Development*, pp. 32–33, 50–1, 54; Wood to Henry Stimson, Jan. 7, 1921; Wood to Nicholas Roosevelt, July 23, 1925; Wood to Guy Murchie, Dec. 11, 1922: all in Wood MSS, Boxes 161, 162, 178; Onorato, *Leonard Wood as Governor General*, pp. 2, 13–14, 80.

57. "Journal of W. Cameron Forbes," series 1, 1:216, 2:401, Forbes MSS; Wood to P. G. McDonald, Mar. 4, 1921; Wood to Mrs. Theodore Roosevelt, May 2, 1921, Wood MSS, Box 157; statement of Frank McCoy, May 19, 1929, Hagedorn MSS, Box 22; W. Cameron Forbes to Leonard Wood, Oct. 5, 1921, copy in Frank McCoy MSS, Box 16.

58. Wood quoted in Katherine Mayo, *The Isles of Fear* (New York: Harcourt & Brace, 1925), pp. 246–47. Edward Bowditch to Hermann Hagedorn, Dec. 18, 1930; two statements of Gen. Johnston Hagood, n.d.: all in Hagedorn MSS,

Boxes 22, 23; Onorato, *Leonard Wood as Governor General,* pp. 6, 29, 30–33, 35–37, 79; Hermann Hagedorn, "Pomp and Circumstance," Nov. 28, 1929, Hagedorn MSS, Box 19; James Weaver to Wood, Dec. 23, 1924, Wood MSS, Box 178; Henry Stimson Diary, Dec. 22, 1926, Stimson MSS; statement of Gordon Johnston, Jan. 25, 1929, Hagedorn MSS, Box 22.

59. John R. White, *Bullets and Bolos* (New York: Century, 1928), pp. 193–94; Mrs. Halstead Dory to Hermann Hagedorn, Jan. 5, 1930, Hagedorn MSS, Box 18; statement of Henry Stimson, Jan. 19, 1926, in Wood MSS, Box 181; Wood to Guy Murchie, Sept. 20, 1922, Wood MSS, Box 161; Victor Heiser, *An American Doctor's Odyssey* (New York: Norton, 1936), pp. 260–61; Wood Diary, July 21, 1927, Wood MSS, Box 1.

60. Edward Bowditch to Hermann Hagedorn, Dec. 18, 1930, Hagedorn MSS, Box 23: Michael J. J. Smith, "Henry L. Stimson and the Philippines" (Ph.D. diss., University of Indiana, 1969), pp. 78, 83.

61. Stimson to Leonard Wood, June 22, 1922, Nov. 30, 1924, Mar. 12, 1925, Oct. 30, 1925: all in Wood MSS, Boxes 162, 172, 198; Stimson to Members of the Skull and Bones of '88, Oct. 29, 1924; Stimson to Mrs. Henry James, Oct. 21, 1927; Stimson to E. H. Crowder, Mar. 23, 1927: all in Stimson MSS.

62. Morison, *Turmoil and Tradition,* pp. 72, 221; Stimson to Members of the Skull and Bones of '88, Oct. 29, 1924, Stimson MSS; Stimson to Leonard Wood, Nov. 30, 1924, Wood MSS, Box 172; O. Mannoni, *Prospero and Caliban: The Psychology of Colonialization* (New York: Praeger, 1964), pp. 100–101; Frantz Fanon, *The Wretched of the Earth* (New York: Grove Press, 1966), p. 204.

63. Stimson quoted in Smith, "Henry Stimson and Philippines," pp. 7, 60; Stimson to Leonard Wood, Nov. 30, 1924, Jan. 1, 1926, Sept. 12, 1926: all in Wood MSS, Box 172, 182; Stimson to William Crozier, Sept. 1, 1927; Stimson to E. H. Crowder, Mar. 23, 1927, Stimson MSS.

64. Stimson to Elihu Root, Nov. 24, 1928, Root MSS, Box 143; Smith, "Henry Stimson and Philippines," pp. 107, 129; "Remarks of Honorable Henry L. Stimson," May 1, 1929, Stimson Diary, "Memorandum by Stimson," May 30, 1946, Stimson MSS.

65. "On Active Service in Peace and War," undated memorandum, Stimson MSS; Smith, "Henry Stimson and Philippines," pp. 147–56; 169–79; Stimson, *Far Eastern Crisis,* p. 89; Stimson Diary, Jan. 7, 1932, Feb. 11, 1932, Stimson MSS. Stimson quoted in Waldo Heinrichs, *American Ambassador: Joseph C. Grew and the Development of the United States Diplomatic Tradition* (Boston: Little, Brown, 1966), p. 185; Robert Ferrell, *American Diplomacy in the Great Depression: Hoover-Stimson Foreign Policy, 1929–1933* (New York: Norton, 1970), p. 184. Stimson to Ernest Wilkins, Sept. 10, 1935; Stimson to Arthur Fischer, Aug. 25, 1935; Stimson to Hermann Hagedorn, Nov. 19, 1935: all in Stimson MSS.

66. Stimson to Arthur Fischer, Aug. 27, 1935; Stimson Diary, Feb. 9, 1942, Stimson MSS: Stimson, "Future Philippine Policy Under the Jones Act," *Foreign Affairs* 5 (Apr., 1927):259; Louis Morton, *The Fall of the Philippines* (Washington: Chief of Military History, Department of the Army, 1953), pp. 149–50; Stimson, Joseph Grew, and Stanely Hornbeck cited in Christopher

Thorne, *Allies of a Kind: The United States, Britain and the War Against Japan* (New York: Oxford University Press, 1978), pp. 79, 209; "Memorandum for the President: A Suggested Analysis of the Best Topics and Their Attendant Problems," in Stimson Diary, Dec. 20, 1941, Stimson MSS. Gen. Booth quoted in James, *Years of MacArthur,* 1:747; Admirals Parker and Upton quoted in Christopher Thorne, *Limits of Foreign Policy: The West, the League and the Foreign Policy Crisis of 1931–1933* (New York: Capricorn, 1972), p. 74; Stimson and Bundy, *On Active Service in Peace and War,* p. 404. Harvey Bundy, "The Reminiscences of Harvey Bundy," p. 258, Oral History Project, Columbia University; Stimson to Marguerite Wolfson, Dec. 6, 1941, Stimson MSS; Stimson quoted in Smith, "Henry Stimson and the Philippines," p. 131. For neutralization, the results of the war, and the quotation from MacArthur, see Carol Morris Petillo, *Douglas MacArthur: The Philippine Years* (Bloomington: University of Indiana Press, 1981), pp. 182, 206–7, 225–26. True, the introduction of the four engine (B-17) bomber in 1941 led some military planners to believe that the Philippines had suddenly become defensible. Unlike these men, who tried to adjust their strategy to new weaponry, Stimson used this innovation to support a position to which he already was emotionally committed. But whatever capabilities these bombers had, there were far better places to deploy their striking powers. If Stimson had not transferred B-17s from Hawaii to the Philippines, their long-range patrols might have blocked the subsequent attack on Pearl Harbor. Japan's aircraft carriers, with hollow decks highly vulnerable to bombing, could have been crippled long before Oahu came within their range; see Gordon W. Prange, *At Dawn We Slept: The Untold Story of Pearl Harbor* (New York: McGraw-Hill, 1982), pp. 188, 292–93, 390.

67. Winston Churchill: *The Second World War: The Hinge of Fate* (Boston: Houghton, Mifflin, 1951), p. 92; *The Second World War: Triumph and Tragedy* (Boston: Houghton, Mifflin, 1951), p. 143; Stimson to John Herr, Aug. 4, 1936, Stimson MSS.

68. Longworth, *Crowded Hours,* p. 13.

69. Roosevelt, Jr., to Mark Kerr, Feb. 8, 1921; Roosevelt, Jr., to J. W. Jackson, Apr. 5, 1921; Roosevelt, Jr., Diary, Oct. 27, 1921; Roosevelt, Jr., to Arthur Lee, May 9, 1922: all in Roosevelt, Jr., MSS, Boxes 1, 44.

70. Roosevelt, Jr., Diary, Jan. 19, 1922; Roosevelt, Jr., to Edwin Denby, Aug. 30, 1923; Roosevelt, Jr., to Mrs. Theodore Roosevelt, July 25, 1923, Aug. 1, 1923: all in Roosevelt, Jr., MSS, Boxes 1, 49, Family Correspondence.

71. Roosevelt, Jr., Diary, May 18, 1922, Jan. 1, 1923, July 11, 1923, Roosevelt, Jr., MSS, Box 1.

72. Roosevelt, Jr., to Philip Bancroft, Apr. 10, 1923; Roosevelt, Jr., Diary, Feb. 2, 1922, Feb. 28, 1922, June 6, 1923, Aug. 22, 1924; Roosevelt, Jr., to R. E. Cunningham, Apr. 1, 1921: all in Roosevelt, Jr., MSS, Boxes 1, 18, 48.

73. Roosevelt, Jr., Diary, May 11, 1923; Roosevelt, Jr., to Richard Tobin, Sept. 20, 1924, Roosevelt, Jr., MSS, Boxes 1, 34; James Lown to James Wadsworth, July 18, 1924, Wadsworth to Lown, July 18, 1924; Wadsworth to Roosevelt, Jr., Oct. 12, 1923; Roosevelt, Jr., to Wadsworth, Oct. 15, 1923: all in Wadsworth MSS, Box 19.

74. *New York Times,* Sept. 20, 1924, Oct. 25, 1924; Mathew and Hannah Josephson, *Al Smith: Hero of the Cities* (Boston: Houghton, Mifflin, 1969), pp. 316–17.

75. Personal interview with Gen. Robert Porter, Sept. 26, 1972. For written examples of Roosevelt's memory, see Arthur Sturdevant to Roosevelt, Jr., Mar. 21, 1932; Roosevelt, Jr., to Sturdevant, Apr. 23, 1932, Roosevelt MSS, Box 60.

76. Roosevelt, Jr., to F. Trubee Davison, Nov. 9, 1932; Roosevelt, Jr., to Mrs. Charles Sumner Bird, Dec. 17, 1924; Roosevelt, Jr., to George C. Marshall, Jan. 24, 1925; Ransom Anderson to Roosevelt, Jr., May 23, 1934: all in Roosevelt, Jr., MSS, Boxes 24, 25, 59.

77. Theodore Roosevelt, Jr., and Kermit Roosevelt, *East of the Sun and West of the Moon* (New York: Blue Ribbon, 1926), pp. 1, 55, 247; Roosevelt, Jr., to Dr. F. W. Bradner, Mar. 12, 1926; Eleanor R. Roosevelt to "Georgie," Dec. 3, 1925; Eleanor to "Mother," Dec. 2, 1925: all in Roosevelt, Jr., MSS, Boxes 25, Family Correspondence. In the war, Roosevelt, Jr., was poison gased and shot twice.

78. Pepper to Edward Bok, Jan. 14, 1921, Pepper MSS, Box 15; Pepper to Frank McCoy, Sept. 15, 1922, McCoy MSS, Box 16. George Wharton Pepper, *Men and Issues: A Selection of Speeches and Articles* (New York: Duffield, 1924), p. 82. John Lukacs, *Philadelphia Patricians and Philistines, 1900–1950* (New York: Farrar, Straus, & Giroux, 1981), pp. 28, 225.

79. Pepper to Joe [sic], n.d.; Pepper to Arthur Bretherick, Apr. 26, 1926: both in Pepper MSS, Box 56; George Wharton Pepper, *In the Senate* (Philadelphia: University of Philadelphia Press, 1930), pp. 25–29; Pepper quoted in the *Daily Princetonian,* Jan. 10, 1931.

80. Pepper to Rep. Guy Campbell, Fall, 1930; Pepper, "Ideals of Churchmanship," Nov. 26, 1928; "Christian Fellowship and Church Unity," May 20, 1930: all in Pepper MSS, Book 17; Richard T. Filler and Marshall W. Fisher, *For Thy Glory: The Building of the Washington Cathedral* (n.p.: Community Press, 1965), pp. 9, 63–64. For democracy and architecture, see Robert M. Crunden, *Ministers of Reform: The Progressives' Achievement in American Civilization, 1889–1920* (New York: Basic Books, 1982) esp. p. 146. Pepper quoted on poster attached to Landon P. Marvin to Franklin D. Roosevelt, Oct. 24, 1929, Group 12, Box 111, Roosevelt Presidential Library; Pepper to Nicholas Murray Butler, Oct. 27, 1927, Butler MSS; Pepper to Rev. H. Carhart, Feb., 1929, Pepper MSS, Book 17.

81. Hornaday: "Eighty Fascinating Years"; unpublished autobiography, Ch. 15, 19: both in Hornaday MSS, Box 21; Hornaday, *Minds and Manners of Wild Animals,* pp. 228, 249–50; Hornaday to Nicholas Murray Butler, Nov. 1, Nov. 4, Nov. 18, 1927, Butler MSS; John Ripley Forbes, *In the Steps of the Great American Zoologist: William Temple Hornaday* (New York: M. Evans, 1969), p. 107.

CHAPTER 10

The 1930s:
From Depression to War

SEVERAL preparedness leaders, as critics of the consumer culture that "made pleasure, not work the chief end of life," initially welcomed the Great Depression. These Jazz Age Jeremiahs, rejecting the twentieth-century trend to attribute depression to underconsumption, felt that America's economic calamity had roots in its "mad rush for wealth, comfort [and] ease." The crash, as a moral crisis, justified their past denunciations and offered them new hope for the future of reform. Consequently some Plattsburgers, in the early 1930s, once again "looked forward to a long, laborious period of regeneration of the national character."[1] When they looked back at the end of the decade, they found that this prediction had been wrong.

In the fight against the Depression, preparedness advocates usually supported President Herbert Hoover's plans for local relief projects and balanced public budgets. This policy, at least, encouraged community cohesion and civic self-denial. Unfortunately, it did not reduce the unemployment rates foreboding a demoralizing dole. Therefore Arthur Woods, chairman of Hoover's Emergency Committee on Employment, tried to increase federal spending to create work.

The New Deal, which came to power shortly thereafter, further expanded the scope of government. With exceptions like the Civilian Conservation Corps, it generally deemphasized moral uplift projects in favor of increasing mass purchasing power. To the extent that it had an ideology other than pragmatism, it stressed welfare and security. Preparedness leaders felt that those objectives subverted their version of the Protestant ethic that emphasized fortitude, resolution, and will. They consequently fought the New Deal with legal briefs, patriotic pageants, and moral rearmament. Finally, to obstruct the growth of federal power, several (but not all) former interventionists opposed America's entry into World War II. War, once thought to produce social improvement, now appeared likely to increase moral decay.

A New Call to Arms: The Benefits of Depression and the Dangers of Unemployment

The belief that economic depression could mean moral elevation was not unprecedented. In 1895, Owen Wister wrote Theodore Roosevelt that the present financial slump might well prevent the nation from degenerating into a mere "strip of land on which a crowd is struggling for riches." The average American citizen, seduced by "material prosperity," needed "'a little misfortune' to bring him back to his good senses." Some forty years later, in 1933, Theodore Roosevelt, Jr., claimed that hard times would eliminate the "silk shirt days" that had replaced family picnics with night club cabarets.²

The "salutary shock" of retrenchment, sustaining Roosevelt, Jr.'s, hopes, initially resurrected a spirit of unity reminiscent of World War I. However, the Great War actually bequeathed an ambiguous legacy to the Great Depression. Its mobilization plans, thrown together in ad hoc haste, used a mosaic of emergency measures from discretionary conservation to enforced taxation. It thus established precedents for both voluntary and government-controlled economic recovery programs. Secretary of State Henry Stimson, a firm believer in the former method, appealing to self-control and patriotism rather than coercion, convinced President Hoover to take his crusade for personal sacrifice directly to the American Legion's cash-bonus lobby. Unreceptive though that audience might be, Stimson said that it was still "composed of people who had been to war. He [Hoover] was their commander and he was now their leader in a great emergency." Hence the President, himself once "certain" that the world war would promote "the purification of men," now asked veterans for new displays of "self-denial" and "courageous service." Unfortunately, this appeal to forego the bonus and "enlist in the fight" for a balanced budget, did not prevent unforeseen analogues to war—the march on Washington by the Bonus Expeditionary Force and the subsequent Battle of Anacostia Flats.³

Although many legionnaires ignored Hoover's battle cry, chanting "we want beer" when he finished his speech, George Wharton Pepper volunteered for duty in the commander-in-chief's economic militia. Too old for the infantry in 1917, Pepper then organized Philadelphia's war chest and liberty loans. In that "blessed age of drives and campaigns" he believed that these charities would "transfigure" Americans into a "decent and God-fearing people." Now in 1931–32, Philadelphia's fund-raiding fight against the Depression resembled its old crusade against the Germans. This new effort "to go over the top," although referring to contribution quotas, seemed to integrate society by resurrecting a bygone "spirit of fighting." Pepper, caught up in these neo-Plattsburg emotions, once again declared that a righteous community cause imposed a chastening sacrifice upon wealthy contributors "privileged" to become philanthropic "veterans." They "mustered out of [their] service," according to him, "better and finer people for the experience through which they passed."[4]

Depression nonetheless proved to be a mixed bag of moral blessings. As the economy faltered, unemployment threatened the American character with subsistence on a debilitating dole. Welfare dependency worried several preparedness advocates but none more directly than Arthur Woods, now the chairman of President Hoover's Emergency Committee on Employment. Woods's assignment has been discussed in most histories of the Hoover Administration. Yet his ideology and actions remain a controversy. Albert Romasco calls Woods "one of Hoover's faithful following" while Irving Bernstein says he quit the administration "in disgust." The evidence in its entirety, however, suggests that Woods both approved and reproved Hoover's policies and programs.[5]

Never a man to solicit criticism, the President had every reason to think he had selected the "faithful" follower whom Romasco depicts. In 1921, when Hoover was secretary of commerce, Woods actively assisted his department's employment program. Their joint effort consciously aped Hoover's wartime conservation drives since, in both instances, the federal government recommended projects for localities to adopt and volunteers to support. Although expansion in the automobile and utility industries brought about the subsequent economic recovery, Hoover's fortuitously timed system of collective individualism assumed credit for the boom it did not create. This sustaining illusion motivated him to continue to apply conferential solutions to the public problems arising between the recession that began the 1920s and the Depression that closed it. In this period he repeatedly asked Woods, then a Rockefeller Foundation executive, to fund his popular education projects on home economics, industrial relations, and "recent social trends" in American life. When massive unemployment reemerged after 1929, Hoover naturally thought that the colonel was the ideal man to exhort the local relief measures which the President envisioned.[6]

Woods, confirming Hoover's assessment, certainly agreed that federal welfare endangered "the most cherished of our American traditions": human character. Convinced that the disadvantaged need personal guidance to prevent charity from destroying their will-to-work, he always used the "visiting" techniques traditionally practiced by New England's philanthropies. In 1900 the poor visited him at the Groton Summer Camp where he instructed them in "cleanliness, discipline and moral strength." In 1919–20, as the secretary of war's special assistant for veterans' reemployment, he had successful entrepreneurs, who "overcame great difficulties in life," visit military hospitals "to encourage and inspire" patients with "their words and presence." In 1930–31, opposing any "great imposing organization that treats people as ciphers," he reendorsed neighborhood aid as the least degrading form of help.[7]

Despite Woods's efforts, community support everywhere began to weaken. Even Pepper's Philadelphia, the paragon of community self-help, exhausted the voluntarily given local resources financing its work relief. Equipment and accident costs could make public works twice as expensive as direct relief. Faltering localities, lacking federal funds, could dispense only welfare. With this dilemma in mind, Woods traveled to England and Germany "to get a human or social side" of the European dole. In Britain, with labor demanding "work or maintenance," Whitehall had relinquished the age-old indictment that welfare sapped the morals of the deserving poor. Complacent officials, otherwise fearful that public works would swell the national debt, told Woods that direct relief prevented revolution by inducing apathy. He himself observed, as did political leftists and academic sociologists alike, that this relatively inexpensive form of social stability had some "terribly dangerous effects." Welfare recipients, young men in particular, were becoming a subculture of idle poor, pacified by an enervating loss of hope, ambition, and faith. Consequently Woods, a moralist who never used custodial forms of social control, returned to America completely convinced that while "distress must be relieved, the dole must not be [used.]." Although he admitted that the President would have to request another $840 million for public employment projects, work had to be the "first principle." Any other alternative seemed to him to threaten an unacceptable "destruction of human values."[8]

Since 1920 Herbert Hoover had also advocated countercyclical spending because he agreed that "public construction is better than relief." Yet, unlike Woods, he now thought it more important "to cut expenses and give the country and the world an exhibit of a balanced budget." Otherwise, Hoover, like most economists, reasoned that deficits and taxes would destroy the investor confidence absolutely necessary for sustained recovery. Recovery, needless to say, was necessary for the reelection which, according to Henry Stimson, "was constantly in [the President's] mind and constantly entered his policy." While Woods agreed with Hoover's orthodox economics, it seemed that he valued character more than financial prosperity and federal appointment. With these impolitic priorities, he could only resign. There was, his widow says, simply nothing else to do. True, he filed no public protest, but gentlemen like Colonel Woods do not attack a beleaguered commander already under fire. Whereas professional soldiers may criticize presidential policies before congressional committees, the martial code of the upper class forbids this "disloyalty." Because Woods soon underwent a prolonged illness, he never held another major public office. Neither did Hoover. Following Woods out of Washington, he left the Depression to the colonel's former Groton pupil, Franklin D. Roosevelt.[9]

The Civilian Conservation Corps: Moral Uplift within the Pragmatic New Deal

By and large the New Deal, priding itself on tough-minded pragmatism, did not try to mobilize or develop moral virtue. The heir to World War I's governmental innovations, it used federal power to balance supply against demand and thereby reestablish the economic equilibrium that the market place alone failed to maintain. Thus, despite the regulatory methods that the Roosevelt administration applied, it represented a new version of the old utilitarian doctrine that government should restrict itself to safeguarding economic growth. "In other words," as Rex Tugwell of the brain trust said, "the New Deal is attempting to do nothing to *people*, and does not seek at all to alter their way of life, their wants and desires." New Dealers, thinking this way, disavowed the Plattsburg political principle that the state must teach its citizens to love virtue. The greatest exception to this general depiction was the Civilian Conservation Corps (CCC), President Roosevelt's favorite project. Normally a consummate broker, offering different interest groups different programs, FDR dealt this "great national movement for the *conservation* of men" largely to himself. After observing the detailed attention that he gave the corps from his first day in office, his secretary of labor concluded: It "was really all his own project."[10]

When talking about the Civilian Conservation Corps, the President tended to emphasize its "moral and spiritual values." Why not? Little else could justify its large appropriation. Excluding the reclamation of timberland, other agencies did more good at less cost. As vocational education, the CCC taught forestry skills that were virtually useless in most labor markets. As public construction, its wilderness works ignored the needs of some 500,000 families who lived without decent homes and hospitals. The National Youth Administration, an agency that taught relevant skills while rehabilitating the urban environment, cost one-half the corps' per capita charge yet received one-fourth its annual appropriation. Unlike the CCC, the neglected NYA embodied the New Deal's true amoral outlook. Its urban-based employment pro-

gram, "reforming the [economic] structure rather than the people," left
the young in the "normal natural connections" that they preferred to
the corps. Although Roosevelt "thought that any man or boy would re-
joice to leave the city and work in the woods," some 20 percent of the
corpsmen deserted their camps despite the loss of room, board, pay,
and medicine. But however expensive, dysfunctional, and unpleasant
the CCC might be as public works construction and a job training program, it remained President Roosevelt's pet welfare project.[11]

The President's hard-core constituents were the urban ethnic groups
whom the abortive military training movement had failed to reform.
Most of his policies consequently served these indigent voters who
satisfied their physical needs in his political marketplace. Roosevelt,
nonetheless, still liked to think of himself as the same steward of high
moral standards who counseled the needy in 1900. Then, at the Groton
Summer Camp, he had returned the poor to their "wretched homes . . .
completely transformed in appearance, cleanliness, decency and civilization." Now, in 1934, the CCC performed "mental, moral and physical"
rehabilitation by helping the young "return to their homes . . . better
citizens with a better chance to meet the various problems of life." As
far as this particular agency was concerned, Roosevelt could feel that
he, like his "greatly loved schoolmaster" Arthur Woods, remained true
to his old patrician ideals.[12]

The CCC, linking the President to his past, shared many moral goals
once articulated by the universal military training movement. In World
War I, Roosevelt supported preparedness organizations which devised
their own plans for "wholesome" work projects during the "hoodlum
period" of adolescence. These groups, then updating the age-old proposal to conscript the unemployed, said that compulsory army service,
in a "slack [season] of idleness," would "substitute a period of helpful
discipline for a period of demoralizing freedom." Twenty years later
the corps itself claimed to make "despondent idlers" into "hard working citizens," thereby eliminating what Roosevelt called "the threat
that enforced idleness brings to spiritual and moral stability."[13]

As part of the UMT tradition, the CCC attracted neither pacifists nor
professional soldiers. Career officers from George Marshall to Douglas
McArthur admired the corps philosophically but still considered it an
inappropriate responsibility for the army to assume, especially at a
time when civilians, radicalized by the Depression, threatened to overturn military discipline. With tactical efficiency its sole concern, the
armed forces once again shrugged off the social welfare programs that
some civilians hoped they would bear. When nonetheless saddled with
the CCC, the army still sought its own self-interest. It used the corps to

prepare its reserves, rather than use its regulars to instruct the corps'
recruits. Because of budget restrictions, many reserve officers previously trained through correspondence courses. Now the service, assigning
them on a rotating basis to the forestry camps, gave these men command experience at the expense of CCC continuity. Those few soldiers
who really supported the corps were often protégés of Leonard Wood,
a hero of FDR's. One of them was Wood's former aide, Frank McCoy,
an officer who had "none of the army man's rigidity" for he "never
gave the impression of being a member of a caste." Another was George
Van Horn Mosley, former architect of the 1916 bill for UMT and present advocate of a compulsory term in a weapons-bearing CCC. His own
proposal, part military indoctrination and part public works, was supposed to develop those "wonderful traits of fundamental character"
which Mosley found "lacking in so many of the city bred."[14]

Civilian Plattsburgers, agreeing with these officers who had been
their instructors, likewise endorsed the CCC. Men such as Theodore
Roosevelt, Jr., and Robert McCormick only asked the agency to be
more extensive and more soldierly. If it added a mandatory military
training component, it would contain McCormick's nostrum for "manly
self-respect and wholesome ... citizenship." Grenville Clark, who
wished that the CCC was both universal and military, brought this request directly to Franklin Roosevelt, his old acquaintance, Harvard
classmate, and former fellow clerk in the same law firm. Specifically,
Clark suggested the unification of the Citizen Military Training Camps
and the CCC into a new institution to be named "Citizen Training
Camps." Because the corps, as an employment program, segregated
the poor into their own work camps, he worried that it inadvertently
nursed a "proletarian spirit" incompatible with his "old stock" traditions. As an alternative proposal, Clark's own "national adventure"
plan for bridging class boundaries would "provide an institution which
will represent the nation as an indissoluble unit against social disintegration." In it, he continued, "the CCC as a relief measure would be
merged into the greater effort of imparting an education for citizenship
to the country's youth. The essence of this education would be to keep
awake the American instinct for the frontier and the joy of overcoming
the obstacles threatening the future of the country through a common
effort."[15]

FDR, who originally built the CCC partly to preoccupy potentially
radical youth, welcomed Grenville Clark's suggestion and, in the late
1930s, tried to make the corps into a permanent institution functionally
independent of the business cycle. But neither Congress nor the public
welcomed the idea. Unlike the President, they thought that it was just

another relief measure. Without a depression, the corps made no sense to them.[16]

The New Deal and the Old Morality: Preparedness Leaders in the 1930s

The CCC, as Franklin Roosevelt's last hurrah for his past, was atypical of his professed tendency "to break foolish traditions." When the pragmatic New Deal did profess a faith, the *New Frontiers* of Henry Wallace clashed with the old frontiers of Henry Stimson. The former preached safety, security, and welfare while the latter lamented the loss of the "initiative, ambition and push which went with pioneer days." Consequently, most Plattsburgers actively opposed the Democratic Party's domestic policies.[17]

If economic interest had been their sole concern, many preparedness patriots might have supported the National Recovery Act, which sanctioned oligopoly, and endorsed Franklin Roosevelt, who preempted the radical left. They also should have accepted the New Deal's disregard for uplift issues since moral indignation would now focus scorn on the rich, their own class. Nonetheless, most of these men were ideologically motivated to protect their dignity, status, and ideals, not just their property. They criticized New Dealers, who tried to regulate big business, on the same grounds they once reproached big businessmen themselves: for emphasizing material growth at the expense of moral principles. Plattsburg leaders cherished fortitude, will, resolution, and the other "basic virtues" which the welfare state appeared to deemphasize. To develop these traits of "character," they underwent discomfort in various degrees from prep school to war. The more pain they endured the more valuable their achievements became. Perhaps this is why Grenville Clark, who never was in combat, could conclude that the New Deal was basically moderate, while Theodore Roosevelt, Jr., and Henry Stimson, both of whom rushed to fight in World War I, were convinced that the same program was morally subversive.[18]

Preparedness leaders, preaching heroism while masses of Americans concentrated on survival, tended to support their besieged social code with the same tenacity by which the army stiffens discipline when under attack. They consequently accused the Roosevelt administration of "insincerity" and "happy-go-lucky" opportunism. Apparently, they could not understand that while indecision (as opposed to resolve) was a military weakness, it was a political virtue at a time when macroeconomic concepts and statistics had yet to be discovered, developed, and refined. Felix Frankfurter told Stimson that the President ("a great trial and error guy") possessed a remarkable "readiness to hear and weigh views which might cross his grain." But the colonel, devoted to the "old school of political economy," could only conclude that Roosevelt "lacked basic political principles."[19]

Most Plattsburgers, having criticized the overconsumption culture of the 1920s, could not fathom the underconsumption crisis of the 1930s. Committed to the "old fashioned principles" of frugality, they rejected the New Deal's experimentation with deficit spending. Such proposals ran counter to their "school day's theory that governments and people were only financially sound when income and outgo were balanced." Yet the economic anarchy that they perceived seemed trivial when compared to the moral condition in which "the virtue of thrift and prudence seems to have been completely lost." These tenets, imbibed at prep schools stressing the *underconsumption* of personal income, prevented these men from objectively assessing the economic merits of fiscal expansion at a time when supply exceeded demand. They therefore thought that increased public spending simply indicated that the country had been "too corrupted and softened by the days of plenty and feast to meet a situation that requires personal sacrifice." In 1938, when Stimson revisited Washington, he found that this once provincial town was inundated with liberal intellectuals of the *New Republic* variety. The place, he said, had grown "less and less attractive. . . . The atmosphere seems very modern and alien to an old-fashioned person like myself."[20]

Because Plattsburgers laid their principles out on a constitutional-political-moral continuum, they could attack the New Deal through law, education, or religion. George Wharton Pepper, doing his duty in the courts, defended violators of National Recovery Act codes and successfully challenged the constitutionality of the Agricultural Adjustment Act. But "satisfied that the life of the practicing lawyer is the happiest life of all," his service entailed little sacrifice. The same could not be said of his good friend Henry Stimson who, in 1933, returned to his "routine practice of law" cursing that "life of drudgery." Feeling "it is better to wear out than rust out," he then was simply grateful for something to do. But down "in the doldrums," he discovered that his legal "harness" provided "a great deal of satisfaction" now that it enabled him to defend utility companies, financial institutions, and individual enterprise "against the power and influence of government." Stimson, having found great social purpose in what was once the "hunt for 'filthy lucre,'" stayed in his law practice until 1940, when fascist aggression eclipsed domestic threats.[21]

Legal suits could hinder the New Deal but not destroy it. Political campaigns, mobilizing the electorate, were also ineffective now that welfare checks "morally debauched" the public's judgment. In search of a solution, patriots once again tried didactic programs for moral uplift. Believing that their social dogma was almost axiomatic, they felt that its defeat sprang from Herbert Hoover's admitted lack of charisma. ("You can't make a Teddy Roosevelt out of me.") They consequently sought to rectify this condition by dramatizing their ideals in more compelling personifications. In Philadelphia, Pepper became involved in his city's Benjamin Franklin memorial projects since, he reasoned, that "nothing but a reincarnation of the man himself will bring about the popular acceptance of [his] teachings." In New York, Hermann Hagedorn's Theodore Roosevelt Memorial Association proclaimed its relevance "to contemporary needs and problems" as it pledged "to do more than tell wistful stories of the happier days of another Roosevelt." Lest present-day "panhandling" continue to undermine "enterprise, self-reliance [and] the pioneering spirit," it planned to "mobilize" works of art that would "galvanize and direct the spiritual energy of American youth." The association unsuccessfully tried the same tactic in the 1920s, when aesthetics "fitted into the business picture" by espousing consumption as artistic "self-expression." Then, as scholars note, "culture" meant a "ceaseless search for a new sensibility," rather than a country's traditional values. Since the Depression, art reflecting increased social involvement became considerably more conscious of the staple themes of RMA productions: national legends, pioneer myths, and "the American Way of Life." Consequently the organization now had reason to hope that this new tendency to use history "as a weapon to effect the present" could avert revolution in the future. Nonetheless, the breach between aesthetics and preparedness remained unbridged. Social concern drove most artists towards the left and political change, not towards the right and moral uplift. Even if the association could have found inspirational works to promote, its pedagogic ambition far exceeded its financial resources. It wanted to strengthen "the American system" by stimulating the national imagination, but only Walt Disney could do that. In the depth of the Depression, Snow White toys were one of the country's few boom industries.[22]

Besides being patrons of art for uplift, some leading members of the Roosevelt Memorial Association supported Reverend Frank Buchman's Moral Rearmament Movement (MRA). If MRA, as Hermann Hagedorn said, could teach politicians to ask "God rather than their constituents what they ought to do," then "fundamental standards" would govern the nation, not just "expediency." In 1935 Hagedorn brought a group of Buchman missionaries out to meet Henry Stimson, his Roosevelt Memorial Association comrade, but by then the colonel already was a convert. After the Manchurian Crisis of 1932–33 turned international politics into "amoral drift," this despondent secretary of state attended an MRA revival meeting. There, on the verge of a job-related breakdown, he recorded that he was ". . . in a position to see the truth they are hammering into all their audience that it is only along these [moral uplift] lines that the world can be saved. Otherwise civilization seems to be pretty bankrupt."[23]

Military training advocates from George Wharton Pepper to James Wadsworth joined the Moral Rearmament Movement because these two programs shared one ideology. Concentrating on what Pepper called the "regeneration of the people," both movements planned to reform the public's character without redistributing the nation's wealth or power. They consequently recruited much of their membership from the elite. But class interest aside, they both tapped class guilt. While some Buchmanites ("the best people and their butlers") used MRA to defend the status quo, others had experienced profound discontent with their pleasant but purposeless lives. Their identity crisis led them to "enlist" in this religious revival whose martial analogues challenged them to forsake their "indulgent" existence and obey "God's orders." Buchman, who claimed that his own "moral equivalent to war" was the "highest form of national service," declared: "What we need today are men of the Plattsburg type, who are willing to train for Moral Re-Armament, and take this message to every city, village and farm, for American to be up and to arm."[24]

MRA not only employed military slogans, it used paramilitary group psychology to accomplish its mission of moral reformation. The fellowship societies, which all members joined, provided their initiates with continuous camaraderie and discipline. The movement thereby gave its "groupers" the same emotional support that a highly motivated army unit gives its soldiers. (One MRA pamphlet said that entering the organization is "like joining the army. You decide there's something worth fighting for. You enlist. You put yourself under orders. Then you are given new equipment. You find new comradeship. Your way of living changes and your whole outlook on life.") In this way the movement could induce exemplary behavior from weak individuals. Once freed from isolation and alienation, these true believers had the strength to answer MRA's challenge to renounce physical pleasures, confess to transgressions, and eschew commercial enterprise for philanthropic service. No wonder Stimson saw this brand of "revitalized Christianity" as an antidote to "the ease and luxury of modern civilization."[25]

MRA, which echoed Plattsburg's moral ideal, also mirrored the UMT plan for economic recovery. Concerning the rich, whom Buchman called "up and outers," it would make them into Christian stewards willing to practice Herbert Hoover's plans for voluntary sharing. As for the jobless who still believed in the work ethic Plattsburgers promoted, MRA could alleviate the self-deprecation to which they were particularly prone. Its religious crusade—a "spiritual world war"—offered "instant enlistment and full-time employment" to everyone. And unlike a government dole, God's WPA preserved man's "fighting spirit."[26]

The Coming of World War II: The New Military Crisis and the Old Preparedness Leaders

While Plattsburgers complained that the New Deal softened the American character, the Roosevelt administration itself used military analogues to portray its welfare state as a warfare state battling a foreign foe. Its depiction of the Depression as an alien force not only justified emergency action, it directed internal class hatred towards an external symbol and thereby helped reunite the country's social order. Most preparedness leaders, nonetheless, assailed this New Deal application of patriotic propaganda. One might suppose they then would have ridiculed the administration as a quartermaster corps of resource mobilization men who never saw combat duty. They could have claimed that while paper wars back in the bureaus might be fought with financial planning, deficit spending, and bureaucratic controls, military and economic wars at the front are won by pain and sacrifice. But despite FDR's attempt to increase mass purchasing power, they failed to contrast the New Deal to wars curtailing civilian consumption. Accepting, instead, the military symbols they might have severed, they attacked the president's program with slogans maligning the army. Henry Stimson berated governmental "regimentation," while Robert McCormick and William Temple Hornaday, respectively, related social security cards to prisoner of war tags and foresaw a national drift towards a "military tyranny ready to shoot and stab any citizen [suspected] of opposition." Falling between these relatively moderate and extreme positions, George Wharton Pepper felt that the "New Deal machine operated [like] mechanized units in modern warfare." Meanwhile Theodore Roosevelt, Jr., called the National Recovery Administration a form of "militaristic Prussianism" whose "ever increasing army of employees" obeyed "German drill sergeant" commands.[27]

Martial analogues used for and against the New Deal may have been rhetorical propaganda sacrificing objectivity for agitation. Nevertheless, they foretold an important realignment in foreign policy. In the late 1930s many populists, trade unionists, and ethnic voters, who formerly held isolationist views, switched to interventionism. Simultaneously, some (but not all) prominent preparedness leaders adopted neutrality. Pepper, Ted Roosevelt, Jr., and others, who had gone into physical or psychological exile after World War I, already had developed an island-of-safety mentality highly compatible with isolationism. Later, the fear of a military accrual to New Deal power reinforced this trend. After 1937, men like McCormick and Hamilton Fish increasingly worried that President Roosevelt would "work up a series of war scares" to obstruct the recent resurgence of congressional conservatism. But, irrespective of Roosevelt, the very process of war threatened to have injurious effects on constitutional government. New Dealers, exploiting the pro-administration windfall of an international crisis, would allegedly use their war powers to turn "America into a totalitarian state." Once the fighting ceased, these rapacious men were not likely to surrender any increased authority. Indeed, the U.S. public, softened in the '20s and corrupted in the '30s, would not want them to do so. If, as most conservatives believed, the aftereffects of the Great War created the Great Depression, even greater economic problems would follow a second world war. The American people, now willing "to surrender their liberties for the sake of a mendacious guarantee of a living," would then support "any political medicine man who promises social security." [28]

In addition to war, the army seemed a peril to former preparedness leaders now afraid of the draft. In 1898, ministers had hoped that the infantry would gather its recruits into pup-tent pulpits for the word of God. In the 1940s, laymen felt that the army could be a forum for New Deal indoctrination. Liberals, once opposing UMT, came to believe that it would promote the "ideals of responsible American citizenship." Meanwhile some conservatives, who once supported the program, worried that it would subjugate citizens to the state. Like the San Francisco newspaper which attacked "a system of barracks regimentation under Government control," George Wharton Pepper worried that the military would produce a generation of "soulless automatons." Like Archibald and Ted Roosevelt, Jr., both refusing to endorse the 1940 draft, David Goodrich, their father's Rough Rider lieutenant, dismissed army life in favor of some form of "universal service which will train our youth to eliminate the Communist tendencies which today are so prevalent." For defense, ex-UMT advocates often supported a technologically intensive military protection which would make arms the purview of professional soldiers: their erstwhile competitors. While some other conservatives emphasized sea and air power, Robert McCormick supported a "small mobile army," based on tanks and artillery, that could deflate "the hysterical appeal for immediate conscription." [29]

These new isolationists, fearing the domestic effects of military institutions, were completing a political cycle. Former Spanish-American War enthusiasts, or relatives of men who were, had come to accept the anti-imperialist position that military intervention abroad would destroy constitutional government at home. Conscriptionists in 1917 came to endorse the argument that conscientious objectors made then and now: that "the very nature of modern war necessitates the abrogation of democracy." Theodore Roosevelt, Jr., now "the most pacifistic type of pacifist," asserted that the first shot of battle "would mark the end of the American republic."[30]

Nonetheless, a form of continuity accompanied their change. In World War I, preparedness leaders felt that war would assist moral reconstruction; in World War II, many of them feared it meant their political destruction. Thus, in both instances, these men were particularly concerned with the domestic by-product of combat overseas. If they were not so preoccupied, they might have been World War I isolationists and World War II interventionists. In 1916, Germany was contained behind a stable Western front and English propaganda in America exuded confidence. By 1940, the undeclared enemy controlled most of Europe, was a subversive force in South America, and a strategic threat on the North Atlantic. In addition, the idea of a self-sufficient fortress America was far less credible. Relative to trench warfare, which puts a premium on simple will and resolution, the mobile tactics of mechanized combat required an extended training period that no embattled nation could afford. And yet, despite foreign danger demanding the foremost attention, several men who once felt that America should wage war now said that it must remain at peace.[31]

Of course, not all Plattsburgers were so obtuse. Several of them remained interventionist sponsors of draft legislation. This group, led by Henry Stimson and Grenville Clark, were not more favorable to the New Deal than were their isolationist comrades, but for a number of reasons, they were less opposed to the army. They not only believed that Roosevelt, compared to Hitler, was *"the lesser of two dangers,"* they felt that war would be less regimenting than a fascist Europe. Whereas combat was temporary, the threat posed by a Nazi superstate would necessitate an indefinite period of political control over thousands of industries, millions of soldiers, and the entire civilian population. A true social analogue to war, this "armed camp over a long period of years" would produce what Clark called America's "permanent impairment."[32]

Some interventionists also felt that isolationists ignored the economic implications of their own foreign policy. Stimson began to fight national planning in 1933 when, to his regret, the "brain trust" advised Franklin Roosevelt to choose autarchy and terminate America's empire in the Philippines. Since then the colonel had been warning others that international commerce was the "only alternative to economic regimentation." If foreign trade were not nurtured, the country would experience "continuing attacks upon our social system of American freedom and renewed efforts for some form of planned economy and greater centralized governmental control."[33]

Because Stimson felt that international relations could prevent internal subjugation, he rebuffed conservative isolationists who feared that New Dealers would use war to tighten industrial controls. According to him, military preparedness would actually require "a radical change" in the administration's policy towards "the business leaders upon whose enthusiastic support any successful program of national defense will necessarily depend." President Roosevelt might have to retire but even if he remained, Stimson felt that FDR would have to sacrifice the New Deal for a coalition government in which the Republican Party would have "direct supervision of the navy and the army." In May, 1940, the prospective appointment of Frank Knox as secretary of the navy seemed "a most effective hostage" for that policy. In June, Republicans Stimson and Knox joined the cabinet together, much to the relief of Hermann Hagedorn. Oblivious to Roosevelt's own rejection of dictatorial powers for industrial mobilization, Hagedorn wrote Stimson, the new secretary of war, that his appointment was an assurance "that the [New Deal] smart alecks will not have an opportunity to use military preparation for political or subversive ends, and that industry will not be hamstrung by open or undercover intrigue."[34]

By mid-1940, men who could not recognize the conservative implications of war were simply self-deceived. "Their distrust of Roosevelt is so deep and incurable," Congressman James Wadsworth said, "that it sways their judgement completely." The President, ironically, benefited from their lapse. The dogmatic right-wing isolationists who assailed Roosevelt's diplomacy enabled him to do what they had feared. Running against Hitler in the 1940 election, he used foreign policy to mend his waning mandate. He won more votes by attacking his opponents as "appeasers" then he lost as an alleged "warmonger" himself. Many ex-preparedness advocates, victims of their own irrationality, held suspicions that apparently had deep subjective roots. If, as psychoanalysis contends, men project their desires onto their enemies, then some critics of the New Deal were accusing the administration of harboring their own political inclinations. Robert McCormick's *Chicago Tribune,* which once welcomed universal military service as a "desirable" measure for "mental conscription," now worried that Roosevelt wished to expand the army for authoritarian reasons. He and his newspaper overlooked the fact that the President was actually a reluctant warrior. Even after Munich, FDR offered mediation. Although rebuffed, he still hoped to avoid sending troops to fight overseas. As late as August, 1941, to the consternation of the War Department, he was obstructing military training in America by shipping weapons for the Allies to stop the Germans on their own. Those conservatives who refused to recognize Roosevelt's restraint possessed fears that were erroneous but nonetheless compelling. To prevent a war that McCormick thought would crush him, he published top secret contingency plans to to send, in an emergency, an army to Europe. This not only helped motivate Hitler to declare war on America, it gave the administration the cause and the means to crush McCormick if it wished.[35]

NOTES

1. The quotations are from James Beck in *United States Congressional Record,* 71st. Cong., 3rd Sess., 1931, pp. 3246–47; John G. Hibben, "Baccalaureate Sermon," June, 1932, Hibben MSS, Box 2; Lloyd Derby to Endicott Peabody, Feb. 21, 1933, Peabody MSS, Box 86. For modern economic thought, see Rogers, *Work Ethic in Industrial America,* pp. 116–22.

2. Wister, *Owen Wister Out West,* pp. 182–82; Wister to Theodore Roosevelt, Feb. 27, 1895, Wister MSS, Box 33; Roosevelt, Jr., "Balancing the Budget," Dec. 28, 1933, Roosevelt, Jr., MSS, Box 3.

3. George Wharton Pepper, "Address Delivered at Luncheon of John H. Mason's Commerce Division, Committee for Unemployment Relief," Mar., 1931, Pepper MSS, Book 15; Stimson Diary, Sept. 16, 17, 19, 1931, Stimson MSS; Herbert Hoover: *An American Epic: Famine in 45 Nations; Organization Behind the Front* (Chicago: H. Regnery, 1960), pp. 261–62; *The State Papers and Other Public Writings of Herbert Hoover,* ed. William Starr Meyers (Garden City: Doubleday & Doran, 1934), p. 620.

4. Pepper: "Liberty Loan Address in Carnegie Hall," Apr. 11, 1918; "Introduction for Myron T. Herrick at a War Chest Meeting in the Metropolitan Opera House," May 24, 1918; "Address Delivered at Luncheon of John H. Mason's Commerce Division," Mar., 1931: all in Pepper MSS, Books 9, 10, 15; Bonnie Fox Schwartz, "Unemployment Relief in Philadelphia, 1930–1932: A Study of the Depression's Impact on Voluntarism," in *Hitting Home,* ed. Bernard Sternsher (Chicago: Quadrangle, 1970), pp. 66, 568, 74–75.

5. Albert Romasco, *The Poverty of Abundance: Hoover, the Nation, the Depression* (New York: Oxford University Press, 1965), p. 146; Irving Bernstein, *The Lean Years: A History of the American Worker, 1920–1933* Baltimore: Penguin, 1966), p. 310.

6. Arthur Woods, "Address of Colonel Arthur Woods at the Unemployment Conference and Luncheon Held Under the Auspices of the Allegheny Chamber of Commerce," Oct. 19, 1921; Herbert Hoover to Woods, Sept. 15, 1923, Jan. 11, 1924, Dec. 10, 1924; Hoover to Ray Lyman Wilbur, May 27, 1930: all in Commerce Papers, Boxes 41, 254, 478, President's Personnel File 541, Hoover Presidential Library.

7. Woods, "Suggestions for the President's Message from the Emergency

Committee for Employment," Nov. 21, 1930, Presidential Papers, Box 273, Hoover Presidential Library; *Announcement of the Groton Summer Camp Committee,* Mar., 1900, Groton Papers, Franklin Roosevelt Presidential Library; United States, War Department, *Jobs for Soldiers: An Account of the Work of Colonel Arthur Woods, Assistant to the Secretary of War in Aiding the Return to Civil Life after the Great War—March–September, 1919* (n.p., n.d.), pp. 14, 40; Arthur Woods, "Unemployment and Its Social Significance," *Proceedings of the American Philosophical Society* 70 (Apr. 23, 1931):289–90.

8. Arthur Woods Diary, May 29, June 4, June 10, June 11, 1931; Woods, "Suggestions for the President's Message from Emergency Committee for Employment," Nov. 21, 1930; Woods to Hoover, Aug. 7, 1931: all in Presidential Papers, Box 275, Hoover Presidential Library; Erving P. Hayes, *Activities of the President's Emergency Committee for Employment: October 17, 1930–August 19, 1931* (Concord: Remford Press, 1936), p. 43. For English welfare and its social effects, see John A. Garrity, *Unemployment In History: Economic Thought and Public Policy* (New York: Harper and Row, 1978), pp. 148, 159, 177–78, 207, 222. Like Woods, Emma Goldman, the radical anarchist, observed that unemployed Germans had lost their "courage" while "waiting in line for a few measly marks," see Richard Drinnon, *Rebel in Paradise* (Boston: Beacon Press, 1970), p. 273.

9. Hoover quoted in William Appleman Williams, *The Contours of American History* (Chicago: Quadrangle, 1966), p. 432; Wilson, *Herbert Hoover,* p. 150. For "expert" economic opinion, see Frank Freidel, *Franklin D. Roosevelt: Launching the New Deal* (Boston: Little, Brown, 1973), pp. 57–58. Stimson Diary, Jan. 16, 1931; Nov. 14, 1932, Stimson MSS; Woods to Hoover, Oct. 29, 1936, Post-Presidential Papers, Box 157, Hoover Presidential Library; personal interview with Mrs. Helen Hamilton Woods Burgess, June 20, 1972. For professional soldiers and criticism, see Morton H. Halperin, *Bureaucratic Politics and Foreign Policy* (Washington, D.C.: Brookings Institute, 1974), pp. 226–27, 231, 257. For the loyalty of elites to their chiefs, see Barnet, *Roots of War,* pp. 61–63, 83.

10. Tugwell quoted in William E. Leuchtenberg, *Franklin D. Roosevelt and the New Deal* (New York: Harper & Row, 1963), p. 339. FDR quoted in Leslie Alexander Law, *The Soil Soldiers: The Civilian Conservation Corps in the Great Depression* (Radnor: Chilton, 1976), pp. 65, 95; Francis Perkins, *The Roosevelt I Knew* (New York: Viking, 1946), p. 177.

11, Edgar B, Nixon, ed., *Franklin D. Roosevelt and Conservation, 1911–1945* (Hyde Park: General Services Administration, 1957), 1:143–44; John Morton Blum, *V Was For Victory: Politics and American Culture During World War II.* (New York: Harcourt, Brace & Jovanovich, 1976), p. 102. For a discussion of the NYA and the quote from its director, Aubrey Williams, see George Rawick, "The New Deal and Youth: The Civilian Conservation Corps, the National Youth Administration and the American Youth" (Ph.D. diss., University of Wisconsin, 1957), pp. 131–33, 195, 215, 391.

12. For Roosevelt's constituents, see Samuel Lubell, *The Future of American Politics* (rev. ed., New York: Harper & Row, 1965), pp. 42–45; Groton Camp announcement in Roosevelt, ed., *F.D.R.,* 1:72; Robert Fechner, director of the

CCC, quoted in John William Killigrew, "The Impact of the Great Depression on the Army, 1929–1936" (Ph.D. diss., University of Indiana, 1960), p. 329; FDR to Mrs. Arthur Woods, May 14, 1942, PPf 8054, Roosevelt Presidential Library.

13. U.S. Chamber of Commerce quoted in Finnegan, *Against the Specter of a Dragon,* p. 186; Address of Secretary of War George Dern, n.d., Dern MSS, Box 1, Library of Congress; FDR quoted in Nixon, ed., *Franklin D. Roosevelt and Conservation,* 1:144.

14. James, *Years of MacArthur, 1880–1941,* pp. 384, 423, 425; Pogue, *George C. Marshall: Education of a General,* pp. 274–79; Killigrew, "Impact of Great Depression on Army," pp. 154–55, 282–83, 330, 334, 348. FDR's admiration of Leonard Wood is described in Langdon P. Marvin, "The Reminiscences of Langdon P. Marvin," p. 37, Oral History Project, Columbia University. The quotation about McCoy is from the statement of Frank Steinhart, May 29, 1929, Hagedorn MSS, Box 17. Frank McCoy to Henry Stimson, June 19, 1933, Stimson MSS; George Van Horn Mosley, "One Soldier's Journey," 2:179–80, 188–95, unpublished autobiography, Mosley MSS, Library of Congress.

15. Roosevelt, Jr., to Daniel Carter Beard, Oct. 26, 1933, Beard MSS, Box 105; *Chicago Tribune,* Jan. 6, 1935, Sept. 9, 1939; Grenville Clark to Eugene Rosenstock-Hussy, Nov. 20, 1934; Clark, "Training-Day of a Nation," n.d.; Clark, "Outline of a Plan for Federal 'Citizens Training Camps' Merging the Civilian Conservation Corps (CCC) and the Citizens Military Training Camps (CMTC)," Sept. 19, 1934: all in Clark MSS.

16. Rex Tugwell's unpublished memoir summarized in Malcom Cowley, *The Dream of the Golden Mountains: Remembering the 1930s* (New York: Penguin Books, 1981), p. 180. John A. Salmond, *The Civilian Conservation Corps, 1933–1942: A New Deal Case Study* (Durham: Duke University Press, 1967), pp. 202–7, 219.

17. Roosevelt quoted in Warren I. Susman, "The Thirties," in *The Development of an American Culture,* ed. Coben and Ratner, p. 192; Henry Stimson to Arthur Fischer, Aug. 27, 1935, Stimson MSS.

18. For the radicalizing effects of moralistic politics, see Robert E. Lane, *Political Ideology: Why the American Common Man Believes What He Does* (New York: Free Press, 1962), pp. 322–30, 345, 448, 453; Clark, "Notes on the Election," n.d., in Stimson MSS; Roosevelt, Jr., to Leslie A. Montgomery, Apr. 7, 1938, Roosevelt, Jr., MSS, Box 45; Stimson Diary, Nov. 1, 1937, Stimson MSS.

19. Richard Derby to Endicott Peabody, Oct. 19, 1936, Peabody MSS, Box 90; Theodore Roosevelt, Jr., to Julian Mason, Dec. 23, 1932, Roosevelt, Jr., MSS, Box 59; Henry Stimson Diary, Mar. 27, 1937, Stimson MSS. FDR described by an associate in Frank Freidel, *Franklin D. Roosevelt: The Apprenticeship* (Boston: Little, Brown, 1952), p. 310; Frankfurter to Stimson, June 10, 1935; Stimson to Maurice Portal, Oct. 27, 1933; Stimson to Pierrepont Moffat, Nov. 17, 1936: all in Stimson MSS.

20. Theodore Roosevelt, Jr., to Benjamin Wallace Douglas, Jan. 4, 1937; Roosevelt, Jr., to Alexander Woolcott, Mar. 12, 1940; Roosevelt, Jr., to H. C. Anderson, Nov. 2, 1933: all in Roosevelt, Jr., MSS, Boxes 30, 50. For the ambi-

ence in Washington, see Matthew Josephson, *Infidel in the Temple: A Memoir of the Nineteen-Thirties* (New York: Knopf, 1977), pp. 247–49. Stimson to Harlen Cooley, Mar. 10, 1938, Stimson MSS.

21. Pepper to Henry Stimson, June 13, 1933; Stimson Diary, Nov. 9, 1932, Apr. 10, 1933; Stimson to Herbert Hoover, June 16, 1934; Stimson to Frank McCoy, Dec. 18, 1934; Stimson to Alex Porter, Mar. 9, 1938: all in Stimson MSS.

22. Theodore Roosevelt, Jr., to L. Lamprey, Jan. 10, 1941, Hoover quoted in Barber, *Pulse of Politics,* p. 240; Pepper to Herbert Hoover, Nov. 8, 1934, Post-Presidential Papers, Box 96, Hoover Presidential Library; Hermann Hagedorn: "The Future of the Association," Oct. 27, 1937; "Confidential Memorandum for the Executive Committee," Jan., 1938: both in Stimson MSS. For art in the 1920s, see Malcolm Cowley, *Exile's Return: A Literary Odyssey of the 1920s* (New York: Viking Press, 1951), p. 62–63; Daniel Bell, "The Cultural Contradictions of Capitalism," in *Capitalism Today,* ed. Bell and Irving Kristol (New York: New American Library, 1971), pp. 28–50. Frederick Lewis Allen, *Since Yesterday* (New York: Bantam Books, 1961), p. 223.

23. Hermann Hagedorn to Henry Stimson, Nov. 15, 1935, Dec. 6, 1935; Stimson Diary, Jan. 17, 1933: all in Stimson MSS.

24. Pepper to John Spargo, Apr. 10, 1934, Pepper MSS, Box 3. Of all the many books on MRA, the two I found most valuable are W. H. Clark, *The Oxford Group: Its History and Significance* (New York: Bookman Associates, 1951) and Allan W. Eister, *Drawing-Room Conversions: A Sociological Account of the Oxford Group* (Durham: Duke University Press, 1950). The quote from Buchman is in ibid., pp. 152–53. The factious description is from Edmund Wilson as quoted in Cowley, *Dream of the Golden Mountains,* p. 41.

25. Clark, *Oxford Group,* passim; Eister, *Drawing-Room Conversions,* passim; Stimson to Francis Sayre, Feb. 4, 1938, Jan. 27, 1939, Stimson MSS.

26. Frank N. D. Buchman, *Remaking the World: The Speeches of Frank N. D. Buchman* (London: Blanford Press, 1961), pp. 46–47, 66, 75–77, 113.

27. William Leuchtenberg, "The New Deal and the Analogue of War," in *Change and Continuity in Twentieth-Century America,* ed. John Braeman, Robert H. Bremner, and Everett Walters (Columbia: Ohio State University Press, 1964), pp. 135, 142; Henry Stimson to Candice Stimson, Apr. 15, 1937, Stimson MSS; Frank Waldrop, *McCormick of Chicago* (Englewood Cliffs: Prentice-Hall, 1966), pp. 220, 224; William Temple Hornaday to Frank and Oliver Seamen, Aug. 17, 1936, Hornaday MSS, Box 4: Pepper, *Philadelphia Lawyer,* pp. 264–65; Theodore Roosevelt, Jr., "Address Delivered to National Republican Club," Apr. 17, 1934, copy in Post-Presidential Papers, Box 108, Hoover Presidential Library.

28. Selig Adler, *The Isolationist Impulse: Its Twentieth-Century Reaction* (New York: Collier, 1961), pp. 269–73; personal interview with Hamilton Fish, June 12, 1972. The first quotation is from a *Chicago Tribune* editorial cited in Joseph Gies, *The Colonel of Chicago* (New York: Dutton, 1979), p. 154. The next quotations are from George Wharton Pepper to Mrs. Elliot Wadsworth, May 23, 1940, Pepper MSS, Box 10; Theodore Roosevelt, Jr., to Eleanor French, Apr. 5,

1939; Roosevelt, Jr., "Address Before the National Conference of Christians and Jews," Apr. 24, 1939: both in Roosevelt, Jr., MSS, Box 40.

29. William A. Karracker, "The American Churches and the Spanish-American War" (Ph.D. diss., University of Chicago, 1940), p. 428; New Dealer Samuel Rosenman quoted in Cunningham, "Army and Universal Military Training," p. 312; *San Francisco Chronicle,* Nov. 18, 1944; Pepper quoted in *New York Times,* June 10, 1940; interview with Archibald Thacher, Oct. 20, 1947, conducted by Samuel Spencer, copy in Grenville Clark MSS; Goodrich quoted in Ralph Bishop to Tom Wyrles (c. June 24, 1940), Military Training Camps Association MSS, Box 12, Chicago Historical Society; McCormick quoted in Gies, *Colonel of Chicago,* pp. 152, 154.

30. Fred Harvey Harrington, "The Anti-Imperialist Movement in the United States," *Mississippi Valley Historical Review* 22 (1935):211–13. For anticonscriptionists in the world wars, see Chambers, "Conscripting for Colossus," pp. 131–32; Wittner, *Rebels Against War,* p. 18. The other quotations are from Roosevelt, Jr., to Felix Frankfurter, Sept. 26, 1938; Roosevelt, Jr., to Van Campen Heiler, June 15, 1940: both in Roosevelt, Jr., MSS, Boxes 38, 40.

31. Osgood, *Ideals and Self-Interest in America's Foreign Relations,* pp. 252–54.

32. Spencer, "Selective Training and Service Act of 1940 from Inception to Enactment," passim; Archibald Thacher to Grenville Clark, Aug. 24, 1941; Clark to Thacher, Aug. 19, 1941, Clark MSS; Clark to Wendell Willkie, Mar. 18, 1941, copy in Henry Stimson MSS.

33. Smith, "Henry Stimson and Philippines," pp. 187–88, 203–4; Stimson to Charles Taft, May 9, 1936; Stimson to Committee on Public Affairs, Feb. 21, 1936: both in Stimson MSS.

34. Stimson to Frank Knox, May 25, 1940; Stimson to Felix Frankfurter, May 21, 1940; Hermann Hagedorn to Stimson, June 22, 1940: all in Stimson MSS; Robert Dallek, *Franklin D. Roosevelt and American Foreign Policy, 1932–1945* (New York: Oxford University Press, 1979), p. 293.

35. Wadsworth to James Wainwright, Sept. 17, 1940, Wadsworth MSS, Box 21; Robert A. Divine, *Foreign Policy and U.S. Presidential Elections, 1940–1948* (New York: New Viewpoints, 1974), pp. 3–89; *Chicago Tribune,* Apr. 24, 1916; Dallek, *Franklin D. Roosevelt and American Foreign Policy,* pp. 217, 293; Gies, *The Colonel of Chicago,* pp. 190–95. Hitler specifically mentioned the war plans that McCormick published in his declaration of war on the United States.

Theodore Roosevelt, Jr., in World War II: A Warrior's Last Campaign

AFTER WORLD WAR I, many preparedness leaders opposed significant aspects of peacetime society, such as consumption ethics in the 1920s and welfare programs in the '30s. Now, in the early 1940s, Theodore Roosevelt, Jr., leaving civilian life behind him, encountered serious problems in the army he professed to love. His subsequent relief from the 1st Infantry Division, despite his heroics on the battlefield, was but one more example of the friction that existed between the military profession and moral reform. Placed in this context, Roosevelt's misfortune resembles the army's prior conflicts with the Rough Riders, his father's prospective World War I division, the Plattsburg and Citizen Military Training Camps, and the Civilian Conservation Corps. It thereby helps reveal the preparedness movement's recurrent failure to foresee that a community of heroes could, at times, become incompatible with military discipline, expertise, and organization. It also shows that war can crush a warrior's ambition. Specifically, Roosevelt neither received the command that he craved nor did he die the way that he wished. Although the army, warily, planned to use his heroics again, this combat soldier perished in his sleep.

From Peace to War

Of all the reversals of opinion about the domestic effects of war, Theodore Roosevelt, Jr.'s, conversion seems the most striking. In 1940 he argued for isolation on more than constitutional and political grounds. Inverting all his old beliefs, he now maintained that hostilities would endanger individual character and social harmony. During the Great War, he said:

> I felt that where men of every faith suffered the same hardships and dangers there would grow a deep understanding and sympathy, a unity of purpose.

I was wrong. Since the war, Americans have drawn apart. . . .

I felt that as all served the nation in that war, offering themselves to her to the last sacrifice of life, there would be bred in us an unselfish loyalty.

I was wrong. Since the war a constantly growing number of Americans have come to look at this nation merely as something that should care for them, without return on their part.[1]

In the 1920s, Roosevelt had used literature to dramatize his defense of the morality of combat. In the 1930s, holding the "soul-satisfying" position of editor at Doubleday and Doran, he continued his politico-literary activities by sponsoring wholesome books "as American as Indian corn." There he discounted the "modern story, which deals perpetually with a sort of sickness of the soul," in favor of Boy Scout tales, pioneer legends, heroic biographies, and anti-New Deal tracts. However, as the new world war developed, Roosevelt published Oloff de Wet's *The Patrol Is Ended,* "one of the least pleasant books that has been written about the Spanish Civil War." This novel-memoir of a Loyalist mercenary resembled nothing so much as a "Lost Generation" depiction of World War I. Earlier, Roosevelt would have called this book a "soul-searching obscenity"; now it was a "brilliantly written article" by a "very gallant gentleman." Once again, Roosevelt was out of step with art. While his new-found fear of martial degradation was leading him towards his own farewell to arms, Ernest Hemingway and other writers were joining a new war which gave them "something that you could believe in . . . and in which you felt as absolute brotherhood with the others engaged in it."[2]

Just once Roosevelt reechoed his World War I feeling that the world crisis "may sweat the softness off our bones and bring us to a keener realization of the finer things of life." More often he spoke, as had the "Lost Generation" when explaining the failures of the postwar world, about brave combatants supporting armies top-heavy with venal bureaucrats. Opportunists would ensure their political futures by ensconcing themselves in service and supply. Meanwhile, the upright men, who might yet reform the nation, would be "killed and maimed by the hundreds" while serving at the front. One in forty would "know anything of the battle and the burden." The rest, engaged in New Deal analogues to war, would just " 'buy bonds till it hurts'—my God what a slogan." Literature now could not breach the gap between front and rear, soldier and civilian, father and son. As Roosevelt said in 1943 on the road to Cassino: "No one who has not been there can know what winter war is for the front-line soldier. It cannot be put into words,—the rain, the filth, the cold and the awful weariness. I think the reason the real front-line soldiers don't talk about war to any but other front-line soldiers is because they know the hopelessness of making anyone else understand."[3]

But while war was a "senseless folly striking down the young, destroying homes, [and] upsetting many so they'll never be normal again," it was still "a man's game." In comparison, the "dreary" office routine —"starting with the 8:25 in the morning and finishing with the 5:45 at night"—was just "something a man should do when he was not doing man's work." Consequently, while Roosevelt was speaking for neutrality, he was also "keeping in top physical condition for the next war." In May, 1940, he asked Army Chief of Staff George C. Marshall, his old 1st Division colleague, to place him on active duty. Thereafter Roosevelt's wife observed that he looked fifteen years younger. "The sober truth," he later said, "is that I am never so happy as when I am with troops."[4]

The Rise and Fall of the 1st Infantry Division

Roosevelt, "entirely happy doing something that he does supremely well," established an exemplary training record which, ironically, was too good for his own good. By winning promotion from colonel to brigadier general, he began the chain of events that eventually led to his tragic relief from command. Initially, Roosevelt did not want a promotion that might take him away from "fighting troops" and the "enlarged family" that was his "beloved regiment." When it nonetheless arrived, he could foresee just one benefit: an extended retirement age allowing him to "fight the next ten years of the war." Soon, however, Roosevelt developed an enormous desire to command the 1st Division in combat and this passion ensnared him in a trap. The army felt that he was not professionally qualified to be a major general, but his own emotional needs made him temperamentally unfit to be an assistant commander— the position to which he was promoted. If Roosevelt had remained a colonel in charge of his own regiment but subject to division level authority, he could have had both a command that he wanted and the restraint which he needed. As a brigadier he had neither. Wanting the devotion of his men and wondering if he had it when he certainly did, he needed a relatively cold and aloof superior to keep his camaraderie and passions within acceptable limits.[5] In the Rough Riders, Leonard Wood did this for his father. However, Terry Allen, the 1st Division commander, was just too much like Roosevelt for Roosevelt's good, Allen's good, and the good of the army itself.

Major General Terry de la Mesa Allen (called a "modern D'Artagnan," the "Army's prize Katzenjammer kid," and more simply, "a fighting son-of-a-bitch") also deemphasized protocol and hierarchy in favor of esprit and charisma. Born, reared, and stationed in western forts with cowboy traditions, he too was an old-fashioned Rough Rider stranded in the infantry. When repellent tanks replaced the horses Allen loved ("good," in modern war, for "eating if you're hungry"), he left the cavalry in body but never in spirit. He always liked to think that he was doing only temporary duty with dismounted troopers. Actually, this remnant of the dying horseman species was lucky to be in the army at all. But for General Henry T. Allen (no relation), an old cavalryman with a streak of fun left in him, he would have been dismissed for his antics in World War I. (According to one comrade: "Other men got sent home for half of the escapades that Terry got away with.") But for George Marshall, he would have been court-martialed in 1940. Although the chief of staff usually displayed "matchless self-control" and professional detachment, he covertly admired "the dashing, optimistic and resourceful" troop leader whose "talents [during peace] are damned by lack of rank." His regard for the warrior's elan, suppressed in his own staff officer career, was frequently expressed in the appointments he made. When Marshall assigned Allen to the 1st Division, the unit in which he served in World War I, he broke the staid mold common to its preceding and succeeding commanders. Allen, however, was not his only protégé. Marshall, also sent to North Africa his other favorite swashbucklers, George Patton and Ted Roosevelt, Jr. "The ARMY," Patton wrote Allen, "HAS CERTAINLY GONE TO HELL when both of us are [promoted]. I guess we must be in for some serious fighting and we are the ones who can lead the way to hell with[out] too much thinking. . . . All that is now needed is a nice juicy war."[6]

With hindsight, Generals Dwight Eisenhower and Omar Bradley said that Allen and Roosevelt should never have served together since they shared the same assets and the same defects. Marshall from the outset suspected as much. After assigning Allen to the 1st, he wrote him: "Theodore Roosevelt and you are very much the same type as to enthusiasm, initiative, and a restless desire to get into things. I am a little fearful that two men so much the same type will probably not get along too well. . . . I hope this doesn't develop for he has a long history with the 1st Division, he is a number one fighting man with rare courage and what is rarer, unlimited fortitude." But instead of transferring either man, Marshall directed Allen to avoid personal conflict with Roosevelt and, by so doing, made him an even more ineffective supervisor.[7]

Similarity can lead to admiration or contention. Thus Roosevelt and Allen vacillated between reciprocal respect and rivalry. Friends at first, they headed separate combat teams in a race to capture Oran (Algeria) and ended the contest with the soldier's friendship rite—getting drunk together. At that time Roosevelt called Allen "a natural fighter" and

Allen praised Roosevelt's "extraordinary executive ability and exceptional leadership." But with time, their friendly competition edged into
mutual jealousy. Allen, still relatively poor and unsophisticated, borrowed Roosevelt's money, listened to his stories about the world's
elite, and, being proud and high-strung, grew to resent his subordinate's wealth and status. Meanwhile, Roosevelt, holding proprietary
feelings about the 1st Division, resented Allen's command. Through
the disappointing days between World Wars I and II, the unit's soldiers,
records, and traditions had been his constant solace. Now, when he
might have been its leader, a neophyte had "his baby." Emotionally
attached to the division, he never took the secondary position naturally
assumed by other brigadiers when assigned to assist a charismatic
commander. Consequently, a "strange competitive feeling," based on
their essential similarities, grew until Roosevelt and Allen, the army's
best-liked generals, were engaged in a popularity contest for the admiration and affection of their men.[8] Poor disciplinarians at best, this exacerbated their defects.

General Bradley, their corps commander, later wrote that Roosevelt
"sinned by loving the division too much." Most of his loved ones, young
urban ethnics from New York and New Jersey, were pillars of the New
Deal coalition he deplored. Yet like his father who led populists in the
Rough Riders, Roosevelt was glad to serve with people whom he politically opposed. In so doing, he demonstrated that he did not stereotype
individuals as he sometimes did groups. "Let them tell my driver [a
Russian-American Jew] I'm anti-Semitic and he'll tell them where to
get off. Let them tell Ben Sternberg, [the Jewish] exec. of the 18 Inf.
I'm anti-bluff, anti-faker, anti-coward, that's all." Roosevelt's life in his
cosmopolitan division also revived his waning faith in his country. No
longer lamenting that the United States resembled "Rome in the days
of degeneracy," he was able to say, for the first time in decades: "I like
Americans—there's no two ways about it."[9]

Roosevelt, who thought his GIs were the best of all citizens, used his
old pedagogic practices to persuade his recruits to admire themselves
as much as he admired them. Convinced that soldiers fight for unit
pride, not for ideology or national interests, he and the other officers
"drilled the hell out of the men with division tradition." Soon, they all
thoroughly knew "the duties of the living to the dead." The heroic historiography, with which he, his father, and his literary friends had
failed to inspire the country, finally triumphed when applied to the 1st
Division—the most tradition-conscious unit in the infantry. Its volunteer
enlisted men and hand-picked officer corps were a devout student body
ensconced in their own little world of heroes, customs, and history. In
this total classroom free from diverting stimuli, Roosevelt was in his

element. He always said that a compelling tradition required a heroic personification. Now he himself, "a legend in the areas he operated," symbolized the division epics that he told. Pleased with his instruction, Roosevelt wrote George Marshall: "There is no doubt in my mind that much of the very splendid performance of the 1st Division in the African campaign has been due to the inspiration that tradition has given the soldiers. Their units are not impersonal to them but personal—intensely personal. . . . Officers and men alike feel they must not let down their regiment and their division. . . . [Thus they can] get up and go after they spent their last resources."[10]

But if, as soldiers say, "the strongest force which keeps a man going in combat is his self-respect and pride," then ironically, the 1st Division's assets were becoming its liabilities. Along with "too much brilliance, too much success [and] too much personality," it had too much pride, too much spirit, and too much tradition. Roosevelt himself, as "relaxed in dangerous situations as anyone [his soldiers] ever saw," showed infantrymen how to accept their travails with a joy more suited to sectarian saints. His elation in the army proved unfortunate. Most other Plattsburgers, dreaming of creating a puritan Sparta, had emphasized the need for a stoic acceptance of military discipline and law. But Roosevelt, going through the war with *Pilgrim's Progress* in his pocket and John Bunyan on his lips, had begun to lead a band of latter-day antinomians. While they could not conceive, let alone claim, that Divine Grace freed them from biblical injunction, they did feel that their battlefield heroism excused them from orders concerning traffic regulations, behavior on leave, care for the uniform, and the customs of the service. As Eisenhower's deputy complained: "They have been told so often that they are the best in the world that, as far as real discipline is concerned, they have become one of the poorest. They look dirty and they never salute an officer if they can help it."[11]

Because this was not a war of spit and polish to be won by shaving, saluting, and shining one's shoes, courage at the front temporarily excused indiscretions in the rear—whether shooting down telephone wires or simply other people. But following the disorder and panic shown at the Battle of the Kasserine Pass in early 1943, the army felt it had to reassess its standards for, without greater discipline, the future looked worse than Kasserine. The draft was gathering a whole generation of lax civilians, most of whom were completely unprepared for military duty. Ideally the best of them would go overseas; in fact the worst were often sent. Stateside officers, passing on their problems, transferred recruits defective in discipline and bearing to North Africa, where their shortcomings exacerbated all the natural problems of induction into combat. Consequently the army's senior commanders, even the so-called "nice guys" like Eisenhower and Bradley, became obsessed with "disciplinary standards both on and off the battlefield." As Eisenhower said at the time: "Saluting, dress, appearance, carriage, deportment—all of these are of transcendent importance because if a unit is produced in which all of these things are exemplary, the teaching of battle technic and methods is a relatively simple thing. . . . [The discipline] that makes a soldier salute properly . . . is the quality that makes him hang onto his machine-gun, firing it to the last round. . . . It is impossible to exaggerate the importance of this subject."[12]

While Eisenhower was imposing these strict new standards for interior discipline, the triumphant 1st Division was taking its boxcar transportation from Bizerte (Tunisia) back to Oran (Algeria). No longer exempted by their heroism, they too now would have to obey. Indeed, as the infantry's elite, they should set, as they did in World War I, military standards for others to follow. If they failed, their leaders would be unceremoniously sacked as was General William L. Sibert, their first commander in World War I. Unfortunately, the 1st never thought much about others. Because, according to Roosevelt, they were "a clan not a Division," Eisenhower could not order their salute, let alone their obedience. Its soldiers obeyed a chain of command that ended with Roosevelt and Allen. And those generals, true to division tradition, tended to feel that "the American army was the 1st Infantry and eleven million replacements." The extraordinary camaraderie that they had with their soldiers was leading them astray. If they had spent some time at army headquarters learning the problems that Eisenhower faced, they might have seen the need for the orders he issued. But contemptuous of men who did not fight no matter what their rank, Roosevelt and Allen spent their time at the front. The "clan" and the army, living by different codes, were on a collision course. Their clash but awaited the right situation.[13]

The open rupture occurred after Eleanor Roosevelt promised relief to the 1st Marine Division decimated by malaria in the Pacific. When *Stars and Stripes* reprinted the story, it deleted the single word "Marine," thus raising expectations that the 1st Infantry Division would soon go home on leave. Told instead to prepare for an amphibious invasion, they naturally were disappointed. Actually, they were only paying the price of their glory. If the army's senior commanders felt they could furlough the 1st, they might have done so just to relieve Roosevelt and Allen. But the high command, in a pinch, believed that no one else could lead the rest of the army ashore. "I want those sons of bitches," Patton told Eisenhower. "I won't go on [into Sicily] without them."[14]

Back in Tunisia awaiting the invasion, Roosevelt tried to cheer up his men by saying: "We'll go back to Oran and beat up every MP in town."

His audience, no doubt, was venting their immediate disappointment. He himself was articulating his chronic contempt for "well-polished little tin soldiers in rear areas." Although most combat soldiers are jealous of support troops, Roosevelt's animosity towards those whom he called "the junk that's come for the ride" was not alloyed with envy. Because his pride depended on the uniform he wore, whatever cheapened that garb reproached his being. When it was worn by "despicable" men who did not fight, he felt truly debased. Since armies run on supplies as well as blood, Roosevelt would admit that support troops are a necessary evil, but his hatred for them was still passionately held. If he could, he might have dressed them as if they were "chocolate soldiers." In essence, this is what Henry Stimson tried to do.[15]

In 1940 Stimson was confident that any wartime president would have to conciliate business and professional men upon whom economic mobilization would inevitably depend. In 1942 he and his War Department coterie of "conspicuously successful" figures from corporate finance and law helped fulfill his prediction by squelching antitrust indictments that "tied up [company] executives and interfered with the war effort." However, Stimson's pleasant prediction of probusiness procedures became a painful experience once the administration chose to placate its political opposition with military status symbols. Reminiscent of the way governors once used their state militias, it "pandered to the itch to wear the Army uniform"—a badge of honor, masculinity, and social rank. It thus gave away commissions to powerful civilians, some of whom, like the president of J. P. Stevens textiles, could suddenly call themselves a colonel. This may not have been outrageous to army officers who later reversed this flow of management by doffing their uniforms to join corporations contracting with the Pentagon in the Cold War. Nor did it seem strange to New Dealers who believed that resource mobilization drives, such as fabric procurement, were moral analogues to war. Nonetheless, all quick commissions to business executives profoundly upset *Colonel* Henry Stimson. He certainly realized that technocrats were indispensible to a "gross national product war" in which 98 percent of the citizens directly involved in the conflict were engaged in research, production, provision, and repair. Indeed, for that reason he persistently supported national service legislation to let the War Department register and allocate civilian manpower. But despite the economic integration of the army and society, separated, for the most part, since the Gilded Age, Stimson still vowed to save "the combat uniform" from "bomb-proof variety patriots."[16]

Unlike professional soldiers who adjusted to the fact that modern wars are economic as well as military contests, Stimson was not content to identify the rear echelon by badge. He resolved instead to develop some unmistakable means of distinction for service and supply. The result was his Army Specialist Corps of "uniformed civilian employees" who wore no U.S. markings, different colored clothing, and "clearly different insignia," such as a silver "non-combatant" decal. Stimson, who picked or approved every detail, called it "a smart looking uniform"; others thought it resembled a messenger boy costume. Because no volunteer wished to wear this "more or less calculated insult," Colonel Stimson had to dissolve the corps and let the specialists join his army. Having already witnessed technology vanquishing the classics and the cavalry, he submitted once again to the necessities of progress. But Ted Roosevelt, Jr., according to Stimson, never had such self-control.[17]

Colonel Stimson, General Roosevelt, Private Jones and every other frontline soldier expects deference from those in the rear. When the 1st Division jumped off their boxcars and entered Oran, they thought themselves especially deserving. Having captured this city in battle, they felt entitled to enjoy it in peace. Instead, they experienced the "bitter disappointment" combat troops cannot abide. While they were at the front, their city "had become populated with a new soldier dressed in fresh khaki and the distinguishing insignia of Service of Supply." The 1st had to stay in pup tents while these trespassers, who lived in billets, barred them from their clubs, their installations, and even their water showers. When the division did go into town wearing filthy, sweaty, tattered, battle woolens—the only clothes they had—MPs enforcing Eisenhower's regulations arrested them for improper dress.[18]

Some fistfights naturally occurred. Exactly how many is disputed. General Bradley called it a major riot; 1st Division soldiers tend to slough it off. They say that "only" some fifty to sixty men were a bit peeved for if the division were really mad, they would have killed somebody. Besides that, whatever did happen was an equitable reprisal for the "dreary tent bivouac" which was their unwarranted fate. But granting the simple justice of their case, a brawl was no way to run an army or to impress the new recruits then streaming into North Africa. Moreover, the division's commanders, not merely their men, were parties to the fracas. Roosevelt and Allen knew trouble was brewing; they even discussed it. Yet they did nothing except create an ambience conducive to the brawl. Their men, reflecting the enormous pride that they had infused, fought if only because "they were the 1st Division and no Goddamned cop was going to tell them what to do." Furthermore, loving their men as they did, Roosevelt and Allen gave them a sense of immunity from punishment for whatever they might do behind the battlefront.

The division, defiant at the very time the high command demanded discipline, angered the senior generals in charge of Roosevelt's fate. Thus his own soldiers helped destroy their beloved "General Teddy's" chance to command them in combat.[19]

On the beach at Sicily, Eisenhower's deputy, Major General John Lucas, buried deeper Roosevelt's dream of command. An amphibious invasion is the most difficult of all military operations and this assault was the first major debarkation facing serious resistance since the Gallipoli disaster of Word War I. Lucas, with future Pacific landings on his mind, was there to learn by its inevitable mistakes. He began to list them weeks before D-Day while observing training in Oran. This self-identified "spit and polish" soldier described the 1st Division as "a dirty looking lot" who neither washed, nor shaved, nor gave him their salute. Its training was sloppy and its planning was poor. He concluded that "Roosevelt has a tendency to spoil the men but they will follow him anywhere. They need a firm and stern disciplinarian. Theodore is not that and neither is Terry."[20]

Lucas landed in Sicily anticipating trouble but found more than he expected down on the beach. The 1st, which had suffered heavy casualties in Africa, attacked with some 7,000 new privates. These expendable garrison replacements suddenly experienced combat in its most terrifying form—an amphibious invasion. But a crisis like this was Roosevelt's forte. Even Eisenhower, one of his strongest critics, granted him "one outstanding quality": when men first enter battle his "personal gallantry is unquestionably an inspiration." Perfectly relaxed no matter what the danger, he projected a truly charismatic aura. Even veterans who really knew better felt that his presence ensured victory.[21]

On D-Day, Roosevelt used this talent as he thought he should. When a man stumbled off his landing craft and desperately flung himself to earth trying to dig up a little sand for protection, Roosevelt limped up (he now had a very bad back), kneeled down, and started a brief conversation about the soldier's home town. Then, after calming a terrified man, he suggested that he had better get off the beach, where he was likely to be killed. As this soldier got up and ran for the sea wall, Roosevelt headed for another.[22]

General Lucas knew that these exploits created a legend. Unfortunately for Roosevelt, he also felt they were producing operational chaos. Because Roosevelt, the senior officer in charge, was down on the beach helping individuals, the invasion as a whole floundered in confusion. At the forward command post, Roosevelt's primary responsibility, men who should have been attacking the enemy's artillery were lying down in slit trenches. On the beach, equipment was cluttered together into targets for the field guns that were free from attack. While

Lucas, in a rough and impersonal manner, was yelling "get the hell out and move against the enemy," Roosevelt was still down at the landing site saying, "Hello soldier; where are you from?"[23]

Actually, things may not have been as bad as Lucas later claimed. All military operations are more or less chaos and amphibious invasions are always more than less. Lucas, however, was Eisenhower's eyes and the "specific and unfavorable" report which he filed confirmed Ike's doubts about Roosevelt's ability. Soon, even George Marshall was saying that Ted Roosevelt, Jr., was thinking too much about his men.[24]

Although Roosevelt was a paternalistic leader always ready to encourage soldiers struggling with their stress, he actually could be tougher than anyone imagined. Common to self-deprecating personalities who repress covert feelings of inferiority behind a heroic mask, Roosevelt overtly denied any weaknesses. Thus he could not understand a nerve-shattered lieutenant who came to see him with a personal problem late in the Sicily campaign. Nothing at first seemed unusual in this encounter since soldiers were constantly bringing Roosevelt their complaints about food, mail, and cigarettes—problems that most professional soldiers ignored. To the consternation of those professionals, Roosevelt would promise to help solve such troubles even when he could not help. This lieutenant, however, had a different problem for he had just deserted his men in battle. When soldiers break down in combat, their self-condemnation usually increases their need for affection. This man probably came to Roosevelt looking for the love that he gave his troops when they were heroes or merely men fighting down their fear. But all this must remain conjecture since, when Roosevelt heard that this officer committed the unforgivable sin, he boiled over in an uncontrollable rage and ordered him immediately shot. There was no malice of forethought in Roosevelt's act. It was just a passionate reaction to someone who betrayed his community of heroes in the 1st Infantry Division.[25]

Other men besides this anonymous lieutenant were breaking down in Sicily, and one of them was Terry Allen. Because America's officers had not been trained to fight on North Africa's barren terrain, compensatory tactics for shelter and deception had to be improvised in all-night planning sessions under flashlight illumination. Consequently Allen grew weary. If the high command had trusted Roosevelt, who craved his job, they would have furloughed Allen "on the spot." Since Roosevelt was his immediate replacement, Allen, a "marked man," was retained. He and the whole division, fatigued before the invasion, were exhausted in Sicily, where, "to take Messina before the British," they were kept in combat day and night for a month. Near collapse, Allen's ingenuity waned and his egocentricity grew until he would have been a problem for any superior, least of all generals Bradley and Patton. The former, corporate infantryman par excellence, ran a team and rugged individualists like Allen were not team players. Patton, on the other hand, an old cavalryman himself, never liked fellow egotists who might cramp his style. With Allen about to be relieved, Roosevelt's great opportunity arrived. A new commander was needed and old "blood and guts" was ready to recommend him.[26]

Patton had his troubles with "those cocky bastards" in the 1st Division. They ignored his dress and deportment orders, and just recently he had given Roosevelt, who in his battle fatigues looked like a battalion cook, a seventy-five dollar fine for leaving his helmet unstrapped beneath his chin. Exasperated, Patton would soon slap a 1st Division private and then he (like Roosevelt and Allen) would also be in trouble. This High Church Episcopalian obviously did not like these antinomians and most of them did not like him. But despite Patton's "gasoline affiliations" as a tank commander, he was "first of all a cavalryman" who believed that "the warrior soul" was "the most important element in war." Having served with cowboy characters in the old horse cavalry, he could live with a Roosevelt-led 1st Infantry Division. He would assign him a tough assistant specializing in organization and discipline but he would tolerate Roosevelt for the same reason others tolerated Patton. The service, promoting in peacetime by seniority, had accumulated numerous tired old veterans "of two decades of easygoing Army posts and country club porches." Roosevelt, according to Patton (and Patton, according to Eisenhower) was a real fighter and the army needed all the real fighters it had. Eisenhower would not have relished Roosevelt in command, but he just might have accepted Patton's recommendation. He did not seem to have anyone else in mind and if he were going to relieve Allen, one of Marshall's favorites, he might have felt more comfortable appointing Roosevelt in his place. However, on July 24, 1943, when Clarence Huebner (described below) suddenly became America's *former* deputy to Sir Harold Alexander, ground forces commander in the Mediterranean Theater, Roosevelt's short-lived opportunity was over.[27]

The Sicilian campaign, from its origins, had been nourishing a showdown between the American and British high commands. Englishmen, having witnessed the battles at Kasserine and Gafsa, were convinced that the United States could not handle major offensive assignments. In late July, the mounting discord erupted when Huebner, "standing up for America," accused General Alexander of denying military equality to the U.S. Army. Because this was the one thing he could not say and still keep his job, he was now available for 1st Division duty. Furthermore, Huebner was everything that Eisenhower, Patton, and Bradley wanted: a World War I 1st Division veteran, another Marshall protégé, a fighter and, most of all, a very strict disciplinarian. At sixteen, he ran away from home to become an army private. During the Great War, his outstanding battlefield record (complete with two Distinguished Service Cross citations) propelled him from sergeant to lieutenant colonel. Yet despite his own career—or perhaps because of it—Huebner had no faith in GI heroism. (If no one is more religious than a convert, no general is a greater martinet than a former enlisted man.) If Roosevelt was John Bunyan's Christian, Huebner was Dostoyevsky's Grand Inquisitor. Roosevelt was soft on his men because he believed they were strong; Huebner was hard because he thought they were weak. In battle—where men are terrified, exhausted, and hurt—Huebner did not expect bravery above and beyond the call of human nature. He only asked for unthinking conformity to his command. To get it, he meticulously drilled men to obey. Roosevelt was courageous but otherwise, Patton now said, he was simply "no soldier."[28]

Whenever Huebner came to the 1st Division, Roosevelt would have to leave. Once they could have made an excellent team, Roosevelt providing love and esprit, Huebner supplying fear and discipline. By now, however, it was far too late for that. Roosevelt wanted to lead too much to be anyone's assistant, and his superiors knew this, for he was constantly campaigning for command. There was nothing to do but push him up or out and the decision was out. On August 5, 1943, notification arrived for Roosevelt, Allen, and all their men. Roosevelt, "thunderstruck and heartbroken," could not face his troops to say goodbye. Allen fell silent "and then burst into tears like a high strung school girl." As for their men, one soldier "felt like my father had died." General Bradley, speaking words that could have been used by Herman Melville's Captain Vere, explained: "In time of war the only value that can be affixed to any unit is the tactical value of that unit in winning the war. Even the lives of those men assigned to it become nothing more than tools to be used in the accomplishment of that mission. War has neither the time nor heart to concern itself with the individual and the dignity of man."[29]

Henry Stimson knew how badly relief hurt Roosevelt and his whole family. Still devoted to Roosevelt's mother and always uneasy that he had not supported his father in the 1912 presidential campaign, Stimson personally intervened to prevent "the humiliation of being sent back to America." So although Roosevelt never knew how or why, he shipped out for liaison duty with the French forces in Italy. Meanwhile the 1st Division was paying for its sins. Before D-Day Sicily, when Eisenhower complained about their lack of discipline, Patton replied: "No one whips a dog just before putting him into a fight." After the fight was over and those battered infantrymen finally got a rest, Huebner arrived and immediately declared: "Everytime we let you jokers loose you tear up the whole damned town." Hereafter, those "jokers" were not let loose again. Veterans of North Africa and Sicily were soon being trained in close-order drill, saluting, military courtesy, and "proper wearing of the uniform." For all intents and purposes, the 1st Infantry Division had rejoined the U.S. Army.[30]

Death and the Final Irony

Roosevelt once said that if he were ever transferred out of the 1st Division, he would leave the war behind him and go home. After his nightmare came true, he stayed despite the fact that he was losing the strength he once had. "A desperate weariness" beset him until all he could "think of is sleep and rest." Rest, however, would show a lack of fortitude which was "the most important quality that a soldier could have." Those who had it—"the men who push themselves up and stumble on and fall, and pick themselves up again and are trying to get up when they die"—were the men he most admired. So "maybe my feet hurt and the way is hard, but I must go on in the Way like Christian, Faithful and Valiant-for-Truth. My soul's peace depends on it, even if at times the Delectable Mountains seem very far away."[31]

Roosevelt, now in Italy, liked the French but hated the "rat's nest" assignment that precluded all chance "to die under an American flag." However pretentious in a Fourth of July oration, that phrase could have been his epitaph, for the people who served with Roosevelt swear that he believed life's greatest honor was to fall in combat for one's country. Indeed, this was the way he and those who knew him were convinced he would die.[32]

His life would probably end in Normandy. Since the assault waves of amphibious invasions usually suffer at least 33 percent casualties, after Roosevelt's third invasion he was likely to be 100 percent dead. Yet he still did all he could to lead the army ashore. In January, 1944, Eisenhower's chief of staff, Walter Bedell Smith, wrote Roosevelt that he was doing his best "to get you in a place such as you want, where you can command troops and be shot over regularly." In February, when Roosevelt was reassigned to England, he could have died reporting to duty. Not privy to the invasion timetable, he ignored the physical pain he felt until Bedell Smith and Bradley personally assured him a place in combat. By that time Roosevelt had a serious case of pneumonia. But possessing an enormous will to live in order to die, he made an astonishing recovery. Soon he was boasting: My doctors "say they've no record of anyone who played the tricks I've played and came through with flying colors and in jig time."[33]

Released from the hospital, Roosevelt reported to the 4th Infantry Division as a "spare brigadier" outside the normal chain of command (and thereby relieved of most disciplinary duties). Its soldiers had never seen combat before. When some of them panicked, as everyone expected, he was there to play his paternal role. "As if he was looking over some real estate," Roosevelt limped around Utah Beach calming, comforting, and exhorting soldiers. At Sicily this had paved his way out of the 1st Division; at Normandy, thanks to Stimson's directions, it won the Congressional Medal of Honor. In both cases, Roosevelt probably received too much responsibility for success or failure. In Sicily, America's first seriously contested invasion, confusion was inevitable. In France, where even Eisenhower said that Roosevelt "absolutely vitalized" the 4th Division, it would prove competent without his presence. This compelling personality, who once had been blamed, now was credited for this unit's surprisingly good performance.[34]

Unlike the 4th, the 90th Division showed little interest in fighting for any officer. When Omar Bradley's staff recommended dissolution, the general thought of Roosevelt, however lax he was enforcing rank and order. Although Bradley sensed that Roosevelt's romanticism might force his relief once again, "a disciplinarian was not what the 90th needed *now*" [italics mine]. Its immediate problem, low esprit, called "for a man with vitality and courage, a man who could pick up the division singlehandedly and give it confidence in itself. Ted," Bradley said, "would have the 90th brawling with the Germans in a couple of weeks." Of course, the 90th was not *the* 1st Division but it was a division and it would soon be his division, and then Roosevelt would learn to love it as he had learned to love the 4th. Moreover, this assignment would enable him to fulfill his ambition to die the way he knew his father had wished to die—as a warrior leading his division in combat. But mere hours before his promotion, Roosevelt died (in Bradley's words) "as no one could have believed he would, in the quiet of his tent."[35]

Even Roosevelt admitted that this new war was much tougher than his last. It entailed destructive new weaponry (the heavy bomber in particular), amphibious landings, extreme climates, and a constant mobility that forbade systematic rest. These conditions, doubling World War I's neuropsychiatric casualty rates, broke young men in their prime, let alone Roosevelt, then fifty-six years old. But since his pain was his glory, he accepted his burden with pride. "I've been comforting myself with the thought that 'muy hombre' describes me. As long as I can fight in the front lines I've still got manhood." Manhood, however, always has its cost. If, as the Surgeon General's Office reported, no infantryman could stand more than 400 days of this combat, Roosevelt was pushing himself past human limitations. His extraordinary bravery proscribed the usual means by which ambulatory men leave the front: the neuropsychiatric symptoms that afflicted some 57.6 percent of the country's disabled soldiers. His courage, however, could not prevent strain and fatigue from taking its toll on his central nervous system. After Normandy, his heartbeat slowed, causing poor circulation and aching pain in his extremities. Now "completely exhausted," even a glorious death seemed less important to him. Once or twice he said that after the army broke out of the hedge-grove country and rolled past Paris, he might ask to be rotated home. From Sicily he wrote: "There's a fool's proverb to the effect that there is always one step more in a doughboy. But how is it when he's taken that step?" On July 13, 1944, he himself took that step; his heart ceased to beat. On July 14, with his GIs gathered in "awe," Roosevelt was buried near the front. George Patton, honorary pallbearer and devout Episcopalian, felt that "one of the bravest men I ever knew" deserved a most "impressive" burial. Unfortunately it was, he thought, "a flop." The orations were poor and the honor guard disorganized. Yet there was "an appropriate requiem to the funeral of a really gallant man." General Patton's aide records that "as the casket was being lowered the reverberations of our anti-aircraft opening up on a German photographic plane re-echoed through the wooded cemetery. 'Roosevelt would have liked that' the General said on the drive home. 'A great leader and a very brave man. Bad luck that he was not killed in action.'"[36]

NOTES

1. Theodore Roosevelt, Jr., "Armistice Day Speech," Nov. 11, 1940, Roosevelt, Jr., MSS, Box 50.

2. Roosevelt, Jr., to Stuart Edward White, Sept. 19, 1935; to Bess Streeter Aldrich, Mar. 3, 1938: both in Roosevelt, Jr., MSS, Box 38. De Wet's book described in the London *Times Literary Supplement* 37 (Dec. 3, 1938):774–75; Roosevelt, Jr., to Lee D. Brown, July 29, 1921; to George Messersmith, Oct. 13, 1939; to Mrs. de Wet, May 13, 1941: all in Roosevelt, Jr., MSS, Boxes 20, 44, 50. Hemingway quoted in Branson and Goethals, ed., *War*, p. 297.

3. Roosevelt, Jr., to Eleanor Butler Roosevelt (hereafter cited as Roosevelt, Jr., to wife), Dec. 23, 1943, Feb. 1, Feb. 14, 1944, May 10, 1944, June 17, 1944: all in Roosevelt, Jr., MSS, Family Papers. For the "Lost Generation," see Wohl, *Generation of 1914*, pp. 113–21.

4. Roosevelt, Jr., to wife, Oct. 6, 1943; Eleanor B. Roosevelt to Cornelius Roosevelt, Apr., 1941: both in Roosevelt, Jr., MSS, Family Papers. Roosevelt, Jr., to George Marshall, n.d., Roosevelt File Marshall Research Library, Arlington, Va. Eleanor B. to Mrs. Theodore Roosevelt, Sr., Nov. 16, 1941; Roosevelt, Jr., to General H. A. Drum, Aug. 28, 1940: both in Roosevelt, Jr., MSS, Family Papers, Box 41.

5. Eleanor B. to Cornelius Roosevelt, May 2, 1941, Roosevelt, Jr., MSS, Family Papers. For Roosevelt, Jr.'s, training record, see his Army 201 Personnel Record that this writer read at the Pentagon. Roosevelt, Jr., to George Marshall, n.d., Roosevelt File, Marshall Research Library. Roosevelt, Jr., quoted in personal interview with Sergeant Theodore Dobol, Jan. 13, 1972. Roosevelt, Jr., to Mrs. Theodore Roosevelt, Sr., Dec. 15, 1941; to Marquis James, Dec. 21, 1941, Roosevelt, Jr., MSS, Family Papers, Box 42.

6. Gerald V, Stamm "Terry Allen's Boys," *Our Army* (Dec., 1943):15; numerous interviews deposited in *Time Magazine*'s archives, July, 1943, copies in possession of this writer. The remark on the "horse" is in Tuchman, *Stilwell and the American Experience in China*, p. 260. A. J. Liebling, "Terry Allen," *New Yorker*, 19 (Apr. 24, 1943):24–25; Terry Allen to George Marshall, Aug. 10, 1940, Allen File, Marshall Research Library. For Henry T. Allen, see Heath Twichell, Jr., *Allen: The Biography of an Army Officer, 1859–1930* (New Brunswick: Rutgers University Press, 1974), passim. Pogue: *George C. Marshall: Education of a General*, pp. 164–65, 251, 256; *George C. Marshall: Ordeal and Hope* (New York: Viking, 1966), pp. 118, 406–7. Marshall is described in Henry Stimson Diary, Dec. 17, 1943, Stimson MSS. The quotations from Marshall are in Marshall, *Memoir of My Service in the World War*, pp. 117–18, 172. Blumenson, ed., *Patton Papers: 1940–1945*, p. 13.

7. Eisenhower to George Marshall, July 28, 1943, Terry Allen File, Eisenhower Presidential Library, Abilene, Kan.; Bradley, *Soldier's Story*, p. 110; Marshall to Allen, June 5, 1942, Allen File, Marshall Research Library; personal interview with General Robert Porter, Sept. 26, 1972.

8. Personal interview with Col. Joseph J. Kohout, Dec. 26, 1972; Allen to Dwight Eisenhower, Feb. 9, 1943; Allen to George Marshall, Feb. 3, 1943: both in Allen File, Marshall Research Library; Roosevelt, Jr., to wife, Nov. 11, 1942, Roosevelt, Jr., MSS, Family Papers; Hanson Baldwin to Tom Dixon, Sept. 24, 1970, copy in possession of this writer; Bradley, *Soldier's Story*, photograph caption opposite page 108; Roosevelt, Jr., to wife, Oct. 14, 1943, Feb. 9, 1944, Roosevelt, Jr., MSS, Family Papers; personal interviews with Gen. Robert Porter, Sept. 26, 1972; Chester Hanson (Gen. Bradley's aide-de-camp), Dec. 24, 1972. Roosevelt wrote home that war correspondent Nick Knickerbocker "told me, which I value coming from him, that *I* was the man most beloved in the Division," [italics mine] see Roosevelt, Jr., to wife, Oct. 29, 1943, Roosevelt, Jr., MSS, Family Papers.

9. Bradley, *Soldier's Story*, p. 155; Drew Middleton, "The Battle Saga of a Tough Outfit," *New York Times Magazine* (Apr. 8, 1945):8, 41: Roosevelt, Jr.: to wife, Nov. 7, 1943; Nov. 28, 1943; to Henry Beston, Feb. 27, 1941: all in Roosevelt, Jr., MSS, Family Papers, Box 48.

10. The first three quotations are from a personal interview with Col. Joseph J. Kohout, Dec. 26, 1972; Hanson Baldwin, "Introduction," in *Danger Forward: The Story of the First Division in World War II* (Atlanta: Albert Love Enterprises, 1947), n.p. Terry Allen to George Marshall, Apr. 27, 1943; Roosevelt, Jr., to Marshall, Apr. 27, 1943: both in Allen File, Marshall Research Library.

11. Capt. J. W. Appel quoted in Menninger, *Psychiatry in a Troubled World*,

p. 333. The next two quotations are from Bradley, *Soldier's Story*, p. 155; former 1st Division Capt. Patrick Riddleberger to Michael Pearlman, Apr. 5, 1973, copy in possession of this writer. For sectarians, see James, *Varieties of Religious Experience,* p. 49. John Dixon to Omar Bradley, Mar. 4, 1970, copy in possession of this writer; John Lucas, "Major-General John Lucas's Diary" (hereafter cited as "Diary"), June 27, 1943, Office of the Chief of Military History, Washington, D.C.

12. Brig. Gen. Elliot D. Cooke, *All But Me and Thee: Psychiatry at the Foxhole Level* (Washington: Infantry Journal Press, 1946), pp. 119–21: Martin Blumenson: *Kasserine Pass* (Boston: Houghton, Mifflin, 1967), pp. 308–9; *Patton Papers: 1940–1945*, pp. 166–67; Alfred D. Chandler, ed., *The Papers of Dwight Eisenhower: The War Years* (Baltimore: Johns Hopkins Press, 1970), 2:1050, 1063–64, 1163.

13. For the 1st Division in World War I, see Millett, *The General*, pp. 317–24. Roosevelt, Jr., to George Marshall, Apr. 27, 1943, Allen File, Marshall Research Library; personal interviews with Sergeant Theodore Dobol, Jan. 13, 1972; General Clarence Huebner, July 23, 1971. Unidentified general quoted in Bruce Jacobs, *Heroes of the Army* (New York: Norton, 1956), p. 130.

14. Personal interviews with Gen. Clarence Huebner, July 23, 1971; Capt. Henry Kelty, Oct. 10, 1971. Patton quoted in Ladislas Farrago, *Patton: Ordeal and Triumph* (New York: Dell, 1971), p. 284.

15. Roosevelt, Jr., quoted in Bradley, *Soldier's Story*, p. 111; to wife, Jan. 30, 1943, Apr. 24, 1944; to Handford McNider, Aug. 26, 1924: all in Roosevelt, Jr., MSS, Family Papers, Box 24. "Chocolate soldiers" is how Harvey Bundy describes Henry Stimson's Army Specialist Corps in Bundy, "The Reminiscences of Harvey H. Bundy," p. 257.

16. Blum, *V Was For Victory*, pp. 120, 123, 133–37; Stimson and Bundy, *On Active Service in Peace and War*, p. 456. For "Colonel" Robert Stevens, see John Kenneth Galbraith, *A Life In Our Times: Memoirs* (Boston: Houghton-Mifflin, 1981), pp. 138–39. The statistics on noncombatants in modern war are from Gen. George C. Marshall in Millis, ed., *American Military Thought*, p. 441. Stimson Diary, Oct. 2, 1942; Stimson to Edgar Crossman, Mar. 18, 1942, Stimson MSS.

17. Stimson Diary, Mar. 18, 19, 1942, Aug. 11, 1942, Stimson MSS; C. B. Mickelwait to the Director of the Army Specialist Corps, June 24, 1942; Dwight Davis, "Memorandum for the Secretary of War," June 26, 1942; Emmett F. Connelly to Col. W. C. McDuffie, Sept. 28, 1942; Ted Dealey to E. F. Connelly, Aug. 3, 1942: all in Army World War II, Record Group 107, Box 182, National Archives; Stimson and Bundy, *On Active Service in Peace and War*, p. 456; Stimson Diary, Mar. 15, 1931, Oct. 29, 1931, Stimson MSS.

18. Stouffer, *American Soldier*, 2:309–10; Gen. Clift Andrus (1st Division's senior artillery officer), "Notes," enclosed in the copy of Bradley, *Soldier's Story*, 1st Division Memorial Museum, Wheaton, Ill.; personal interview with Capt. Henry Kelty, Oct. 10, 1971; Col. Stanhope Mason, "Algeria: The Record," in *Danger Forward*, pp. 5–6; Bradley, *Soldier's Story*, pp. 109–11.

19. Ibid; personal interviews with Gen. Robert Porter, Sept. 26, 1972; Capt.

Henry Kelty, Oct. 10, 1971; Gen. Clarence Huebner, July 23, 1971.

20. Lucas, "Diary," June 7, 28, 1943, July 2, 4, 1943.

21. Personal interview with Gen. Robert Porter, Sept. 26, 1972; Eisenhower to Marshall, July 28, 1943, Terry Allen File, Eisenhower Presidential Library; personal interview with Sgt. Theodore Dobol, Jan. 17, 1973.

22. Albert Wedemeyer, *Wedemeyer Reports* (New York: Henry Holt, 1958), p. 224; personal interview with Gen. Wedemeyer, Jan. 17, 1973.

23. Lucas, "Diary," July 10, 1943, July 21, 1943; Eisenhower to Marshall, July 28, 1943, Terry Allen File, Eisenhower Presidential Library.

24. Harry C. Butcher, *My Three Years with Eisenhower* (New York: Simon & Schuster, 1946), p. 148; Roosevelt, Jr., to wife, Nov. 7, 1943, Roosevelt, Jr., MSS, Family Papers.

25. As to Roosevelt's personality: most people who knew him as "the most self-confident man in the world" would say that this writer does not know what he is talking about. However, at times, even Roosevelt admitted to an "inferiority complex" and a hypersensitivity that caused him "suffering and humiliation," see Roosevelt, Jr., to Dallas McGrew, May 12, 1927; to Sherrard Billings, Dec. 2, 1932; Bill O'Reilly, "Palabras Neighbors," undated newspaper column: all in Roosevelt, Jr., MSS, Boxes 44, 59, newspaper file.

The story about the lieutenant was reluctantly told to me by Kurt Show (Roosevelt's orderly), Dec. 23, 1971. For Roosevelt's promises to his troops see General Ray McLain cited by Albert Garland, who is editing McLain's papers for publication, in Garland to Michael Pearlman, Sept. 28, 1971, letter in possession of this writer. For the feelings of deserters, see S. Kierson Weinberg, "The Combat Neurosis," *American Journal of Sociology* 51 (Mar., 1946):465.

26. H. R. Nickerbocker, "Algeria: As I Saw It," in *Danger Forward,* pp. 45–46; personal interviews with Gen. Robert Porter, Sept. 26, 1972; Gen. Clarence Huebner, July 23, 1971; Omar Bradley and Clay Blair, *A General's Life: An Autobiography* (New York: Simon & Schuster, 1983), p. 158; Lucas, "Diary," July 28, 30, 1943; Blumenson, ed., *Patton Papers: 1940–1945,* pp. 249, 263, 306.

27. Farrago, *Patton,* pp. 284, 323; Brad Day, "Death of a Warrior," *Infantry* (Nov.–Dec., 1966):53; Andrus, "Notes," p. 44: personal interview with Capt. Henry Kelty, Oct. 10, 1971; Blumenson, ed.: *Patton Papers: 1940–1945,* pp. 9, 21, 270, 428; *Patton Papers: 1885–1940,* pp. 647, 771, 796. The quotation on the peacetime army is cited in Tuchman, *Stilwell and the American Experience in China,* p. 345.

28. Lucas, "Diary," July 14, 15, 16, 20, 23, 28, 29m 1943; Forrest Pogue, *George C. Marshall: Organizer of Victory* (New York: Viking, 1963), p. 647; *Washington Post,* Sept. 26, 1972; *Washington Evening Star,* Sept. 25, 1972; personal interview with Gen. Huebner, July 23, 1971; Blumenson, ed., *Patton Papers: 1940–1945,* pp. 218, 301, 309.

29. Roosevelt, Jr., to wife, n.d., Roosevelt, Jr., MSS, Family Papers; Andrus, "Notes," pp. 149; personal interview with Sgt. Theodore Dobol, Jan. 13, 1972; Bradley, *Soldier's Story,* p. 154.

30. Stimson Diary, July 31, 1918, Oct. 10, 1943, Stimson MSS; George Marshall to Dwight Eisenhower, July 28, 1943, Roosevelt File, Marshall Research Library; Blumenson, ed., *Patton Papers: 1940–1945*, p. 272; Huebner quoted in personal interview with Col. Joseph Kohout, Dec. 26, 1972; "First Division Periodic Report," Aug. 8, 11, 13, 1943, First Division World War II Papers, Box 5953, National Archives, Suitland, Md.

31. Personal interview with Marcus O. Stevenson (Roosevelt, Jr.'s, aide-de-camp), Nov. 15, 1972; Roosevelt, Jr., to wife, Dec. 19, 1943, Jan. 1, 1944, Feb. 1, 1944: all in Roosevelt, Jr., MSS, Family Papers. Roosevelt's imagery comes from his moral roadmap—Bunyan's *Pilgrim's Progress*.

32. Roosevelt, Jr., quoted in Bradley, *Soldier's Story*, p. 333; to wife, Jan. 22, 1944, Feb. 22, 1944, Roosevelt, Jr., MSS, Family Papers; former 1st Division Col. John Bowen cited in Albert Garland to Michael Pearlman, Sept. 28, 1971, letter in possession of this writer. For Roosevelt's own comments on death in combat, see *New York Times*, July 19, 1918, Sept. 8, 1918.

33. Bedell Smith quoted in Roosevelt, Jr., to wife, Jan. 15, 1944; Roosevelt, Jr., to wife, Mar. 16, 1944: both in Roosevelt, Jr., MSS, Family Papers; personal interview with Marcus Stevenson, Nov. 15, 1972.

34. Sgt. Henry Brown quoted in Cornelius Ryan, *The Longest Day, June 6, 1944* (New York: Simon & Shuster, 1959), p. 232; Eisenhower quoted in Butcher, *My Three Years with Eisenhower*, p. 612. The European Theater Command recommended that Roosevelt receive an oak leaf cluster on his Distinguished Service Cross for his exploits on D-Day. By the time their proposal reached Washington, Roosevelt was dead. In memoriam, Stimson and Marshall personally ordered the army's commission on decorations to bestow the Medal of Honor posthumously, see Roosevelt, Jr.'s, Army Personnel (201) File.

35. Bradley, *Soldier's Story*, p. 333; personal interview with Chester Hanson (Bradley's aide and editor of his book), Dec. 24, 1972; Henry Stimson to Mrs. Theodore Roosevelt, Sr., Feb. 1, 1936; Roosevelt, Jr., to Stimson, Feb. 5, 1936, both in Stimson MSS. When making his admittedly risky selection of Roosevelt, Bradley was not giving him a free reign. He, not Roosevelt, Jr., would appoint the assistant commander, "a thick skinned disciplinarian," who would try to enforce order, contain Roosevelt's romanticism, and be, in effect, Bradley's spy. Bradley also might have pondered that Roosevelt, Jr., would probably not live to command very long. Everybody thought he was already living on borrowed time.

36. Menninger, *Psychiatry in a Troubled World*, pp. 130, 132, 339, 345; Roosevelt, Jr., to wife, Apr. 5, 1944, Roosevelt, Jr., MSS, Family Papers; personal interview with Marcus Stevenson, Nov. 15, 1972; Day, "Death of a Warrior," pp. 50–53; Blumenson, ed., *Patton Papers: 1940–1945*, pp. 480–81; Charles Codman, *Drive* (Boston: Little, Brown, 1957), p. 156.

Summary and Conclusions

☆

THE WORLD WAR I military preparedness movement tried to solve America's social problems without redistributing its wealth and power. It felt it could do this by strengthening the individual's will to renounce personal pleasure. Normally, such moral reform projects do not attempt to utilize the army. However, other institutions, at the turn of the twentieth century, seemed even more unsuited to its goals. Political parties, having lost elections in the Gilded Age by endorsing prohibition and pietism, now were reluctant "to pass [any] law which the bulk of the people do not want, even though they *ought* to want it."[1] Educational institutions, at this time, also appeared inadequate. Changes in curricula, from primary schools to the colleges, were deemphasizing moral training in order to develop whatever skills produced the goods and services in demand. As alternative ways of building social righteousness were thereby circumscribed, civilian leaders of preparedness organizations advocated military programs to perform the uplift functions that other associations shunned. Those prominent members of the upper class who led these societies wanted to nurture national unity, discipline, and heroism—qualities which they found lacking in pampered students, unassimilated immigrants, the idle rich, the idle poor, and many other Americans. To accomplish their objectives, they formulated a conservative (if not reactionary) plan for reform based on the theory that physical sacrifice and suffering creates solidarity and virtue. They specifically prescribed military preparedness for the moral restoration of a body politic whose malaise seemed to lie in its preoccupation with creature comforts.

Unlike evangelical Christians who have faith in their forgiving God's benevolent gift of Grace, many preparedness leaders were raised in Congregational, Episcopal, and other high-status churches whose proscriptive morality and exacting authority dovetailed with the social code of scarcity capitalism. In post-Civil War America, where old religious concepts received a secular interpretation, these men rendered attributes of sanctity into traits of character. In an age of growing affluence, they felt that universal military training could restore the principles of their inner-directed Protestant work ethic which made duty, not comfort, man's foremost concern. They conceived the army regimen to be a functional equivalent for the vanishing frontier that allegedly bred America's finest legacy—the hardy virtues of its pristine national character. If resurrected in military institutions, this neo-puritan form of social purgatory might forge a type of man opposed to the pleasure ethic of consumer capitalism.

Different historic epochs have had different notions of human nature. In the early and medieval Christian eras, when "to comfort" meant "to strengthen," man was thought to be a spiritual being devoted to salvation. Now, in the age of marketing and commerce, where "comfort" meant "convenience," the genius of the human race became the "economic man" driven by hopes of material gain. To avoid strenuous tasks of discipline, this utilitarian creature procured doctors, athletes, and army officers to dispense professionally produced health, recreation, and national security. Preparedness leaders, deploring what observers called modern man's "constant cry to make things easy," hoped that a military experience could remedy the headlong pursuit of pleasure.[2] These reformers, who earlier supported other uplift programs, from heroic literature to outdoor camping and football, endorsed total war as a matchless opportunity to make the American citizen into the "heroic man" whose nature is self-sacrifice.

During World War I, at home and abroad, preparedness leaders organized patriotic programs both inside and outside the army. While some taught military discipline to young recruits and immigrants, others displayed heroism on the battlefield. At least a few of these men, hoping to expedite the country's moral elevation, physically repressed those whom they could not convert. When the armistice arrived, almost all of them believed that their political strength would grow as they gathered support from the American Legionnaires. The Plattsburgers who initially reorganized these former doughboys felt that the latter were veterans of martial purification. As such they would surely solidify the wartime revival of patriotism and the movement for UMT. If the expectations of preparedness leaders proved correct, they would have solved their great conundrum by popularizing their unpopular plans to reduce the public mania for private goods. Rather quickly, however, their faith proved unfounded. High-technology war, making human "will" seem helpless, did little to support their calls for "character." The American Legion itself reflected this fact in the 1920s. Having then outgrown its initial sponsors, the organization became a self-interested lobby chiefly concerned with a cash bonus for veterans and corporate growth for itself. Moreover the nation, having developed "a pleasure or surplus economy,"[3] became a body politic largely committed

to the outer-directed consumption ethic that the preparedness movement tried to forestall. Their hopes crushed, their ideals scorned, and
their policies ignored, members of the National Security League blamed
their failure on a mythical radical menace which, after 1920, sank into
the same national oblivion that engulfed UMT itself. But not all preparedness leaders were so obtuse. Rather than suffer the futility of
paranoid politics, many of them sought self-exile instead. While patriotic expatriates Leonard Wood and Henry Stimson labored in the Philippines and Theodore Roosevelt, Jr., hunted in the Himalayas, other
Plattsburg advocates found sanctuaries at home. Through censorship,
John G. Hibben, Endicott Peabody, and Samuel Drury hoped to shield
their schools from modern social pollution. At the Washington Cathedral or the Bronx Zoo, George Wharton Pepper and William Temple
Hornaday sought moral satisfaction within the confines of magnificent
monuments. From bitter experience these men now learned the old
adage that moralists who try too hard to change a flawed human nature
are likely to be vanquished by the nature they defy.

   In the next decade, this last principle was as valid as it was in the
1920s. Despite initial hopes to the contrary, the presence of the Depression did not ensure the absence of materialism. In fact, the Franklin
Roosevelt administration, stressing welfare and security, chose to rebuild purchasing power through deficit spending, public employment,
and bureaucratic controls, all of which were contrary to the moral uplift ideals that most Plattsburgers tenaciously held. To curtail these
deleterious trends, several former interventionists became leading isolationists preceding World War II. By then they had decided that war
would corrupt the country by increasing the power of the New Deal.

   The social reform effort described above was not the only objective
of the preparedness movement. Several of its leaders believed that its
program could uplift themselves as well as the nation. They specifically
hoped that the military life, which they themselves endured, would
forge or verify their virtue beyond all doubt. Many of these men previously had tested their mettle in the wilderness and on the playing fields.
A few of them even took the cure at William Muldoon's health camp—
an institution that embodied Dr. Leonard Wood's old dictum that therapists should treat character, not just disease. Hoping to pass the ultimate test of manhood, they turned towards the battlefield, where they
sometimes found that war could be disappointing. Although Robert
Bacon died content that he had finally done his duty, other men, whose
demands for self-confirmation may well have been insatiable, were not
so fortunate. If it were possible for the Theodore Roosevelts, father
and son, to have satisfied themselves, their combat records would have
done so. By all accounts, no one who witnessed their exploits ever ques-

tioned their courage. Yet, their expectations to the contrary, war did not provide the definitive proof they sought; no matter what they did, they could not rest content. Indeed, their futile pursuit of a conclusive satisfaction led them toward their greatest disappointments—the punishments they received from the army that they loved. Partly because Roosevelt, Sr., in his final grasp for glory, tried to horde the army's best officers, he was not allowed to lead his great division into the Great War. Largely because Roosevelt, Jr.'s, own heroics became detrimental to military organization, he was relieved from his own division in a still greater war. Try as they might, neither man could die in combat.

These observations suggest that the civilian leaders of the World War I universal military training movement, despite some contributions they made to the service, should not have entrusted their social and personal ambitions to military institutions. Arthur Woods may have helped cadets live through flight school and both Roosevelts led frightened men to battlefield victories. Nonetheless, in the final analysis, the army in which they served could not improve their country because its professional soldiers were no better than civilians. During the Gilded Age, when commercial America exiled the army to a string of "hitching post" forts, the service responded to disfavor by converting its exclusion into exclusivity. Proclaiming that soldiers alone embodied selfless sacrifice, it professed a chivalric and communal code of life.[4] This doctrine appealed to those particular civilians who would later lead the military training movement. However, the army's claim to be free from commonplace greed was not completely valid for its true ethic was more professional than Spartan. It actually resembled all the other guilds which have also disdained amateurs, denigrated new men with new interests, and resisted any change in their traditional function. Consequently, from 1898 to 1943, when civilians from Roosevelt, Sr., to Roosevelt, Jr., tried to use the army for the sake of public uplift, professional soldiers usually neglected the civic responsibilities which these men wished to impose upon them. In the Spanish-American War, jealous army regulars resented the Rough Riders, whose exploits inspired national unity. Subsequently, from 1913 through the 1930s, they resisted service in the Plattsburg citizen-soldier camps and the Civilian Conservation Corps, lest these moral uplift projects interfere with national defense and their own prerogatives. Finally, in World War II, the army discharged Roosevelt, Jr., from his 1st Division post. Preoccupied with strategic problems, the service (unlike Roosevelt) had not the time, the heart, nor the wish "to concern itself with the dignity of man."[5] On all these occasions the army expressed its professional bias, not a Spartan code. It was citizen-soldiers like Henry Stimson and

Theodore Roosevelt, Jr., who took the martial ethic seriously. When, during World War II, they tried to shame noncombatants who dared wear the military uniform, they encumbered the total war effort. Shortly thereafter, Eisenhower the professional relieved Roosevelt the warrior from his command.

NOTES

1. Morison, ed., *Letters of Theodore Roosevelt,* 2:1438. For the partisan rejection of pietistic politics, see Lewis L. Gould, "The Republican Search for a National Majority," in H. Wayne Morgan, ed., *The Gilded Age* (New York: Syracuse University Press, 1970), pp. 181–84.

2. Siegfried Giedion, *Mechanization Takes Command: A Contribution to Anonymous History* (New York: Oxford University Press, 1948), pp. 260, 265, 301, 310. Mrs. Thomas Edison quoted in May, *Screening Out The Past,* p. 22.

3. Economist Simon Patten and others quoted in Rodgers, *Work Ethic in Industrial America,* pp. 120–22.

4. Huntington, *Soldier and the State,* pp. 222–70.

5. Bradley, *Soldier's Story,* p. 154.

Appendix

Individual Leaders and their Institutional Position in the Preparedness Movement

Lyman Abbott	publicist for universal military training (UMT)
Robert Bacon	executive member: National Security League (NSL), American Defense Society (ADS), and Military Training Camps Association (MTCA)
James Beck	executive member: NSL and ADS
Charles Henry Brent	member MTCA; founding member American Legion (AL)
Grenville Clark	executive secretary MTCA
Joseph Howland Coit	chairman ADS
Frederic Rene Coudert	executive member NSL
Harvey Cushing	spokesman UMT
Roger Alden Derby	member MTCA
Henry Sturgis Drinker	executive secretary MTCA's Advisory Committee of College Presidents (ACCP)
Samuel S. Drury	founder Junior Plattsburg Training Camp (JP)
Hamilton Fish	director Junior Patriots of America; executive member NSL; member MTCA
David Goodrich	executive member MTCA
William Guggenheim	executive member ADS
Arthur Hadley	executive member ACCP
Hermann Hagedorn	founder Vigilantes; executive director Theodore Roosevelt Memorial Foundation
Albert Bushnell Hart	chairman NSL's Committee on Patriotism through Education (CPE)
John Grier Hibben	chairman ACCP
David Jayne Hill	executive member NSL
Henry S. Hooker	member: MTCA and JP
William Temple Hornaday	executive member ADS; chairman Junior Naval Reserve (JNR)

Delancey Kane Jay	executive member MTCA
A. Lawrence Lowell	executive member ACCP
Robert McCormick	publicist UMT; member NSL
Robert McElroy	director CPE
S. Stanwood Menken	founder and president NSL
John Purroy Mitchel	member: NSL and MTCA
William Muldoon	spokesman UMT
Endicott Peabody	spokesman UMT
George Wharton Pepper	executive member: NSL and MTCA
Ralph Barton Perry	executive member MTCA
Raymond Price	executive member NSL
Corrine Roosevelt Robinson	president Women's League for UMT; executive member Women's Roosevelt Memorial Association (WRMA)
Franklin D. Roosevelt	spokesman UMT
Theodore Roosevelt	spokesman UMT; honorary president ADS
Theodore Roosevelt, Jr.	member MTCA; founder AL
Jacob Gould Schurman	executive member ACCP
Horace Stebbins	member MTCA; director JP
Henry Stimson	member: NSL and MTCA
Archibald Thacher	executive member MTCA
John Wanamaker	president Philadelphia NSL
Owen Wister	publicist UMT
Henry Alexander Wise Wood	executive member NSL; chairman Conference Committee on Preparedness
Leonard Wood	founder and military commander Plattsburg training camp
Arthur Woods	executive member JPA: member MTCA and NSL

TABLE I. PRIMARY OCCUPATIONS

Categories	Number out of 45-Man Group	Percentage of Preparedness Leaders	Categories' Approximate Percentage of America as a Whole in 1910
A. Education	13	31.0%	1.2%
B. Politics	6	13.3%	---
C. Business	11	24.4%	6.3%
D. Professionals	10	22.2%	10.0%
E. Publicist	5	11.0%	.10%
Total	45	100.0%	17.6%

TABLE II. RELIGION

A. Episcopal	16	35.5%	2.0%
B. Presbyterian	7	15.5%	1.4%
C. Congregational	4	8.8%	.8%
D. Roman Catholic	3	6.7%	14.3%
F. Other	7	15.5%	---
G. Unknown	8	18.0%	---
Total	45	100.0%	---

TABLE III. ECONOMIC STATUS

A. Moderate	11	24.4%	31.0%
B. Substantial	10	22.2%	3.0%
C. Wealthy	24	53.4%	1.0%
Total	45	100.0%	35.0%

TABLE IV. FAMILY ORIGINS

A. Working Class	1	2.2%	65.0%
B. Middle Class	20	44.4%	34.0%
C. Upper Class	24	53.4%	1.0%
Total	45	100.0%	100.0%

TABLE V. PRESTIGE ACHIEVED

Categories	Number out of 45-Man Group	Percentage of Preparedness Leaders	Categories' Approximate Percentage of America as a Whole in 1910
A. Moderate	9	17.7%	---
B. Prominent	36	82.3%	---
Total	45	100.0%	---

TABLE VI. EDUCATION

A. Pre-College	3	6.7%	96.0%
B. College	8	20.0%	3.5%
C. Advanced	32	68.8%	1.5%
D. Unknown	2	4.5%	---
Total	45	100.0%	100.0%

Definition of Terms Used in Tables

Most of the categories used under the heading "primary occupations" are self-explanatory. "Professionals" refers to men like Dr. Harvey Cushing and lawyer S. Stanwood Menken. They had an extended education for a white-collar occupation which can be practiced only by those licensed by some regulatory body. "Publicist" refers to Lyman Abbott and others who conveyed their opinions to a mass audience through the popular printed media. John Grier Hibben, on the other hand, was an "educator" since he usually communicated to a relatively small group through lectures or academic monographs. When a man fell within two or more categories, as did lawyer-politician James M. Beck, I have chosen a predominant category. In Beck's case it was politics.

To determine one's "economic status," I have, whenever possible, used bank accounts and probated wills. Certainly multimillionaries Robert Bacon and Horace Stebbins fall among the wealthy. In other cases, where precise quantitative data is missing, I had to make judgments based on general life style. Those of "moderate" or middle-class status usually employed a servant and lived in a house in a residential district. Most "substantial" citizens could afford to join an exclusive social club or own a summer home. Obviously the "wealthy" possessed objects which only they could buy. S. Standwood Menken's wife had a very expensive jewelry collection and Henry Alexander Wise Wood owned a large yacht.

The religion categories are largely self-defined. "Others" refers to those from

Jewish, Baptist, Unitarian, and Quaker backgrounds. Respective examples are Menken, Jacob Gould Schurman, A. Lawrence Lowell, and Henry S. Drinker.

"Family origins" have been determined by the income, education, and prestige of one's parents. Because William Muldoon's family had little of each, he was classified as coming from "the working class." Since James Beck's father was considered somewhat successful, I classified his background as "middle class." Robert Bacon and others who came from wealthy families headed by leading men of their communities were born into the "upper class."

"Prestige achieved" has been measured by such indices as the newspaper space one received in both life and death. For example, when Grenville Clark died the *New York Times* gave him a glowing multicolumn obituary. Other indicators of prestige that were used were the exclusivity of the social clubs a man joined and the public testimonials given to him.

Out of the forty-five selected leaders, only Muldoon, Stebbins, and Wise Wood did not have a higher education. All the others attended a college or university where they acquired a bachelor's degree, if not a professional or postgraduate education.

Selective Bibliography

I. MANUSCRIPT COLLECTIONS

Allen, William H. Memoir, Oral History Collection, Columbia University.
American Legion Papers. National Legion Library, Indianapolis, Ind.
Army Air Force Papers. World War I, National Archives.
Brent, Charles. Papers, Library of Congress.
Bullard, Robert. Papers, Library of Congress.
Bundy, Harvey H. Memoir, Oral History Collection, Columbia University.
Butler, Nicholas Murray. Papers, Columbia University.
Clark, Grenville. Papers, Dartmouth College.
Coudert, Frederic Rene. Memoir, Oral History Collection, Columbia
   University.
Eisenhower, Dwight David. Papers, Eisenhower Presidential Library, Abilene,
   Kans.
Forbes, W. Cameron. Papers and Journal, Library of Congress.
Hagedorn, Hermann. Papers, Library of Congress.
Hoover, Herbert. Papers, Hoover Presidential Library, West Branch, Ia.
Hornaday, William Temple. Papers, Library of Congress.
Lowell, Abbott Lawrence. Papers, Harvard University.
Lucas, John. Diary, Office of the Chief of Military History, Washington, D.C.
McCoy, Frank. Papers, Library of Congress.
Marshall, George C. Papers, Marshall Research Library, Arlington, Va.
Military Training Camps Society. Papers, Chicago Historical Society.
Mitchel, John Purroy. Papers, Library of Congress.
Nicholson, E. E. Papers, University of Minnesota.
Palmer, John McAuley. Papers, Library of Congress.
Peabody, George Wharton. Papers, University of Pennsylvania.
Perry, Ralph Barton. Papers, Harvard University.
Roosevelt, Franklin D. Papers, Roosevelt Presidential Library, Hyde Park, N.Y.
Roosevelt, Theodore. Collection, Harvard University.
Roosevelt, Theodore. Papers, Library of Congress.
Roosevelt, Theodore, Jr. Papers, Library of Congress.
Seventy-Seventh Infantry Division. Papers, World War I, National Archives.
Stimson, Henry L. Papers, Yale University.
Wadsworth, James. Papers, Library of Congress.
Wood, Leonard. Papers, Library of Congress.
Woods, Arthur. Papers, Library of Congress.

II. GOVERNMENT PUBLICATIONS

New York City Police Department. *The Junior Policeman.* 1917.
———. *The Official Handbook of the Junior Police of the City of New York.* Nov. 1917.
———. *Report, 1914–1917.* 1917.
U.S. Congress, House Appropriations Committee. *War Department Appropriations Bill for 1923: Hearings.* 67th Cong., 2nd Sess., Washington, D.C., 1922.
———. *War Department Appropriations Bill for 1929: Hearings.* 70th Cong., 1st Sess., Washington, D.C. 1928.
U.S. Congress, Senate Military Affairs Committee. *Army Reorganization: Hearings.* 66th Cong., 1st Sess., Washington, D.C., 1919.
———. *Universal Military Training: Hearings.* 64th Cong., 2nd Sess., Washington, D.C., 1917.
U.S. Congress, Special Committee to Investigate the National Security League. *National Security League: Hearings.* 65th Cong., 3rd Sess., Washington, D.C., 1919.
U.S. War Department. *Jobs For Soldiers: An Account of the work of Colonel Arthur Woods, Assistant to the Secretary of War in aiding the return to Civil life after the Great War—March–September, 1919.*

III. PROCEEDINGS AND REPORTS

Association of the American Universities. *Journal of the Proceedings and Addresses of the 20th Annual Convention,* Dec. 4 and 5, 1918.
Laura Spellman Rockefeller Memorial Final Report. New York: n.p., 1933.
National Collegiate Athletic Association. *Proceedings of the 12th Annual Convention,* Dec. 28, 1917.
———. *Proceedings of the 13th Annual Convention,* Dec. 27, 1918.
———. *Proceedings of the 15th Annual Convention,* Dec. 29, 1920.
National Security League. *Annual Report of the President of the National Security League,* May 3, 1916. New York: National Security League, 1916.
———. *Proceedings of the Congress of Constructive Patriotism.* New York: National Security League, 1917.
———. *Proceedings of the National Security Congress.* New York: National Security League, 1916.
New York Zoological Society. *First Annual Report of the New York Zoological Society,* Mar. 15, 1897.

IV. PAMPHLETS

American Defense Society: History, Purpose and Accomplishments. New York: American Defense Society, 1918.
Beck, James M. *The Six Fundamental Principles of the Constitution.* New York: National Security League, 1919.
Carter, Burnham. *The Berkshire Industrial Farm, 1886–1926.* n.p.: n.p., n.d.

Cashman, Joseph. *Give the Constitution a Chance.* New York: National Security League, 1927.

Easley, Ralph. *The Youth Movement: Do We Want It Here?* n.p.: n.p., n.d.

Hill, David Jayne. *The National Association for Constitutional Government: A Statement of Its Aims and Purposes.* Washington: n.p., n.d.

————. *Our National Development.* Philadelphia: Anvil Printing, 1902.

Mayor Mitchel's Police Bills: Why They Should Become Law. New York: City Club of New York, 1914.

Menken, S. Stanwood. *A Concept of National Service.* n.p.: National Security League, 1918.

————. *Knowledge by the People: True Basis of National Security.* n.p.: National Security League, 1917.

National Security League Future Work, New York: National Security League, 1919.

Stimson, Henry L. *The Issues of the War.* New York: National Security League, n.d.

Thacher, Archibald. *The Cadets of Plum Island.* New York: Junior Division of the Military Training Camps Association of the United States, 1916.

Wood, Henry Alexander Wise. *Progress in Newspaper Manufacture and Its Effects upon the Printing Industry.* New York: Wood Newspaper Manufacturing, 1932.

V. PRIMARY SOURCES: ARTICLES

Abbott, Ernest Hamlin. "The Boys of Plum Island." *Outlook* (Aug. 23, 1916): 950–58.

Alger, George W. "Preparedness and Democrat Discipline." *Atlantic Monthly* (Apr., 1916):482–91.

"The American Army." *Outlook* (July 1, 1903):645.

Beatty, Jerome. "William Muldoon." *American Magazine* (Jan., 1930):28–29, 136–39.

Beck, James. "The Age of Lawlessness." *Current History* (Oct., 1921):61–68.

————. "America's Need of Youth." *Saturday Evening Post* (May 14, 1921):7, 77–80.

————. "A Yearning for World Peace." *Annals of the American Academy of Political and Social Science* 72 (1917):214–16.

Briggs, L. B. "Intercollegiate Athletics and the War." *Atlantic Monthly* (Sept., 1918):303–9.

Bronson, T. B. "The Value of Military Training and Discipline in Schools." *School Review* 2 (1894):281–85.

Cowell, James R. "The New Undergraduate: An Interview with John Grier Hibben." *Saturday Evening Post* (Jan. 14, 1928):123–31.

Day, Brad. "Death of a Warrior." *Infantry* (Nov.–Dec., 1966):50–53.

Drinker, Henry Sturgis. "The Student's Military Instruction Camp at Gettysburg." *New York Times* (Aug. 17, 1913).

Drummond, Henry. "Manliness in Boys—By a New Process." *McClure's Magazine* (Dec., 1893):68–77.

Glass, Albert. "Psychotherapy in the Combat Zone." *American Journal of Psychiatry* 60 (1954):725–30.

Hadley, Arthur T. "Education in Germany." *Youth's Companion* (Jan. 6, 1910): 3–4.

Harbord, James G. "Theodore Roosevelt and the Army." *Review of Reviews* (Jan., 1924):65–75.

Hibben, John G. "The Colleges and the National Defense." *Independent* (June 28, 1915):532–33.

———. "The University Cantonment: Princeton." *Bookman* (Nov., 1918): 288–91.

Howard, Sidney. "Our Professional Patriots." *New Republic* (Aug. 20, 1924): 346–53, (Sept. 3, 1924):12–16, (Sept. 10, 1924):37–41, (Sept. 17, 1924): 71–75, (Sept. 24, 1924):93–95, (Oct. 1, 1924):119–23, (Oct. 15, 1924), pp. 143–45.

Johnson, Willis Fletcher. "Students at Camp Upton." *North American Review* (Jan., 1920):44–50.

Liebling, A. J. "Terry Allen." *New Yorker* (Apr. 24, 1943):22–26, (May 1, 1943):24–28.

Lippmann, Walter. "Leonard Wood." *New Republic* (Mar. 17, 1920):78–79.

McCormick, Robert. "Ripe for Conquest." *Century* (Apr., 1916):833–39.

Mather, Frank J. "Rear-Rank Reflections." *Unpopular Review* (Jan., 1916):15–25.

Menken, S. Stanwood. "National Defense and Efficiency." *Scientific Monthly* (Apr., 1916):355–58.

———. "The Russian Dilemma: Why I Favor Recognition." *North American Review* (Dec., 1930):660–64.

Middletown, Drew. "The Battle Saga of a Tough Outfit." *New York Times Magazine* (Aug. 8, 1945):8–9, 11.

"A Moral Miracle." *Outlook* (June 11, 1898):362.

"The New York City Junior Police." *Outlook* (July 12, 1916):588.

Perry, Ralph Barton. "The American Legion in Politics." *Outlook* (Jan. 14, 1920):62–63.

———. "The Colleges and the New Age." *Harvard Alumni Bulletin* (Feb., 1919):490–91.

———. "The Student Army Training Corps." *National Service* 6 (1919):84.

———. "What Is Worth Fighting For?" *Atlantic Monthly* (Dec.. 1915):822–31.

"A Physical Culturist Who Steadies 'Jumpy' Nerves by 'Treating 'Em Rough.'" *Literary Digest* (Apr. 3, 1920):84–87.

Putnam, George Palmer. "The Birth of the American Legion." *Outlook* (May 21, 1919):104–5.

Roosevelt, Theodore, Jr. "A Boy's Book Rambles." *Bookman* (Feb., 1925): 687–91.

Schurman, Jacob Gould. "Every College Should Introduce Military Training." *Everybody's Magazine* (Feb., 1915):179–83.

———. "The University Cantonment: Cornell." *Bookman* (Nov., 1918):291–95.
"Sedition." *Outlook* (May 1, 1917):10–11.
"Some Advantages of War." *Outlook* (June 25, 1898):461–62.
Stamm, Gerald V. "Terry Allen's Boys." *Our Army* (Dec., 1943):15–17.
Stimson, Henry L. "Artillery in a Quiet Sector." *Scribner's* (June, 1919):709–16.
———. "Future Philippine Policy under the Jones Act." *Foreign Affairs* 5 (1927):257–67.
"Therepeutic Value of War." *Boston Medical and Surgical Journal* 168 (1913): 400.
Thwing, Charles. "The Colleges as War Camps." *Independent* (Oct. 5, 1918):12.
Whidden, Graham. "Our Schoolboy Soldiers." *Munsey's Magazine* (July, 1896): 459–66.
White, Frank Marshall. "A Man Who Has Achieved the Impossible." *Outlook* (Sept. 26, 1917):124–26.
Williams, John D. "An American Admiral Crichton." *Century* (Oct., 1922):899–911.
Wisehart, M. K. "William Muldoon Has Brought Thousands Back to Health." *American Magazine* (Dec., 1924):14–15.
Wister, Owen. "Safe in the Arms of Croesus." *Harper's* (Oct., 1927):539–51.
Wood, Henry Alexander Wise. "Planning the Future of America." *Annals of the American Academy of Political and Social Science* 72 (1917):19–23.
———. "What the Army Needs." *Independent* (Feb. 19, 1917):303–4.
Woods, Arthur. "The Making of Good Police Force." *Weekly Review* (Sept. 29, 1920):642–43.
———. "Unemployment and Its Social Significance." *Proceedings of the American Philosophical Society* 70 (1931):289–90.

VI. PRIMARY SOURCES: BOOKS

Abbott, Lyman. *Christianity and Social Problems.* Boston: Houghton, Mifflin, 1896.
———. *The Twentieth Century Crusade.* New York: Macmillan, 1918.
Adler, Julius Ochs, ed. *History of the Seventy-Seventh Division.* New York: 77th Division Association, 1919.
———. *History of the 306th Infantry.* New York: 306th Infantry Association, 1935.
Beck, James M. *The Constitution of the United States.* New York: George H. Doran, 1924.
Blumenson, Martin, ed. *The Patton Papers: 1885–1940.* Boston: Houghton, Mifflin, 1972.
———. *The Patton Papers: 1940–1945.* Boston: Houghton, Mifflin, 1974.
Bradley, Omar. *A Soldier's Story.* New York: Henry Holt, 1951.
Bramson, Leon, and George Goethals, Jr., ed. *War: Studies from Psychology, Sociology and Anthropology.* New York: Basic Books, 1968.
Brent, Charles Henry. *The Mount of Vision.* New York: Longmans, Green. 1918.

Brieger, Gert H., ed. *Medical America in the Nineteenth Century.* Baltimore: Johns Hopkins Press, 1972.

Bowen, Catherine Drinker. *Family Portrait.* Boston: Atlantic-Little, Brown, 1970.

Bullard, Robert L. *Personalities and Reminiscences of the War.* Garden City: Doubleday, Page, 1925.

Butcher, Harry C. *My Three Years with Eisenhower.* New York: Simon & Schuster, 1946.

Butler, Nicholas Murray. *A World in Ferment.* New York: Scribner's, 1917.

Chandler, Alfred D., ed. *The Papers of Dwight David Eisenhower: The War Years.* Baltimore: Johns Hopkins Press, 1970.

Coudert, Frederic Rene. *A Half Century of International Problems.* New York: Columbia University Press, 1954.

Creel, George. *Rebel at Large: Recollections of 50 Crowded Years.* New York: Putnam's, 1947.

Cushing, Harvey. *Consecratio Medici.* Boston: Little, Brown, 1928.

————. *From a Surgeon's Journal: 1915–1918.* Boston: Little, Brown, 1937.

————. *The Medical Career and Other Papers.* Boston: Little, Brown, 1940.

Davis, Richard Harding. *The Cuban and Puerto Rican Campaigns.* Reprint. Freeport: Books for Libraries, 1970.

Derby, Roger A. *Memoirs of Roger Alden Derby.* n.p.: privately printed, 1959.

Feuss, Claude. *Independent Schoolmaster.* Boston: Little, Brown, 1952.

Fosdick, Raymond. *Chronicle of a Generation: An Autobiography.* New York: Harper & Brothers, 1958.

Gray, J. Glenn. *The Warriors: Reflections on Men in Battle.* New York: Harper & Row, 1967.

Heiser, Victor. *An American Doctor's Odyssey.* New York: Norton, 1936.

Hill, David Jayne. *Americanism, What It Is.* New York: D. Appleton, 1916.

Hornaday, William T. *Awake! America.* New York: Moffat, Yard, 1918.

————. *The Man Who Became a Savage.* Buffalo: Peter, Paul, 1896.

————. *The Minds and Manners of Wild Animals.* New York: Scribner's, 1922.

————. *Wild Life Conservation in Theory and Practice.* New Haven: Yale University Press, 1914.

Knickerbocker, H. R., et al. *Danger Forward: The Story of the First Division in World War II.* Atlanta: Albert Love Enterprises, 1947.

Kolbe, Parke R. *The Colleges in Wartime and After.* New York: D. Appleton, 1919.

Longworth, Alice Roosevelt. *Crowded Hours: The Reminiscences of Alice Roosevelt Longworth.* New York: Scribner's, 1933.

Marshall, Edward. *The Story of the Rough Riders.* New York: G. W. Dillingham, 1899.

Marshall, George C. *Memoirs of My Service in the World War, 1917–1918.* Boston: Houghton, Mifflin, 1976.

Mayo, Katherine. *The Isles of Fear.* New York: Harcourt, Brace, 1925.

Menninger, William. *Psychiatry in a Troubled World: Yesterday's War and To-day's Troubles.* New York: Macmillan, 1948.

Miles, L. Wardlaw. *History of the 308th Infantry.* New York: Putnam's, 1927.

Millis, Walter, ed. *American Military Thought.* Indianapolis: Bobbs-Merrill, 1966.

Morrison, Elting E., ed. *The Letters of Theodore Roosevelt.* 8 Vols. Cambridge, Mass.: Harvard University Press, 1951.

Nixon, Edgar, ed. *Franklin D. Roosevelt and Conservation: 1911–1945.* 2 Vols. Hyde Park: General Service Administration, 1957.

Onorato, Michael, ed. *Leonard Wood as Governor-General: A Calendar of Selected Correspondence.* n.p.: McS Enterprises, 1969.

Parker, John. *History of the Gatling Gun Detachment: Fifth Army Corps, at Santiago.* Kansas City: Hudson-Kimberly, 1898.

Pepper, George Wharton. *In the Senate.* Philadelphia: University of Pennsylvania Press, 1930.

———. *Men and Issues: A Selection of Speeches and Articles.* New York: Duffield, 1924,

———. *Philadelphia Lawyer: An Autobiography.* Philadelphia: University of Pennsylvania Press, 1944.

Perry, Ralph Barton. *The Plattsburg Movement.* New York: Dutton, 1921.

———. *Puritanism and Democracy.* New York: Vanguard, 1944.

Pershing, John J. *My Experiences in the World War.* 2 Vols. New York: Frederick A. Stokes, 1931.

Post, Charles J. *The Little War of Private Post.* Boston: Little, Brown, 1960.

Rainsford, W. Kerr. *From Upton to the Meuse: With the 307th Infantry.* New York: D. Appleton, 1920.

Robinson, Corrine Roosevelt. *My Brother Theodore Roosevelt.* New York: Scribner's, 1921.

Roosevelt, Eleanor Butler. *The Day before Yesterday: The Reminiscences of Mrs. Theodore Roosevelt, Jr.* Garden City: Doubleday, 1959.

Roosevelt, Eliot, ed. *F.D.R.: His Personal Letters.* 4 Vols. New York: Duell, Sloan & Pearce, 1947–50.

Roosevelt, Theodore. *The Works of Theodore Roosevelt.* Ed. Hermann Hagedorn. 29 Vols. New York: Scribner's, 1926.

Roosevelt, Theodore, and Henry Cabot Lodge. *Selections from the Correspondence of Theodore Roosevelt and Henry Cabot Lodge.* New York: Scribner's, 1925.

Roosevelt, Theodore, Jr. *Average Americans.* New York: Scribner's, 1921.

———. *Rank and File: True Stories of the Great War.* New York: Scribner's, 1925.

Scott, James Brown, ed. *Robert Bacon: Life and Letters.* Garden City: Doubleday & Page, 1923.

Stimson, Henry L. *The Far Eastern Crisis.* New York: Harper & Brothers, 1936.

———. *My Vacations.* n.p. privately printed, 1946.

Stimson, Henry, and McGeorge Bundy. *On Active Service in Peace and War,* New York: Harper and Brothers, 1948.

Thwing, Charles. *The American Colleges and Universities in the Great War.* New York: Macmillan, 1920.

Villard, Oswald Garrison. *Fighting Years: Memoirs of a Liberal Editor.* New

York: Harcourt, Brace, 1939.
Wheat, George S. *The Story of the American Legion.* New York: Putnam's, 1919.
Wister, Owen. *The Pentecost of Calamity.* New York: Macmillan, 1915.
————. *Owen Wister Out West: His Journals and Letters.* Ed. Fanny Kemble Wister. Chicago: University of Chicago Press, 1958.
————. *Roosevelt, the Story of a Friendship.* New York: Macmillan, 1930.
Wood, Henry Alexander Wise. *The Book of Symbols.* Boston: Plimpton Press, 1904.
————. *Fancies.* London: Elkin Mathews, 1903.
————. *Money Hunger: A Brief History of Commercial Immorality in the United States.* New York: Putnam's, 1908.
————. *A Philosophy of Success.* New York: William Ritchie, 1905.
Wood, Leonard. *The Military Obligation of Citizenship.* Princeton: Princeton University Press, 1915.
————. *Our Military History: Its Facts and Fallacies.* Chicago: Reilley & Breiton, 1916.
Woods, Arthur. *Crime Prevention.* Princeton: Princeton University Press, 1915.
————. *The Policeman and the Public.* New Haven: Yale University Press, 1919.
Young, Hugh Hampton. *A Surgeon's Autobiography.* New York: Harcourt, Brace, 1940.

VII. SECONDARY SOURCES: ARTICLES

Bell, Daniel. "The Cultural Contradictions of Capitalism," in Daniel Bell and Irving Kristol, ed. *Capitalism Today.* New York: New American Library, 1971, pp. 28–50.
Cawelti, John G. "America on Display: The World's Fairs of 1876, 1893 and 1933," in Frederic Jaher, ed. *The Age of Industrialism in America.* New York: Free Press, 1968, pp. 317–63.
George, Alexander. "Primary Groups, Organization and Military Performance," in Roger Little, ed. *Handbook of Military Institutions.* Beverly Hills: Russel Sage, 1971, pp. 293–318.
Gillette, Howard, Jr. "The Military Occupation of Cuba, 1899–1902: Workshop for American Progressivism," *American Quarterly* 25 (1973):27–33.
Harrington, Fred Harvey. "The Anti-Imperialist Movement in the United States." *Mississippi Valley Historical Review* 2 (1935):211–30.
Judd, Charles H. "Education," in *Recent Social Trends in the United States.* New York: McGraw-Hill, 1933, pp. 325–81.
Katzenback Edward L. "The Horse Cavalry in the Twentieth Century," in Carl Friedrich and Seymour Harris, ed. *Public Policy: A Yearbook of the Graduate School of Public Administration.* Cambridge, Mass.: Harvard University Press, 1958, pp. 120–50.
Leuchtenberg, William. "The New Deal and the Analogue to War," in John Braeman, Robert Bremner, and Everett Waters, ed. *Change and Continuity in Twentieth Century America.* Columbus: Ohio State University Press, 1964, pp. 95–123.

Mooney, Chase C., and Martha F. Lyman. "Some Phases of the Compulsory Military Training Movement, 1914–1920." *Mississippi Valley Historical Review* 38 (1952):633–56.

Morris, Brian. "Ernest Thompson Seton and the Origins of Woodcraft." *Journal of Contemporary History* 5 (1970):187–94.

Ross, Murray. "Football Red and Baseball Green." *American Way* (Oct., 1971): 31–36.

Schwartz, Bonnie Fox. "Unemployment Relief in Philadelphia, 1930–1932: A Study of the Depression's Impact on Voluntarism," in Bernard Sternsher, ed. *Hitting Home.* Chicago: Quadrangle, 1970, pp. 66–75.

Skolnick, Richard. "George Edwin Waring, Jr.: A Model for Reformers." *New York Historical Society Quarterly* 52 (Oct., 1968):354–78.

Steiner, Jesse. "Recreation and Leisure Time Activities," in *Recent Social Trends in the United States.* New York: McGraw-Hill, 1933, pp. 912–58.

Stone, Robert C. "Status and Leadership in a Combat Fighter Squadron." *American Journal of Sociology* 51 (1946):383–93.

Tucker, Rufus S. "A Balance Sheet of the Philippines." *Harvard Business Review* 8 (1929):10–23.

Vesey, Laurence R. "The Academic Mind of Woodrow Wilson." *Mississippi Valley Historical Review* 49 (1963):613–34.

White, Bruce. "The American Military and the Melting Pot in World War I," in J. L. Granatstein and R. D. Cuff, ed. *War and Society in North America.* Toronto: Thomas Nelson, 1971, pp. 37–51.

VIII. SECONDARY SOURCES: BOOKS

Abrahamson, James L. *America Arms for a New Century: The Making of a Great Military Power.* New York: Free Press, 1981.

Adler, Selig. *The Isolationist Impulse: Its Twentieth Century Reaction.* New York: Collier, 1961.

Allmendinger, David. *Paupers and Scholars: The Transformation of Student Life in Nineteenth Century New England.* New York: St. Martin's, 1975.

Ashburn, Frank. *Peabody of Groton.* Boston: Coward-McCann, 1944.

Barber, James. *The Pulse of Politics: Electing the President in the Media Age.* New York: Norton, 1980.

Barnet, Richard J. *Roots of War.* Baltimore: Penguin Books, 1972.

Beaver, Daniel R. *Newton Baker and the American War Effort, 1917–1919.* Lincoln: University of Nebraska Press, 1966.

Bercovitch, Sacvan. *The American Jeremiad.* Madison: University of Wisconsin Press, 1978.

Bledstein, Burton. *The Culture of Professionalism: The Middle-Class and the Development of Higher Education in America.* New York: Norton, 1976.

Blum, John Morton. *The Republican Roosevelt.* New York: Atheneum, 1963.

———. *V Was for Victory: Politics and American Culture during World War II.* New York: Harcourt, Brace & Jovanovich, 1976.

Boorstin, Daniel. *The Americans: The Democratic Experience.* New York: Vintage, 1974.

Boyer, Paul. *Urban Masses and Moral Order in America, 1820–1920.* Cambridge, Mass.: Harvard University Press, 1978.

Bridges, William. *Gathering of Animals: An Unconventional History of the New York Zoological Society.* New York: Harper & Row, 1974.

Challener, Richard. *Admirals, Generals and American Foreign Policy, 1898–1914.* Princeton: Princeton University Press, 1973.

Clark, W. H. *The Oxford Group: Its History and Significance.* New York: Bookman Associates, 1951.

Clifford, John Garry. *The Citizen Soldiers: The Plattsburg Training Camp Movement.* Lexington: University of Kentucky Press, 1972.

Coben, Stanley, and Lorman Ratner, ed. *The Development of an American Culture.* Englewood Cliffs: Barnes & Noble, 1970.

Cochran, Thomas. *200 Years of American Business.* New York: Basic Books, 1977.

Coffman, Edward M. *The War to End All Wars: The American Military Experience in World War I.* Madison: University of Wisconsin Press, 1966.

Cohen, Ronald, and Raymond Mohl. *The Paradox of Progressive Education: The Gary Plan and Urban Schools.* Port Washington: Kennikat, 1979.

Cosmas, Graham. *An Army for Empire: The United States and the Spanish-American War.* Columbia: University of Missouri Press, 1971.

Cunliffe, Marcus. *Soldiers and Civilians: The Martial Spirit in America, 1775–1865.* Boston: Little, Brown, 1968.

Dallek, Robert. *Franklin D. Roosevelt and American Foreign Policy, 1932–1945.* New York: Oxford University Press, 1979.

Davies, Wallace Evan. *Patriotism on Parade: The Story of Veterans' and Hereditary Organizations in America, 1793 to 1900.* Cambridge, Mass.: Harvard University Press, 1955.

Drury, Roger W. *Drury and St. Paul's: The Scars of a Schoolmaster.* Boston: Little, Brown, 1964.

Dubbert, Joe L. *A Man's Place: Masculinity in Transition.* Englewood Cliffs: Prentice-Hall, 1979.

Duffy, John. *The Healers: The Rise of the Medical Establishment.* New York: McGraw-Hill, 1976.

Dyer, John P. *'Fighting Joe' Wheeler.* Baton Rouge: Louisiana State University Press, 1941.

Dyer, Thomas G. *Theodore Roosevelt and the Idea of Race.* Baton Rouge: Louisiana State University Press, 1980.

Eister, Allen W. *Drawing-Room Conversions: A Sociological Account of the Oxford Group Movement.* Durham: Duke University Press, 1950.

Ekrich, Arthur A. *The Civilian and the Military.* New York: Oxford University Press, 1956.

Ewen, Stuart. *Captains of Consciousness: Advertising and the Social Roots of the Consumer Culture.* New York: McGraw-Hill, 1976.

Farrago, Ladislas. *Patton: Ordeal and Triumph.* New York: Dell, 1971.

Ferrell, Robert. *American Diplomacy in the Great Depression: Hoover-Stimson Foreign Policy, 1929–1933.* New York: Norton, 1970.

Finnegan, John P. *Against the Specter of a Dragon: The Campaign for American*

Military Preparedness, 1914–1917. Westport: Greenwood Press, 1974.

Friedson, Eliot. *The Profession of Medicine: A Study of the Sociology of Applied Knowledge.* New York: Dodd, Mead, 1970.

Fussell, Paul. *The Great War and Modern Memory.* New York: Oxford University Press, 1975.

Genthe, Charles. *American War Narratives, 1917–1918.* New York: David Lewis, 1969.

Gies, Joseph. *The Colonel of Chicago.* New York: Dutton, 1979.

Gilbert, James B. *Work without Salvation: America's Intelletuals and Industrial Alienation.* Baltimore: Johns Hopkins University Press, 1977.

Grob, Gerald. *Mental Institutions in America: Social Policy to 1895.* New York: Free Press, 1973.

Hagedorn, Hermann. *The Bugle That Awoke America.* New York: John Day, 1940.

————. *Leonard Wood.* 2 Vols. New York: Harper & Brothers, 1931.

————. *The Roosevelt Family of Sagamore Hill.* New York: Macmillan, 1954.

Hall, J. K., ed. *One Hundred Years of American Psychiatry.* New York: Columbia University Press, 1944.

Harbaugh, William H. *The Life and Times of Theodore Roosevelt.* New York: Collier Books, 1963.

Hartmann, Edward G. *The Movement to Americanize the Immigrant.* New York: AMS Press, 1967.

Hawes, Joseph W. *Children in Urban Society: Juvenile Delinquency in 19th Century America.* New York: Oxford University Press, 1971.

Healey, David F. *The United States in Cuba: 1898–1902.* Madison: University of Wisconsin Press, 1963.

Herner, Charles. *The Arizona Rough Riders.* Tucson: University of Arizona Press, 1970.

Hobsbawn, E. J. *The Age of Capital, 1848–1975.* New York: Scribner's, 1975.

Hofstadter, Richard. *The American Political Tradition and the Men Who Made It.* New York: Vintage, 1955.

Holl, Jack M. *Juvenile Reform in the Progressive Era: William R. George and the Junior Republic Movement.* Ithaca: Cornell University Press, 1971.

Horney, Karen. *Neurosis and Human Growth: The Struggle for Self-Realization.* New York: Norton, 1950.

Huntington, Samuel P. *The Soldier and the State: The Theory and Politics of Civil-Military Relations.* New York: Vintage, 1957.

Jaher, Frederic Cople. *The Urban Establishment: Upper Strata in Boston, New York, Charleston, Chicago, and Los Angeles.* Urbana: University of Illinois Press, 1982.

James, D. Clayton. *The Years of MacArthur, Vol. 1, 1880–1941.* Boston: Houghton, Mifflin, 1970.

James, William. *The Varieties of Religious Experience.* New York: New American Library, 1958.

Johnson, Donald. *The Challenge to American Freedoms: World War I and the Rise of the American Civil Liberties Union.* Lexington: University of Kentucky Press, 1963.

Jones, Howard Mumford. *The Age of Energy: Varieties of American Experience, 1865-1915*. New York: Viking, 1973.

Jones, Richard Seelye. *A History of the American Legion*. Indianapolis: Bobbs-Merrill, 1946.

Jones, Virgil Carrington. *Roosevelt's Rough Riders*. Garden City: Doubleday, 1971.

Kett, Joseph. *Rites of Passage: Adolescence in America: 1790 to the Present*. New York: Basic Books, 1977.

Kevles, Daniel J. *The Physicists: The History of a Scientific Community in Modern America*. New York, Knopf, 1977.

Leed, Eric J. *No Man's Land: Combat and Identity in World War I*. Cambridge: Cambridge University Press, 1979.

Lewinson, Edward R. *John Purroy Mitchel, the Boy Mayor of New York*. New York: Astra Books, 1965.

Linderman, Gerald. *The Mirror of War: American Society and the Spanish-American War*. Ann Arbor: University of Michigan Press, 1974.

Link, Arthur. *Wilson: Campaigns for Progressivism and Peace, 1916-1917*. Princeton: Princeton University Press, 1965.

Lynd, Robert S. and Helen M. Lynd. *Middletown: A Study in Modern American Culture*. New York: Harcourt, Brace & World, 1929.

McCullough, David. *Mornings on Horseback*. New York: Simon & Schuster, 1981.

McLachlan, James. *American Boarding Schools: A Historical Study*. New York: Scribner's, 1970.

Malin, James C. *Confounded Rot about Napoleon: Reflections upon Science and Technology, Nationalisn, World Depression of the Eighteen-Nineties and Afterwards*. Lawrence, Kans.: privately printed, 1961.

Marchland, Roland C. *The American Peace Movement and Social Reform, 1898-1918*. Princeton: Princeton University Press, 1972.

May, Ernest. *Imperical Democracy: The Emergence of America as a Great Power*. New York: Harper & Row, 1973.

————. *The World War and American Isolation, 1914-1917*. Chicago: Quadrangle, 1966.

May, Henry. *The End of American Innocence: A Study of the First Years of Our Time, 1912-1917*. Chicago: Quadrangle, 1964,

May, Lary. *Screening Out the Past: The Birth of Mass Culture and the Motion Picture Industry*. New York: Oxford University Press, 1980.

Mechanic, David. *Medical Sociology*. New York: Free Press, 1968.

Millett, Allan R. *The General: Robert L. Bullard and Officership in the United States Army, 1881-1925*. Westport: Greenwood Press, 1975.

Millis, Walter. *The Martial Spirit: A Study of Our War with Spain*. New York: Viking, 1965.

Morison, Elting E. *From Know-How to Nowhere: The Development of American Technology*. New York: Basic Books, 1974.

————. *Men, Machines and Modern Times*. Cambridge, Mass.: Massachusetts Institute of Technology Press, 1966.

————. *Turmoil and Tradition: A Study of the Life and Times of Henry L.*

Stimson. New York: Atheneum, 1964.

Morris, Edmund. *The Rise of Theodore Roosevelt.* New York: Coward, McCann & Geoghegan, 1979.

Murray, Robert. *Red Scare: A Study in National Hysteria, 1919–1920.* New York: McGraw-Hill, 1964.

Onorato, Michael. *A Brief Review of American Interest in Philippine Development and Other Essays.* Berkeley: McCutchan, 1968.

Osgood, Robert. *Ideals and Self-Interest in America's Foreign Relations: The Great Transformation of the Twentieth Century.* Chicago: University of Chicago Press, 1953.

Palmer, John McAuley. *America in Arms: The Experience of the United States with Military Organization.* New Haven: Yale University Press, 1942.

Peterson, H. C., and Gilbert Fite. *Opponents of the War, 1917–1918.* Seattle: University of Washington Press, 1968.

Pogue, Forrest C. *George C. Marshall: Education of a General.* New York: Viking, 1963.

———. *George C. Marshall: Ordeal and Hope.* New York: Viking, 1966.

Putnam, Carleton. *Theodore Roosevelt: The Formative Years, 1858–1886.* New York: Scribner's, 1958.

Quandt, Jean B. *From the Small Town to the Great Community; The Social Thought of Progressive Intellectuals.* New Brunswick: Rutgers University Press, 1970.

Ravitch, Diane. *The Great School Wars: New York City, 1885–1973.* New York: Basic Books, 1974.

Rochester, Stuart I. *American Liberal Disillusionment: In the Wake of World War I.* University Park: Pennsylvania State University Press, 1977.

Rodgers, Daniel T. *The Work Ethic in Industrial America: 1850–1920.* Chicago: University of Chicago Press, 1978.

Romasco, Albert. *The Poverty of Abundance: Hoover, the Nation, the Depression.* New York: Oxford University Press, 1965.

Rosen, George. *From Medical Police to Social Medicine.* New York: Science History Publications, 1974.

———. *A History of Public Health.* New York: M. D. Publications, 1958.

Rosenberg, Charles. *No Other Gods: On Science and American Social Thought.* Baltimore: Johns Hopkins Press, 1976.

Rudolph, Frederick. *The American College and University: A History.* New York: Vintage, 1962.

Shryock, Richard. *The Development of Modern Medicine.* New York: Knopf, 1947.

———. *Medicine and Society in America: 1660–1860.* New York: New York University Press, 1960.

Smythe, Donald. *Guerrilla Warrior: The Early Life of John J. Pershing.* New York: Scribner's, 1973.

Solomon, Barbara. *Ancestors and Immigrants: A Changing New England Tradition.* Chicago: University of Chicago Press, 1972.

Stallings, Laurence. *The Doughboys: The Story of the AEF, 1917–1918.* New York: Harper & Row, 1963.

Starr, Paul. *The Social Transformation of American Medicine.* New York: Basic Books, 1982.

Stouffer, Samuel, et al. *The American Soldier: Combat and Its Aftermath.* Princeton: Princeton University Press, 1949.

Sward, Keith. *The Legend of Henry Ford.* New York: Atheneum, 1968.

Trachtenberg, Alan. *The Incorporation of America: Culture and Society in the Gilded Age.* New York: Hill & Wang, 1982.

Trask, David F. *The War with Spain in 1898.* New York: Macmillan, 1981.

Tuchman, Barbara. *Stilwell and the American Experience in China, 1911–45.* New York: Bantam Books, 1975.

Twichell, Heath, Jr. *Allen: The Biography of an Army Officer.* New Brunswick: Rutgers University Press, 1974.

Vandiver, Frank E. *Black Jack: The Life and Times of John J. Pershing.* College Station: Texas A. & M. University Press, 1977.

Van Every, Edward. *Muldoon: The Solid Man of Sport.* New York: Frederick Stokes, 1929.

Veysey, Laurence R. *The Emergence of the American University.* Chicago: University of Chicago Press, 1965.

Waldrop, Frank C. *McCormick of Chicago.* Englewood Cliffs: Prentice-Hall, 1966.

Wagenknecht, Edward. *The Seven Worlds of Theodore Roosevelt.* New York: Longmans, 1958.

Wecter, Dixon. *The Hero in America: A Chronicle of Hero-Worship.* New York: Scribner's, 1941.

————. *When Johnny Comes Marching Home.* Boston: Houghton, Mifflin, 1944.

Weigley, Russell. *History of the United States Army.* New York: Macmillan, 1967.

White, G. Edward. *The Eastern Establishment and the Western Experience: The West of Frederick Remington, Theodore Roosevelt and Owen Wister.* New Haven: Yale University Press, 1968.

Wilson, Joan Hoff. *Herbert Hoover: Forgotten Progressive.* Boston: Little, Brown, 1975.

Wittner, Lawrence S. *Rebels against War: The American Peace Movement, 1941–1960.* New York: Columbia University Press, 1970.

Wohl, Robert. *The Generation of 1914.* Cambridge, Mass.: Harvard University Press, 1979.

Zabrinski, Alexander C. *Bishop Brent: Crusader for Christian Unity.* Philadelphia: Westminster Press, 1948.

IX. UNPUBLISHED MATERIAL

Andrus, Clift. "Notes on Omar Bradley's *A Soldier's Story*, First Infantry Division Memorial Museum Library, Wheaton, Ill.

Axeen, David. "Romantics and Civilizers: American Attitudes toward War, 1898–1902." Ph.D. diss., Yale University, 1969.

Baldwin, Fred Davis. "The American Enlisted Man in World War I." Ph.D. diss., Princeton University, 1964.

Buenning, Steven. "John Grier Hibben: A Biographical Study." Senior Honors Paper, Princeton University, 1971.

Chambers, John W. "Conscripting for Colossus: The Adoption of the Draft in the United States in World War I." Ph.D. diss., Columbia University, 1973.

Collin, Richard H. "The Image of Theodore Roosevelt in American History and Thought, 1885–1965." Ph.D. diss., New York University, 1966.

Cunningham, Frank. "The Army and Universal Military Training, 1942–1948." Ph.D. diss., University of Texas, 1976.

Fry, Richard T. "Community through War: A Study of Theodore Roosevelt's Rise and Fall as a Prophet and Hero in Modern America." Ph.D. diss., University of Minnesota, 1969.

Gruber, Carol S. "Mars and Minerva: World War I and the American Academic Man." Ph.D. diss., Columbia University, 1968.

Hotchkiss, Eugene. "Jacob Gould Schurmann and the Cornell Tradition." Ph.D. diss., Cornell University, 1960.

Killingrew, John William. "The Impact of the Great Depression on the Army, 1929–1936." Ph.D. diss., University of Indiana, 1960.

Lewis, Guy. "The American Intercollegiate Football Spectacle." Ph.D. diss., University of Maryland, 1954.

Minot, Rodney G. "The Organized Veterans and the Spirit of Americanism, 1898–1959." Ph.D. diss., Stanford University, 1960.

Parkman, Aubrey L. "David Jayne Hill." Ph.D. diss., University of Rochester, 1961.

Rawick, George P. "The New Deal and Youth: The Civilian Conservation Corps, the National Youth Administration and the American Youth." Ph.D. diss., University of Wisconsin, 1957.

Skolnick, Richard S. "The Crystallization of Reform in New York City, 1894–1917." Ph.D. diss., Yale University, 1954.

Smith, Michael J. J. "Henry Stimson and the Philippines." Ph.D. diss., University of Indiana, 1969.

Vogel, Morris. "Boston's Hospitals, 1870–1930: A Social History." Ph.D. diss., University of Chicago, 1974.

Watkins, George T. "Owen Wister and the American West: A Biographical and Critical Study." Ph.D. diss., University of Illinos, 1959.

Index

162–63; attacks Bolshevism as radical democracy, 169; alienation in 1920s; attacks New Deal, 237
Huebner, Clarence: described, 257–58; replaces Theodore Roosevelt, Jr., and Terry Allen in World War II, 258–59

Immigrants: social problem for preparedness leaders, 3, 108, 109, 128–29, 134
Industrial mediation and arbitration: under Mayor John P. Mitchel, 124; affinity to military training, 127; mentioned, 121. *See also* National Civic Federation
International law: conservative affinity to preparedness movement, 122–24, 170. *See also* Coudert, Frederic Rene

James, Edmund: and Plattsburg, 59; as conservative humanist, 89
Jay, Delancey Kane: in World War I 77th Division, 153; mentioned, 7, 28n3
Junior Plattsburg movement: philosophy and purpose, 101–2, 116n8; program at Ft. Terry, 102–3; becomes a national movement, 103–4; mentioned, 106, 110
Juvenile delinquency: corrected by military training, 15, 107–8; mentioned, 15

Lindbergh, Charles, hero for preparedness leaders, 201
Literature (heroic): as moral therapy, 14–15; to reform youth in 1920s, 196–99; and "lost generation" writers, 198–99; conflicts with radical art in 1930s, 235
Lowell, A. Lawrence: supports military training only for defense, 84, 158; verbally attacks commercial football, 92, 192

McCormick, Robert: World War I advocate of universal military training, 100, 232, 240; army scholarships to Groton, 100; in American Legion, 175; supports CCC, 232; attacks FDR and New Deal, 237; pre-World War II isolationism, 237–38, 240–41, 245n35
McKinley, William : believes Spanish-American War unites America, 17; uses Spanish-American War for partisan advantage, 25; mentioned, 38
Marshall, George Catlett: relationship

with Theodore Roosevelt, Jr., 71, 248, 249, 251; covert romanticism, 249
Medicine: relationship to military training, 35, 44; growing impersonality of, 37, 45, 46, 47: practitioners support universal military training, 44, 45, 46, 47. *See also* Military medicine.
Menken, S. Stanwood: uses military training to Americanize immigrants, 129, 150; described, 137–39; organizes National Security League, 138; uses military training to reform America, 138–39; admires Soviet dictatorship, 170; mentioned, 121
Military medicine: concern for community health, 37; impersonal nature of, 46; frontline psychotherapy, 50–51. *See also* Medicine
Military Training Camps Association: 1, 7, 28n3, 62, 75, 150, 160, 175, 189. *See also* Plattsburgers
Mitchel, John Purroy: at Plattsburg, 48, 125, 128, 139n5; advocates junior military training, 108–9, 124–25, 126; supports Gary school system, 109–10; personal characteristics, 124; political reforms fail, 124–25; wants to join army, 125–26; killed at flight school, 126, 154; and New York City police, 130, mentioned, 121
Moral Rearmament Movement: affinity to Plattsburg and military training, 235–37
Muldoon, William: background, 48; military characteristics, 49, 50; drills patients, 49, 50, 71; endorses universal military training, 51; mentioned 99, 105

National Civic Federation: and preparedness leaders, 127; and Red Scare, 173
National Security League: founded by Menken, 138; demands American declaration of war, 145; represses dissidents, 161–62; in post-World War I America, 169, 179; eclipsed by post-war prosperity, 179–82; philosophical reactionaries in 1920s, 181–82; decline and fall, 180, 181–82; mentioned, 28n3, 75, 111, 122, 123, 126, 133, 134, 149
New York City Junior Police, 107–8

War I, 84, 159–60; as a moral educator, 100, 101, 158, 159, 204; has wayward sons, 100–101; activities for junior military training, 100–102, 112; at Plattsburg, 128, 132; in American Legion, 174; candidate for president, 188, 203; to be president of University of Pennsylvania, 204, 205; as governor-general of Philippines, 204–9; death of, 209; mentioned, 1, 2, 3, 11, 21, 62, 75, 172, 232

Woods, Arthur: background, 106; as Groton schoolmaster, 106–7, 130–31, 132, 228–29, 231; as police commissioner of New York, 107–8, 130–33; supports quasi-military training for delinquents, 107–8, 109, 110, 112; military training for policemen, 131–32; in World War I, 154–55; as a Harvard trustee, 158; in American Legion, 177–78; as post-World War I Rockefeller Foundation executive, 190, 194, 228; reforms physical education at Harvard, 191–92; as chairman of Hoover's Emergency Committee on Employment, 228–30; mentioned, 21, 128

A Note on the Author

MICHAEL PEARLMAN received his B.A. degree
from Wichita State University, his M.A. degree from
the University of Chicago, and his Ph.D. degree from
the University of Illinois. His articles have appeared in
the *New England Quarterly,* the *Canadian Review of
American Studies,* and the *Journal of Psychohistory. To
Make Democracy Safe for America* is his first book. He
is now working on a study of the relationship between
political rhetoric and melodrama in the twentieth century.